AF254316

FAMILY PORTRAIT

The Lost Sketchbooks of BOB CAMBLIN
1956 - 1973

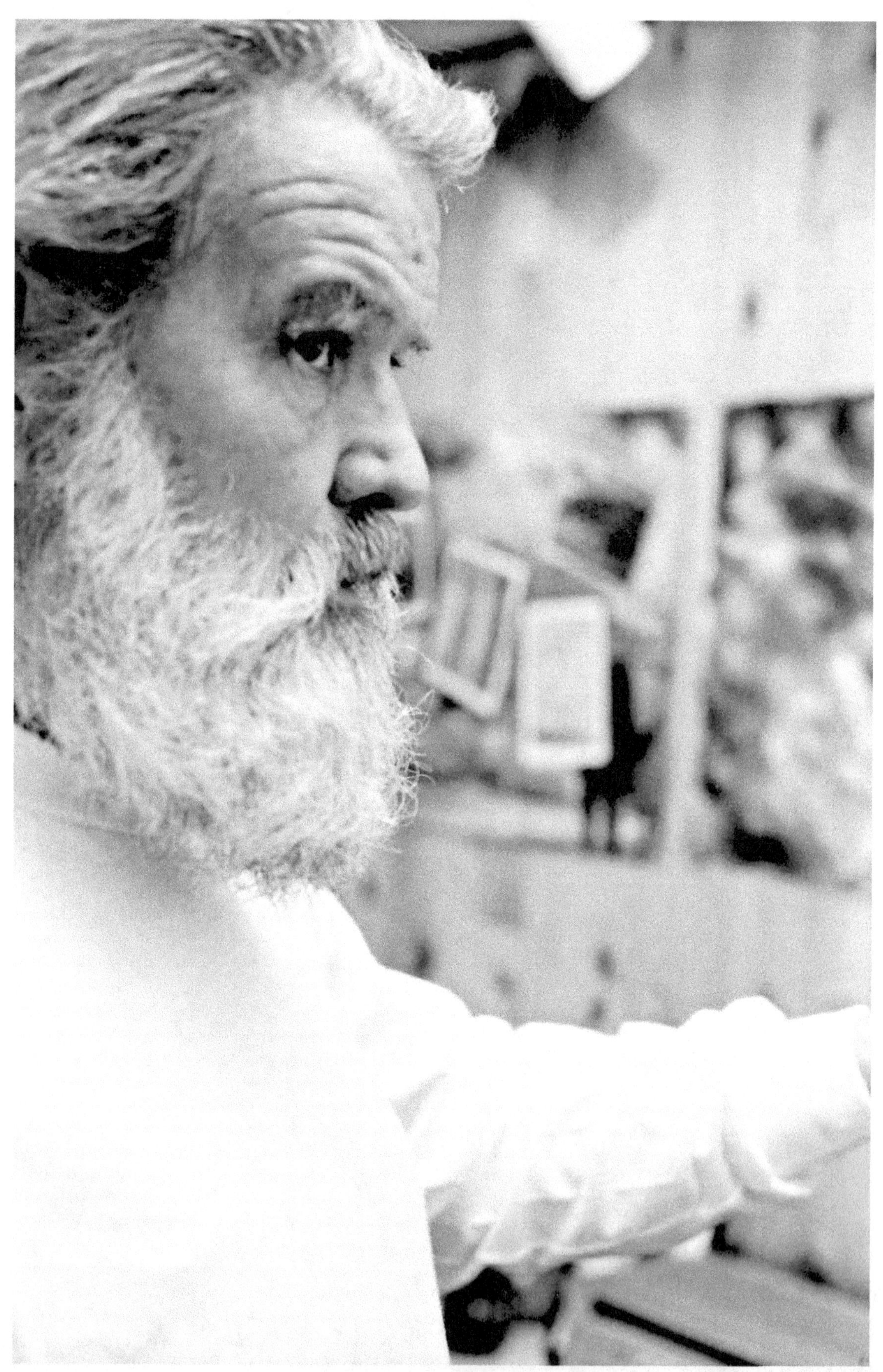

Bob Camblin in his Oregon studio, c. 1990s, by Nancy Giordiano Echegoyen

FAMILY PORTRAIT

The Lost Sketchbooks of BOB CAMBLIN

1956 - 1973

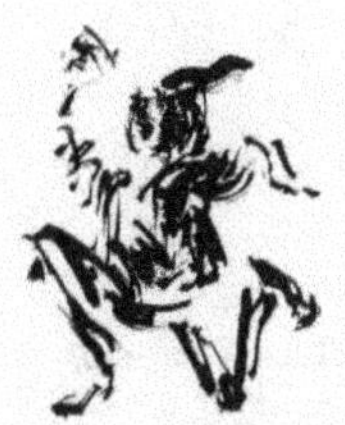

RUNNING MAN PRESS, MICHIGAN

Family Portrait The Lost Sketchbooks of Bob Camblin 1956-1973
is published by Running Man Press.

Cover: Family Portrait, c. 1970s

Frontispiece: Bob Camblin in his Oregon studio, c. 1990s,
photo by Nancy Giordano Echegoyen

Distributed by Ingram Content Group
United States: ingramsparksupport@ingramcontent.com
Australia: ingramsparkaustralia@ingramcontent.com
International: ingramsparkinternational@ingramcontent.com

© 2017 Running Man Press
All rights reserved. No part of this publication may be reproduced in
any form or by any electronic or mechanical means, including
information storage and retrieval systems, without permission in
writing from the publisher, except by a reviewer who may quote
passages and use drawings in a review.

All artwork by Bob Camblin © 2017 by the estate of Bob Camblin

ISBN-10: 0-9988949-0-7
ISBN-13: 978-0-9988949-0-4

Foreword by Eliot Whitehead
Editors: Jillian Rodriguez and Beau Lukas

Running Man Press
Royal Oak, MI
hello@runningmanpress.com

CONTENTS

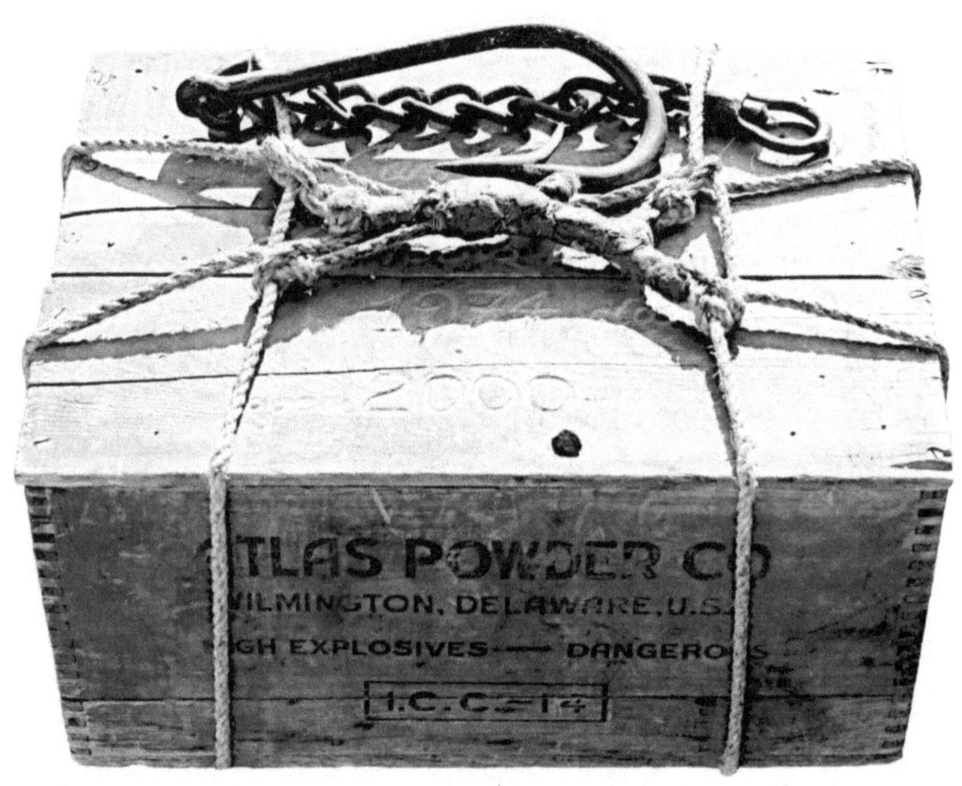

How do you know how much to pay if you don't know what it's worth?

- Peter Carey, *Theft: A Love Story*, 2006

In 1974, this renowned artist's artist, packed and sealed with rope and
wax, a dynamite crate of Atlas Powder's. The top carved:

All Fool's Day

1974 closed

Open 2000

Was it his intent the crate not be opened until his death? Perhaps. It
remained unopened for forty years, contents unknown. Wrapped in fishing
nets, protected by hooks and anchors was artistic gold - his sketchbooks
from 1956-1974.

Widely known, controversial, iconoclastic and often imitated by those in
his sphere, little is known of his immense body of work. Literally
thousands of oils, acrylics, watercolors, drawings, prints, and painted
paper are scattered to the four corners - yet none can be found for sale.
The rare instant a Camblin shows up on eBay or other sites, it is
immediately snatched up, price never questioned. Like his explosive, time
capsule crate, it is an adventure many undertake to uncover an original.
Those in museums, private collections, and the Smithsonian are never for
sale. Like all beautiful, masterful and unique art, they remain closely held.
Like a modern-age pirate, his treasures were often hidden and abandoned,
left to be discovered by future treasure hunters.

This book is an effort to give this extraordinary artist a wider recognition – to bring him to an audience of those with discriminating sensibility, who will know, "Yes, he was the real thing." Bob Camblin was truly gifted. Few artists are. He began one leg up on all but those who were also born with the golden touch. Adept in all mediums, it was the ink line, the fundamental line, pure and shaded, that took him above and beyond the everyman ability.

Camblin was born in Oklahoma. As a young man, he left for Kansas City Art Institute, received a prestigious Fulbright to live in Italy, returned to live and teach at Ringling in Sarasota, Florida, moved on to University of Detroit, University of Illinois, University of Utah and, finally, Rice University (Yale of the South). Through all of this, he kept a private studio. When not engaged in teaching, which he claimed nigh impossible, there were one-man shows and seminal collaborations with other artists.

"Nothing terribly unusual here," you may think. However, one day in 1976, out of the blue, he walked away from all stability - Rice, friends, personal comforts - and lived the life of artist on the edge. Art or nothing. Devil take the rest.

"We have nothing to fear, but fear ourself." - Camblin, 1971.

During the 1970s and 1980s, using the sales of paintings and commissions, he would travel, drawing and painting in Italy, France, Ireland, Mexico, and across the South Pacific.

This book is an abridgment of drawings from 1950-1974: intimate drawings and musings never intended for the public eye; unmediated, spontaneous expressions of joy in free hand. He ran with this gift unto death.

It is not our desire to write art-babble. We believe the sensitive person can look at these images and be deeply pleased, without having to be told how they should react and why. This facsimile of original manuscripts will speak to you without intermediary, as the artist himself would have desired.

Additional books by other publishers are in progress and will ideally fill in the details of the artist's life and his oeuvre. In the interim, please find the most extensive collection of his images available at camblin.com.

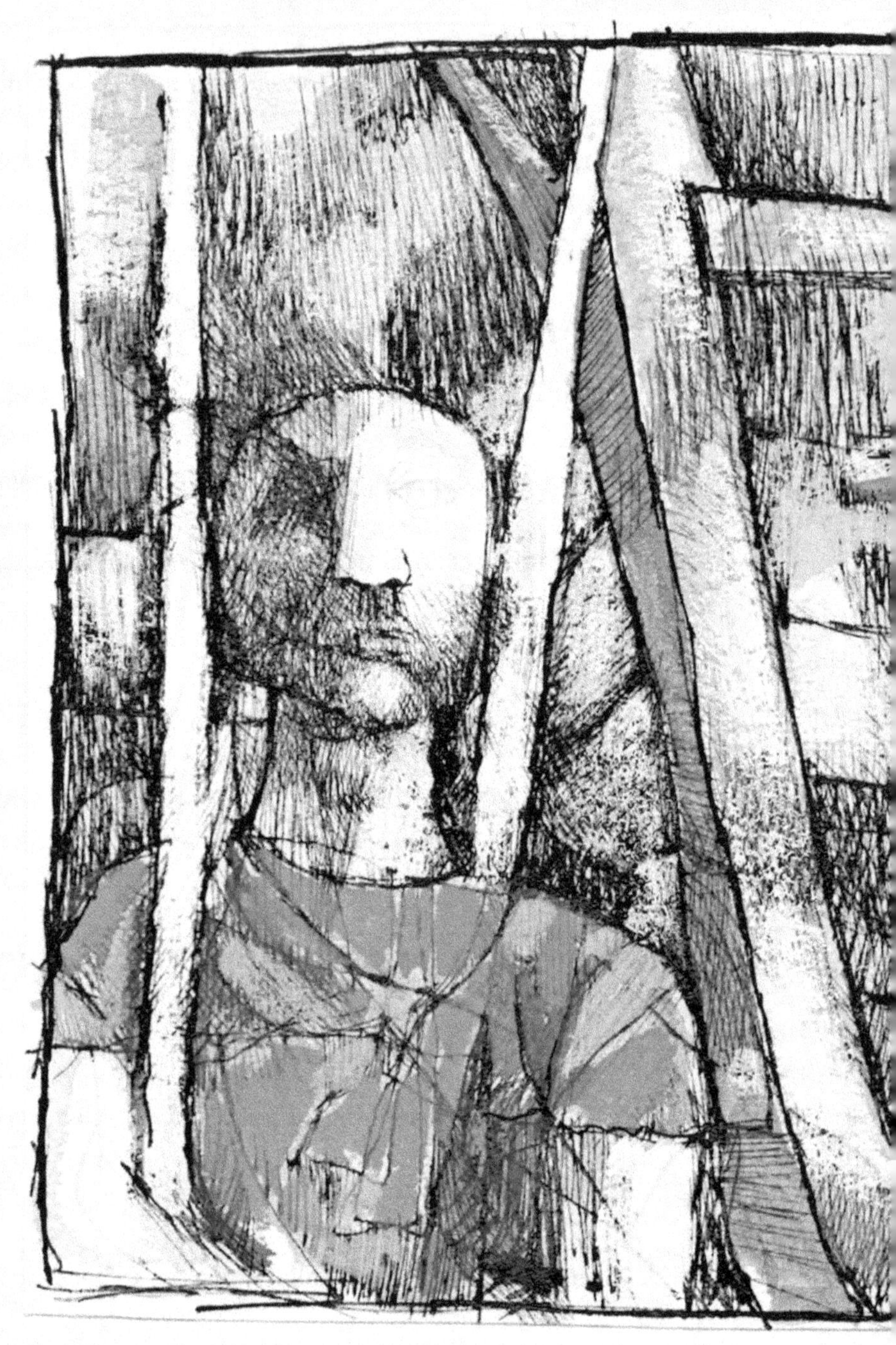

The painted eye sees
more than mine and g...
I see nothing ... yet

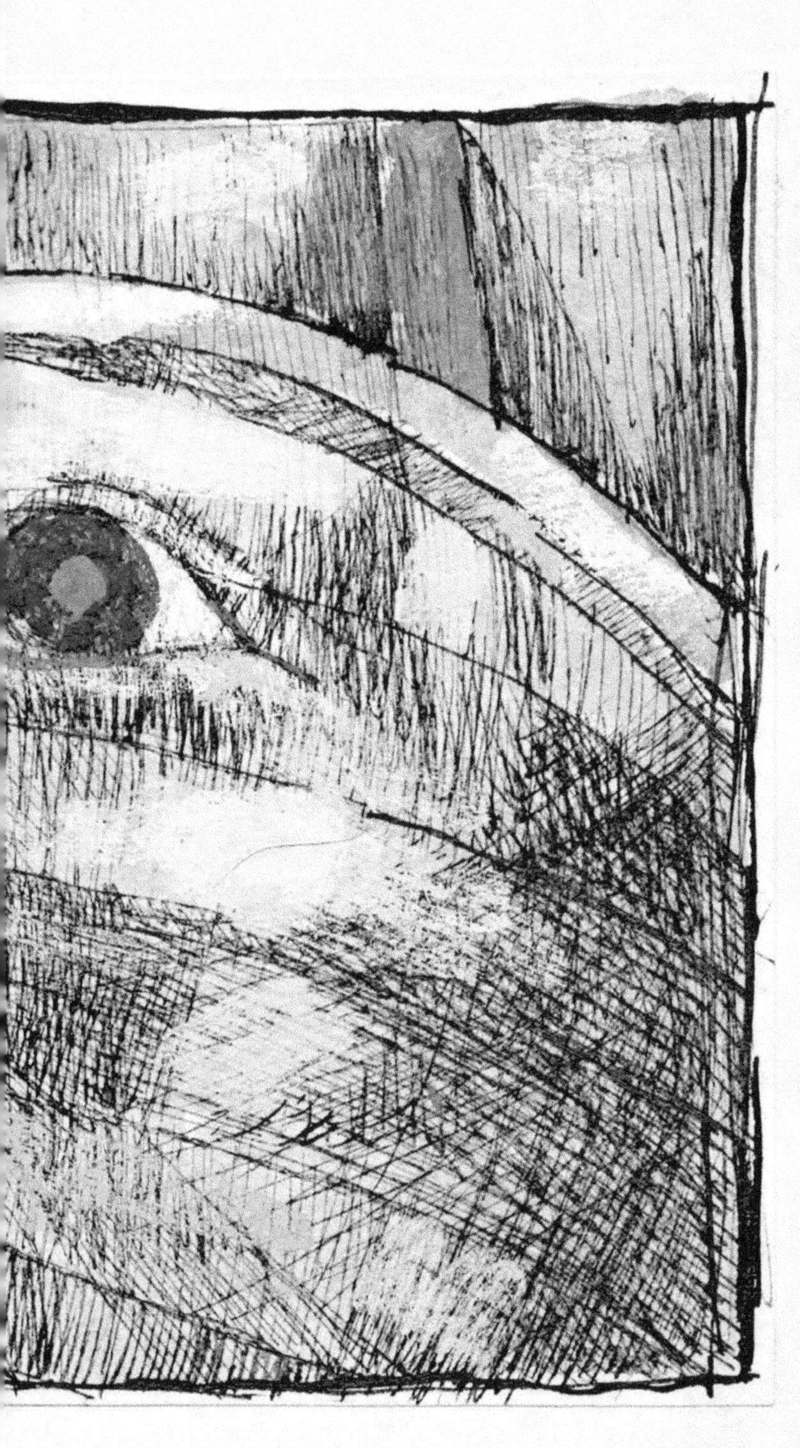

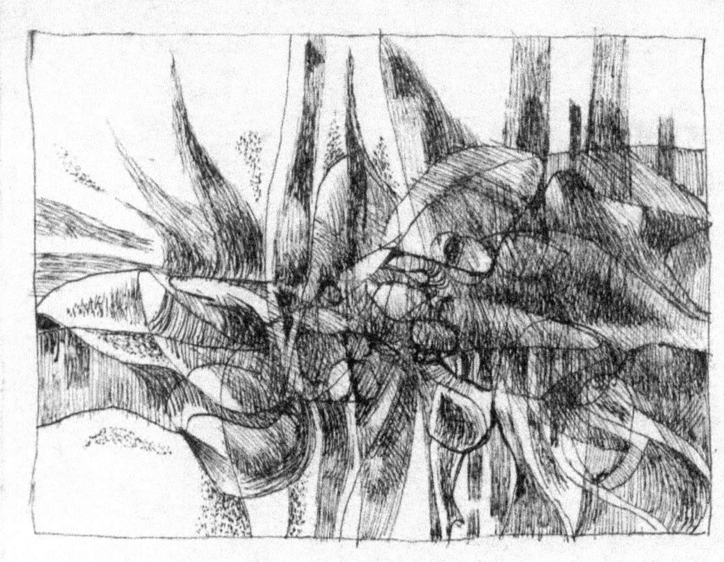

Venice – 1957

chŏk, chŏk, water tongue...
chŏk, chŏk, sound of foot to stone,
This marble island.

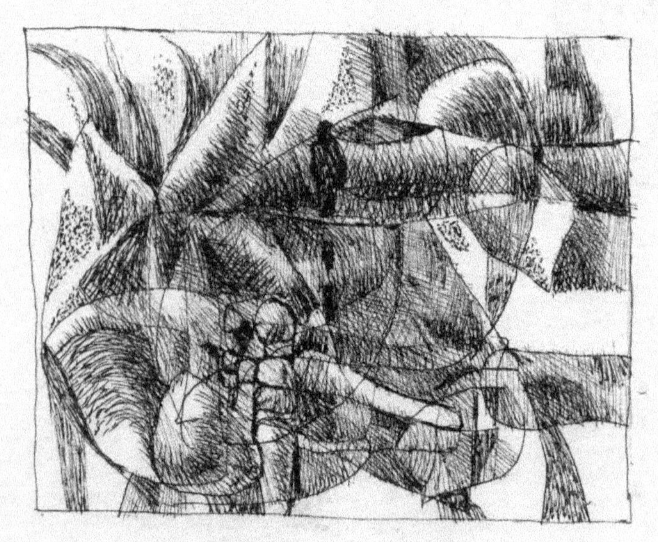

veil of August's heat
weaves the widest dragonfly.
Banyan trees are flat!

Handa – 1959

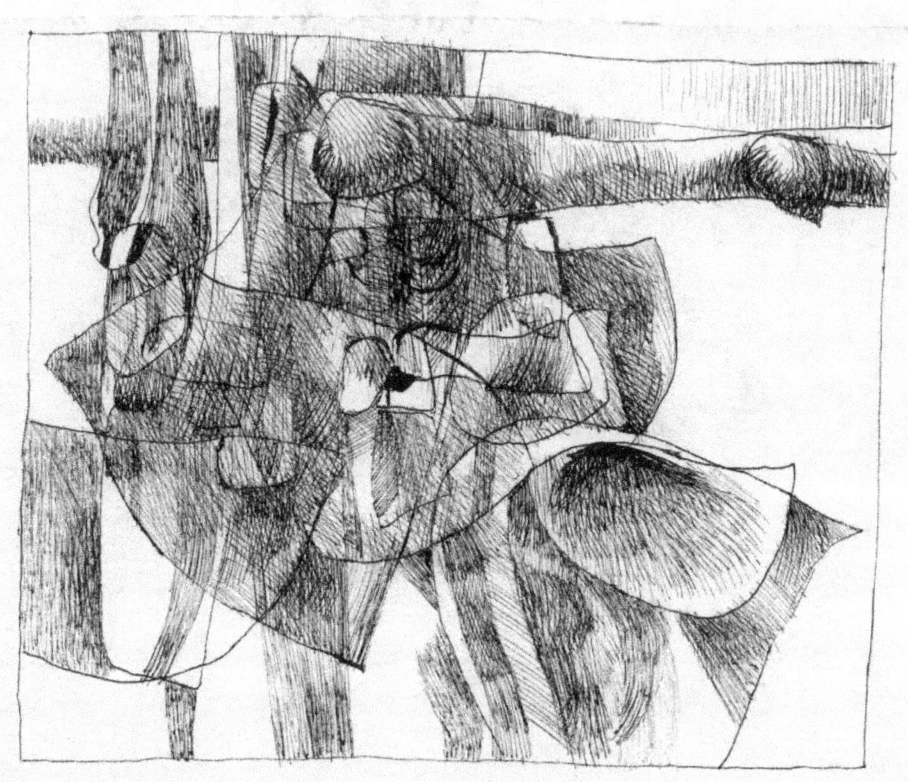

Sarasota 58-60

Canvas rectangle...
Summer light; calligraphy...
Mystic and complete?

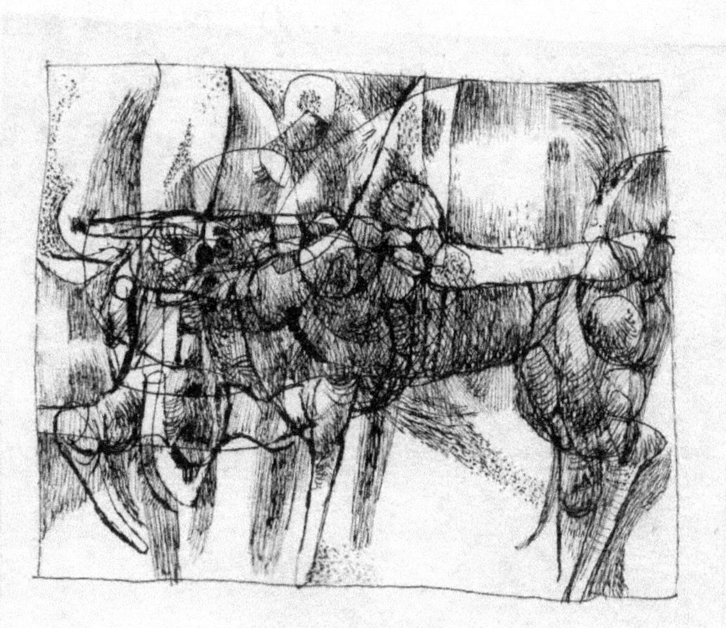

Eater of Christians
Chimera Byzantium...
warm, cold childrens'
                chair.

Venice, Italy - 1956

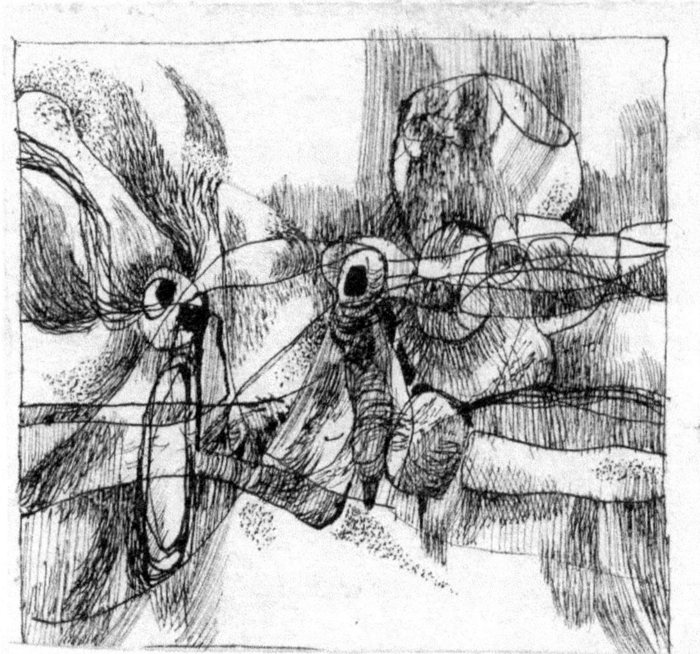

San Gimignano...
Calamari to oblivion.
Strange ways of magic.

Honda - 1959

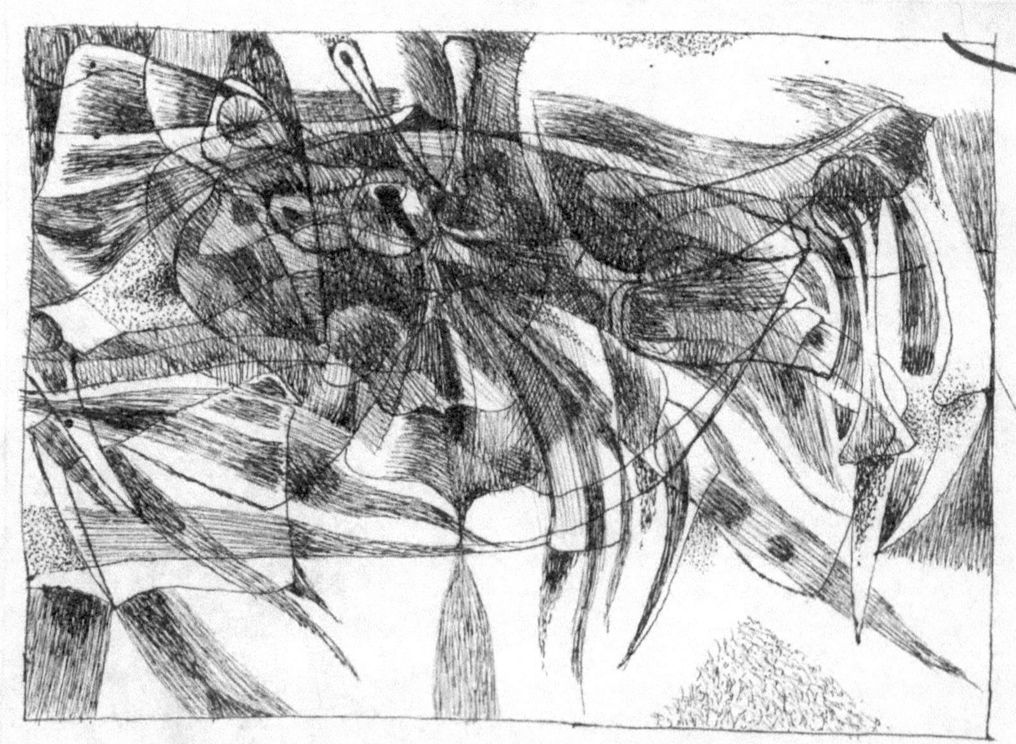

Fragile grayed lady...
Now tiptoe, now skirts high, side-
wise hasty retreat.

O sandpiper, why
Do you dance at ocean's edge?
Come, the water's fine.

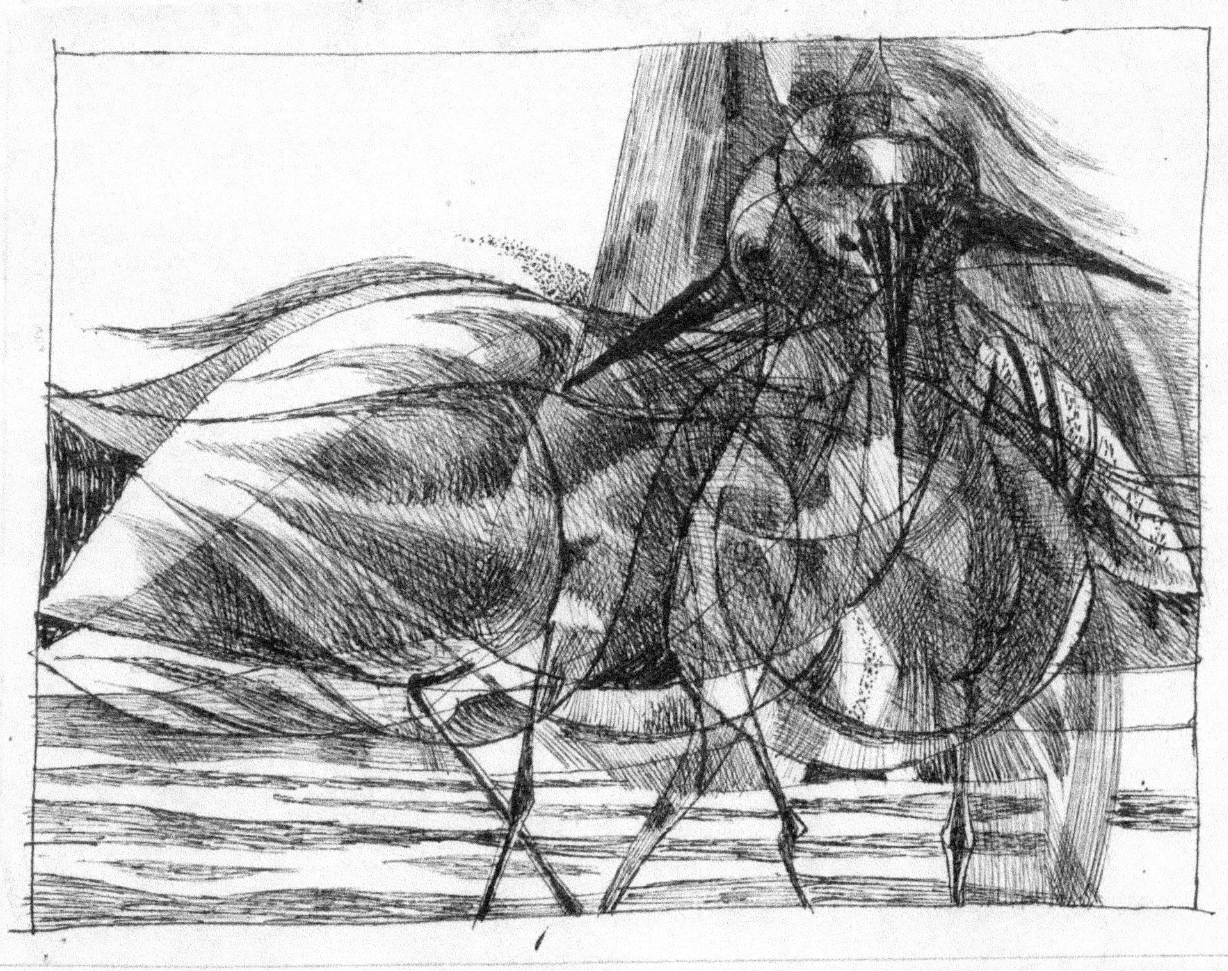

Sarasota, Florida 1959

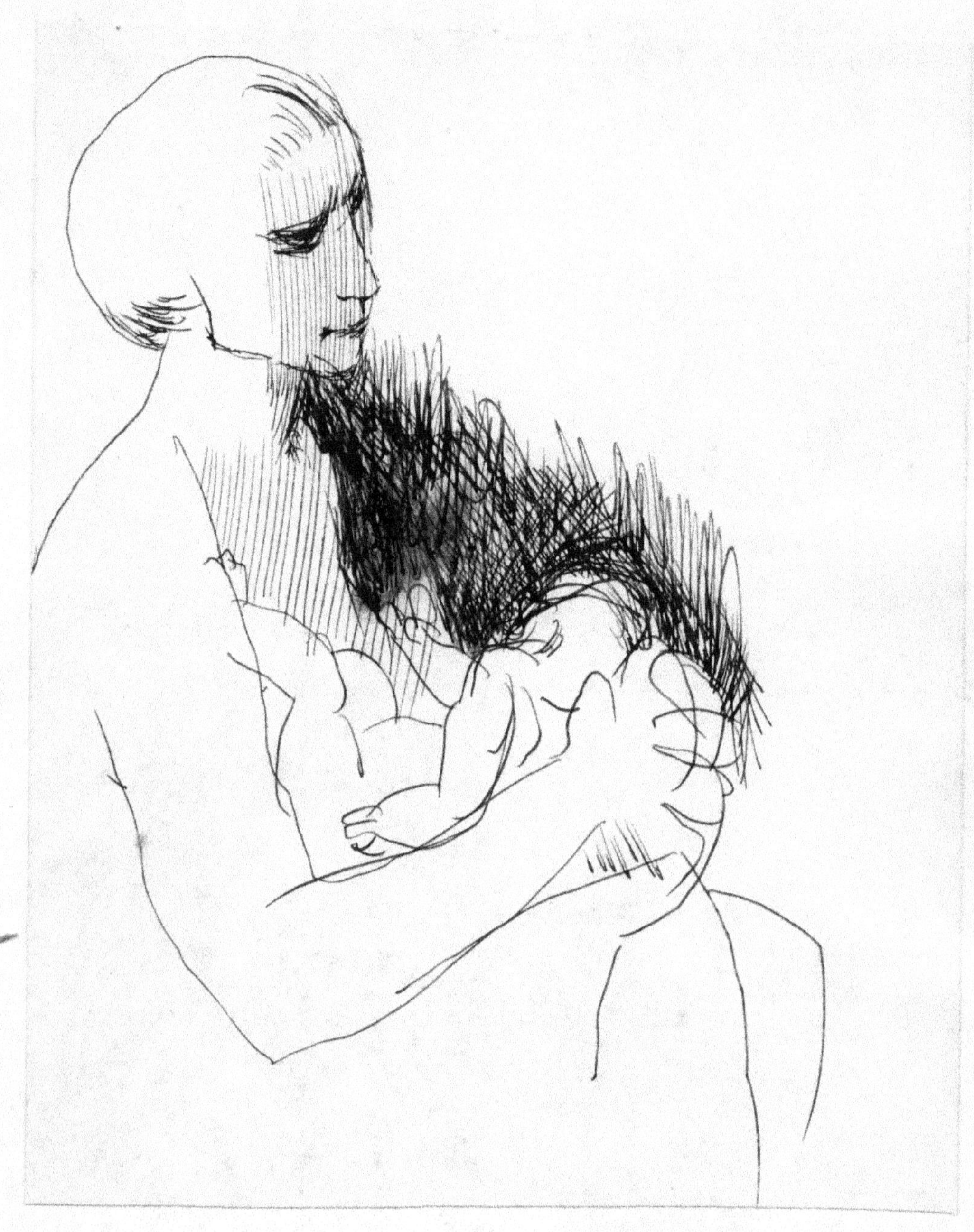

First child. Glory be!
Seven years deprived (my dear)
For economy.

White magic, white lies...
Thoughts of twisted limbs and mind.
The hidden fear seen.

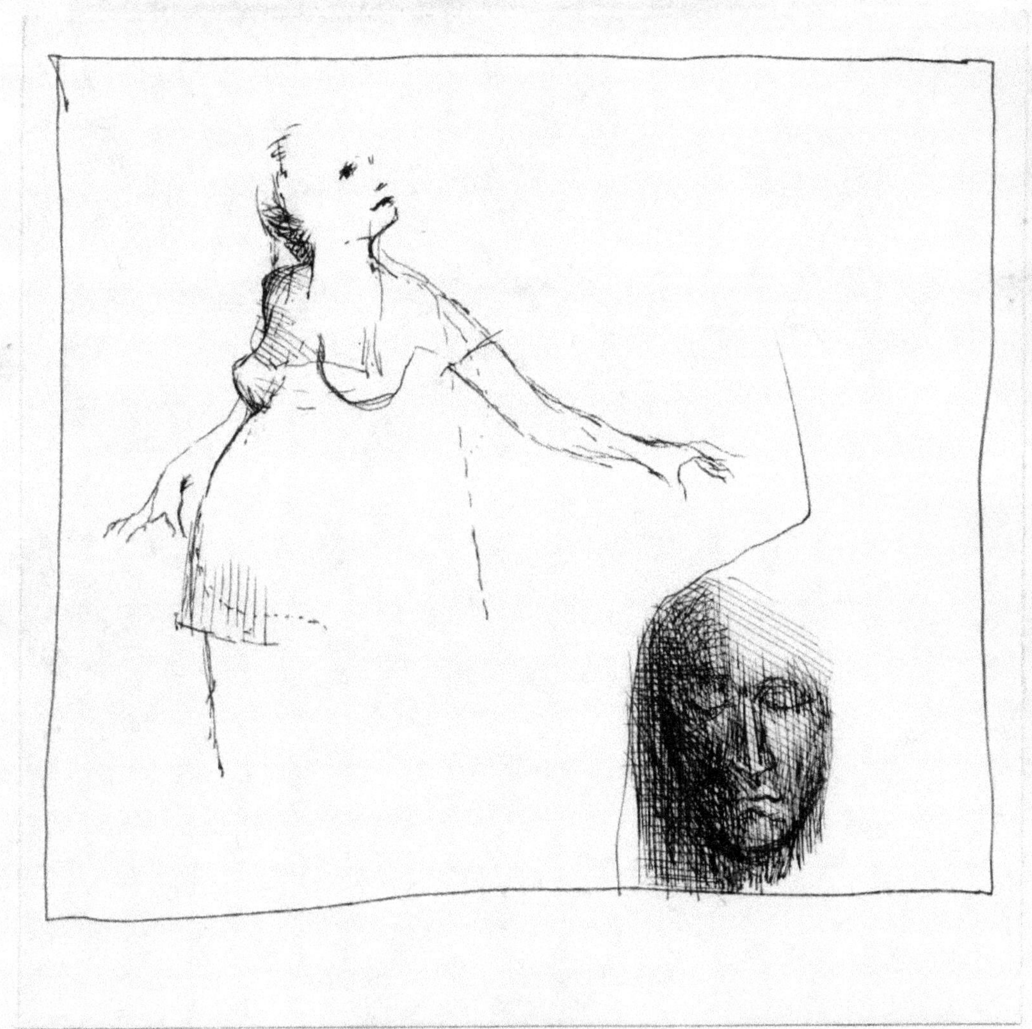

Florida – 1960

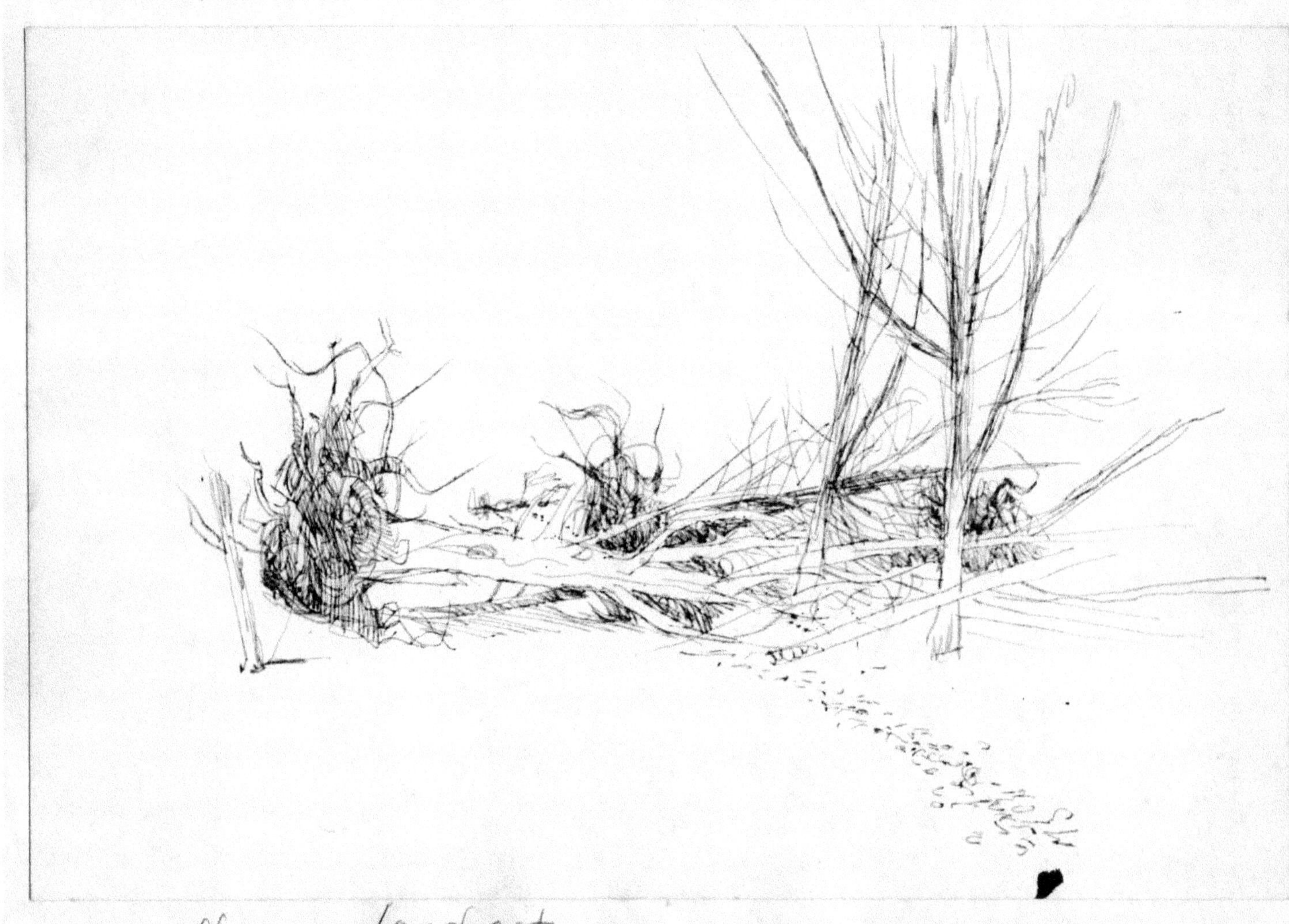

Alone on Longboat...
Memory of summer walks –
I hear this is gone...

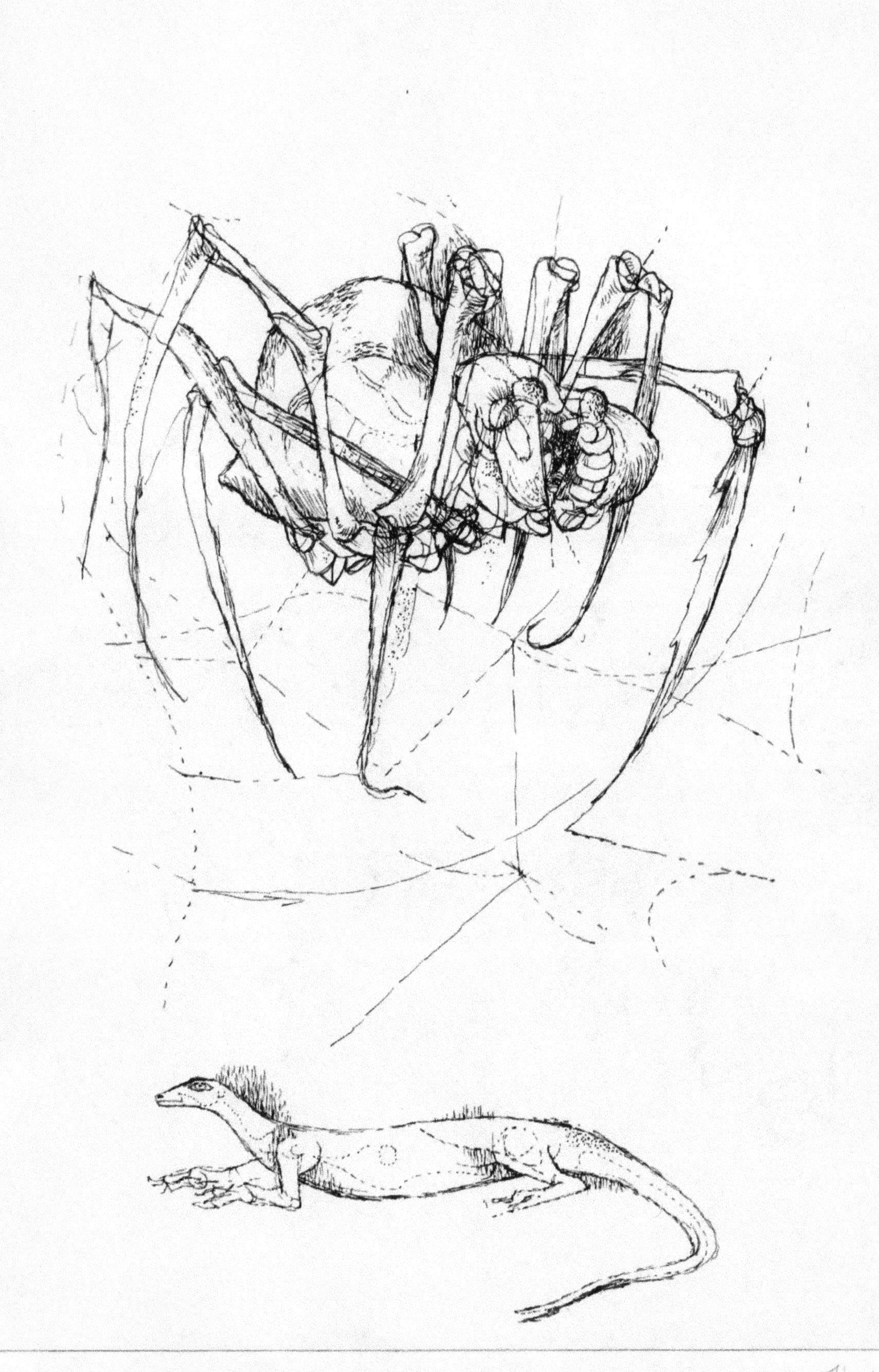

Ragged wheels of silk...
Minuscule dragons observed
By buddha spiders

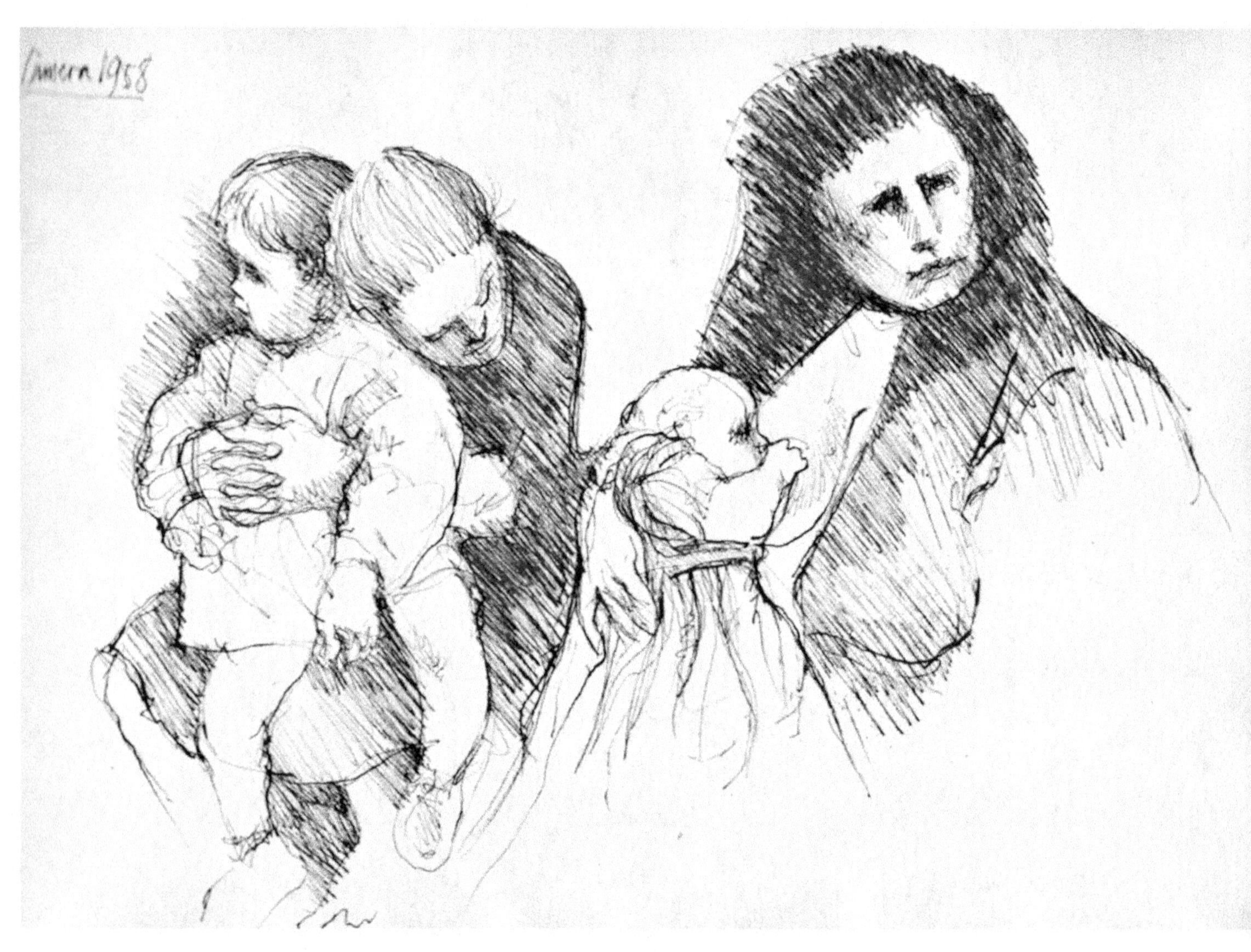

Camern 1958

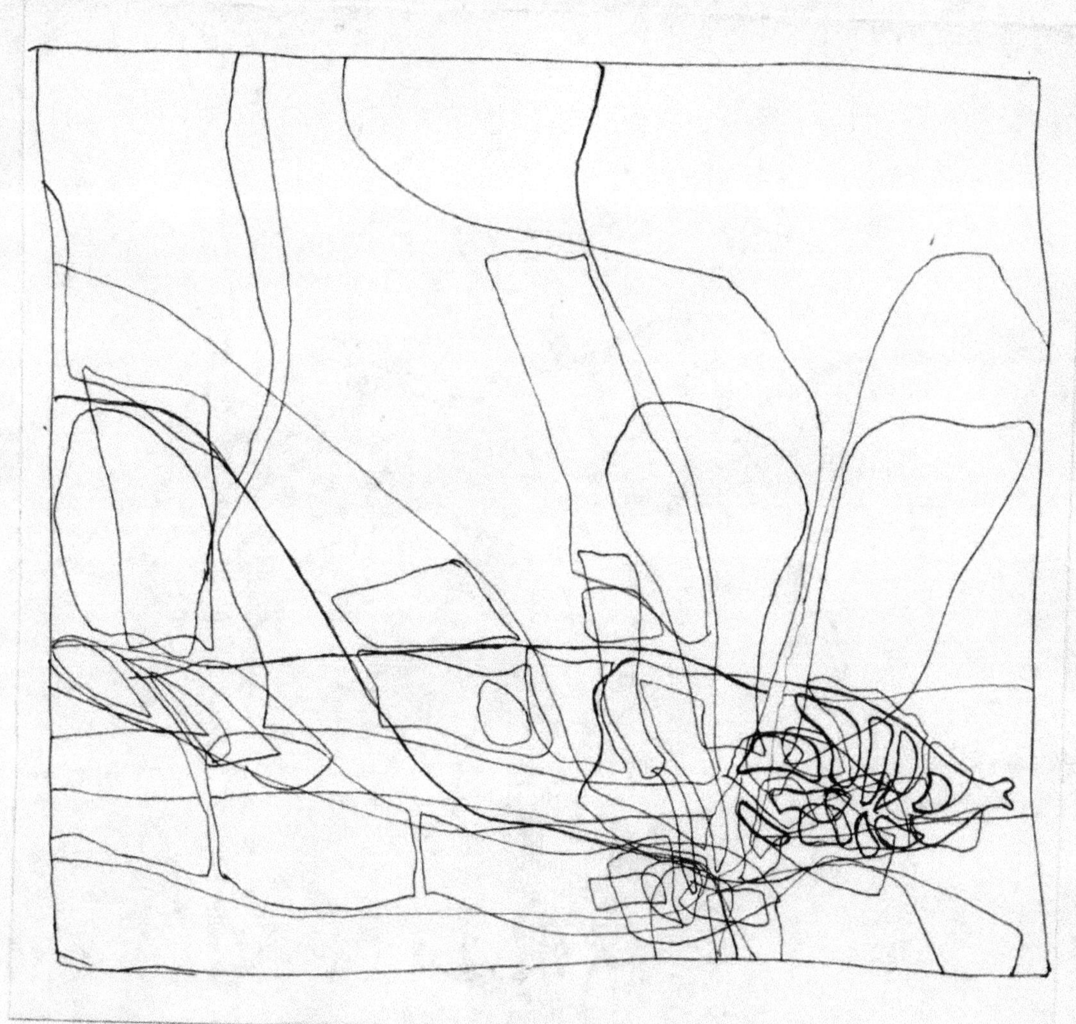

This dragon never
lived — on paper or flowers.
Well, perhaps next time.

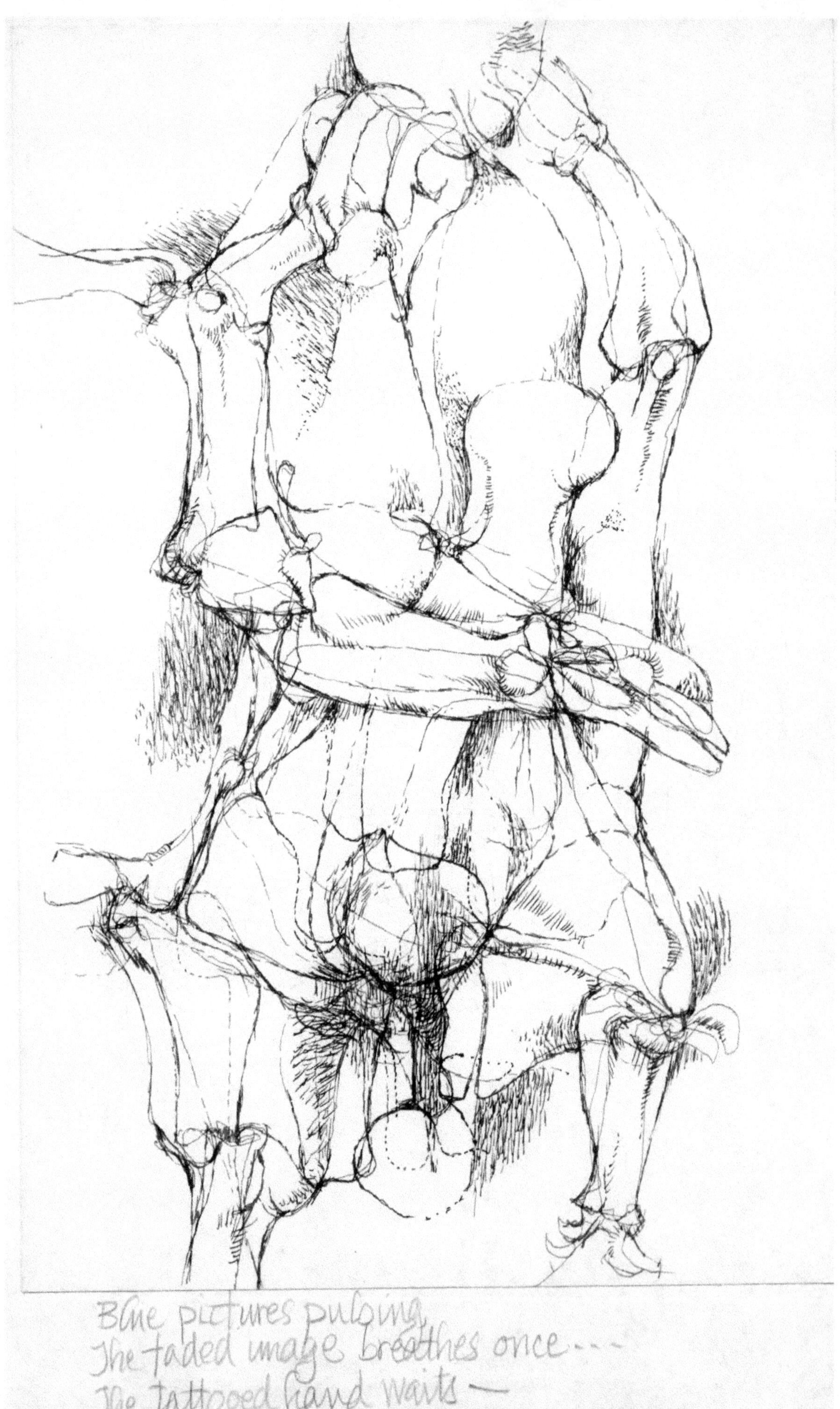

Bone pictures pulsing,
The faded image breathes once....
The tattooed hand waits —

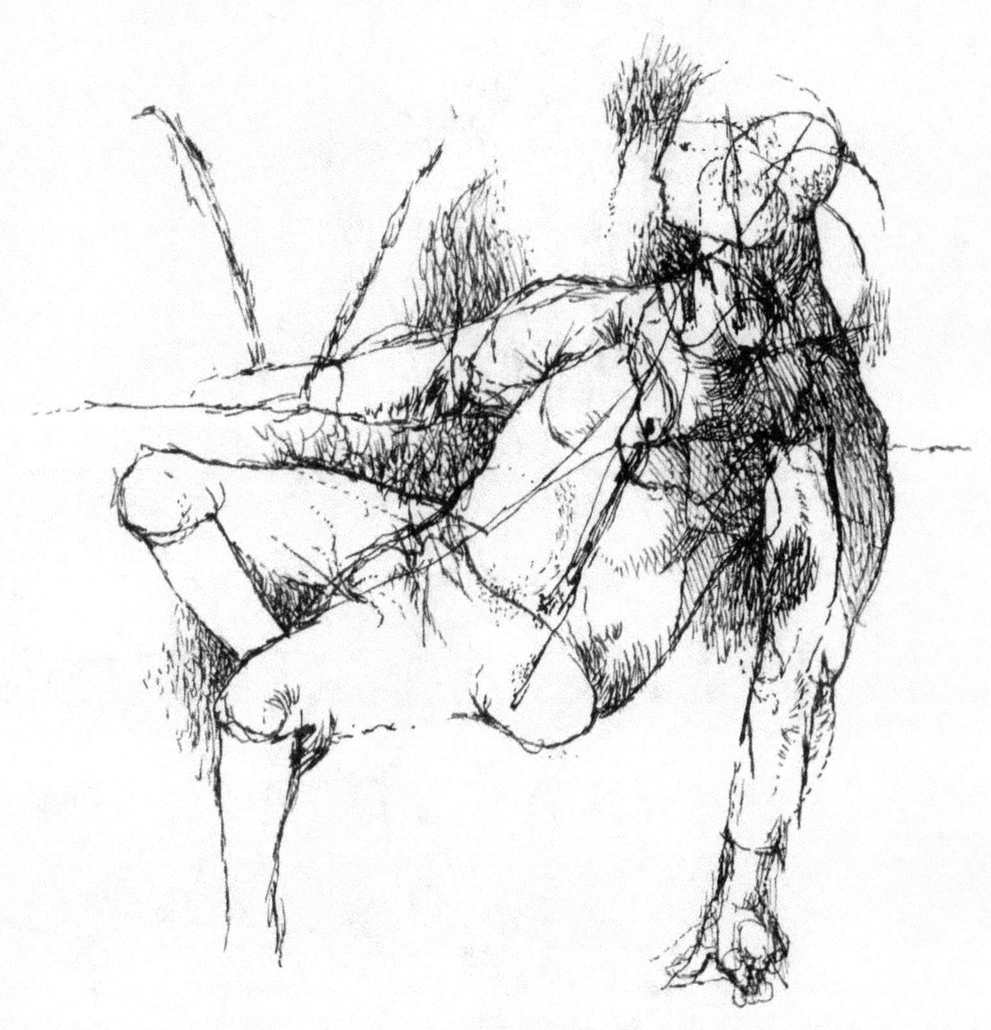

Hmm? Since I drew him –
Wonder why he never moved.
Perhaps we've died . . .

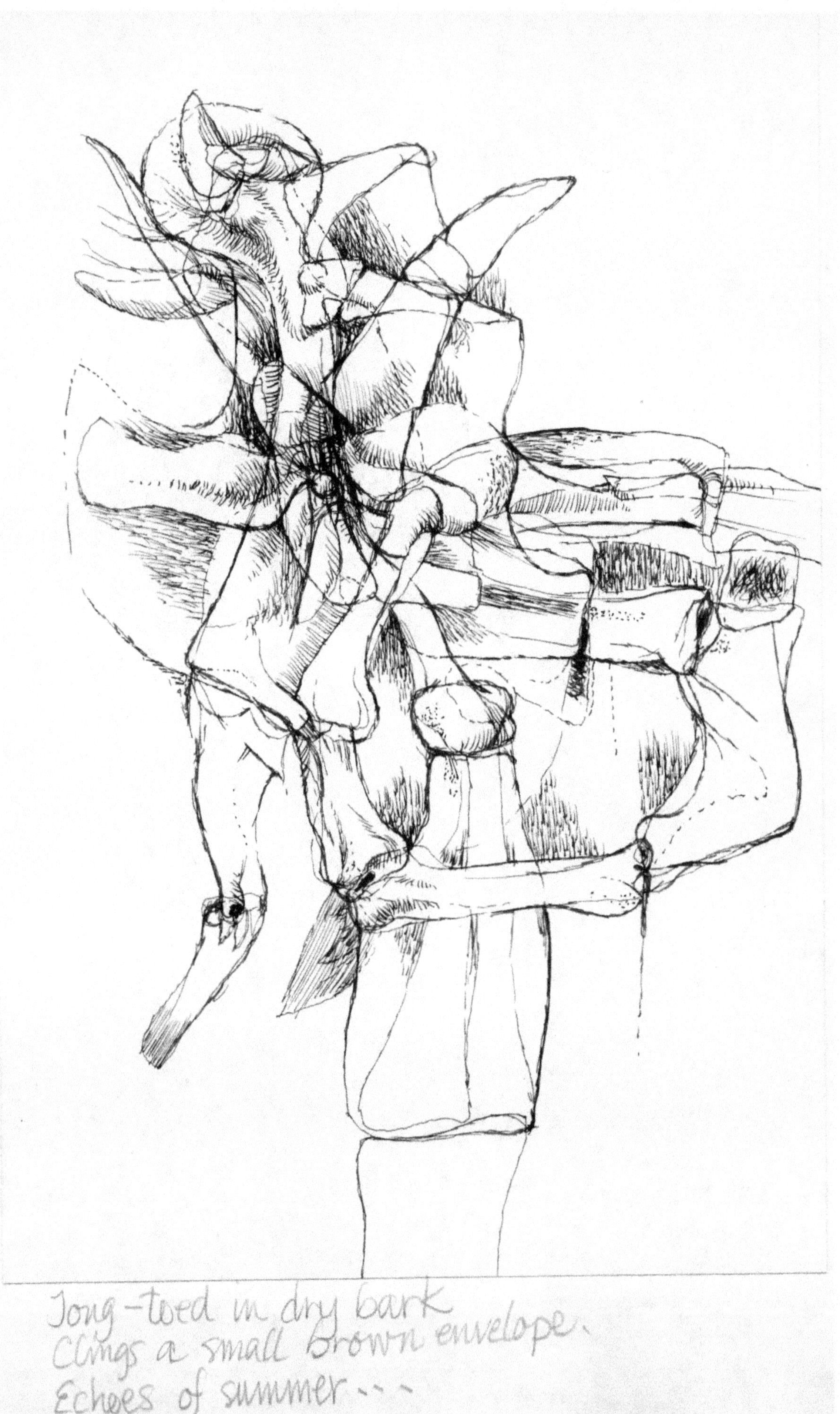

long-toed in dry bark
clings a small brown envelope.
Echoes of summer~~~

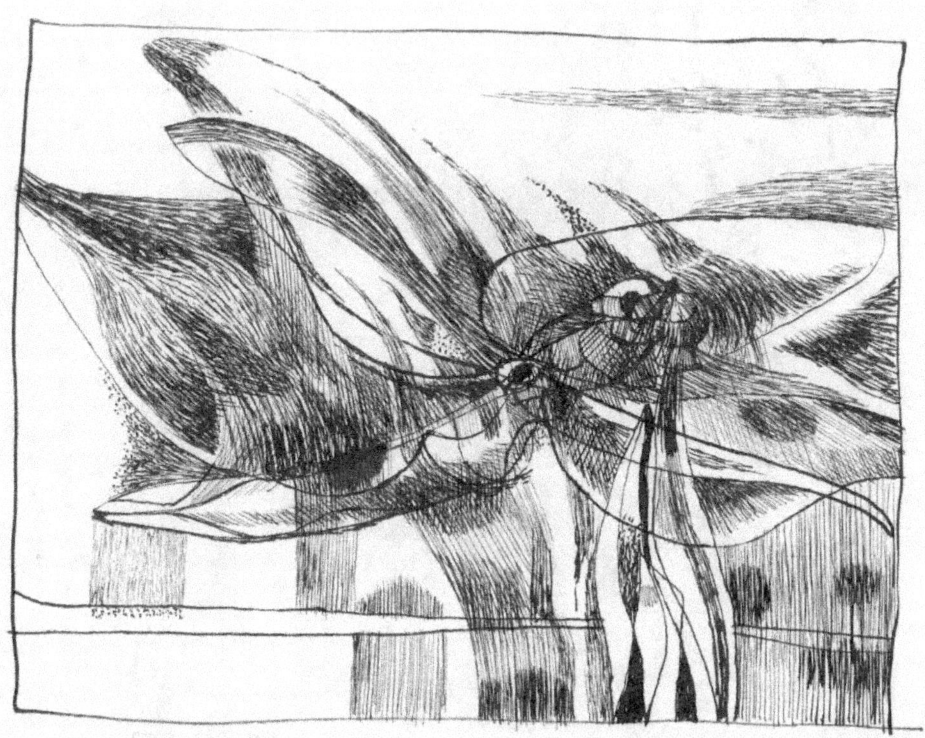

Darning needles sew
Shimmering tapestries... of
Blue, green and white bands.

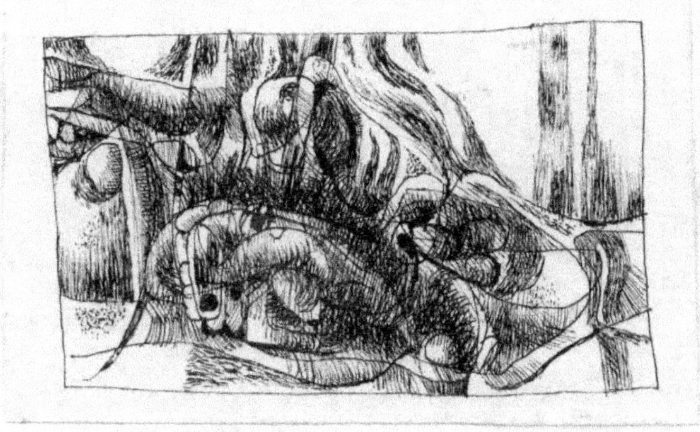

Bleached, textured and white
To taste and sight. Pray ever
Avoid the lamp's fate.

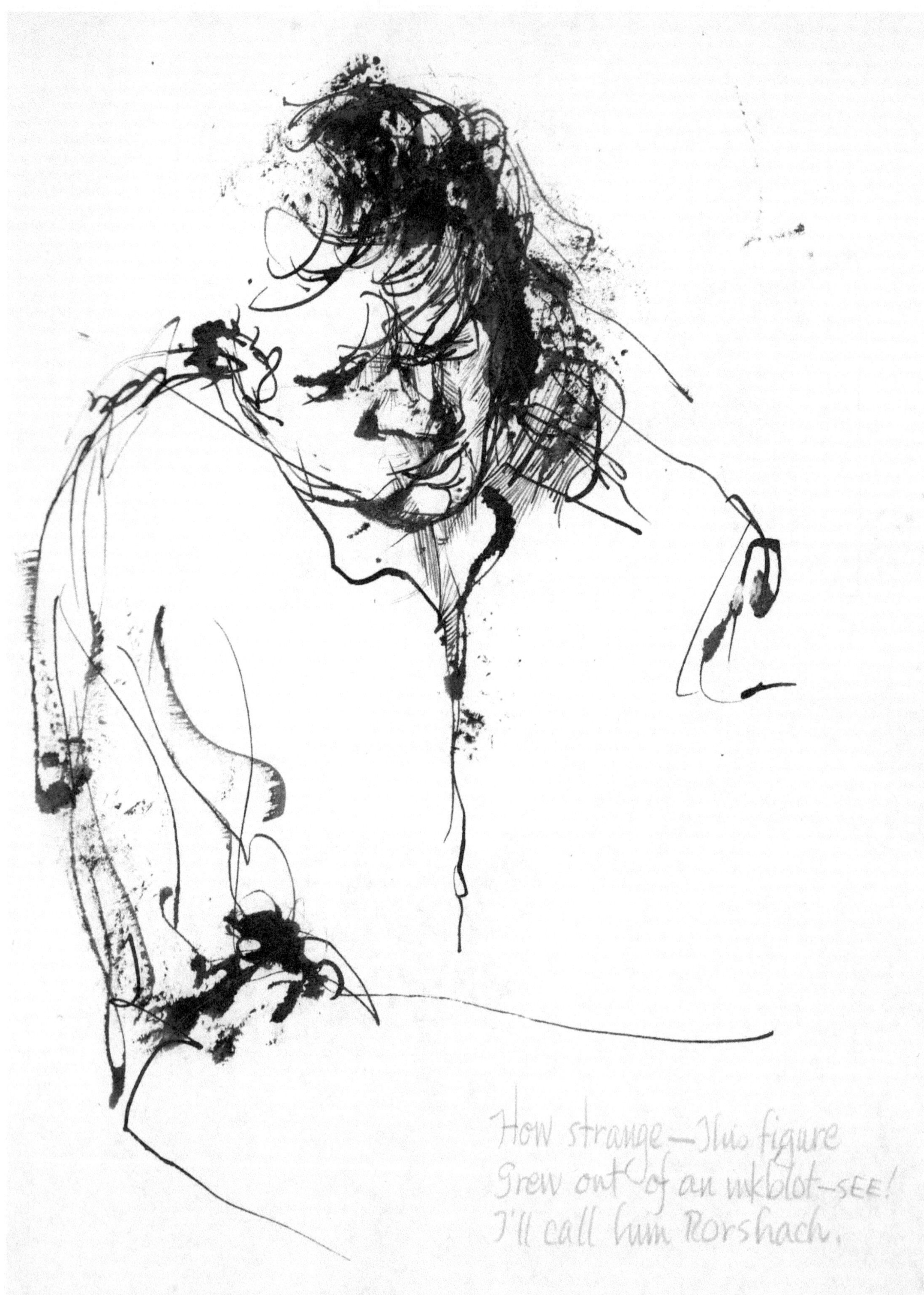

How strange—this figure
grew out of an inkblot—SEE!
I'll call him Rorshach.

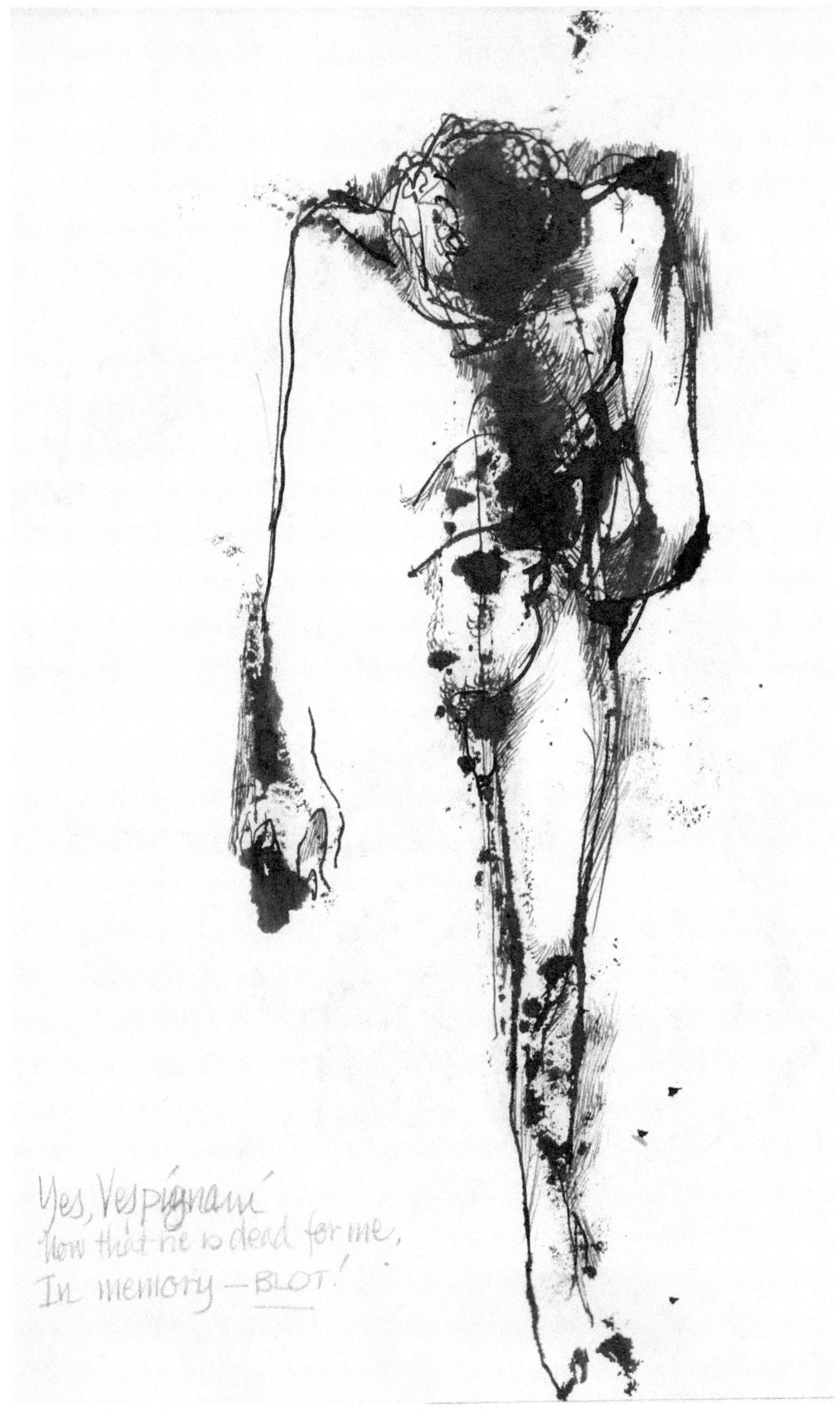

Yes, Vespignani
"Now that he is dead for me,
In memory — BLOT!"

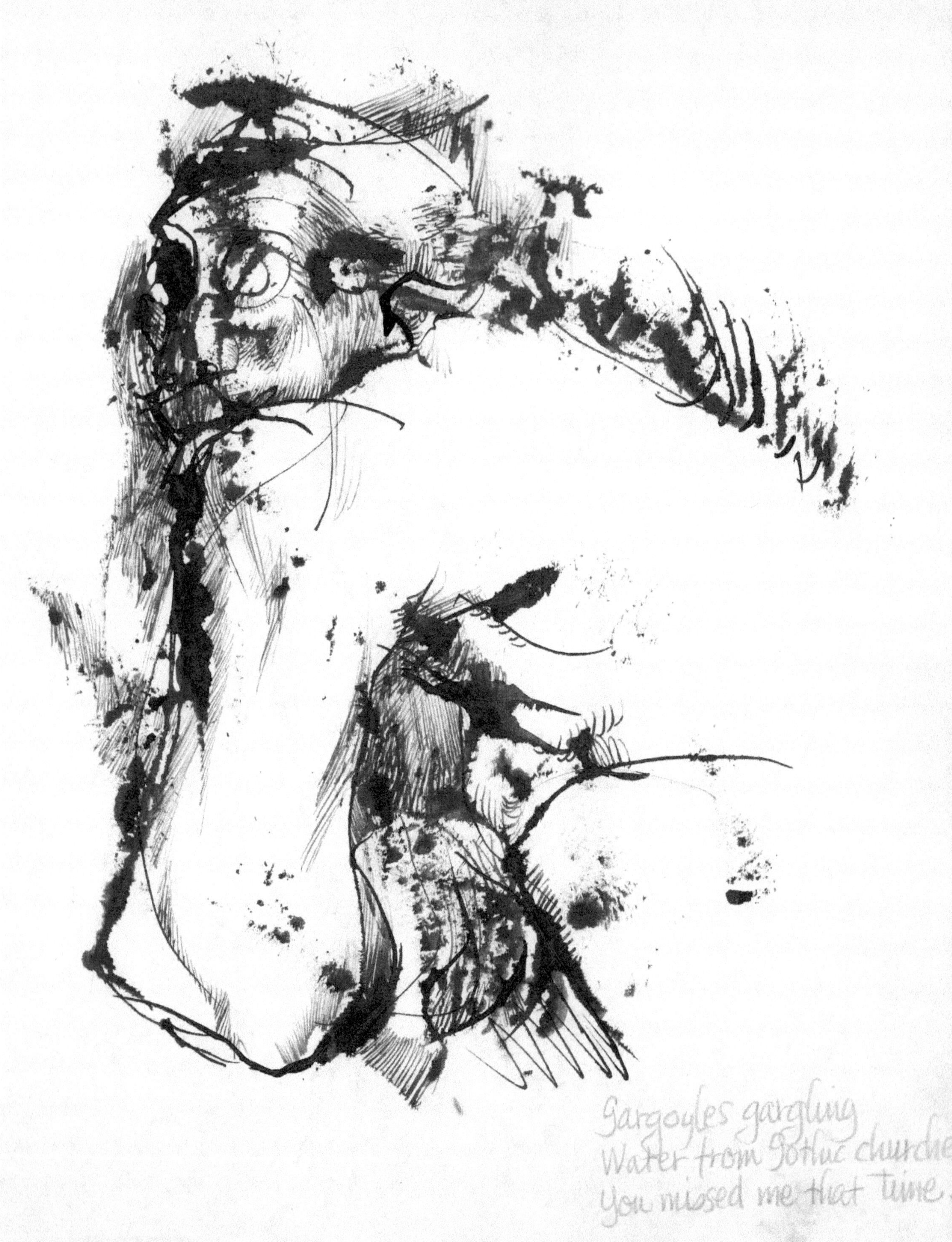
Gargoyles gargling
Water from Gothic churches
You missed me that time.

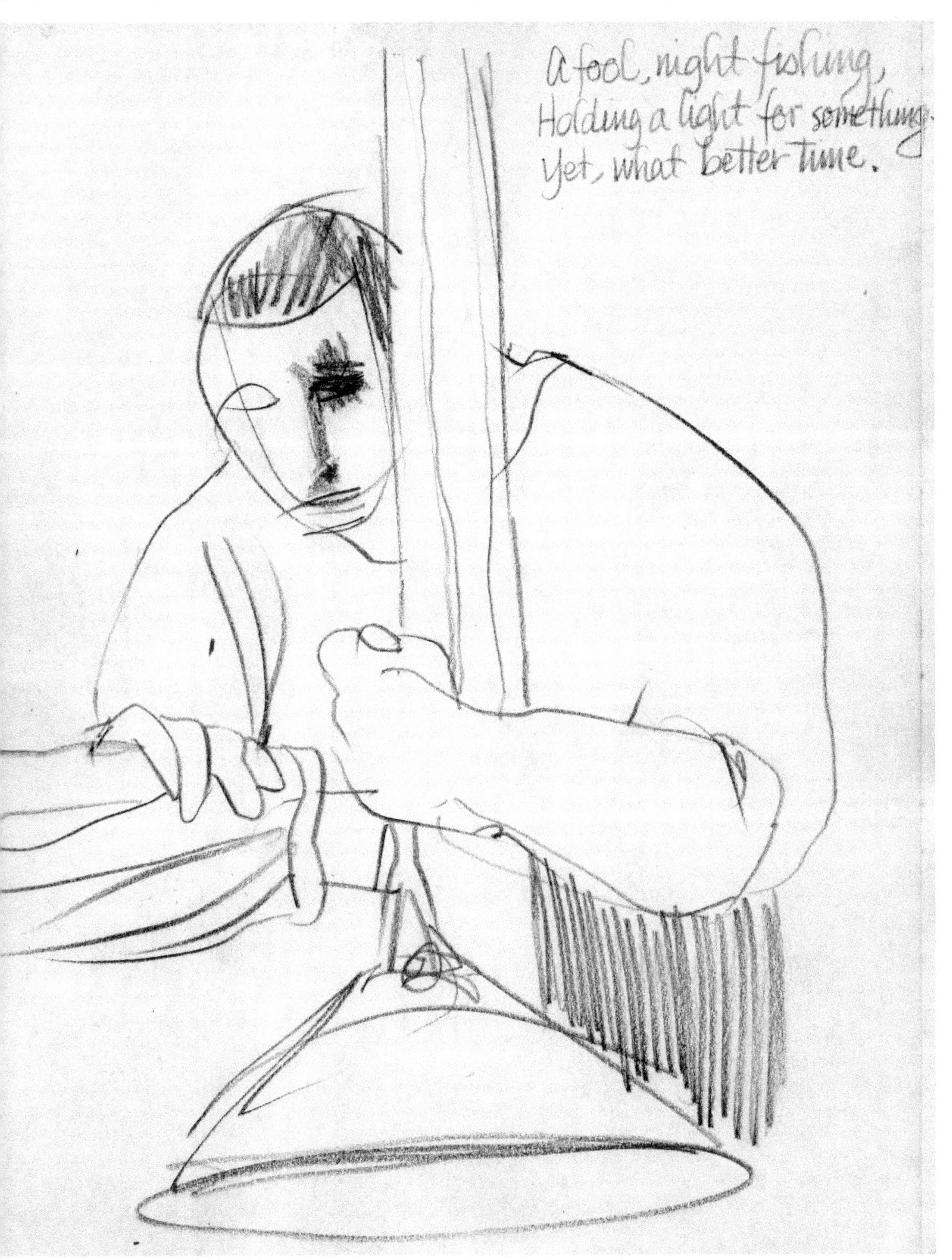

A fool, night fishing,
Holding a light for something.
Yet, what better time.

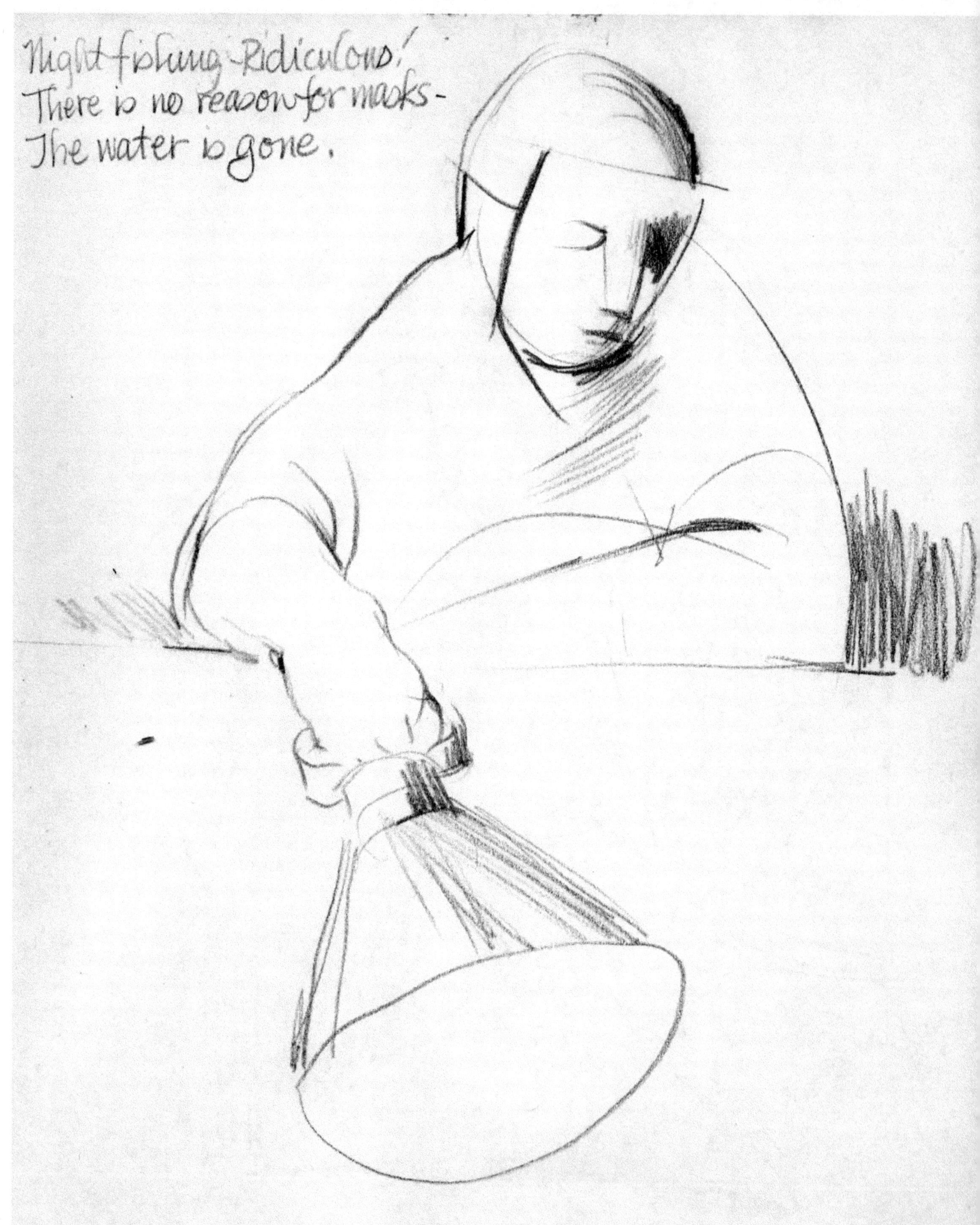

Night fishing - Ridiculous!
There is no reason for masks -
The water is gone.

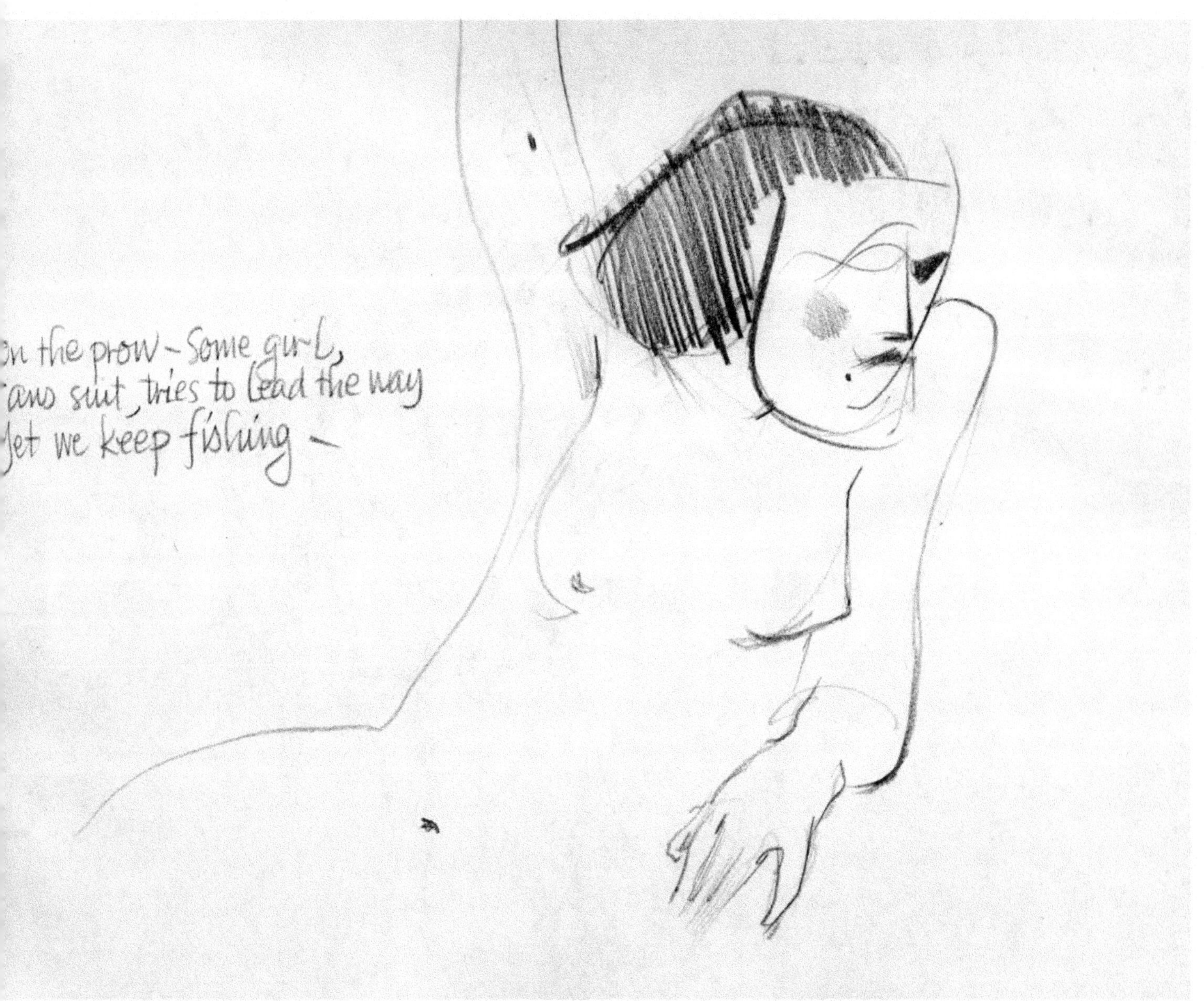
on the prow ~ some girl,
ans suit, tries to lead the way
yet we keep fishing ~

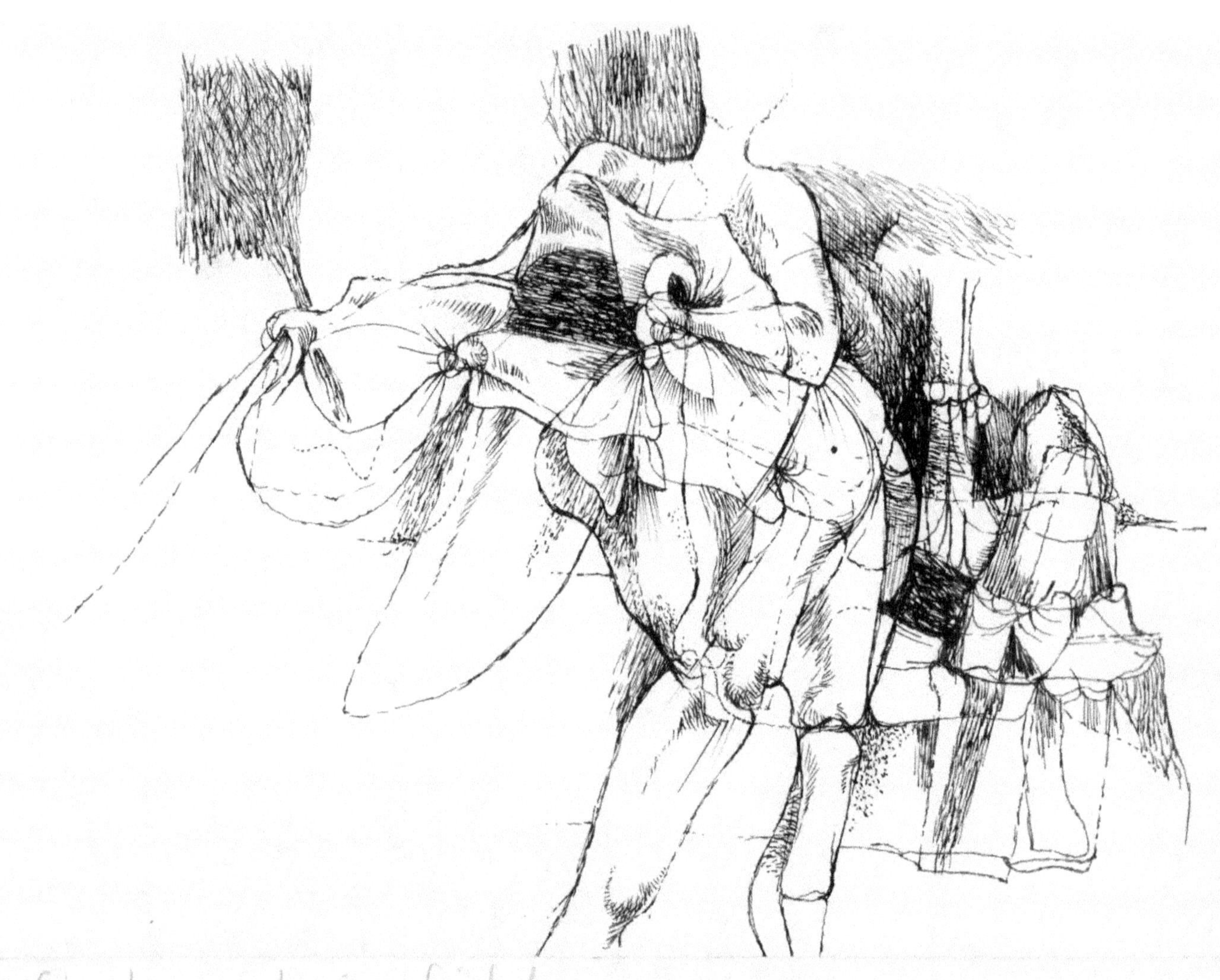

This strange device whirled
by a figure of my mind—
a beautiful dance!

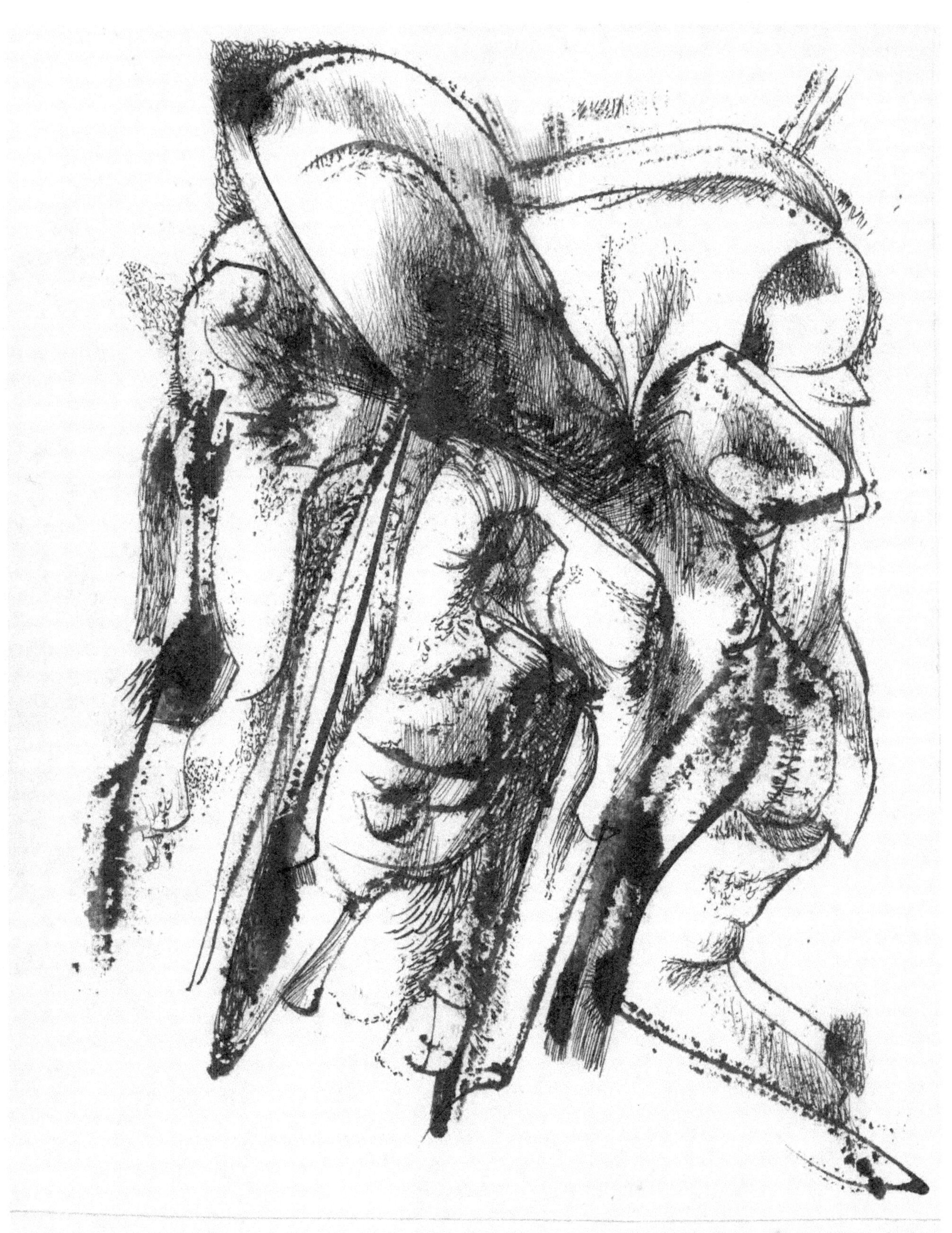

Iridescent wings...
Green buzzing bodies announce
Summer requiem.

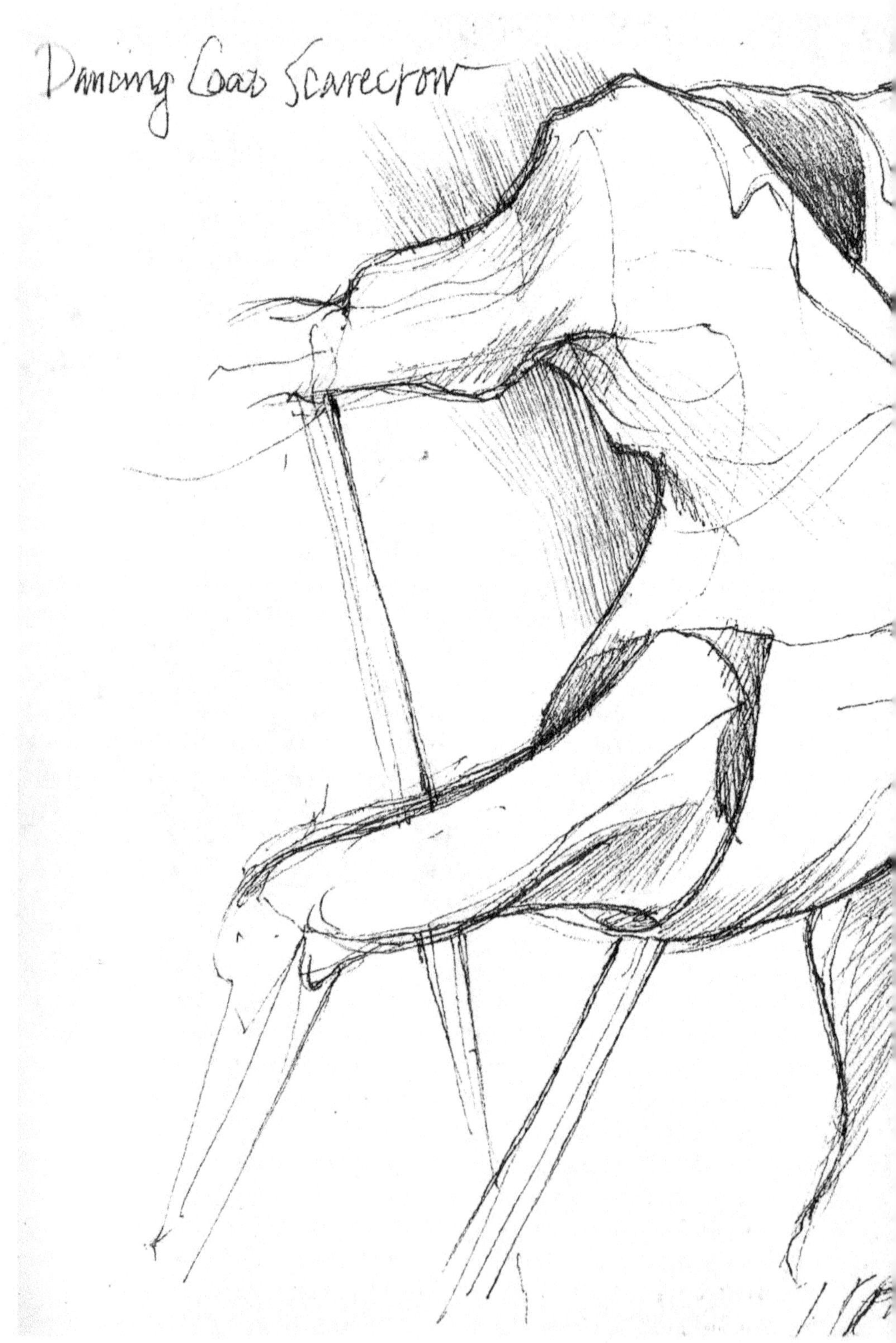

Dancing Coat Scarecrow

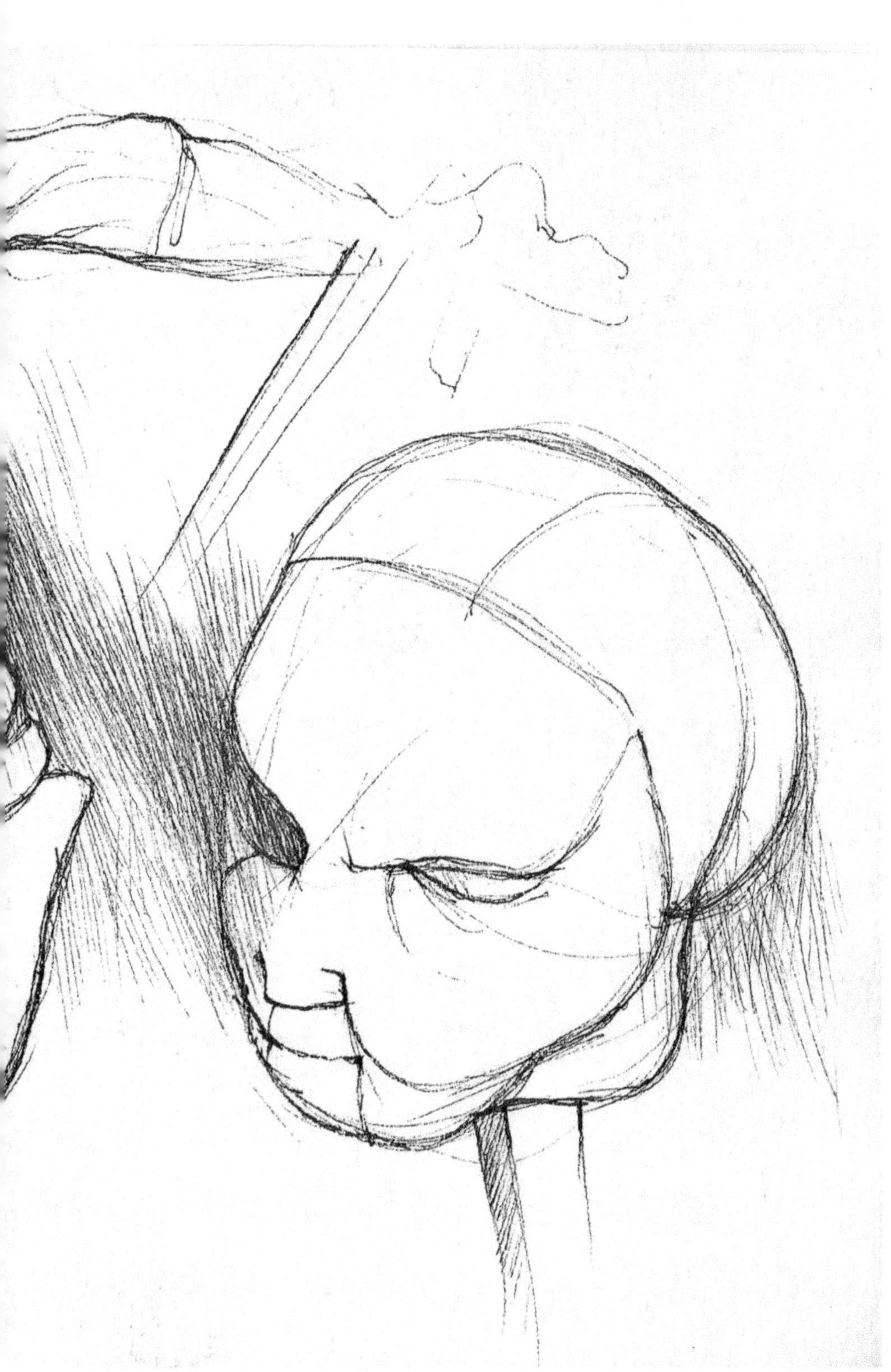

BOOK 2 drawings from 1962 to 1966

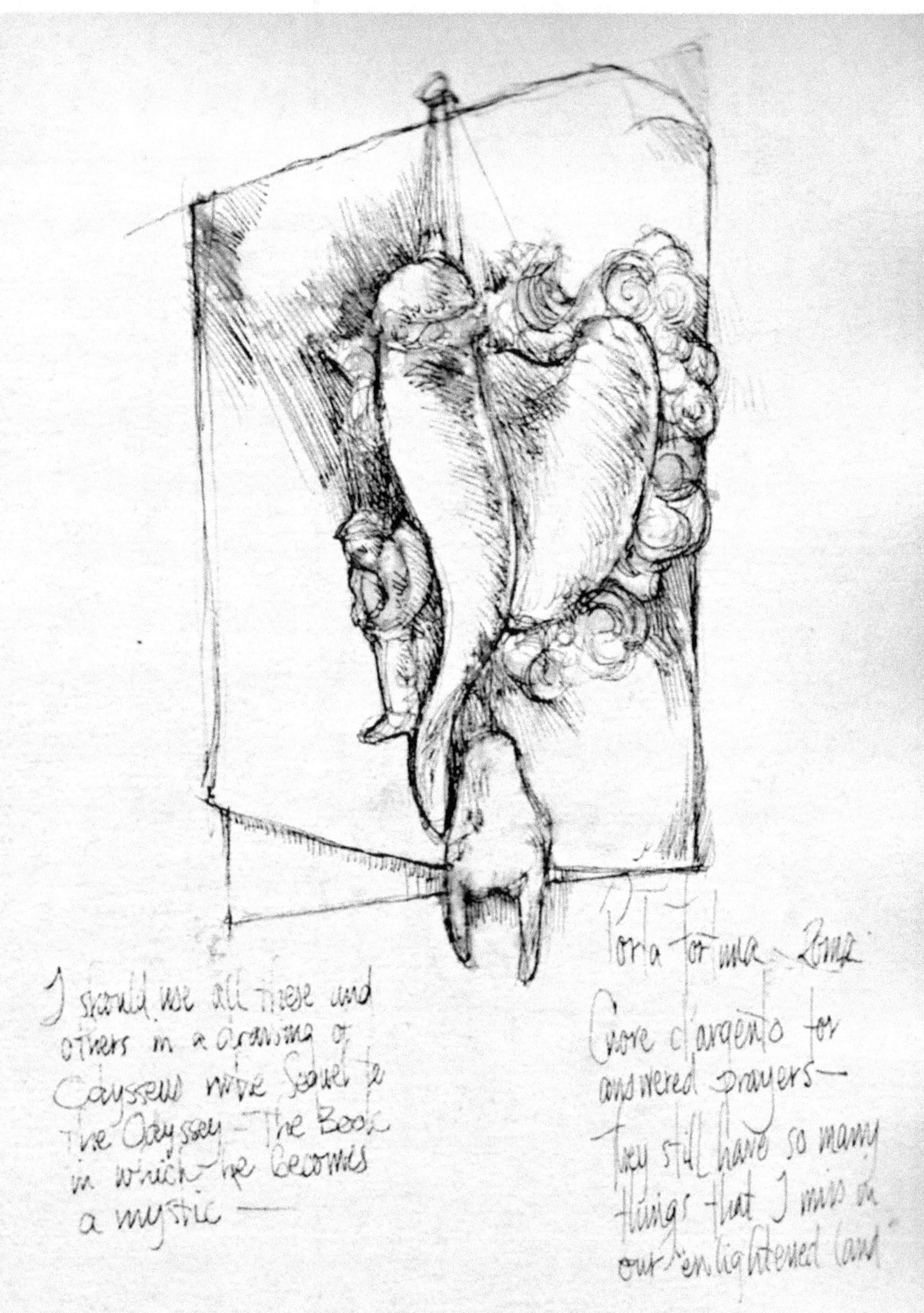

I should use all these and others in a drawing of Calypso more Sequel to The Odyssey — The Book in which he becomes a mystic —

Porta Fortuna ~ Rome
Cuore d'argento for answered prayers —
They still have so many things that I miss in our "enlightened" land.

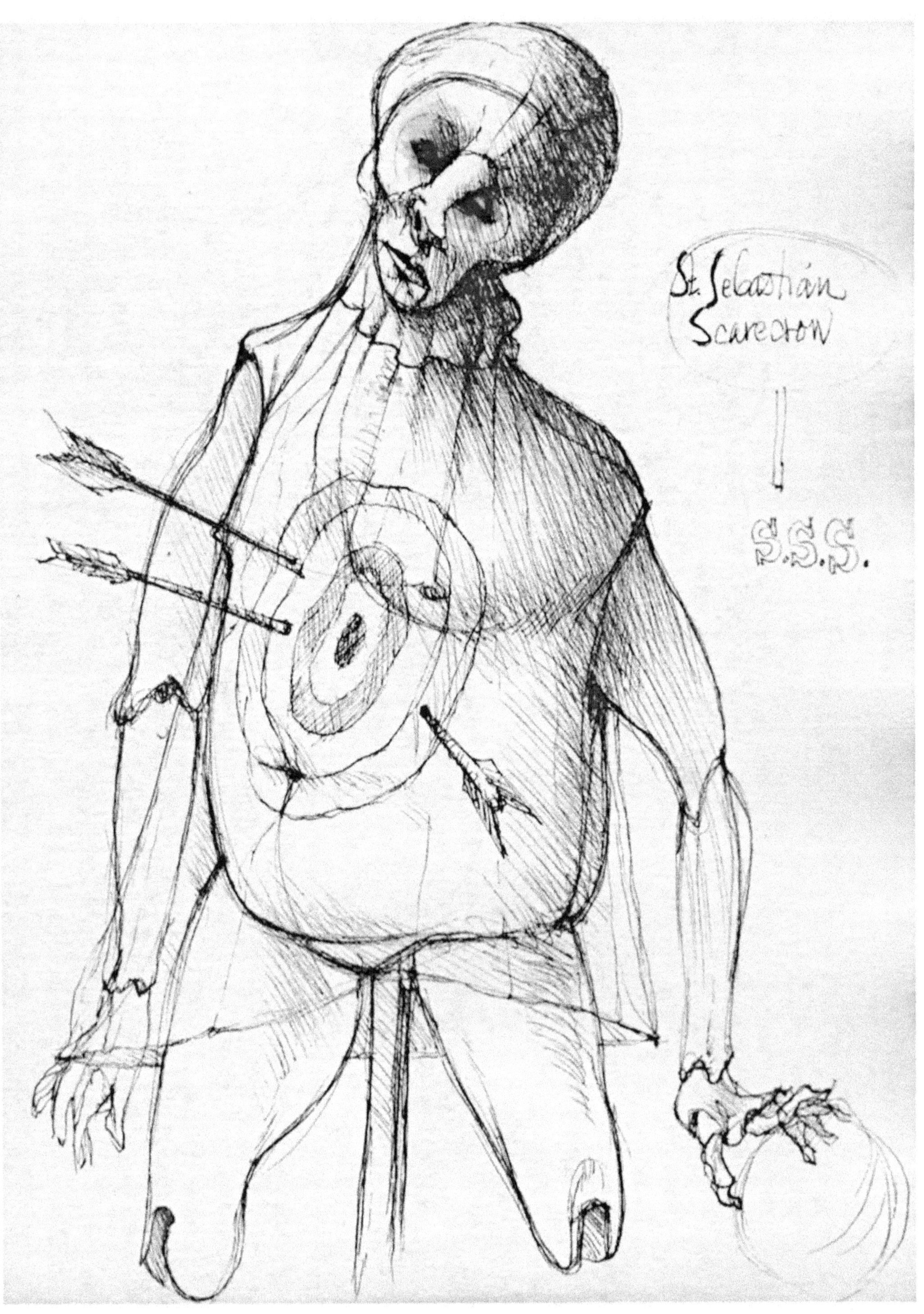

St. Sebastian
Scarecrow

S.S.S.

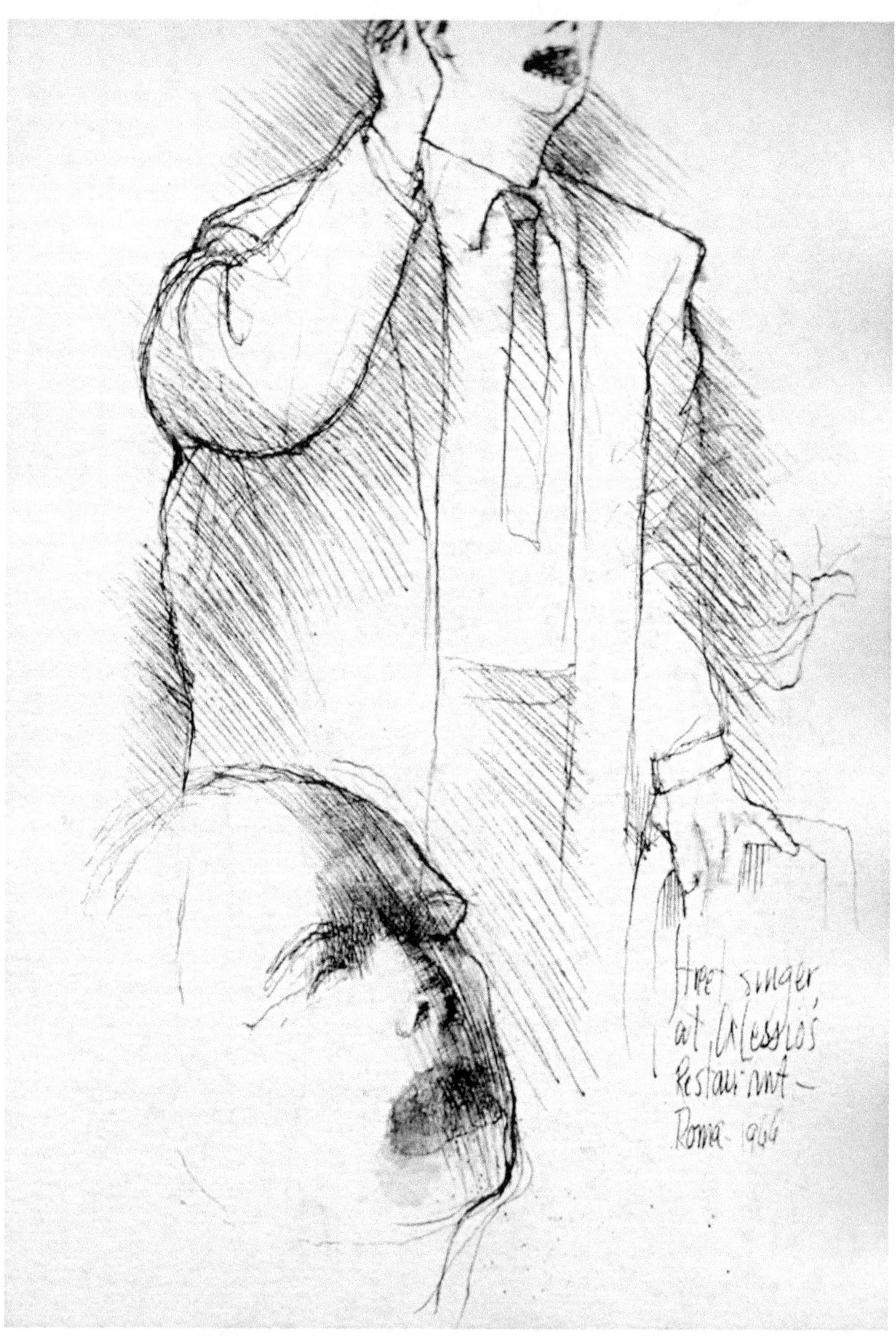

Street singer
at Alessio's
Restaurant —
Roma - 1966

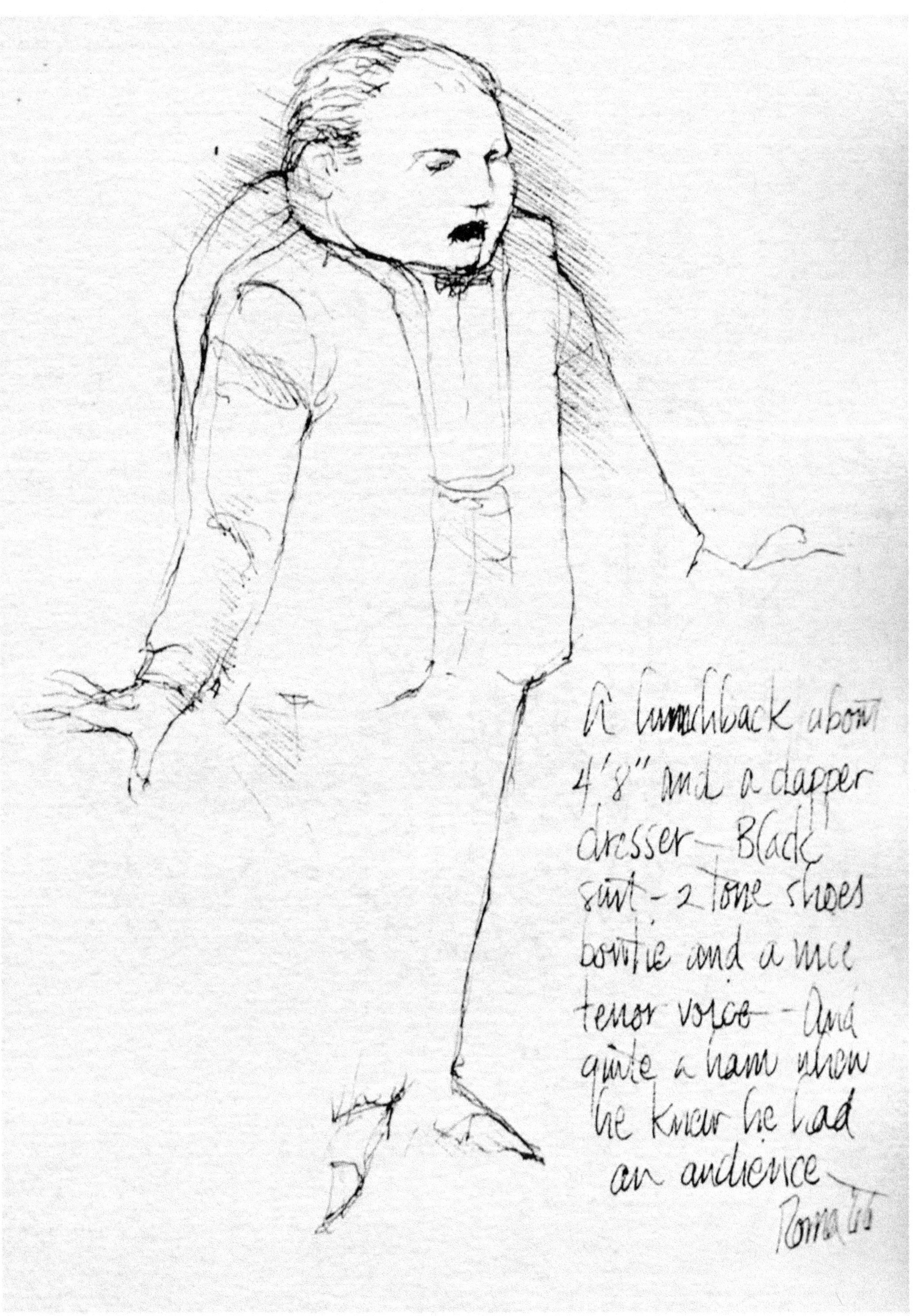

A hunchback about
4'8" and a dapper
dresser - Black
suit - 2 tone shoes
bowtie and a nice
tenor voice - And
quite a ham when
he knew he had
an audience.
Ronald

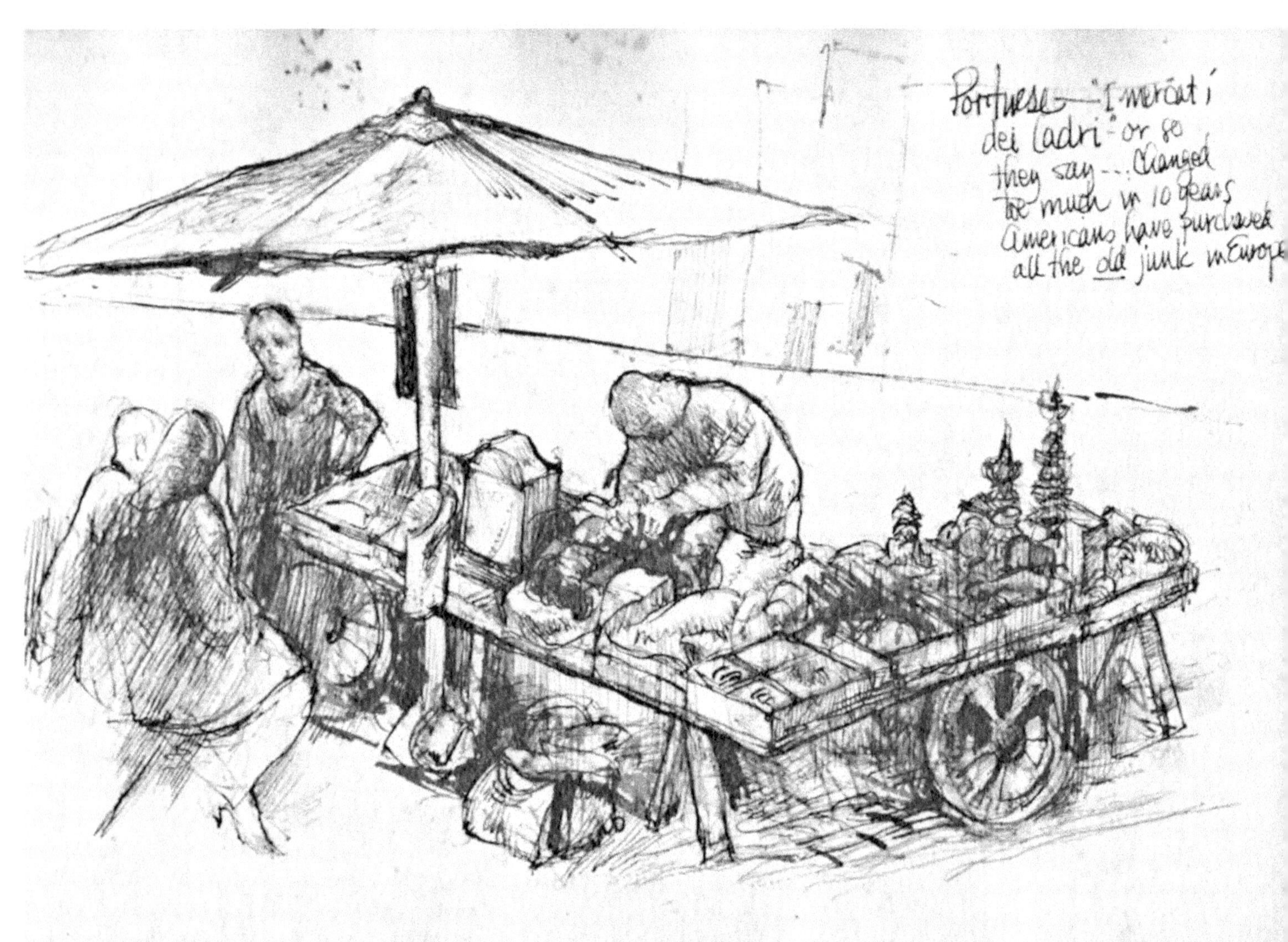

Portuese — "I mercat i
dei ladri" or so
they say ... Changed
too much in 10 years
Americans have purchased
all the old junk in Europe

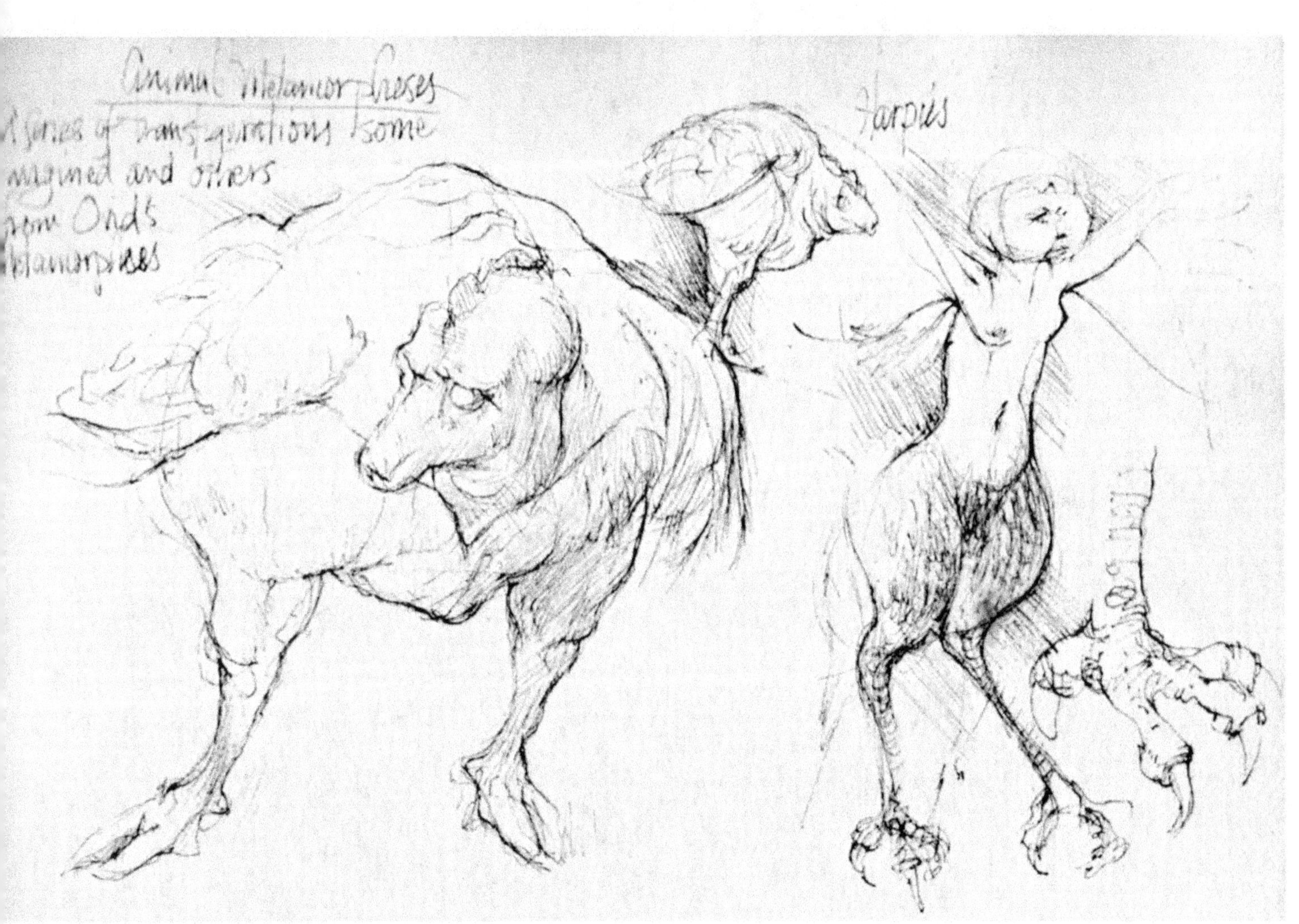

Animal Metamorphoses
A series of transfigurations, some
imagined and others
from Ovid's
Metamorphoses
Harpies

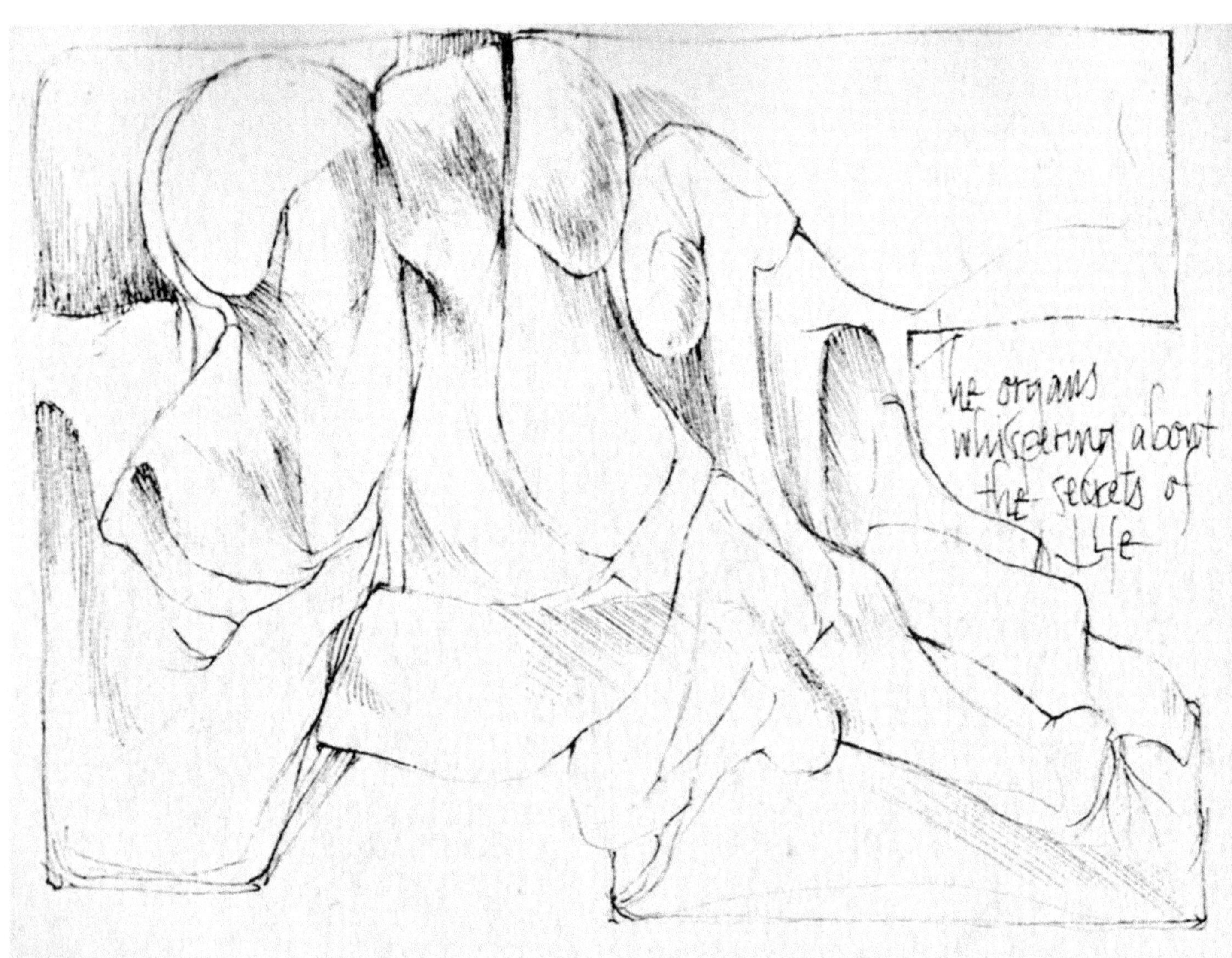

The organs
whispering about
the secrets of
life

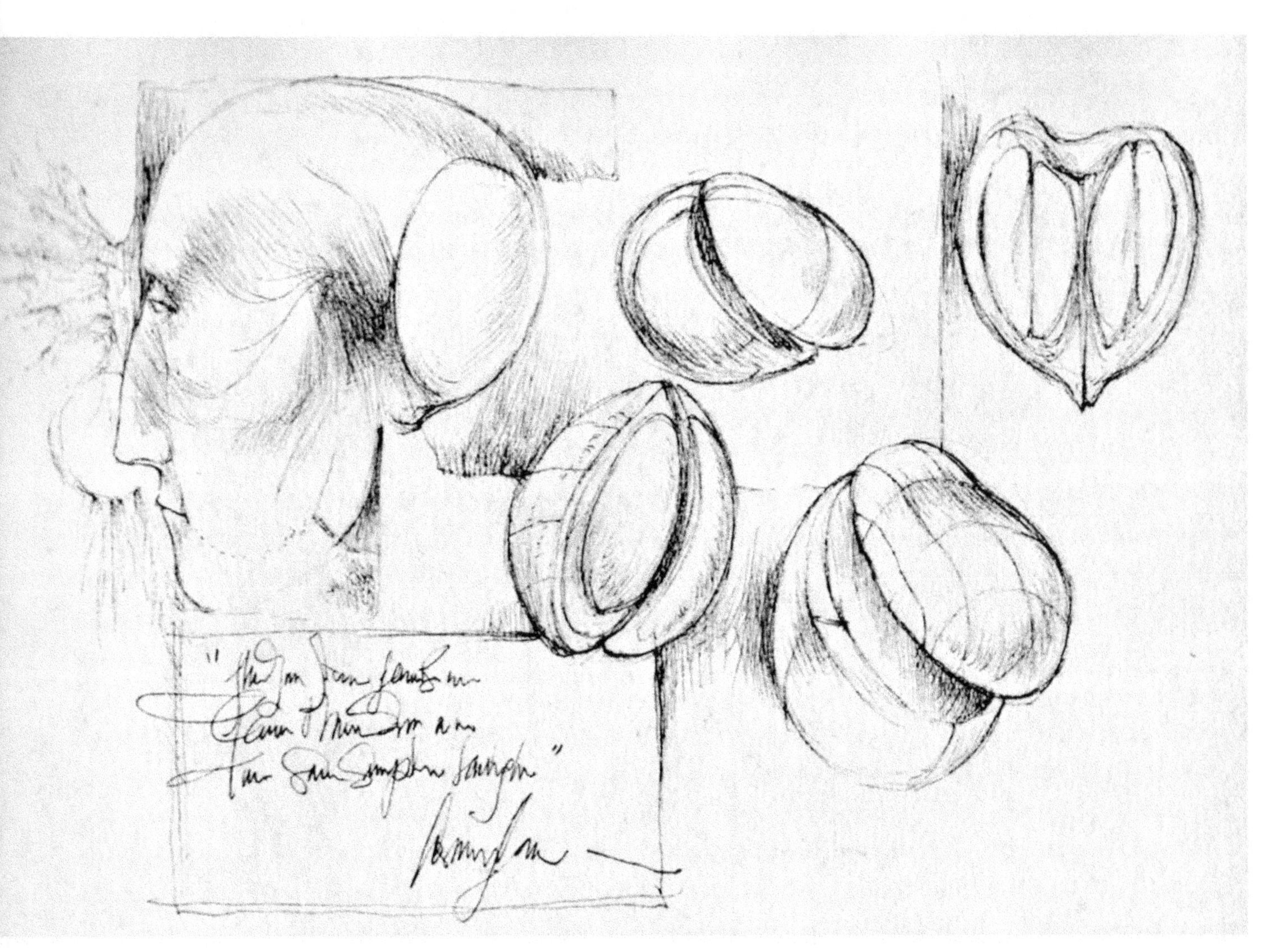

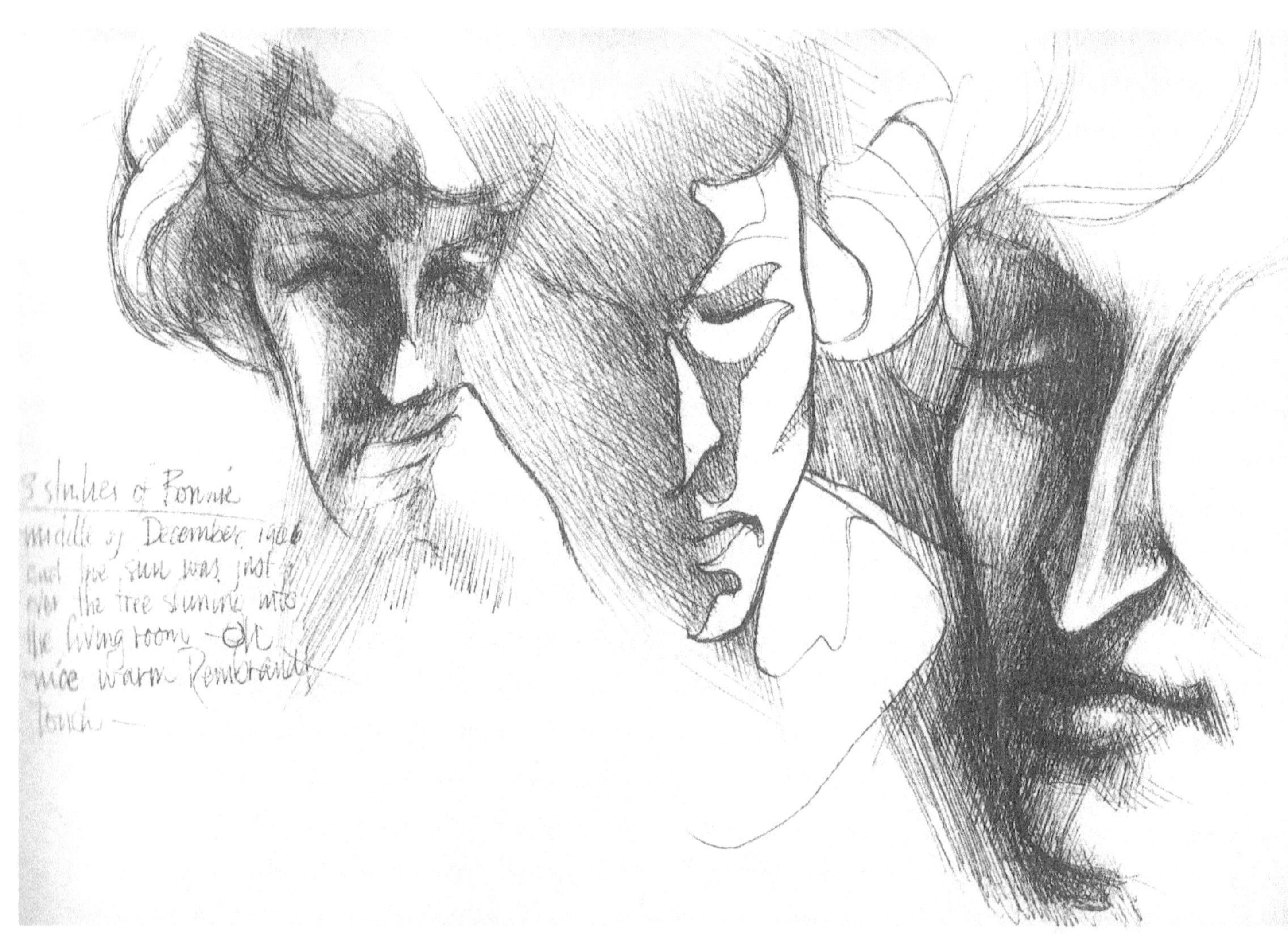

3 studies of Ronnie
middle of December 1966
and the sun was just
over the tree slanting into
the living room — Oh
nice warm Rembrandt
touch —

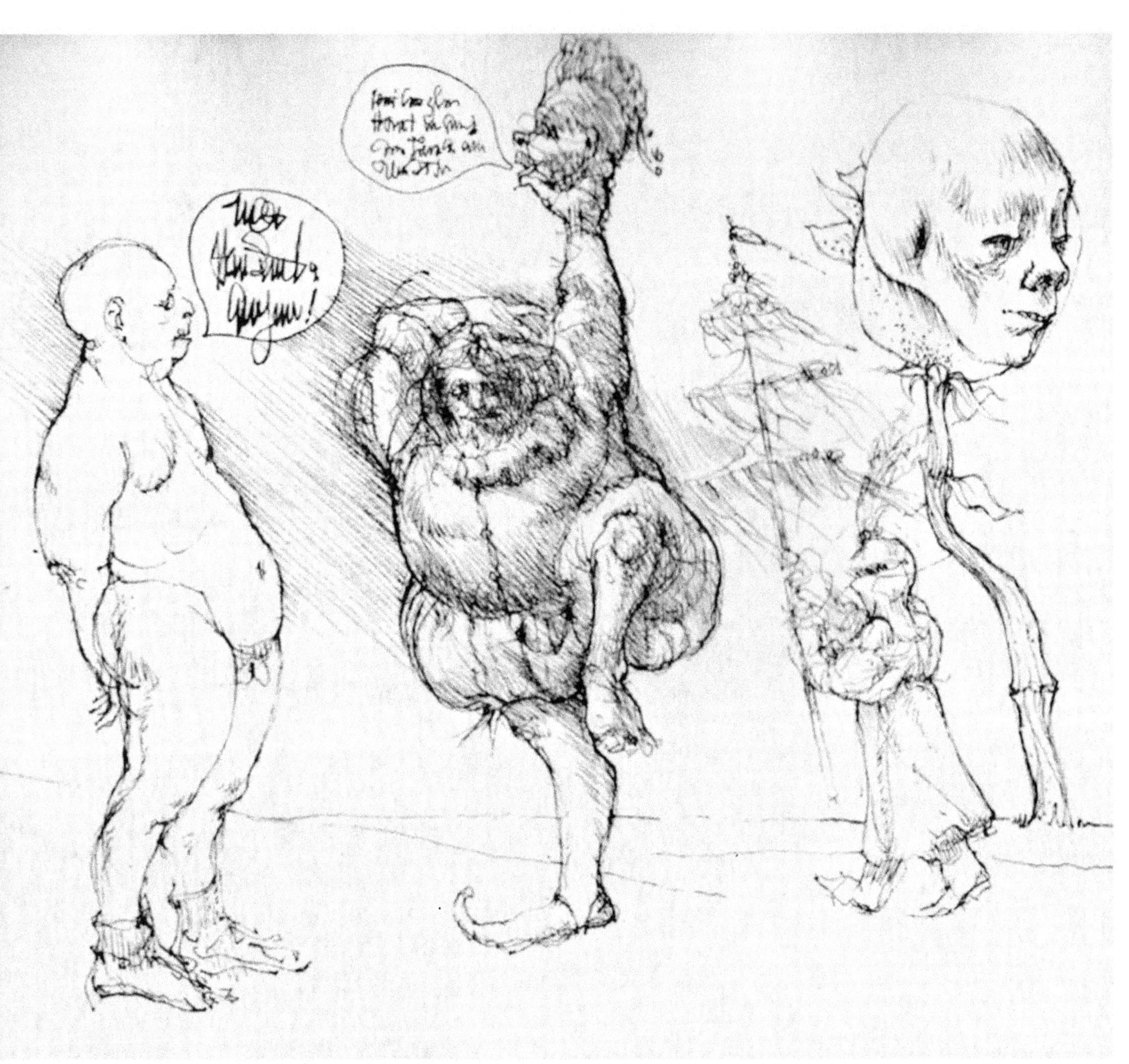

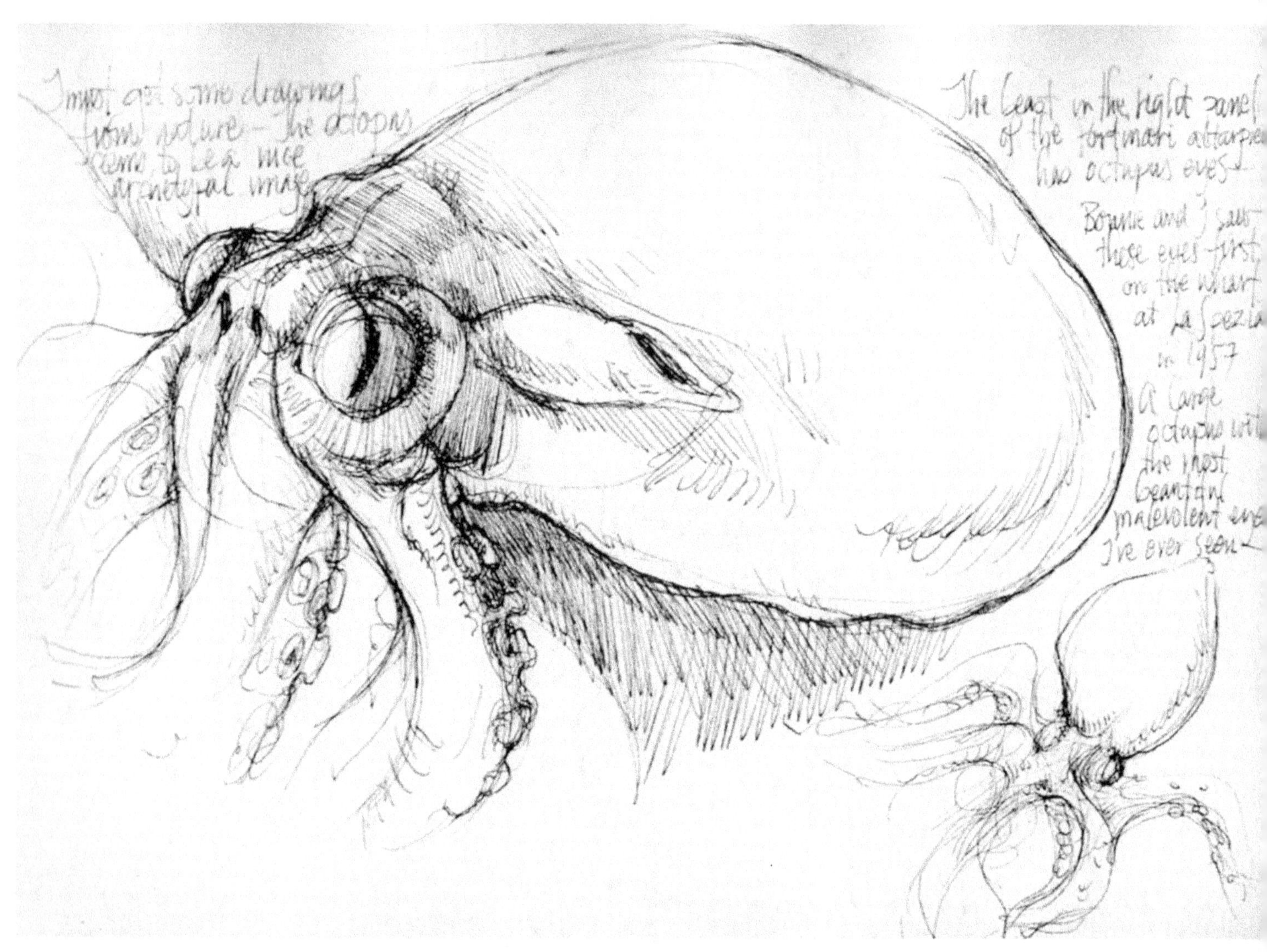

I must get some drawings from nature — the octopus seem to be a huge archetypal image

The beast in the right panel of the Portinari altarpiece has octopus eyes

Bonnie and I saw these eyes first on the wharf at La Spezia in 1957

A large octopus with the most Giant and malevolent eyes I've ever seen

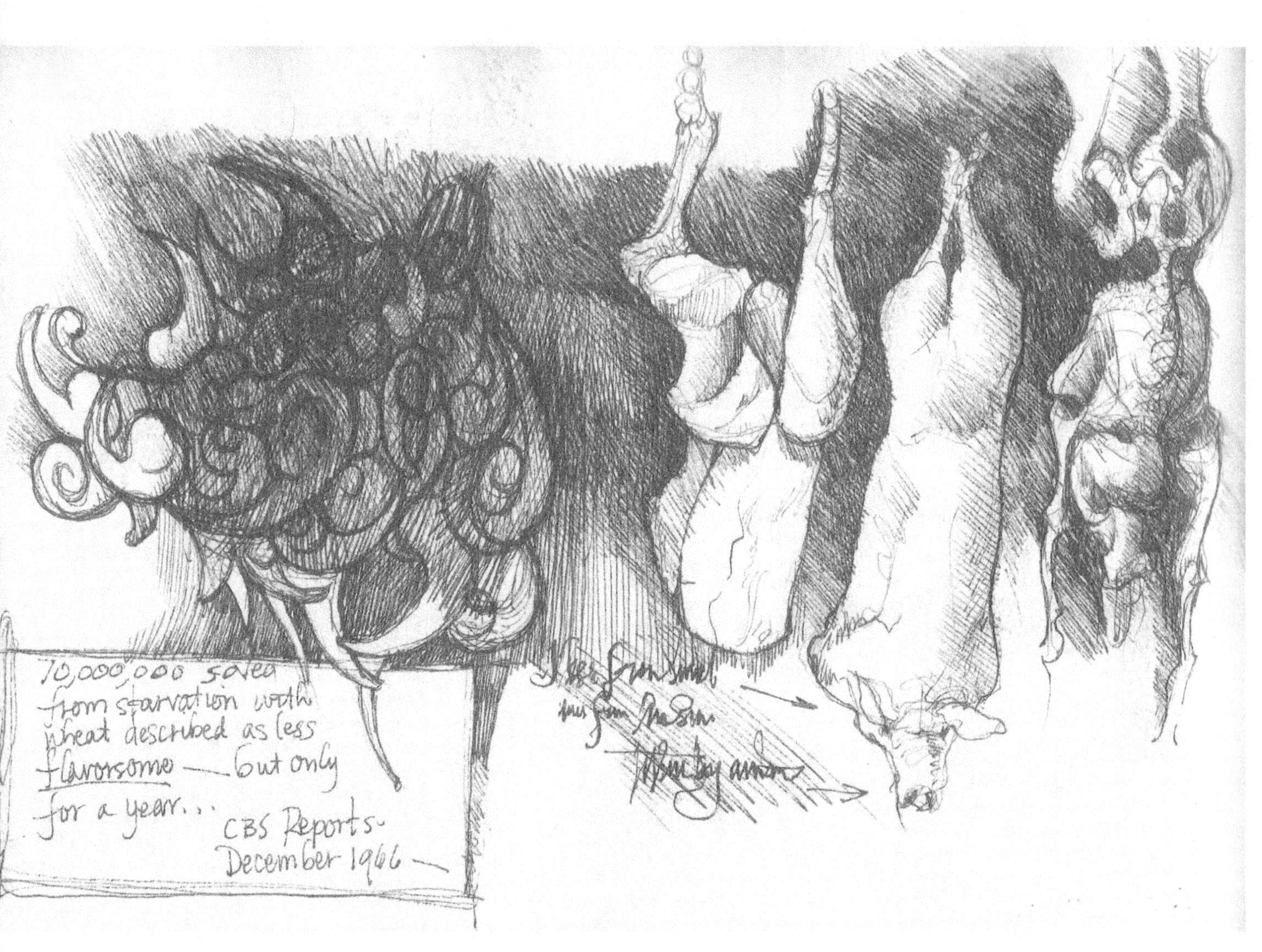

70,000,000 saved
from starvation with
wheat described as less
flavorsome — but only
for a year...
CBS Reports.
December 1966 —

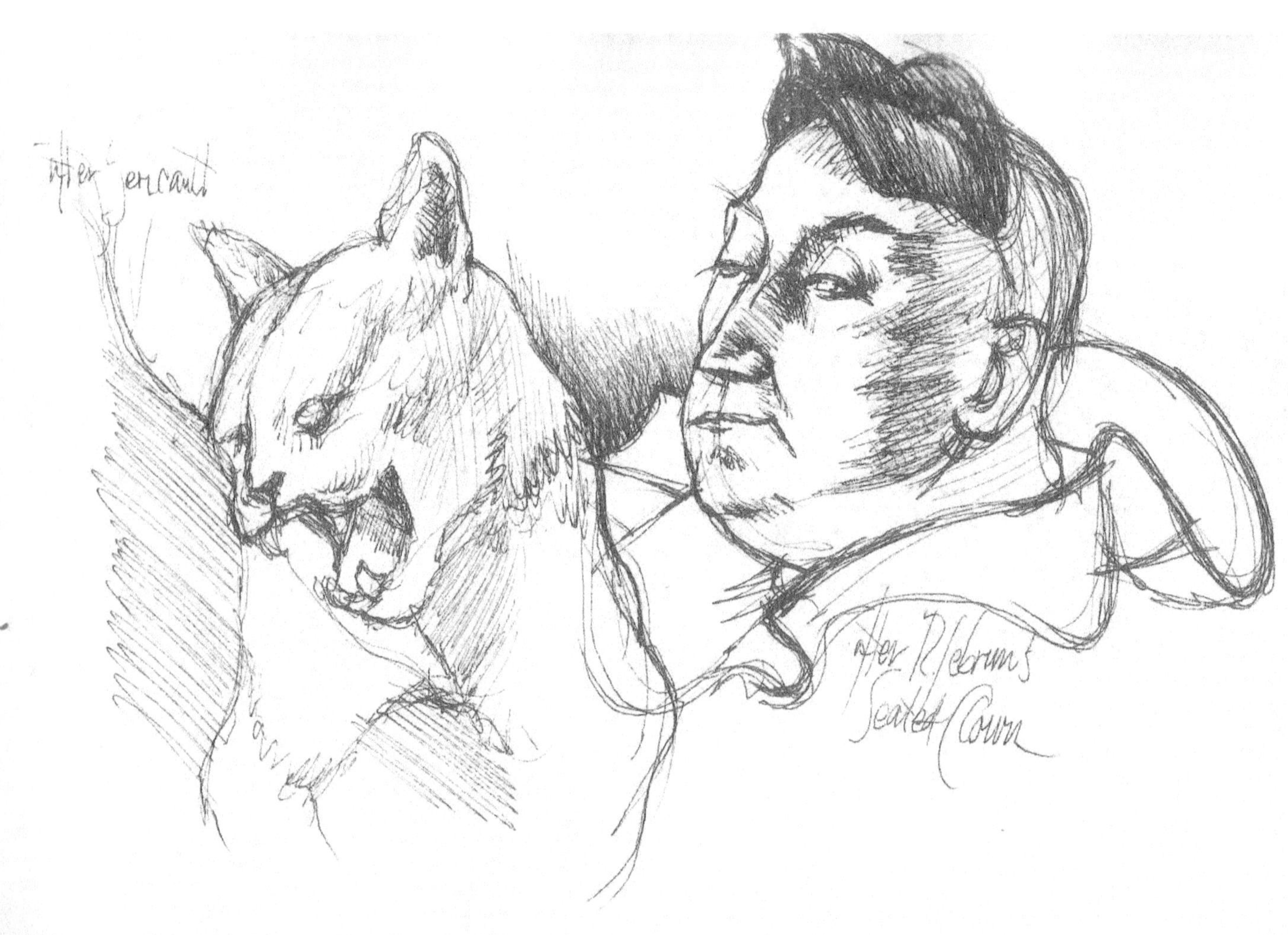
after Bercault
after R Verum's
Seated Cown

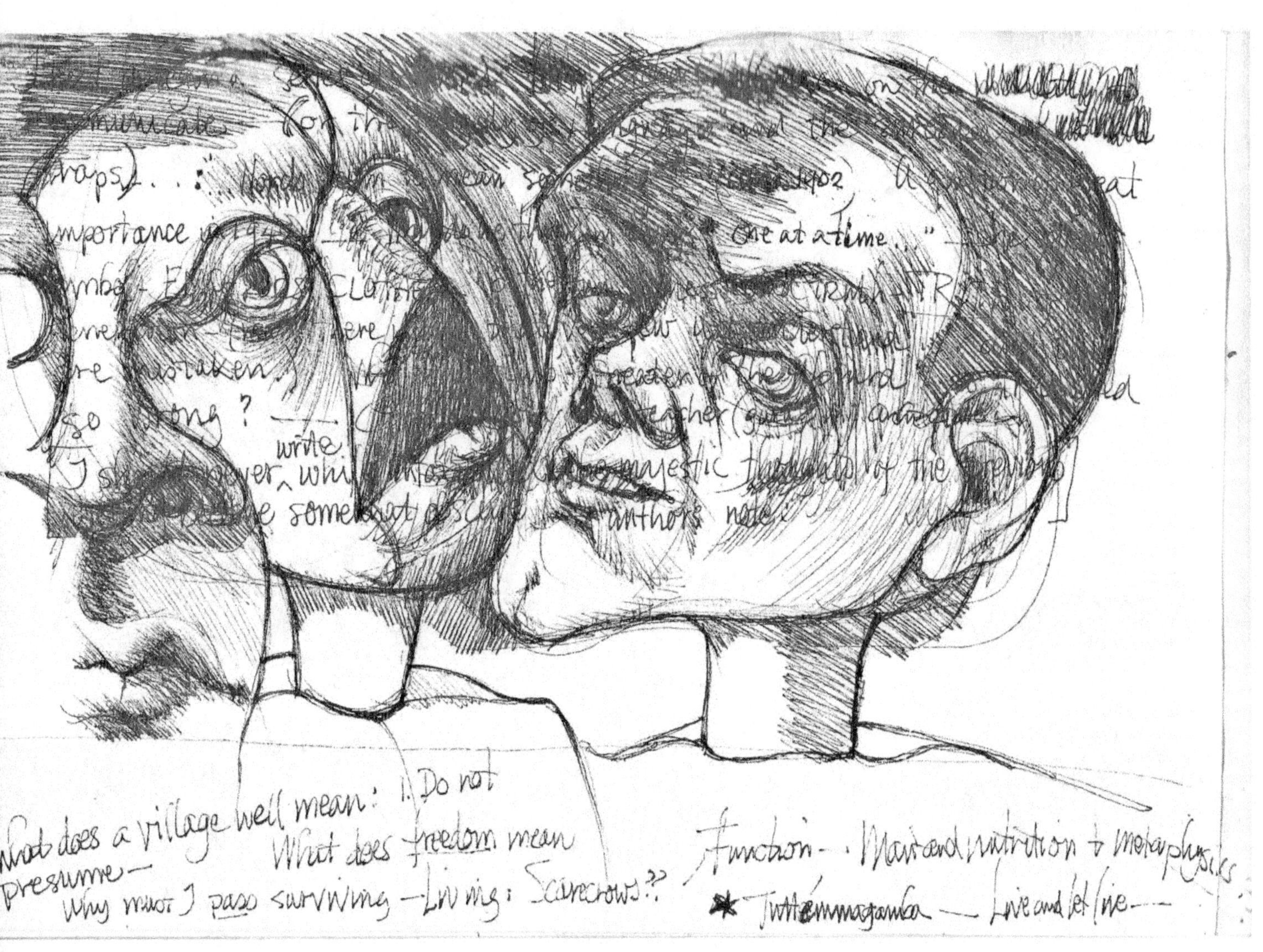

What does a village well mean? 1. Do not presume—
What does freedom mean
Why must I pass surviving — Living: Scarecrows??
Function— Mair and nutrition + metaphysics
* Tuttiemmagamba — Live and let live—

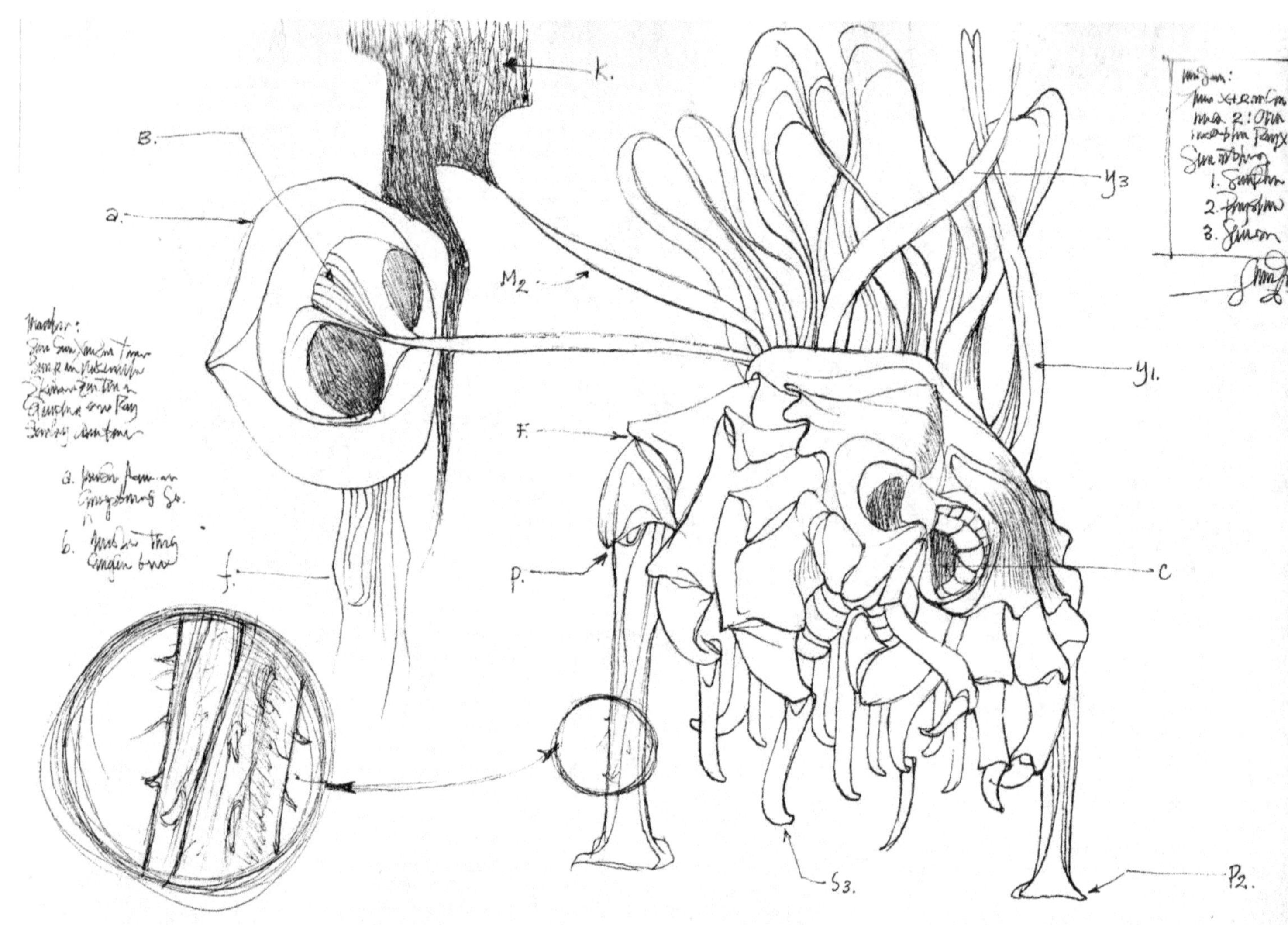

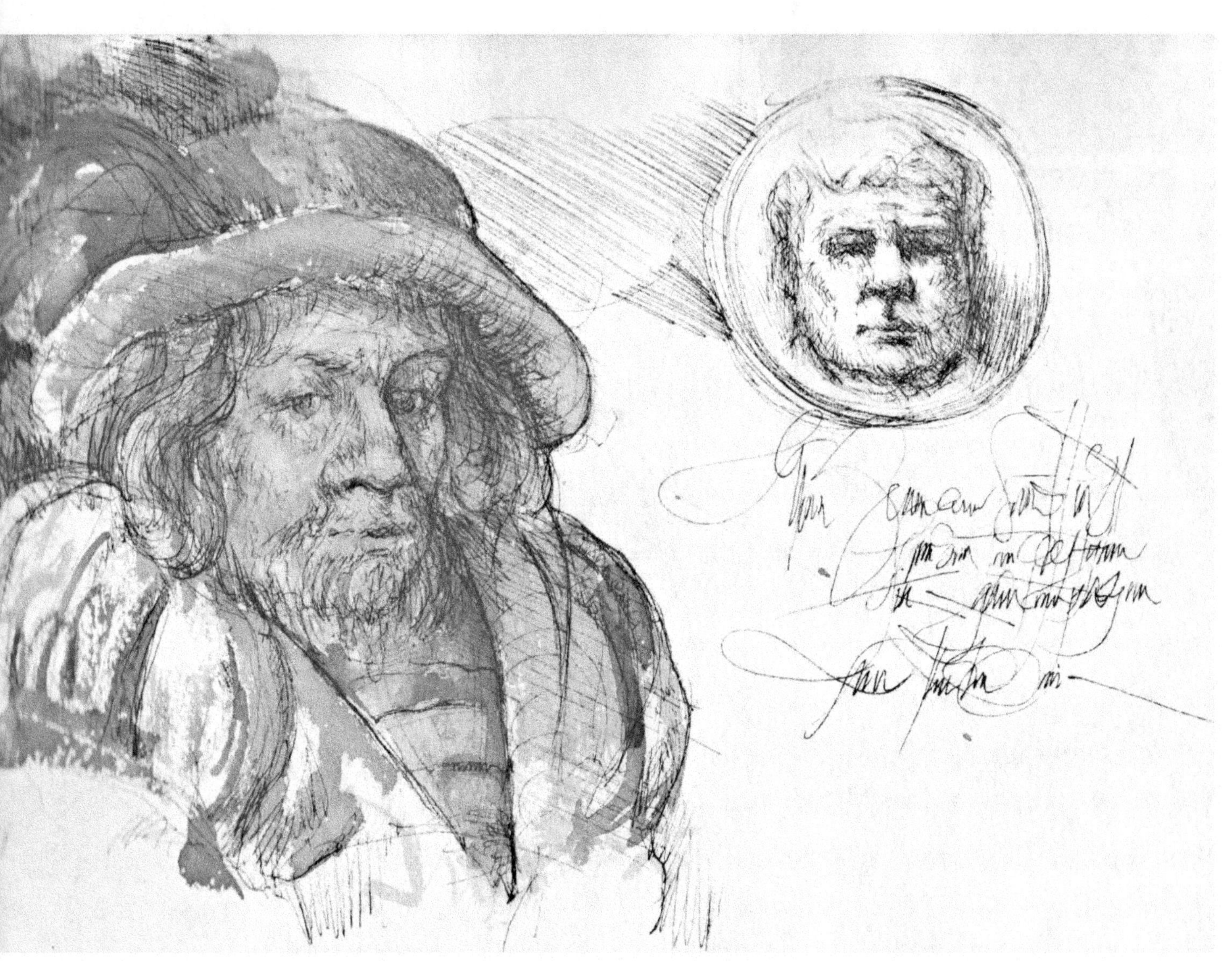

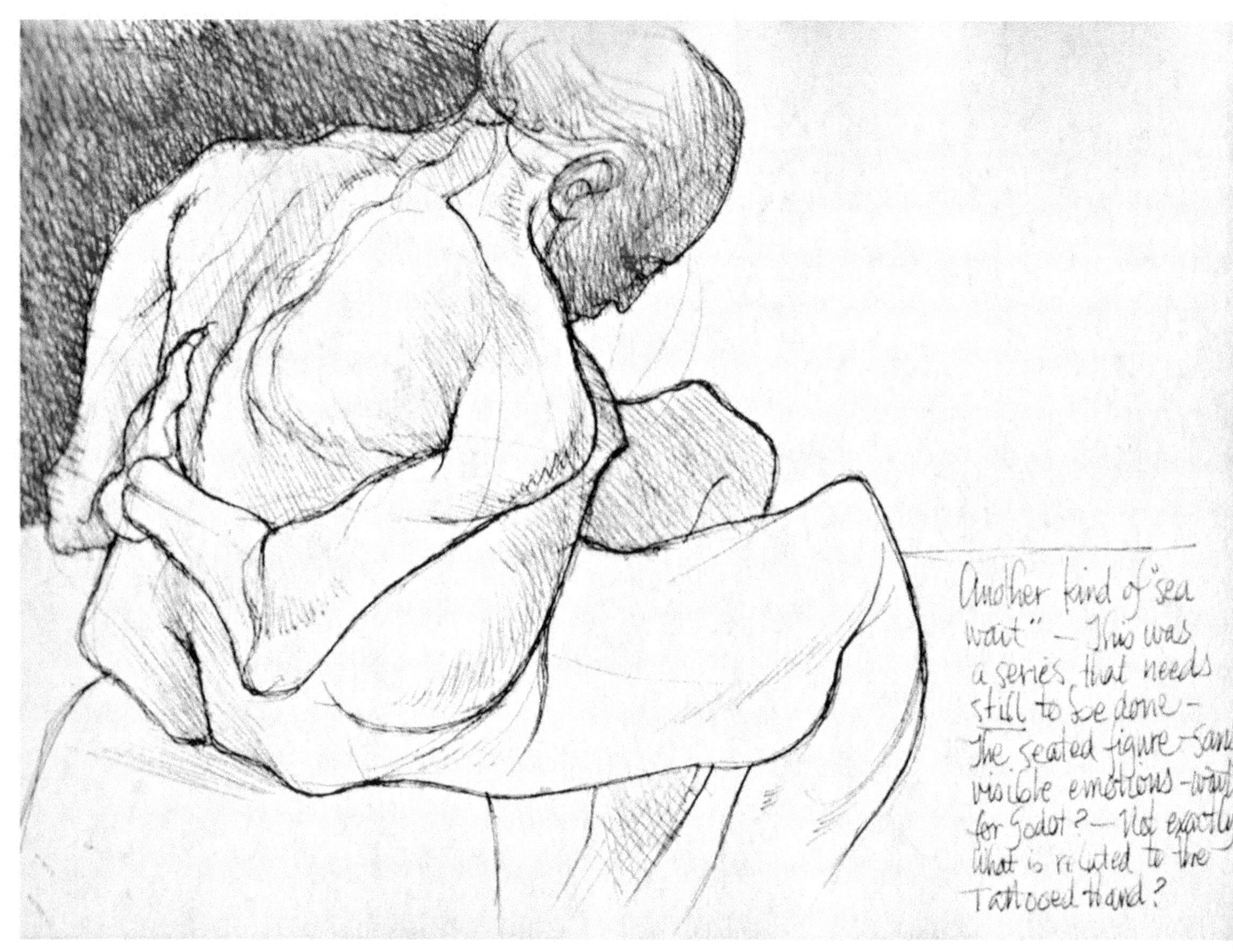

Another kind of "sea
wait" — This was
a series, that needs
still to be done —
The seated figure — same
visible emotions — wait
for Godot? — Not exactly
what is related to the
Tattooed Hand?

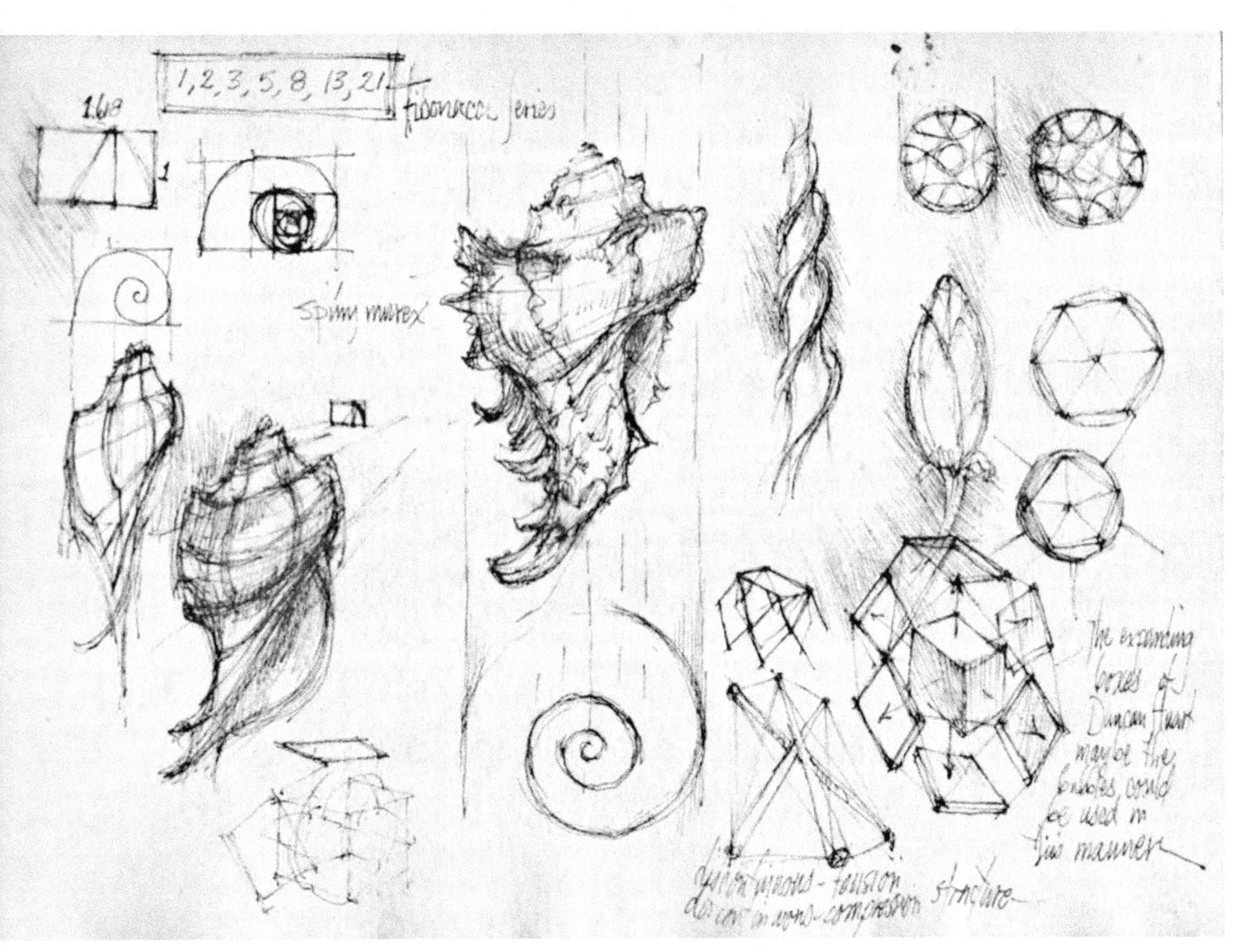

1, 2, 3, 5, 8, 13, 21
fibonacci series
1.618
1
Spiny murex
The expanding
bones of
Duncan Hunt
maybe the
bridges, could
be used in
this manner
continuous - tension
discontinuous - compression structure

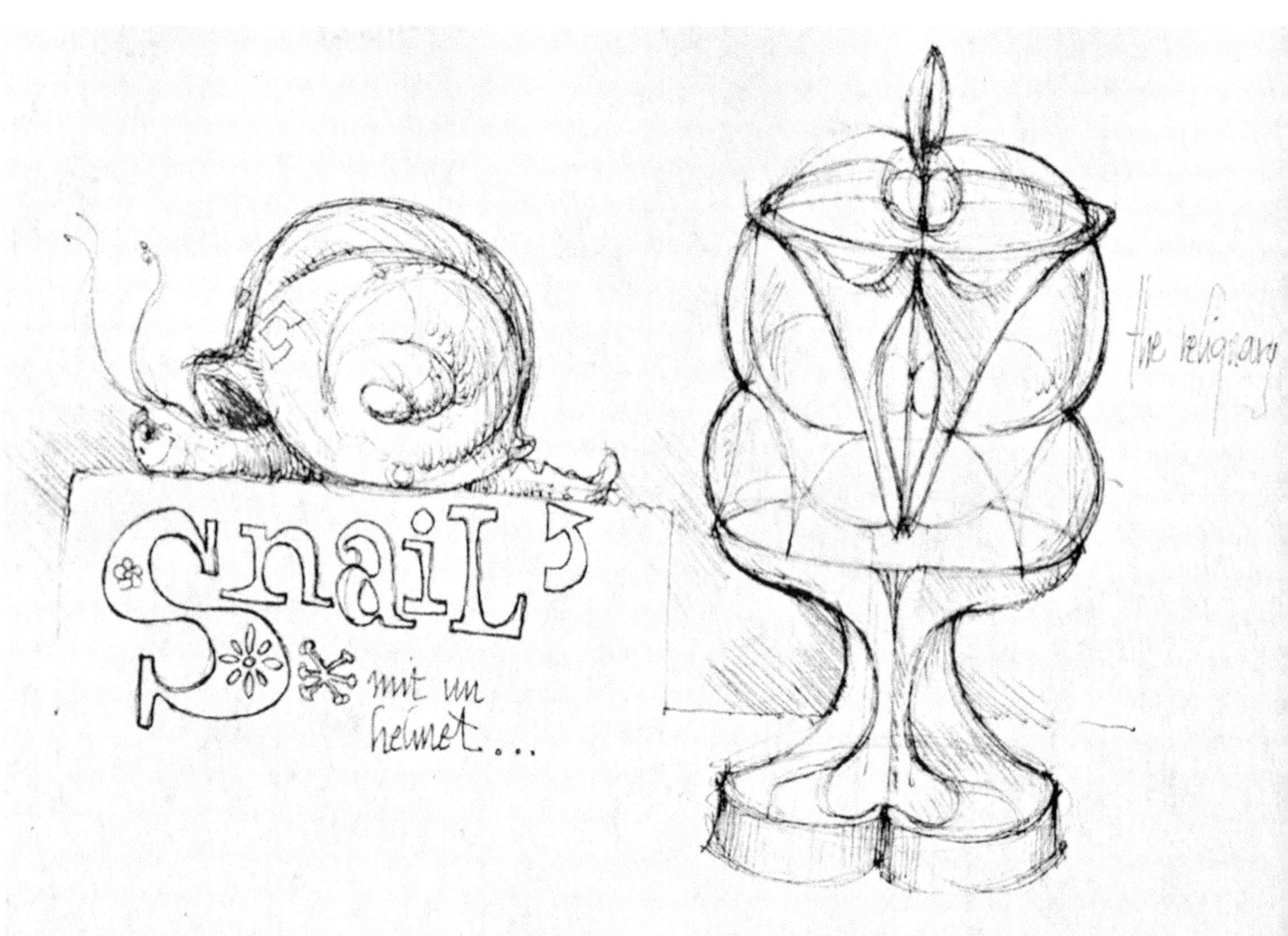
Snail
mit un
helmet...
the reliquary

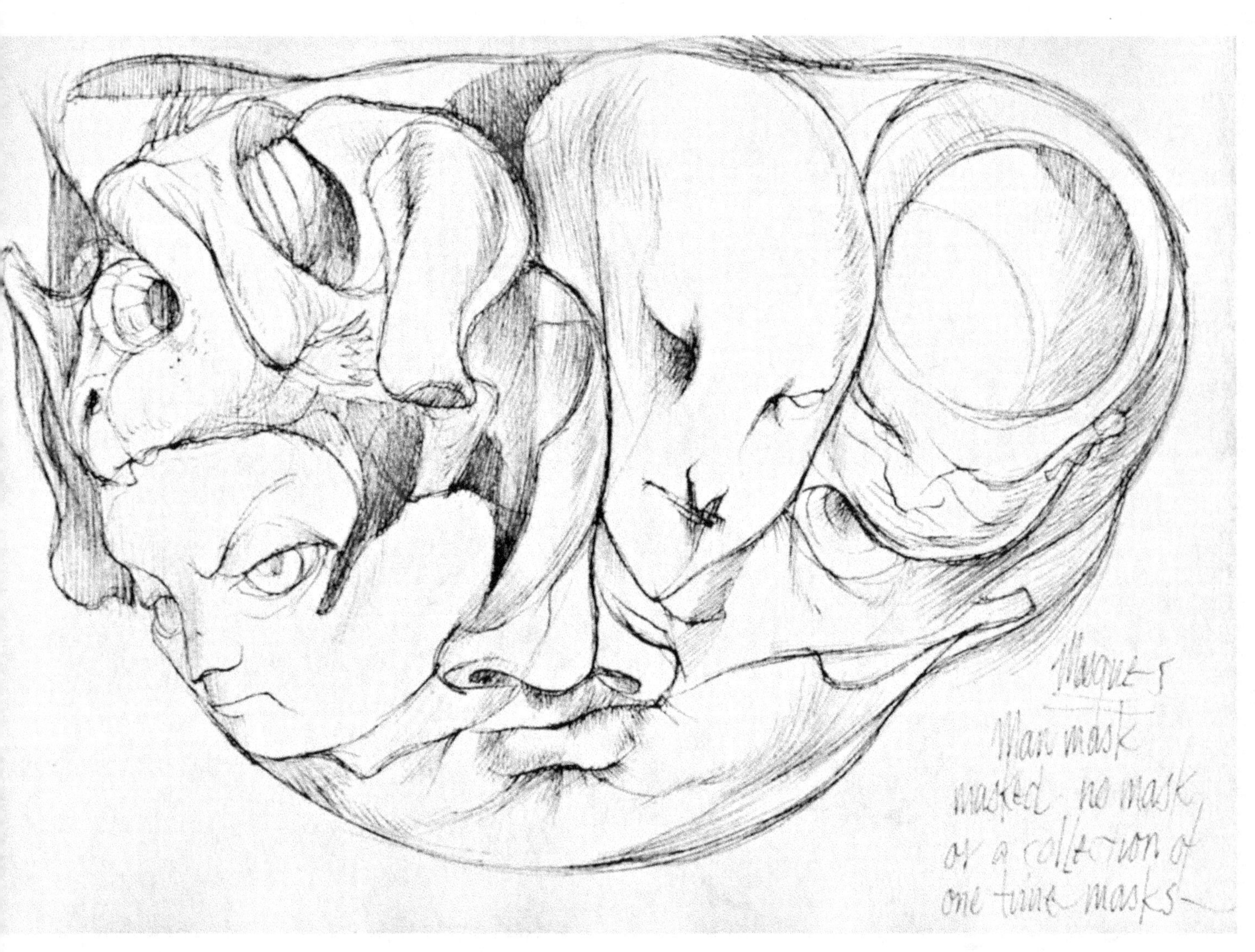

Marquis
Man mask
masked, no mask
or a collection of
one time masks

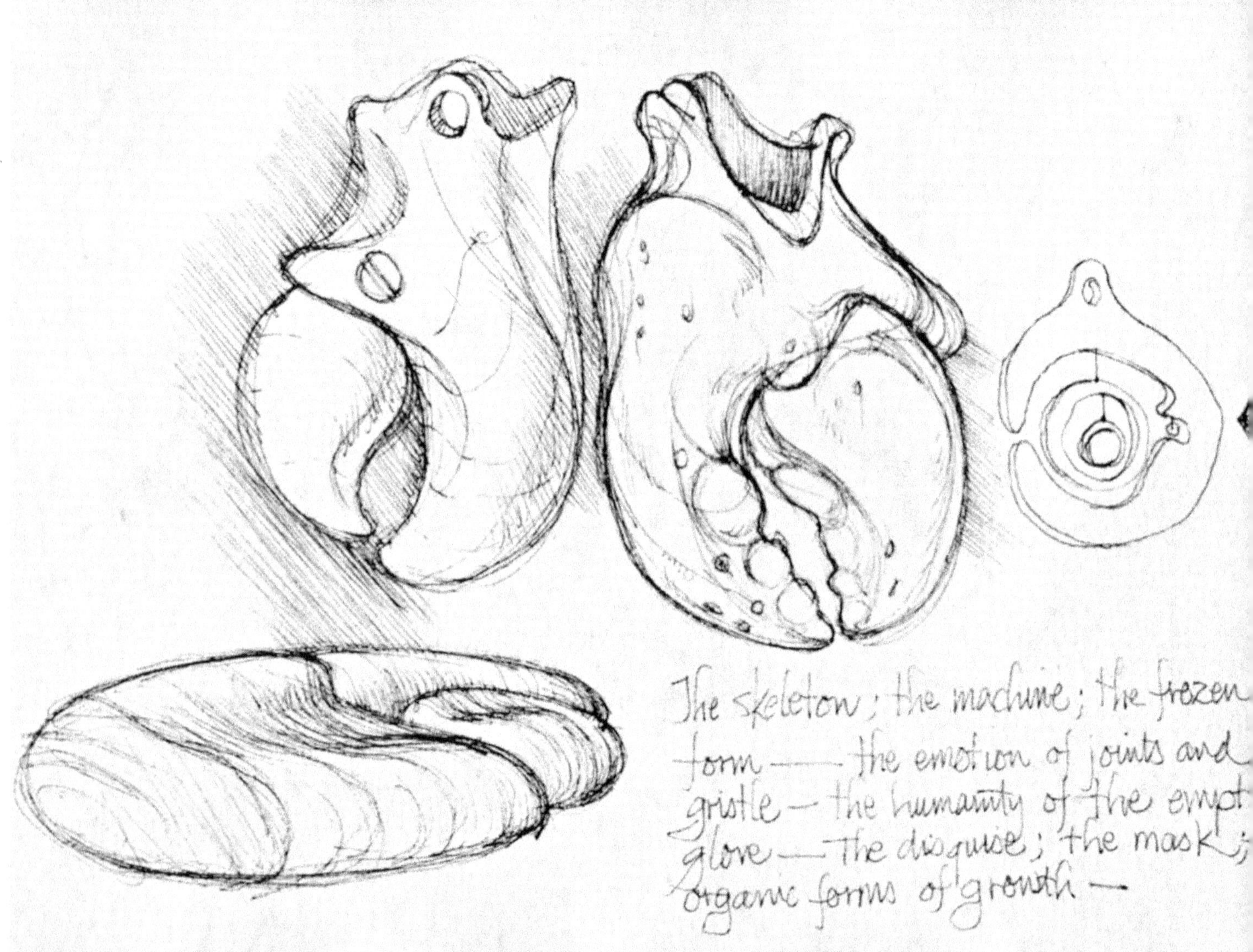

The skeleton; the machine; the frozen
form —— the emotion of joints and
gristle — the humanity of the empty
glove — The disguise; the mask;
organic forms of growth —

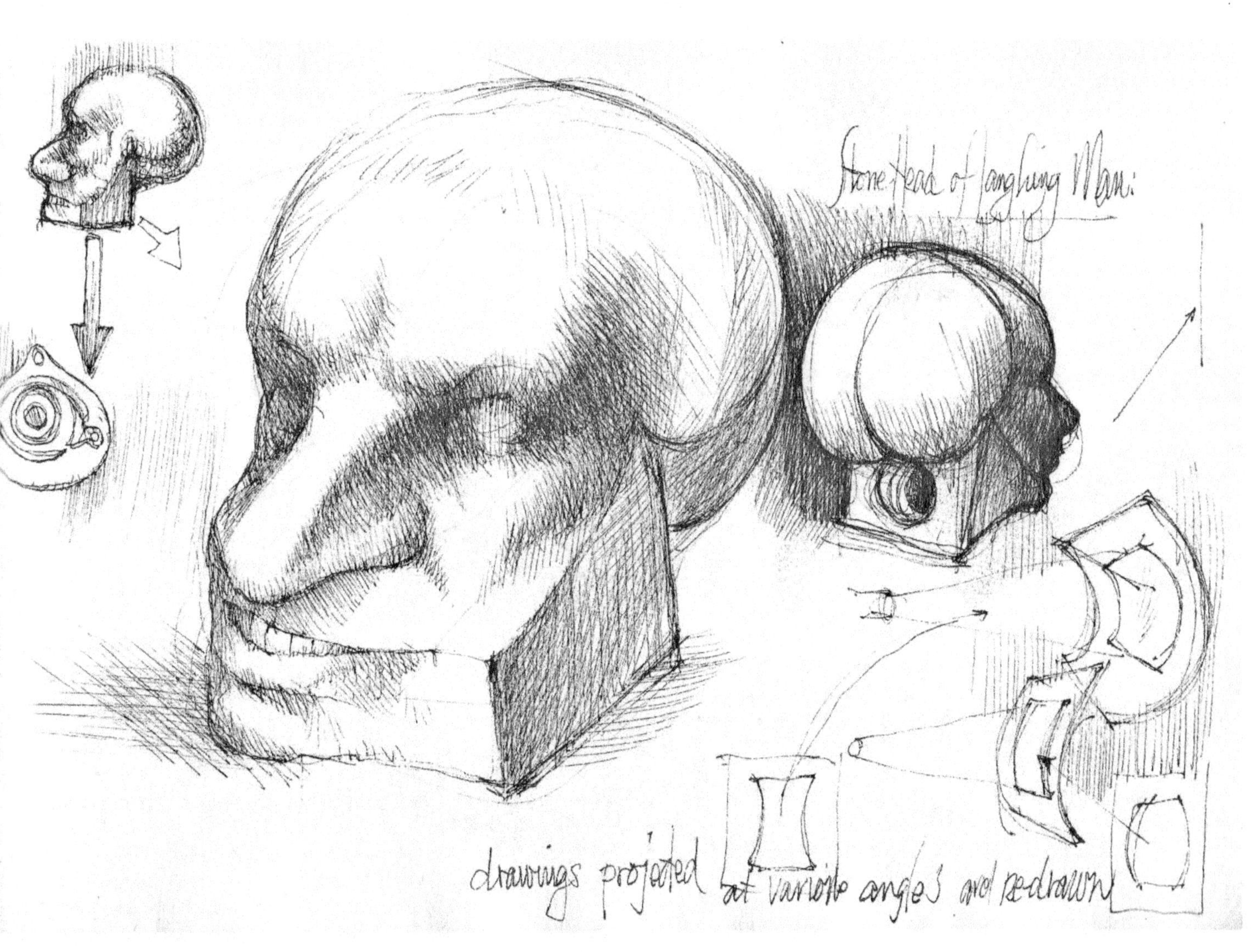

Stone Head of Laughing Man.
drawings projected at various angles and redrawn

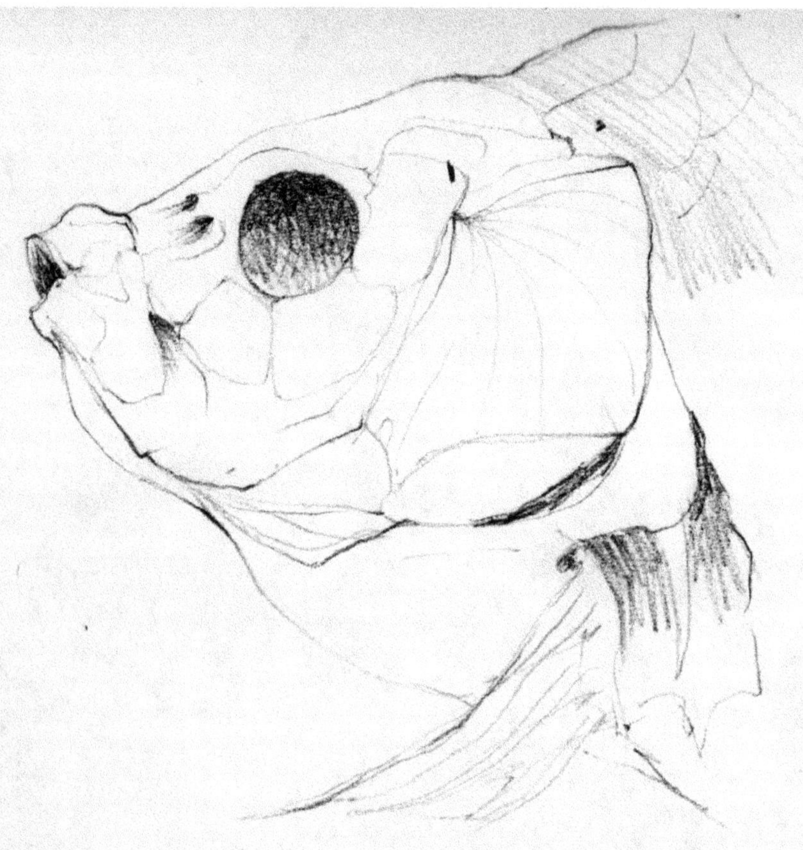

There; beneath those rocks -
Poor fish! Trapped by changing
Tides ... So much like us.

Grosse Ile - 1963

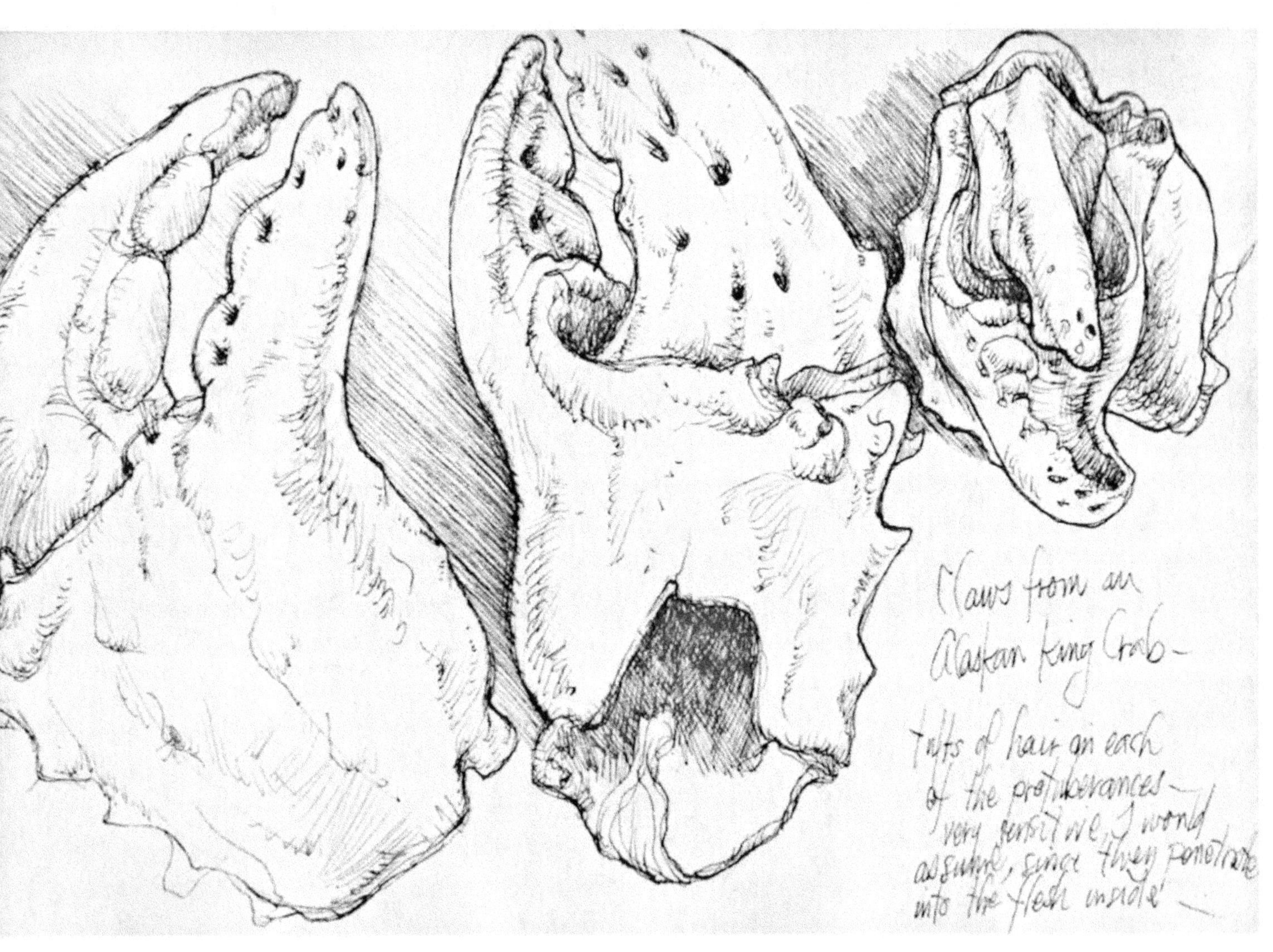

Claws from an
Alaskan King Crab —

Tufts of hair on each
of the protuberances —
very sensitive, I would
assume, since they penetrate
into the flesh inside!

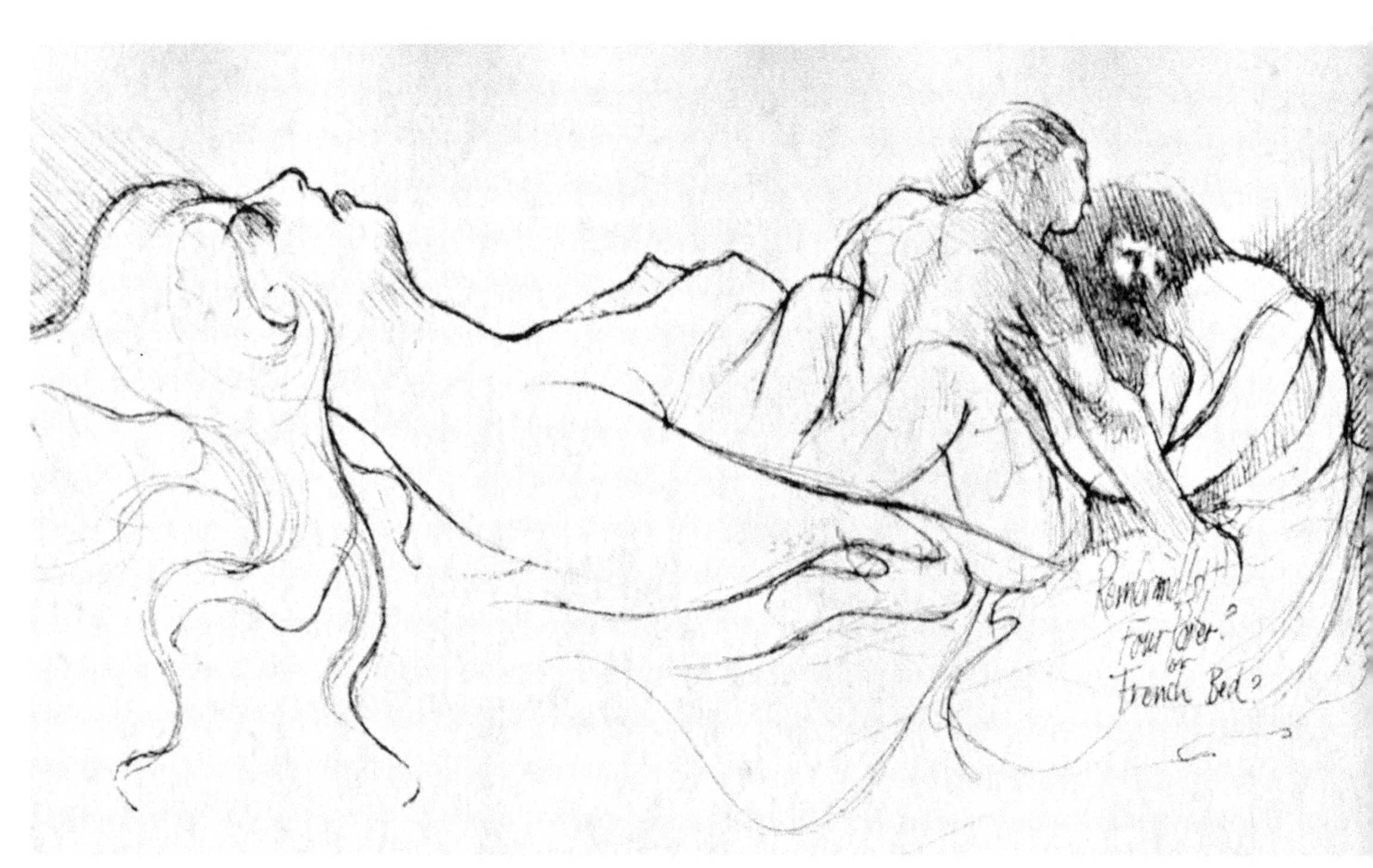

Rembrandt?
Your lover?
or
French Bed?

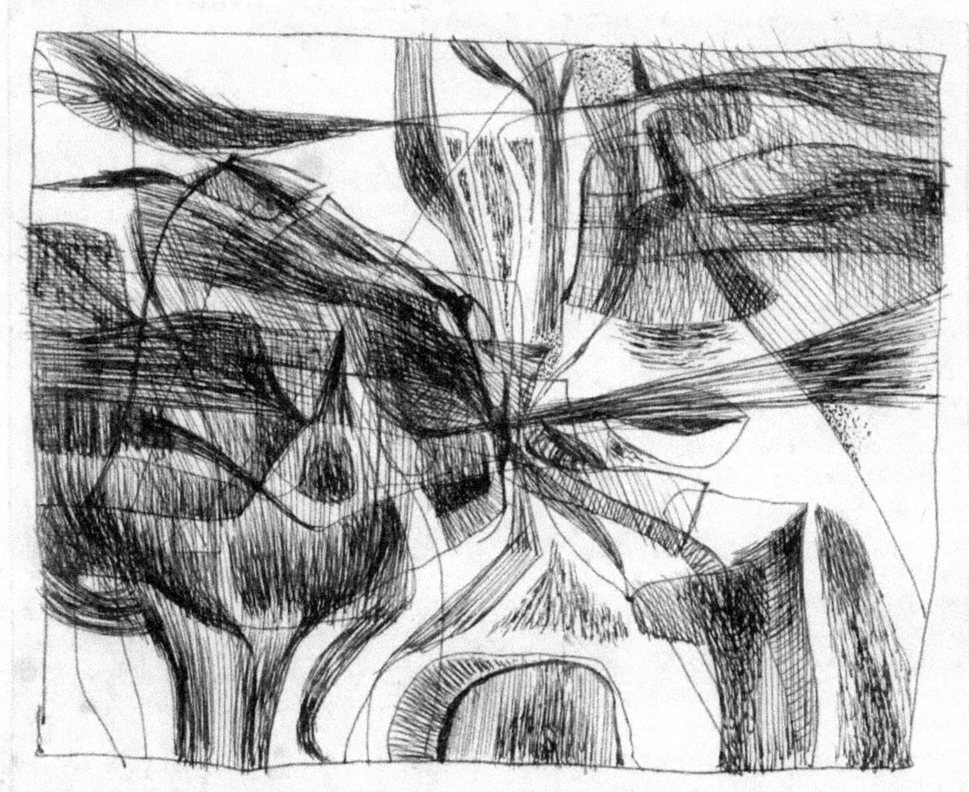

Ah! This strange mirror.
Bright face clipped between my hands
Makes me seem so young...

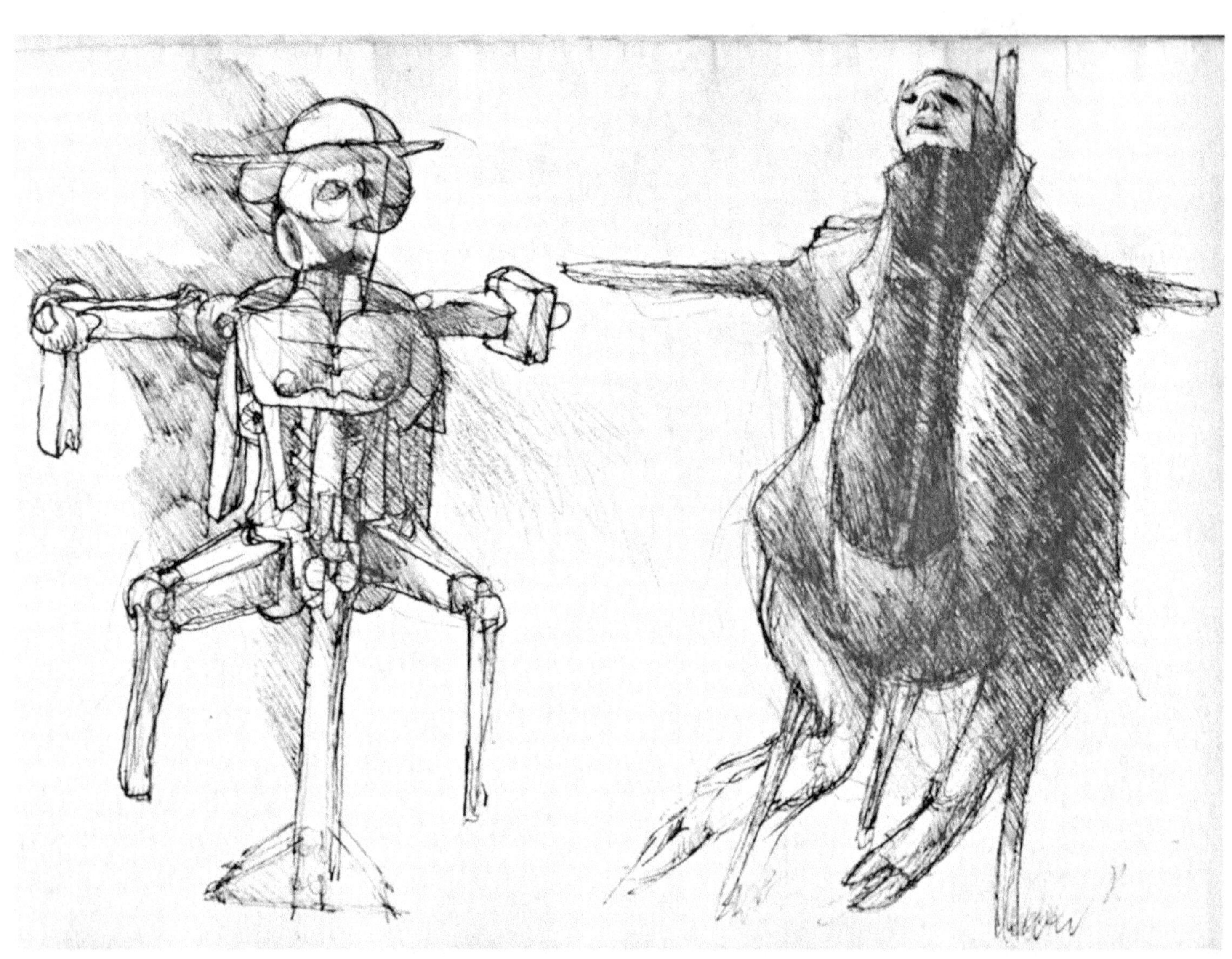

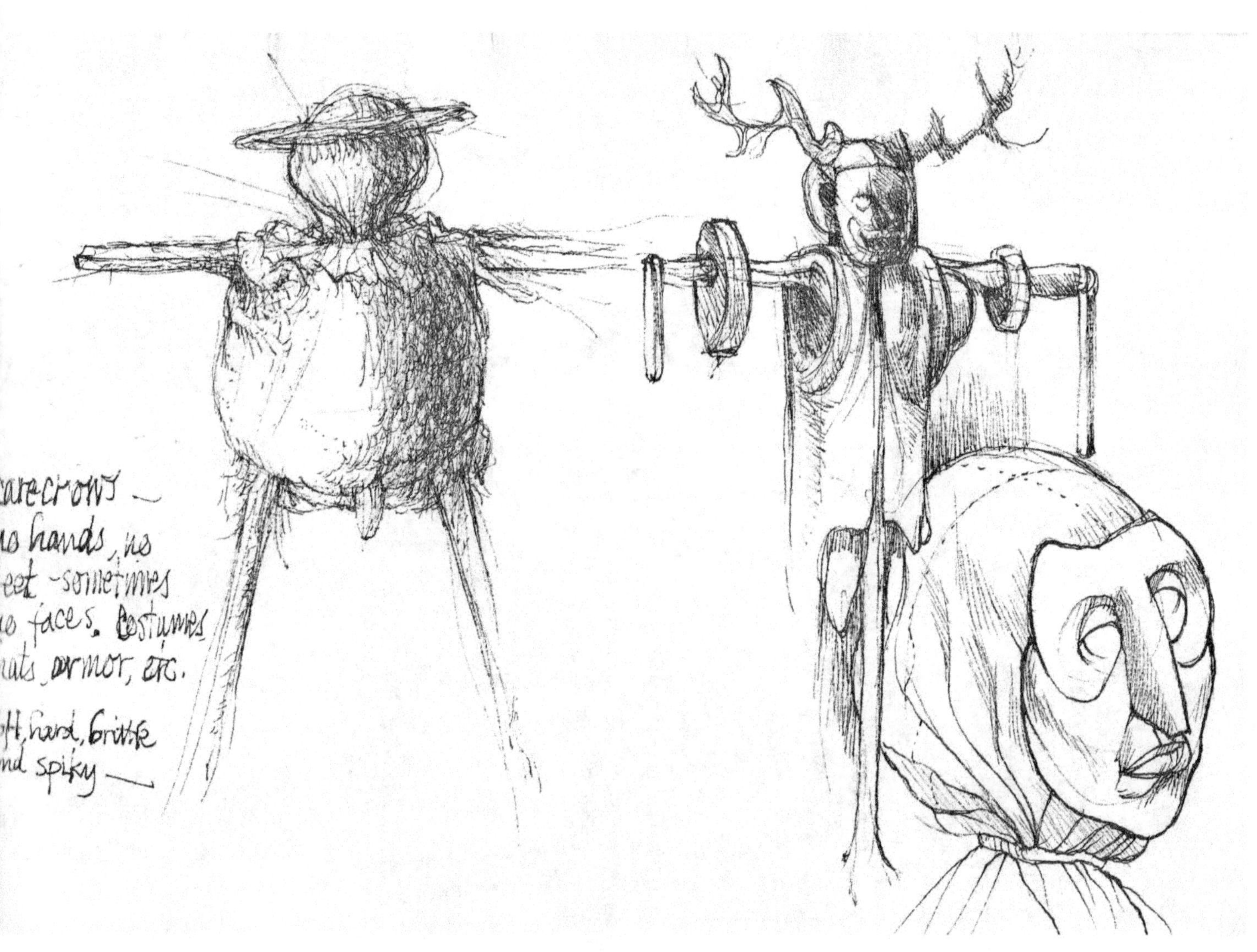

arecrows —
o hands, no
eet - sometimes
o faces. Costumes
ats, armor, etc.

ft, hard, brittle
nd spiky —

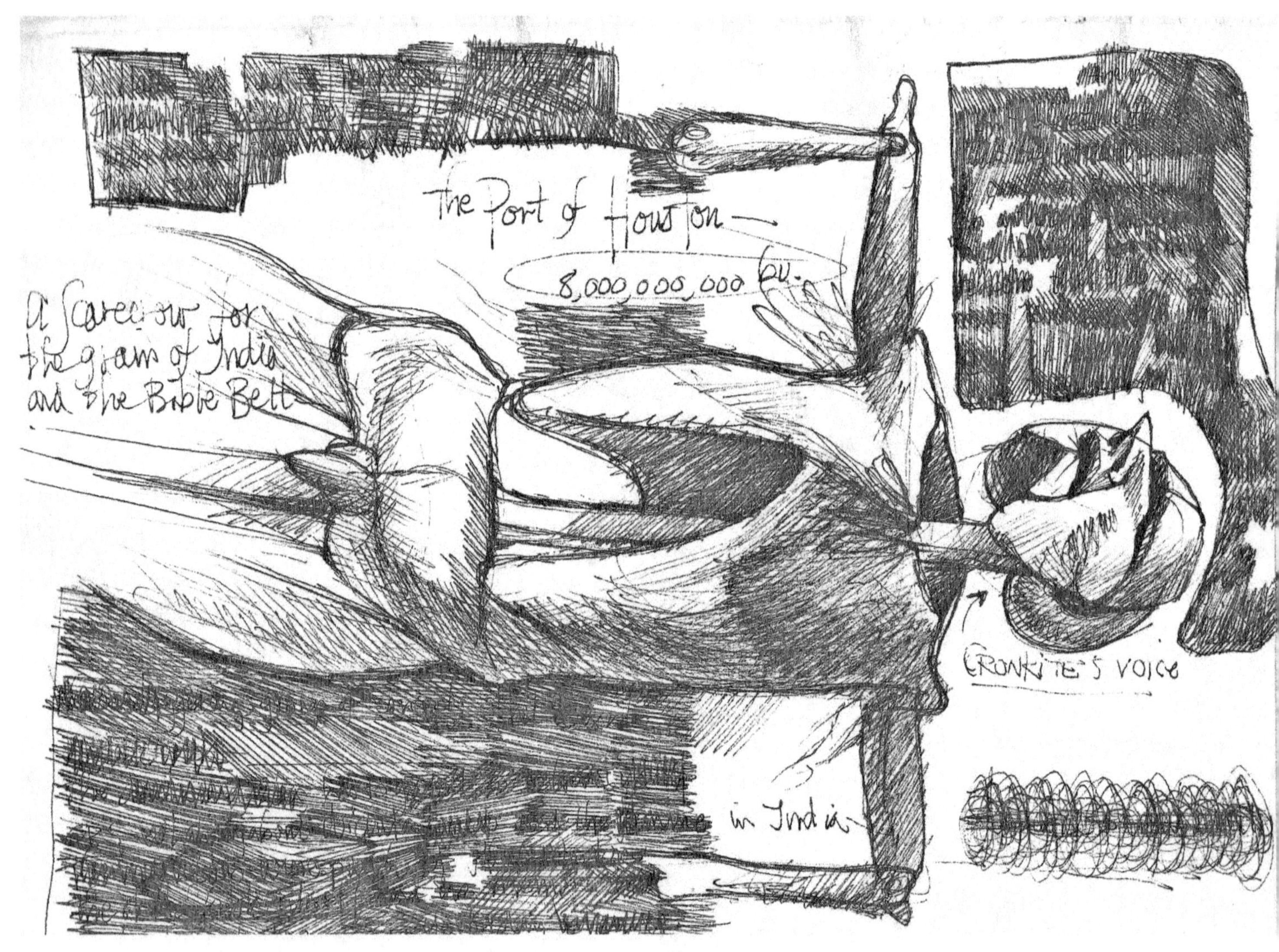

A Scarecrow for
the grain of India
and the Bible Belt
The Port of Houston —
8,000,000,000 bu.
in India
CRONKITE'S VOICE

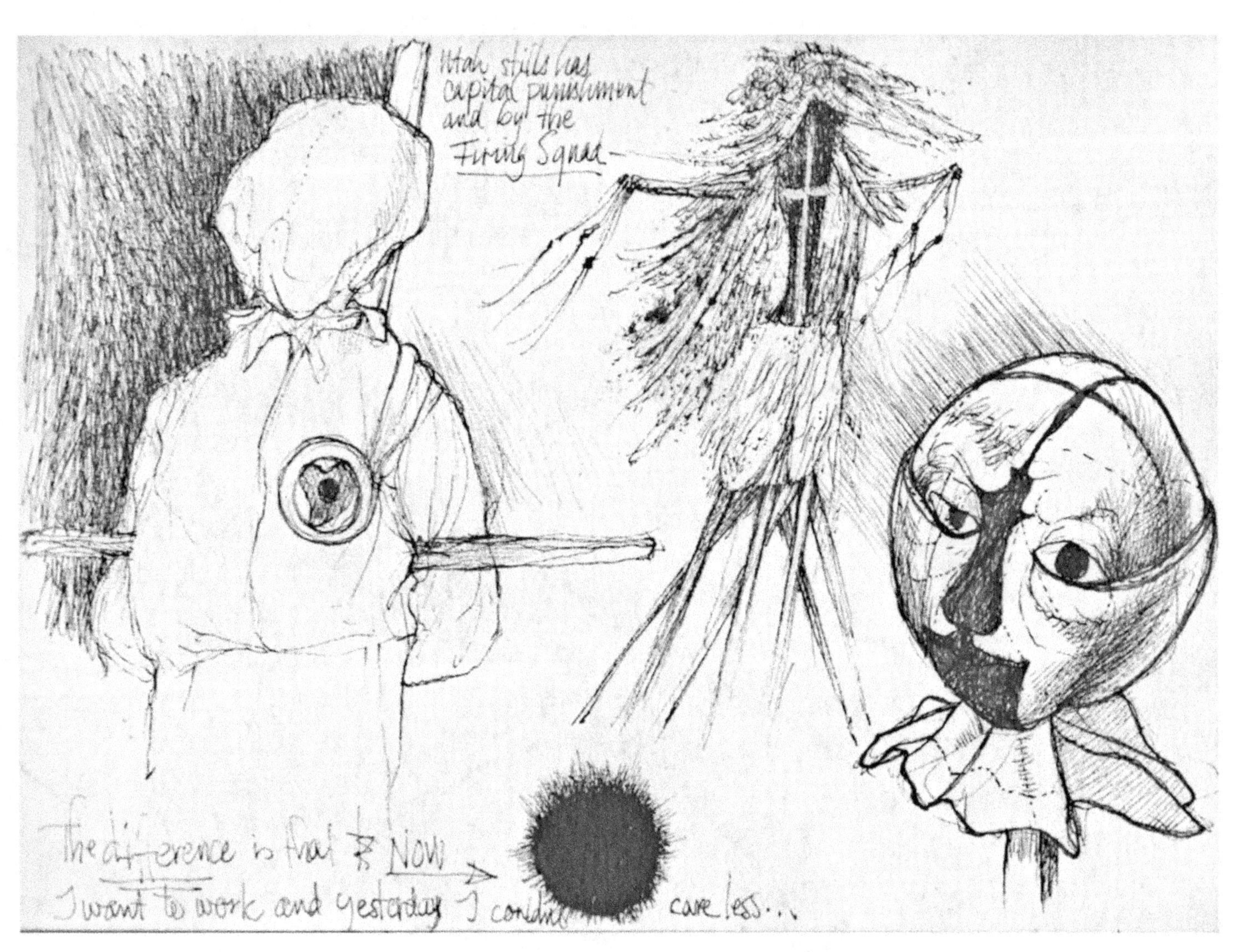

Utah stills has capital punishment and by the Firing Squad —
The difference is that NOW I want to work and yesterday I couldn't care less...

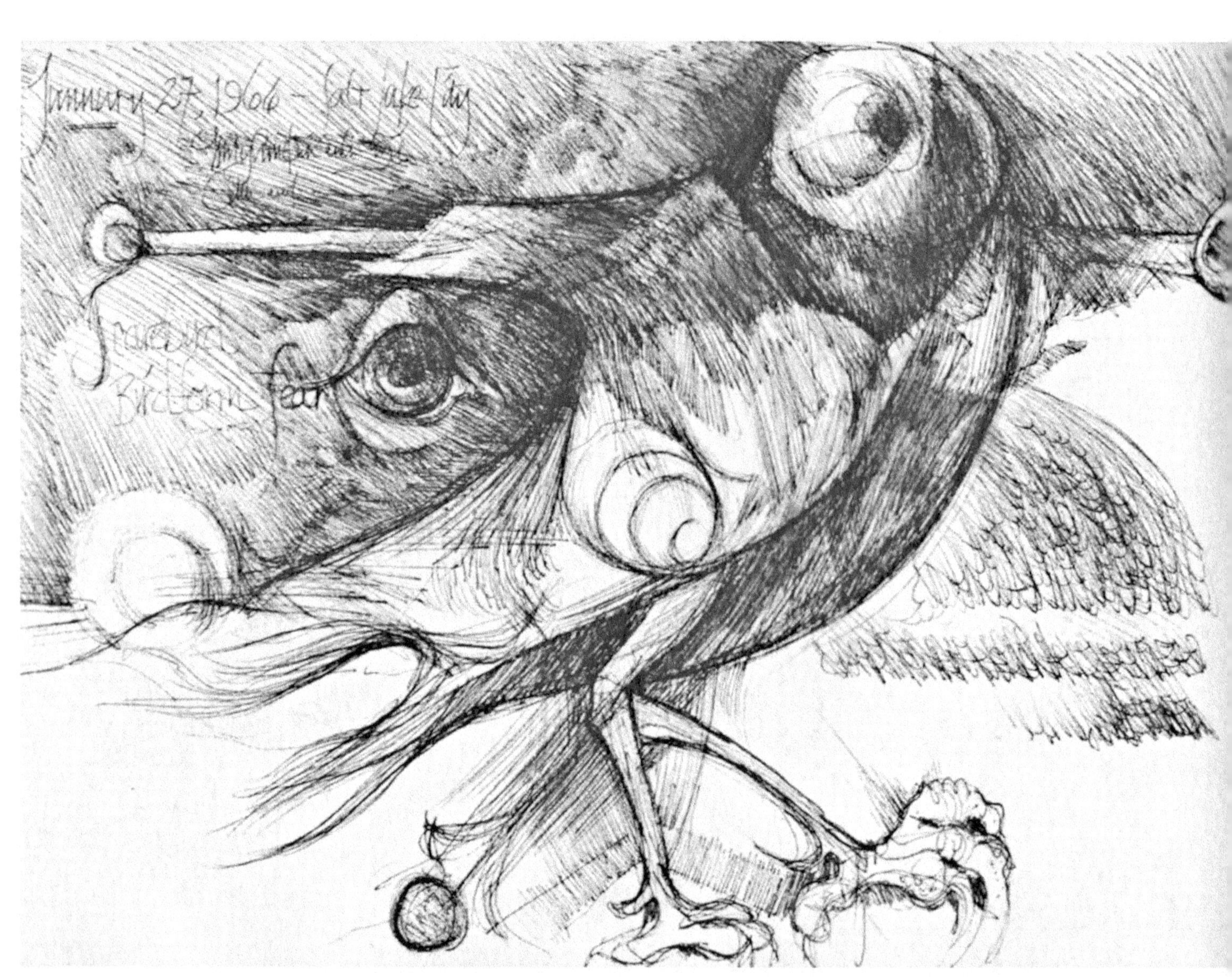

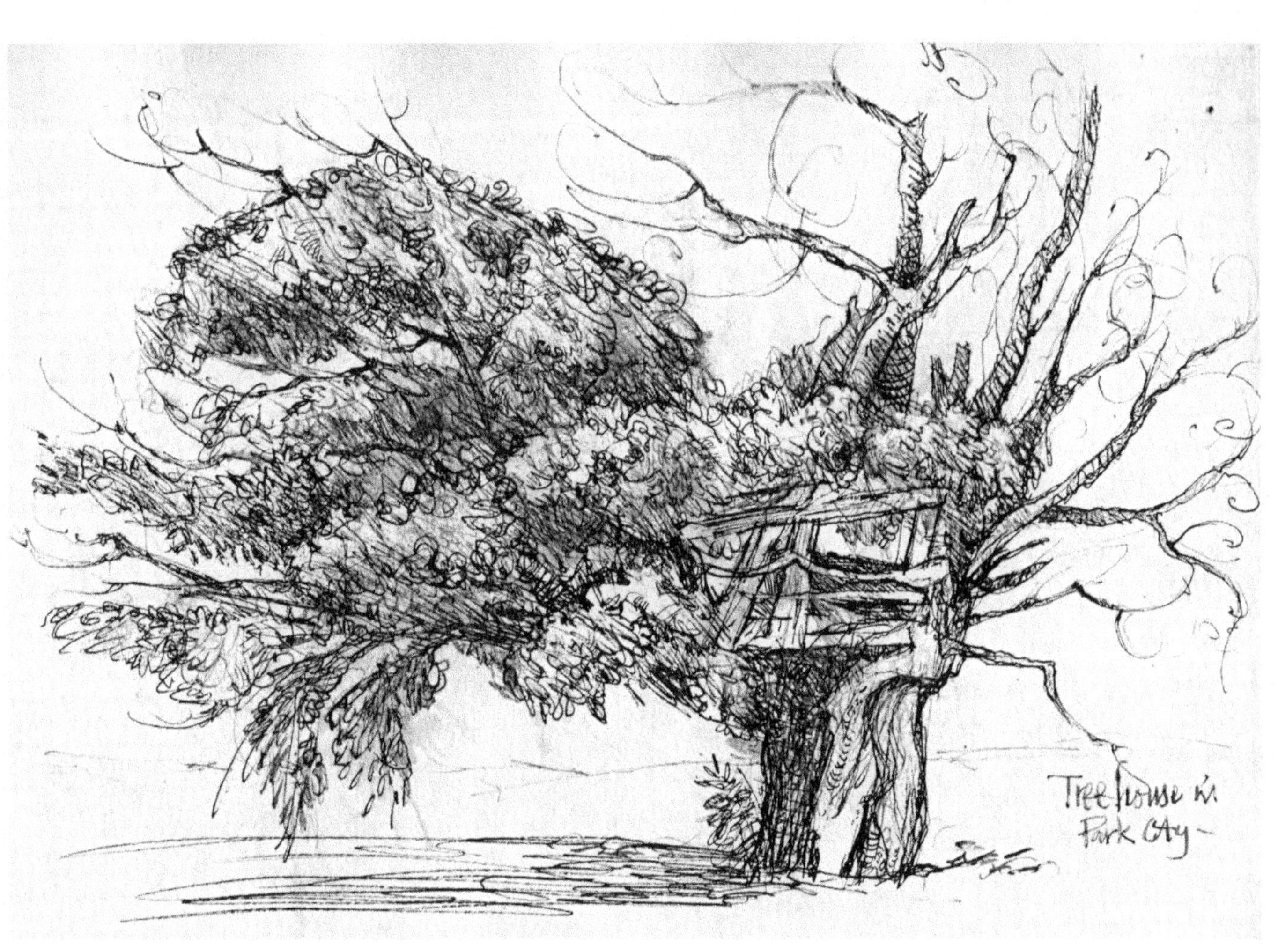
Treehouse in
Park City—

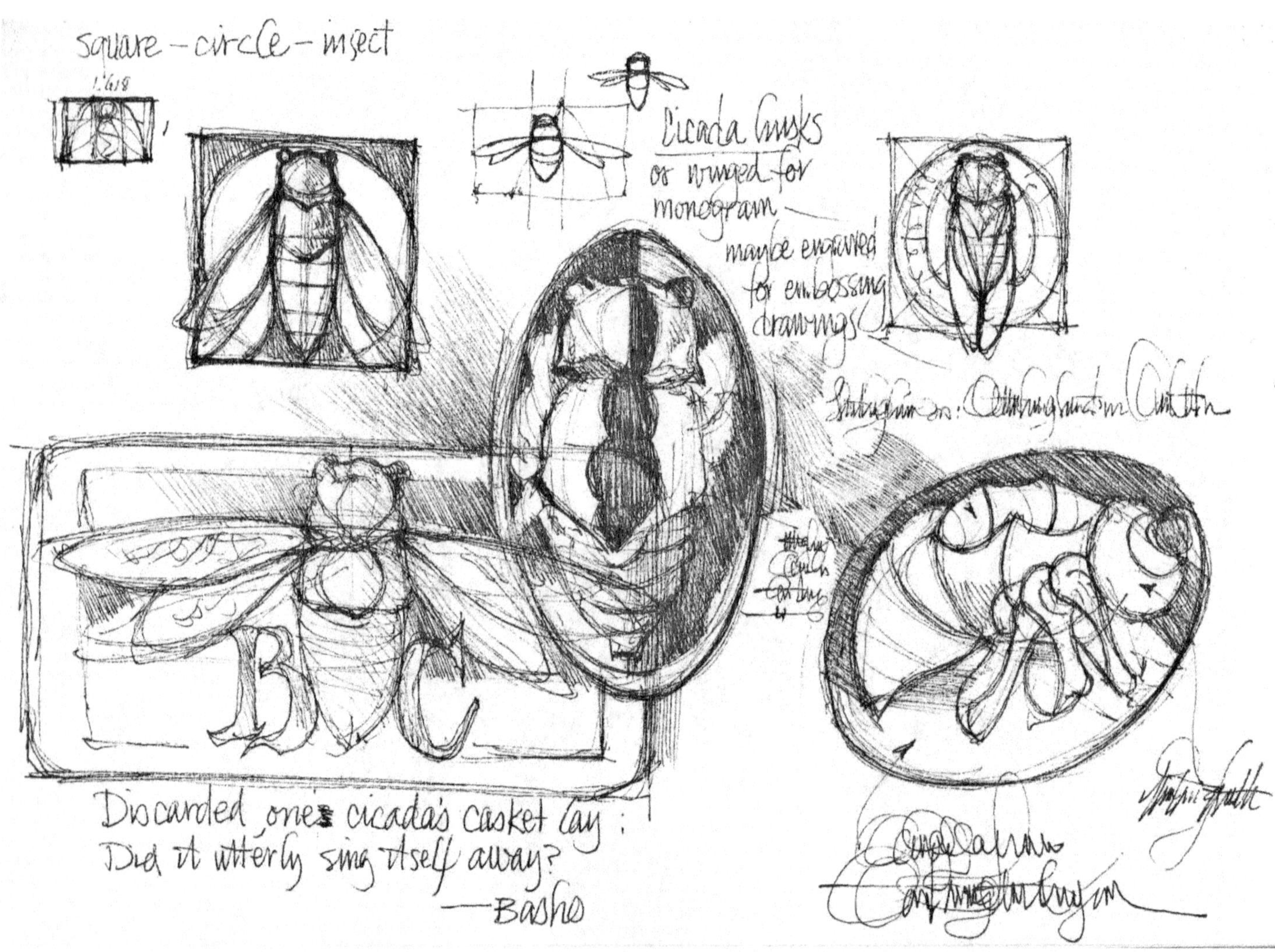

square — circle — insect
1:618
Cicada husks
or winged for
monogram —
maybe engraved
for embossing
drawings
Discarded ones cicada's casket lay:
Did it utterly sing itself away?
—Basho

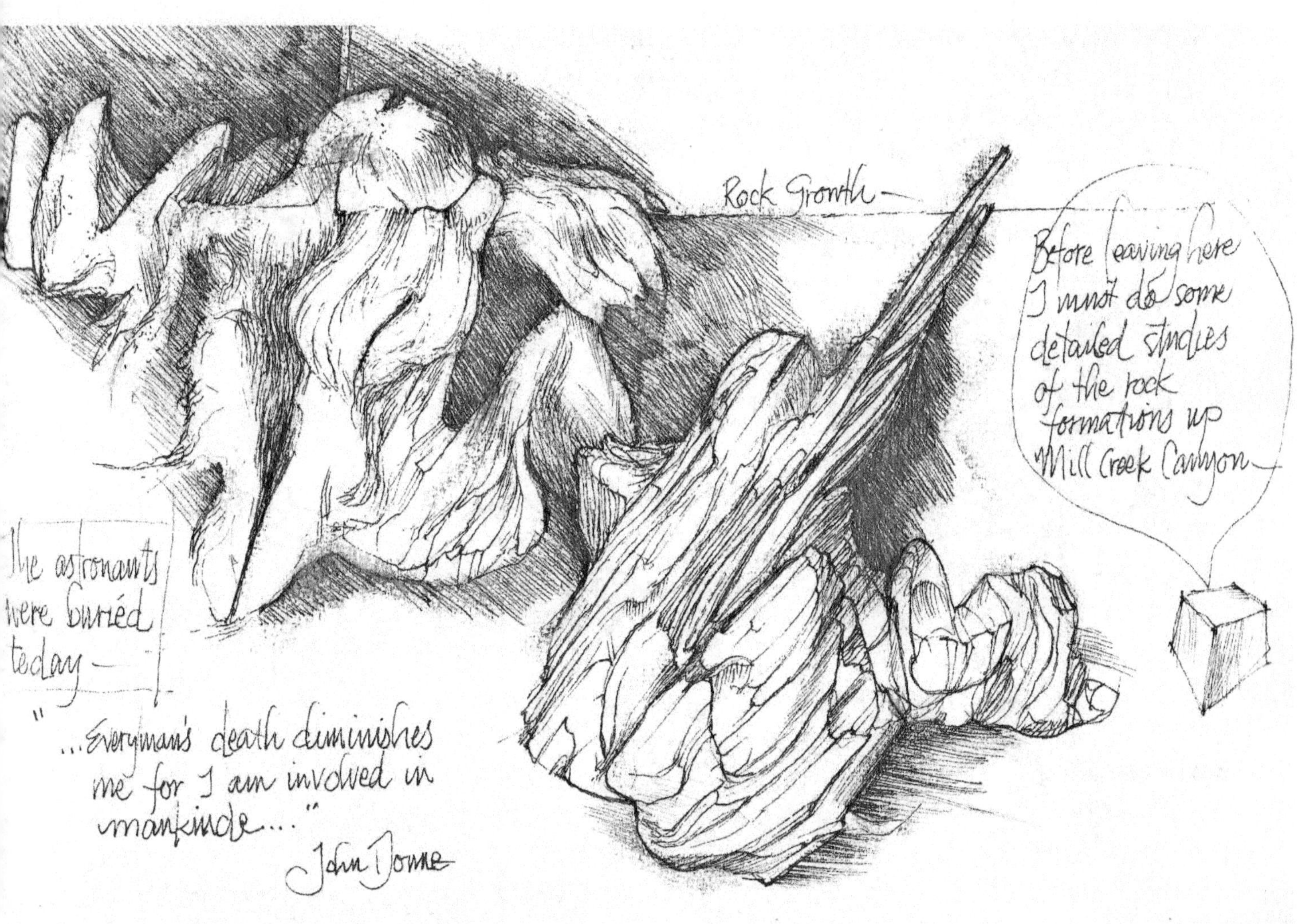

Rock Growth —
Before leaving here
I must do some
detailed studies
of the rock
formations up
Mill Creek Canyon
The astronauts
were buried
today —
"...Everyman's death diminishes
me for I am involved in
mankind..."
John Donne

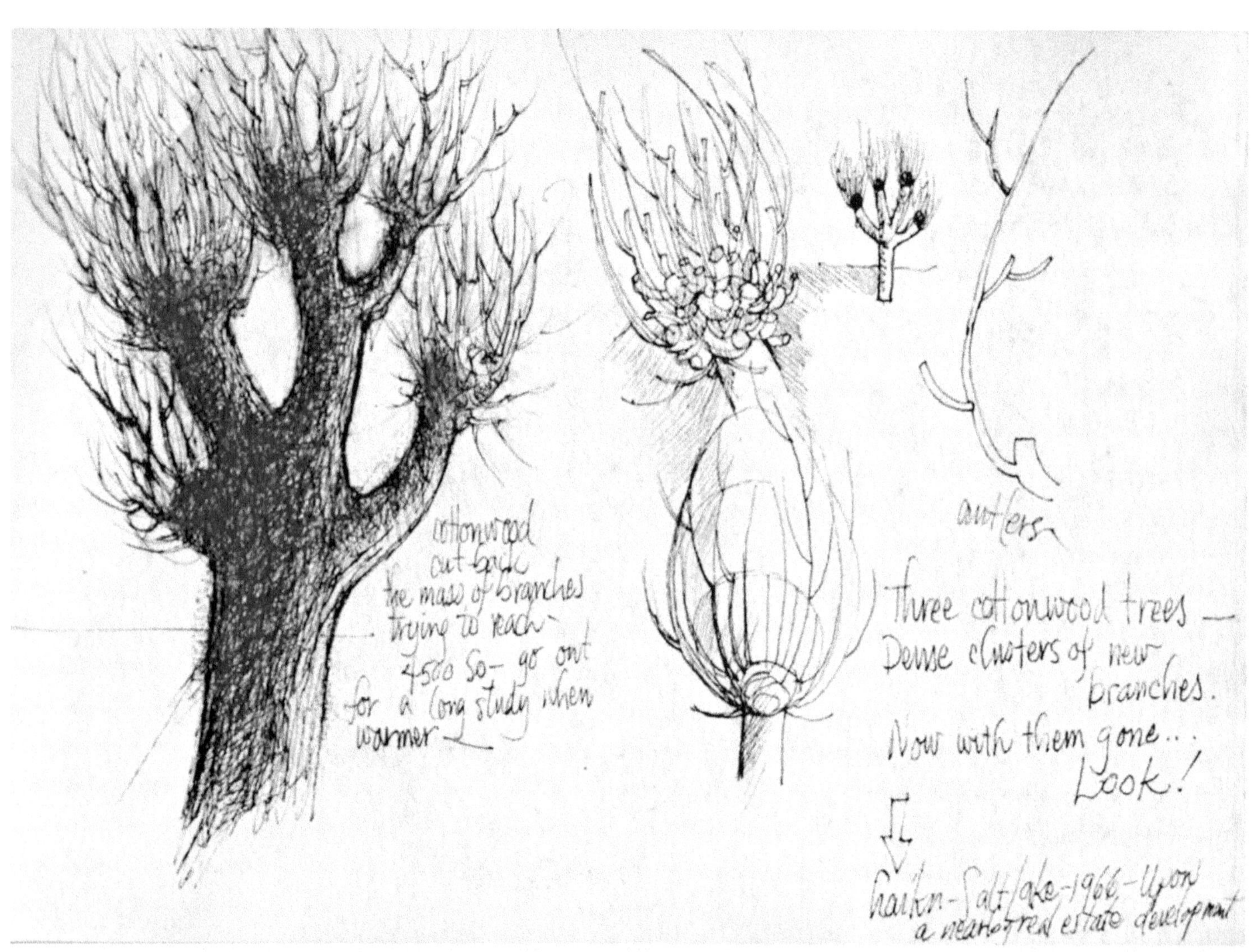

cottonwood
cut back
the mass of branches
trying to reach—
4500 So— go out
for a long study when
warmer—
antlers
Three cottonwood trees —
Dense clusters of new
branches.
Now with them gone...
Look!
Harkin—Salt/ake—1966—Upon
a near-dead estate development

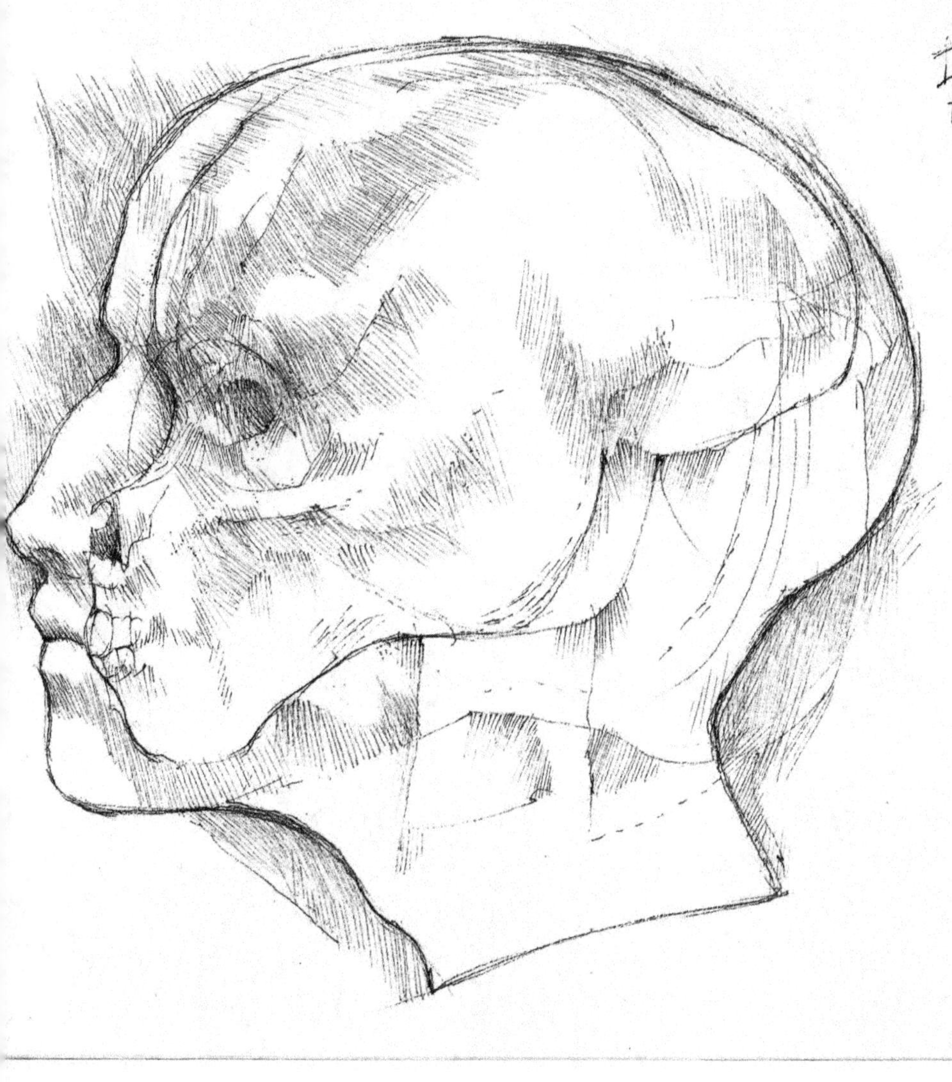

In the most recent scarecrow drwngs —
the written description of them
as sculptures is a delight —
They describe exactly what it is
and the viewer sees the drawings
as a means to another end.
That is not the case — it
becomes a disguise — The
words Guide the drawing
as most words have
always hidden the
experience of the art.
The books of copy and typography
are part of the drawing,
not to inform as in Shahn,
but perhaps nearer to
Steinberg's documents. They
tell you something, but it
may or may not relate
to the drawing. They
are really first of all
shapes on the surface
I see a direct relation to the
plastic bubbles over the shaped
drawings — Which was like making
people see the glass over a print

& also important — The emperors new clothes were also invisible —

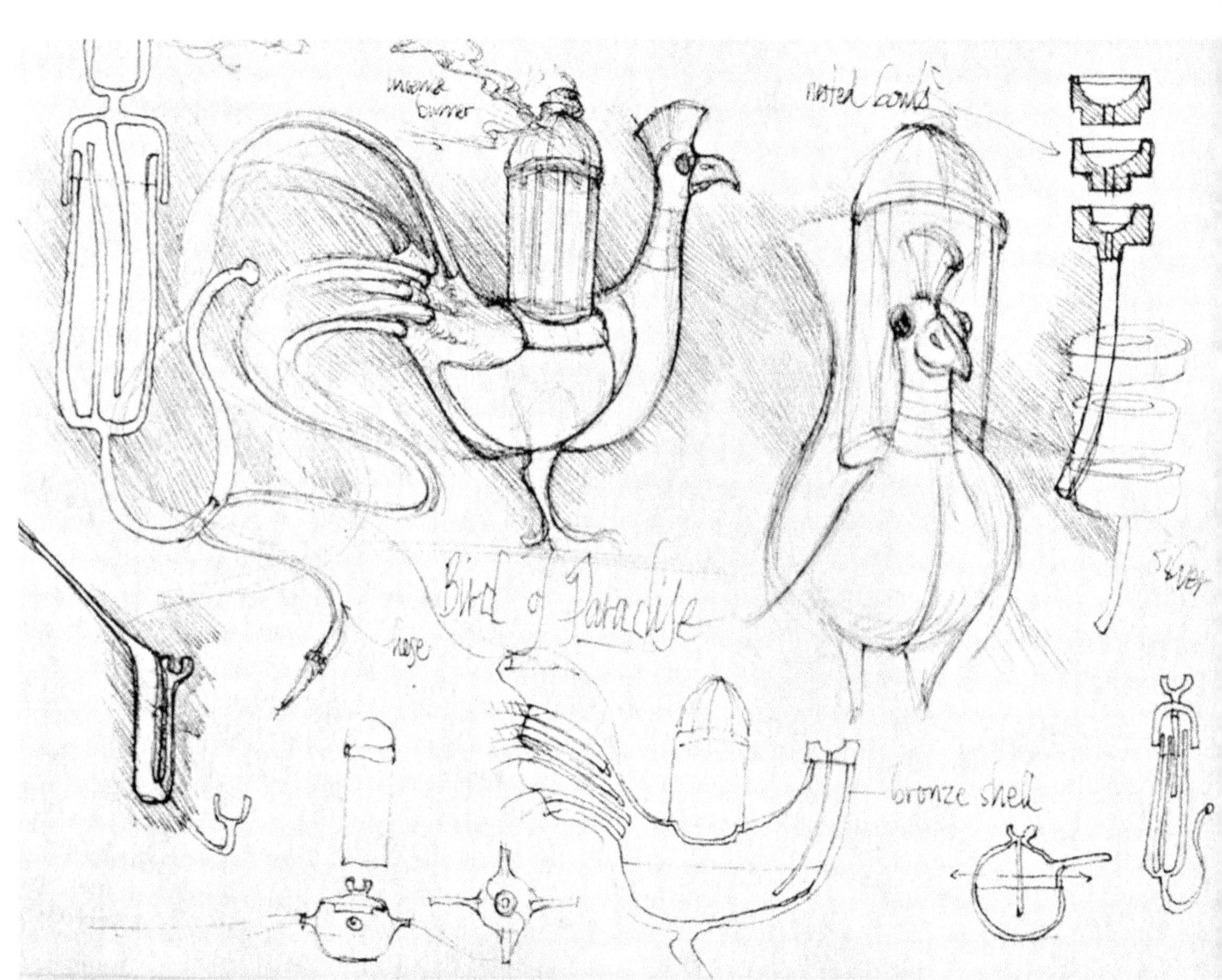

incense burner
nested bowls
Bird of Paradise
nose
silver
bronze shell

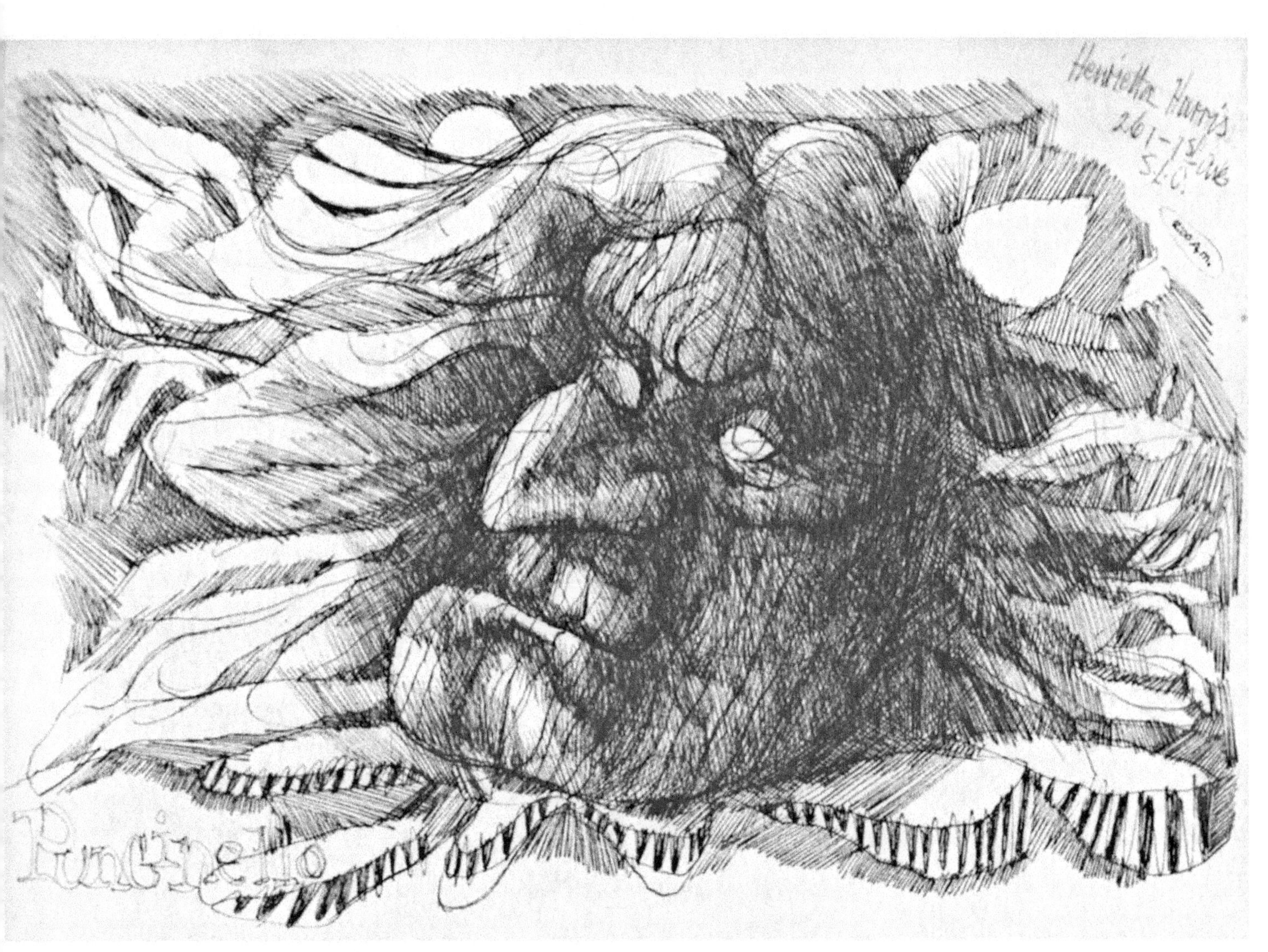

Henrietta Harry's
261-1st ave
S.L.C.
Puncinello

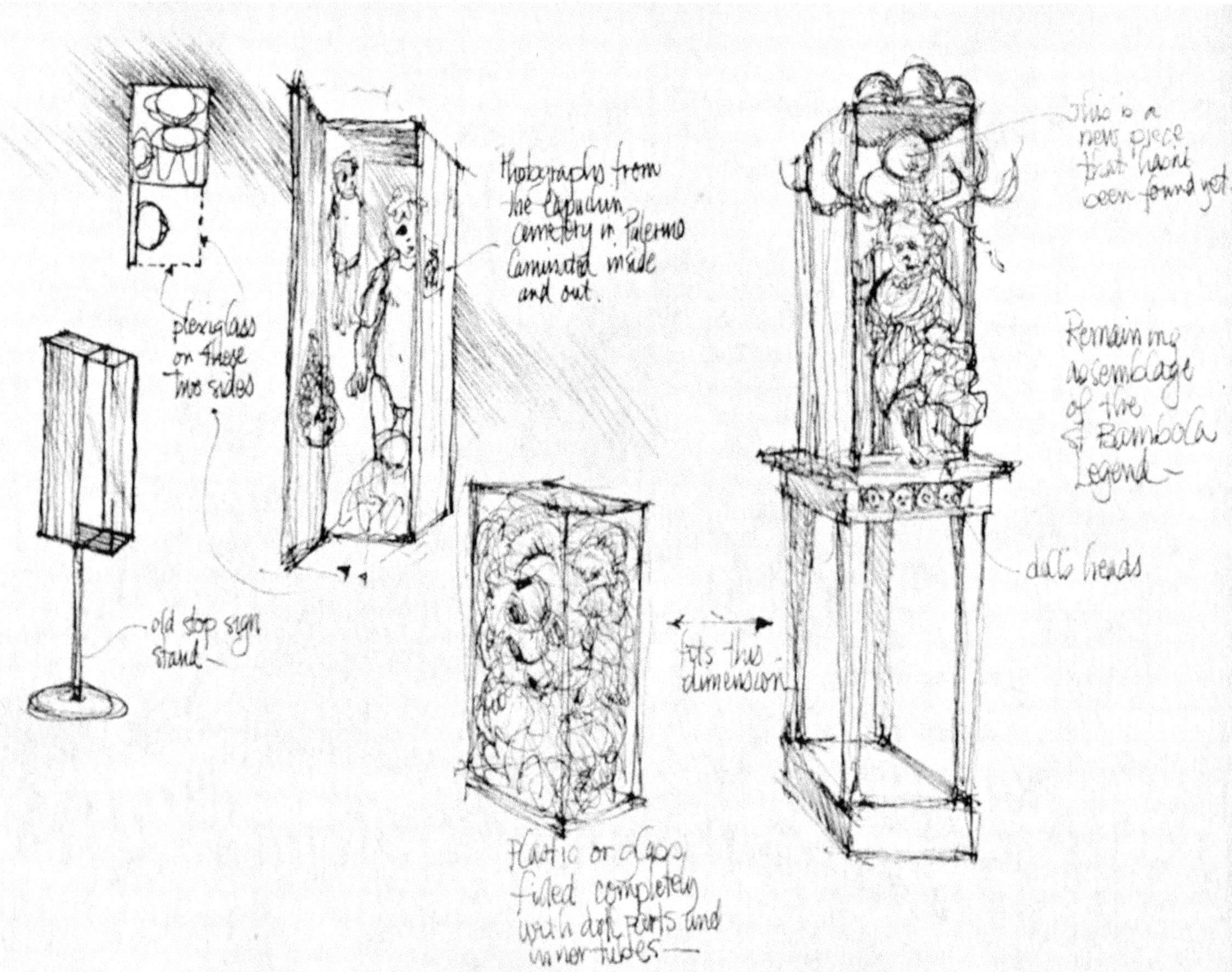

plexiglass on these two sides
old stop sign stand
photographs from the Capuchin cemetery in Palermo laminated inside and out.
This is a new piece that hasn't been found yet
Remaining assemblage of the Bambola Legend
dolls heads
fits this dimension
Plastic or glass filled completely with doll parts and inner tubes

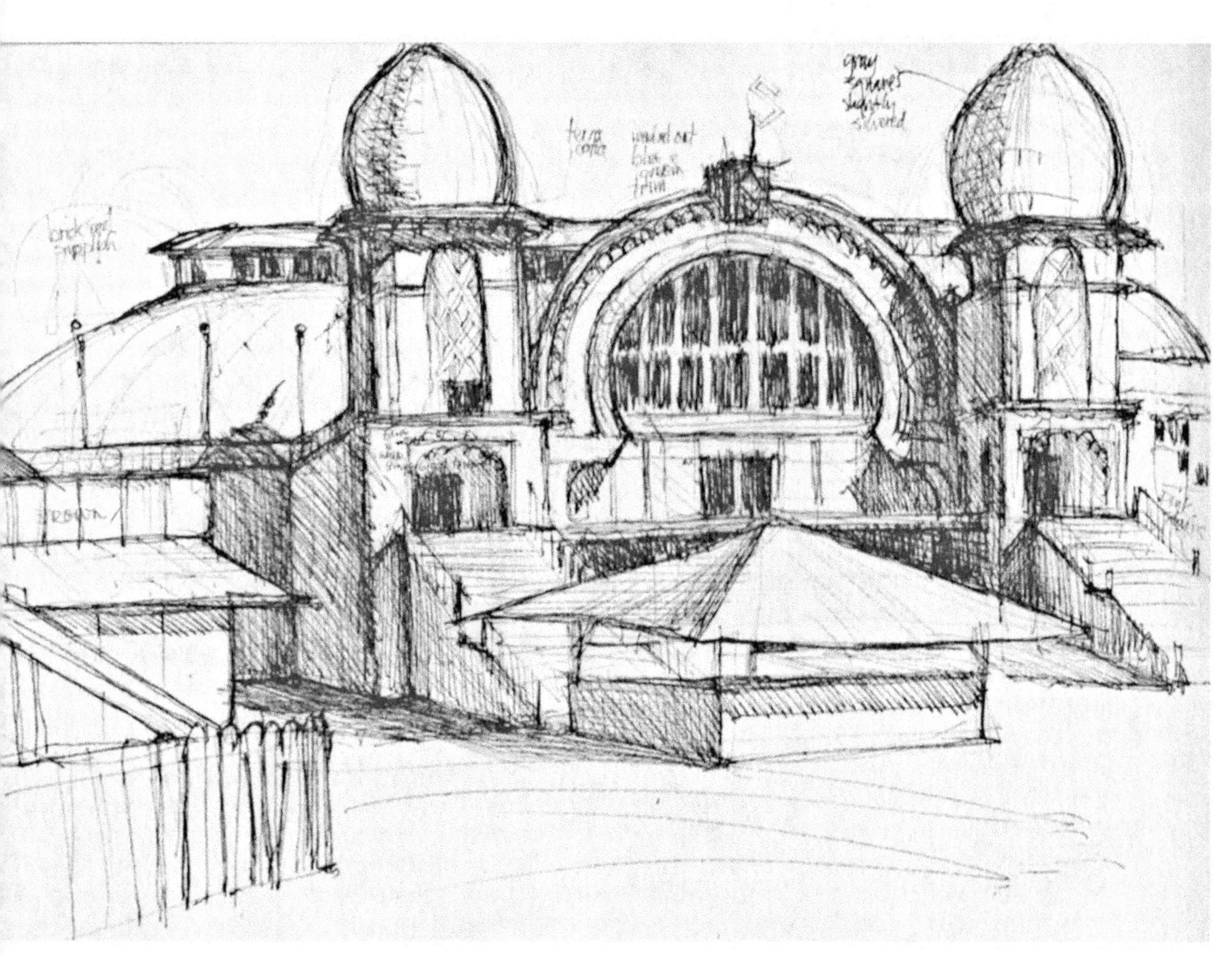

brick red
pavilion
terra
cotta
washed out
blue & green
trim
gray
& shades
slightly
silvered

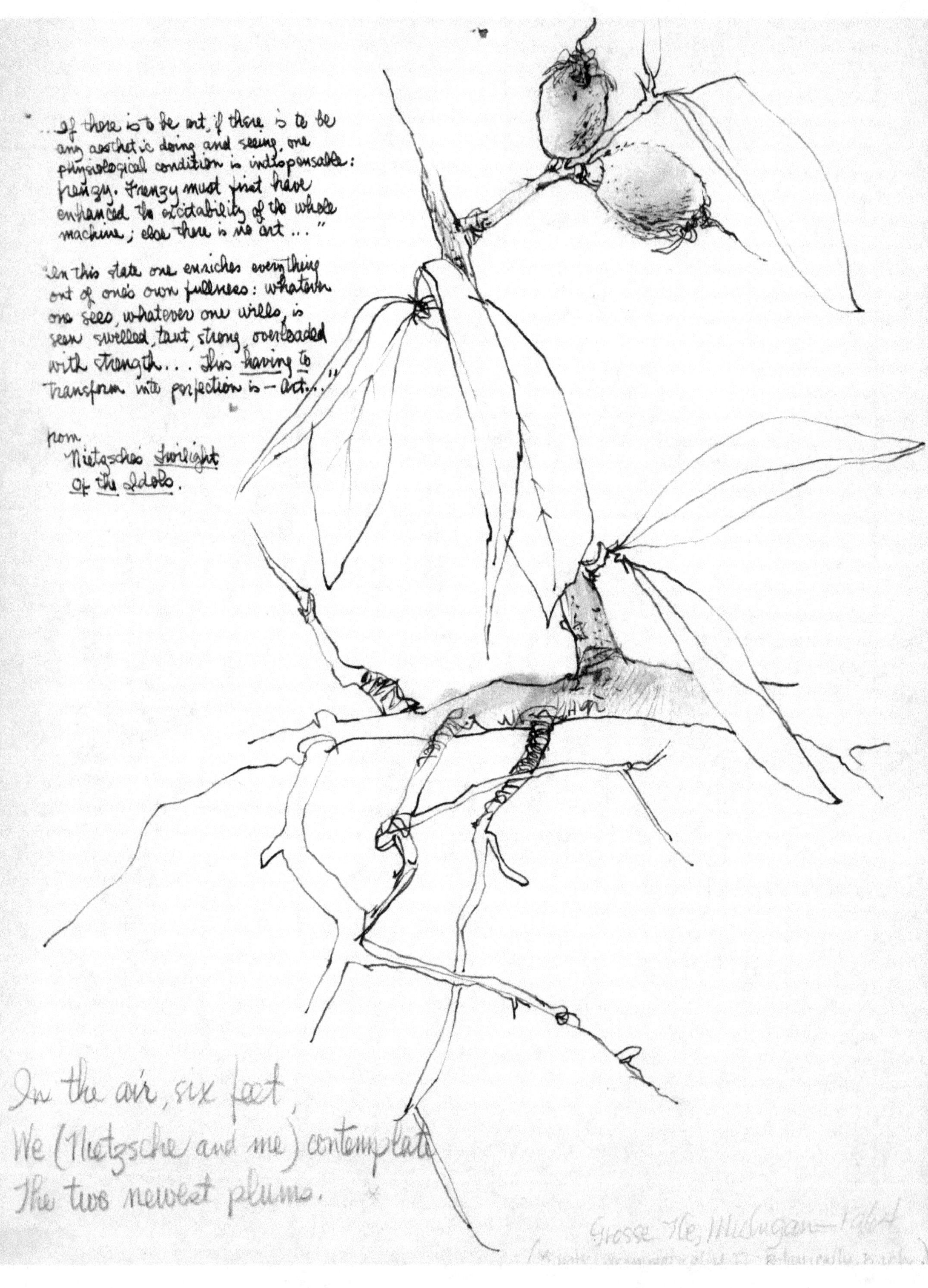
"...if there is to be art, if there is to be
any aesthetic doing and seeing, one
physiological condition is indispensable:
frenzy. Frenzy must first have
enhanced the excitability of the whole
machine; else there is no art ..."

"In this state one enriches everything
out of one's own fullness: whatever
one sees, whatever one wills, is
seen swelled, taut, strong overloaded
with strength... This having to
transform into perfection is — art..."

from
Nietzsche's Twilight
Of the Idols.

In the air, six feet,
We (Nietzsche and me) contemplate
The two newest plums.

Grosse Ile, Michigan—1988

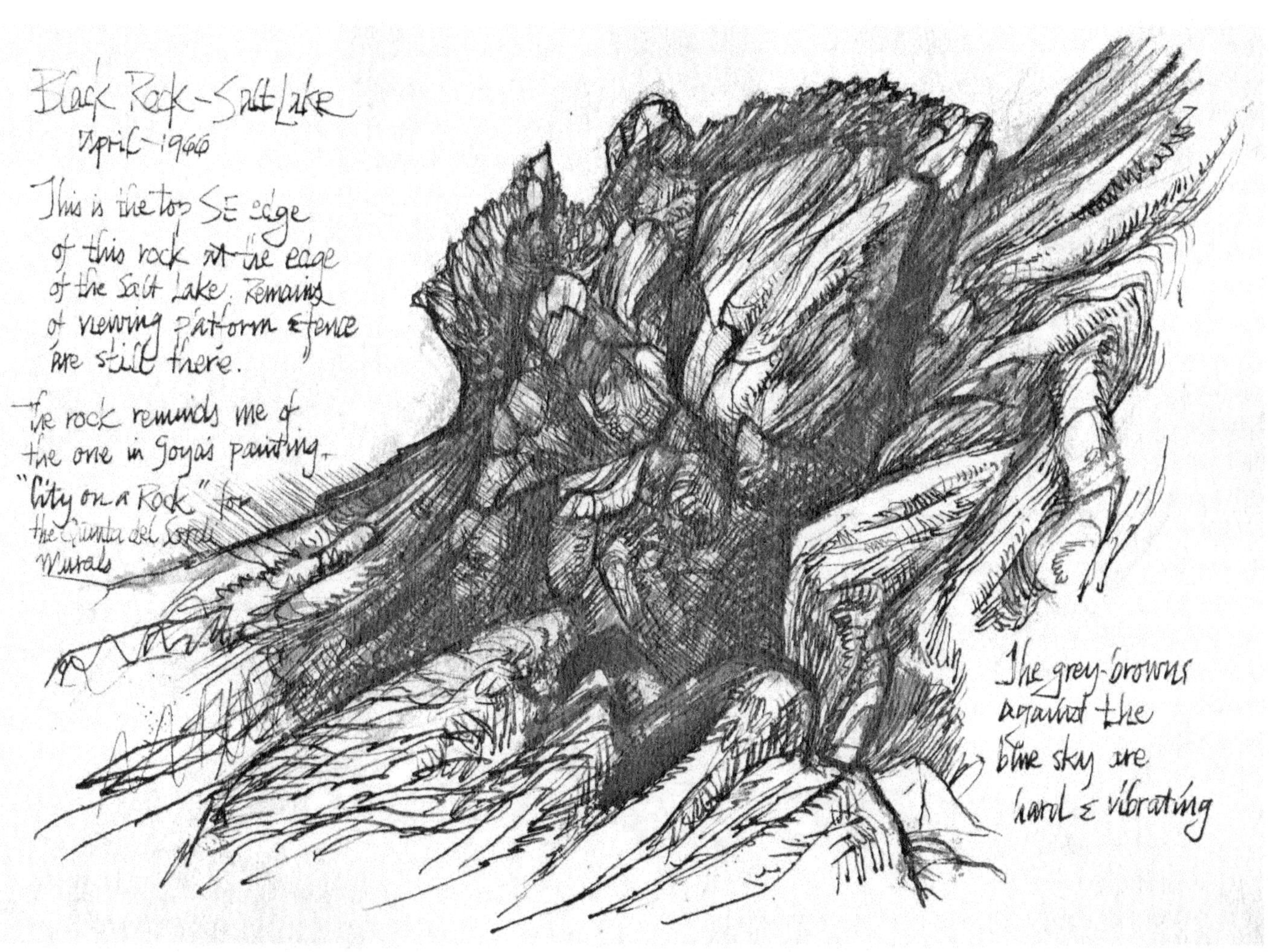

Black Rock - Salt Lake
April - 1966

This is the top SE edge
of this rock at the edge
of the Salt Lake. Remains
of viewing platform & fence
are still there.

The rock reminds me of
the one in Goya's painting
"City on a Rock" for
the Quinta del Sordi
Murals

The grey-browns
against the
blue sky are
hard & vibrating

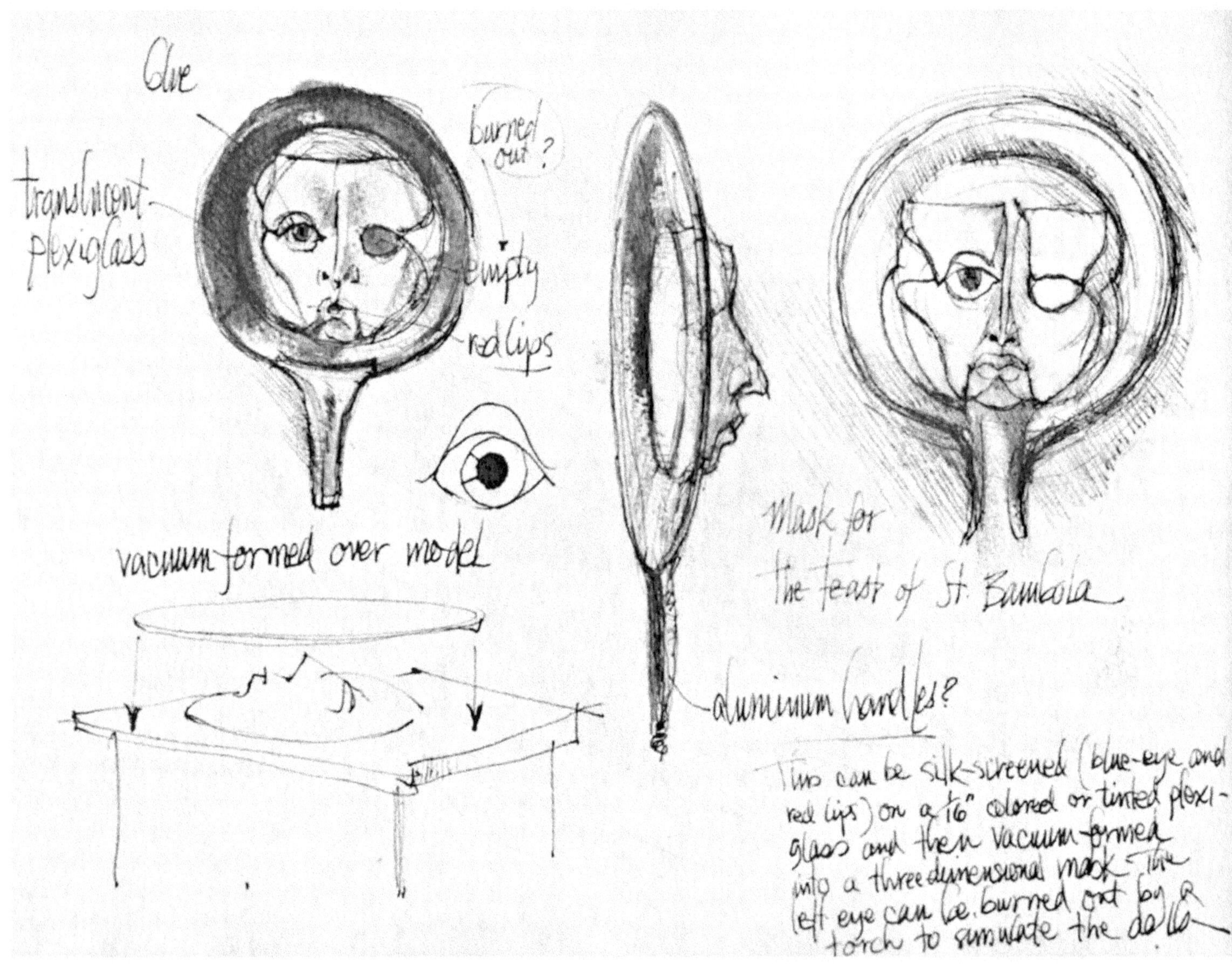

Glue
translucent plexiglass
burned out?
empty
red lips
vacuum formed over model
Mask for the Feast of St. Bambola
aluminum handles?
This can be silk-screened (blue-eye and red lips) on a 16" colored or tinted plexi-glass and then vacuum-formed into a three-dimensional mask. The left eye can be burned out by a torch to simulate the death

The weekend following Hurricane Beulah. — The
shore was a mass of small dead things — a
bat, bird, stingray — thousands of small fish
thrown up by hightides — I feel abt like a
colossal grim reaper striding along . . .

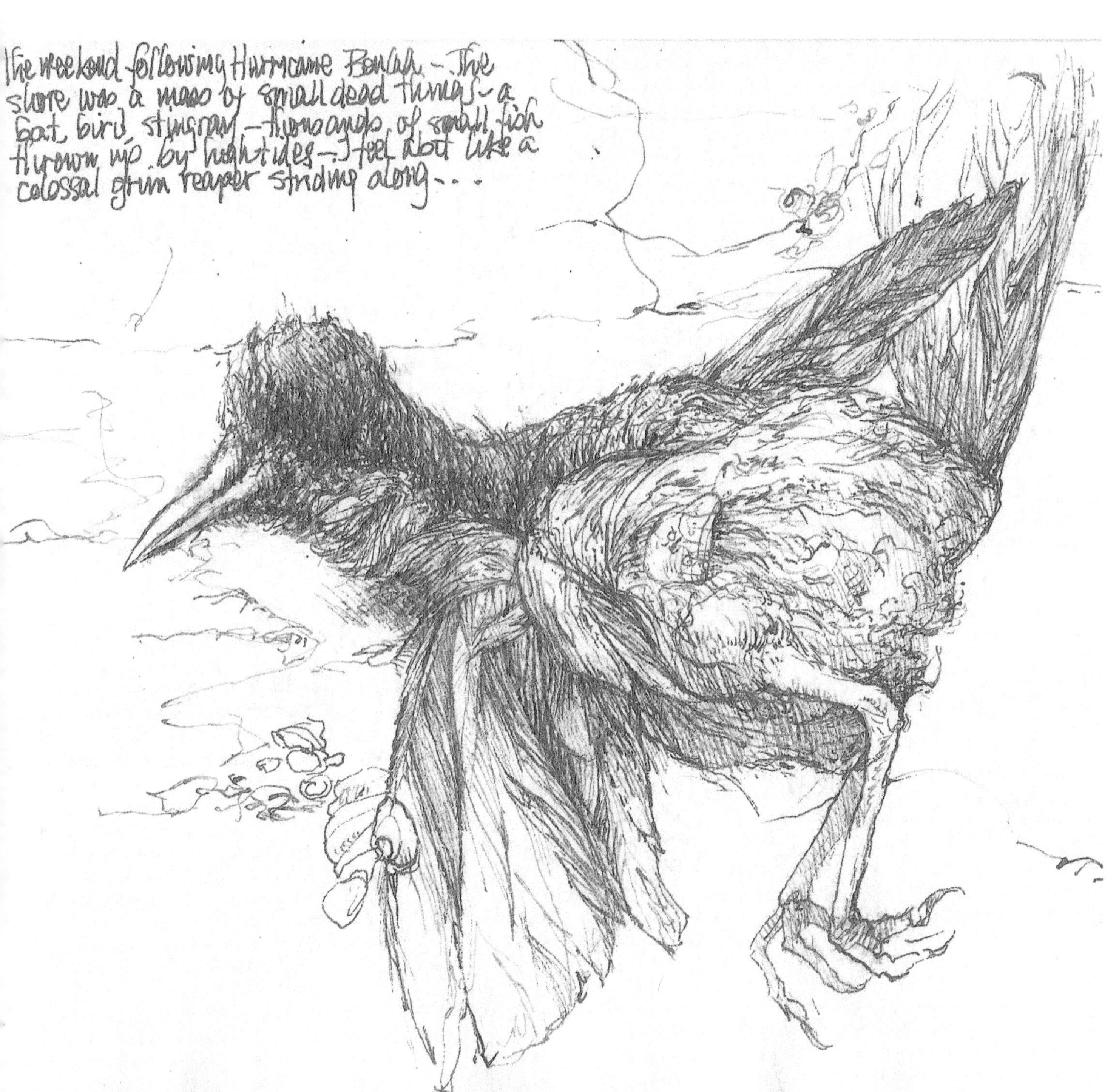

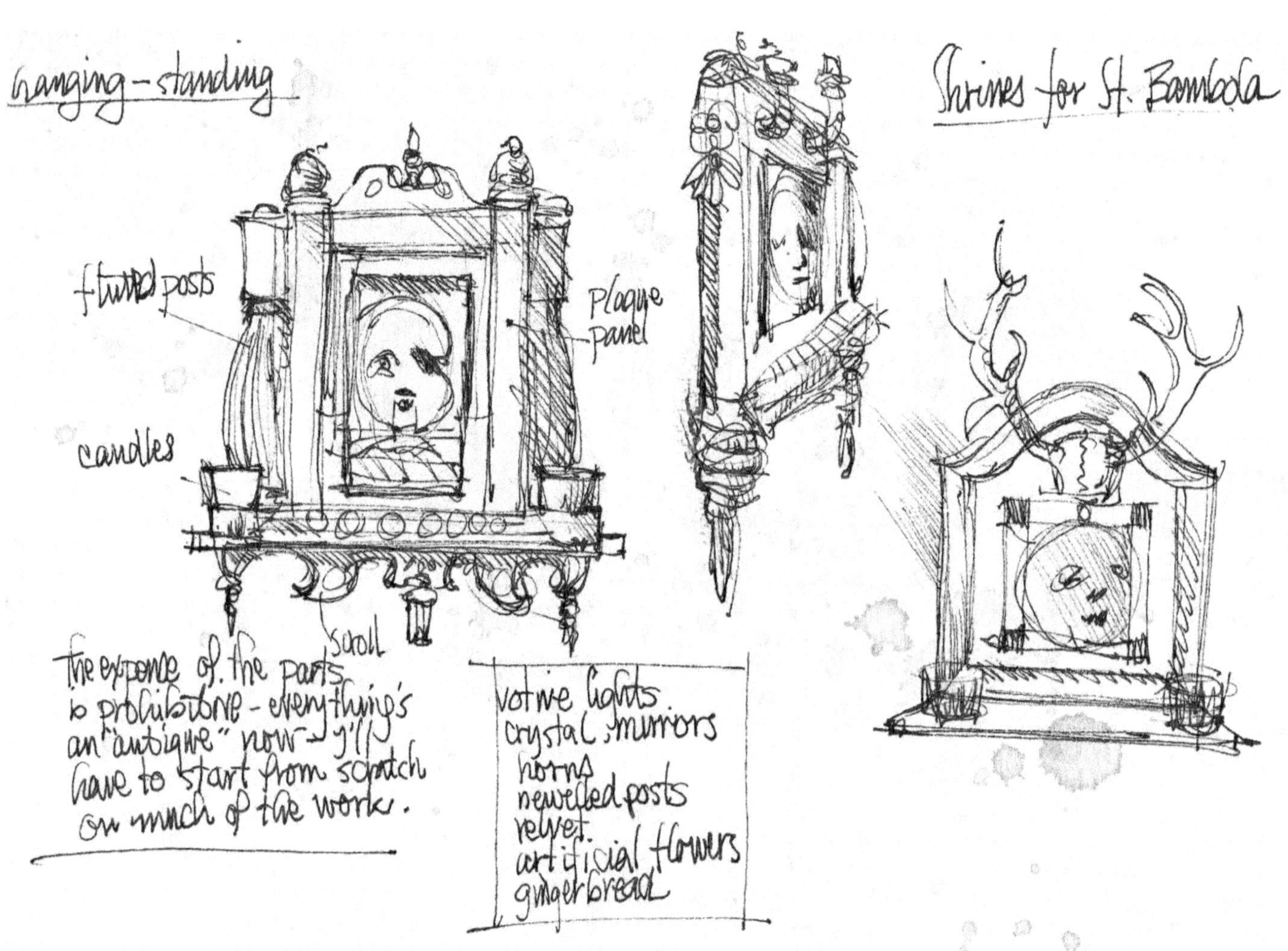

hanging - standing
Shrines for St. Bambola
f luted posts
Plaque
Panel
candles
scroll
The expence of the parts
is prohibitive - everything's
an "antique" now - y'll
have to start from scratch
on much of the work.

votive lights
crystal mirrors
horns
newelled posts
velvet
artificial flowers
gingerbread

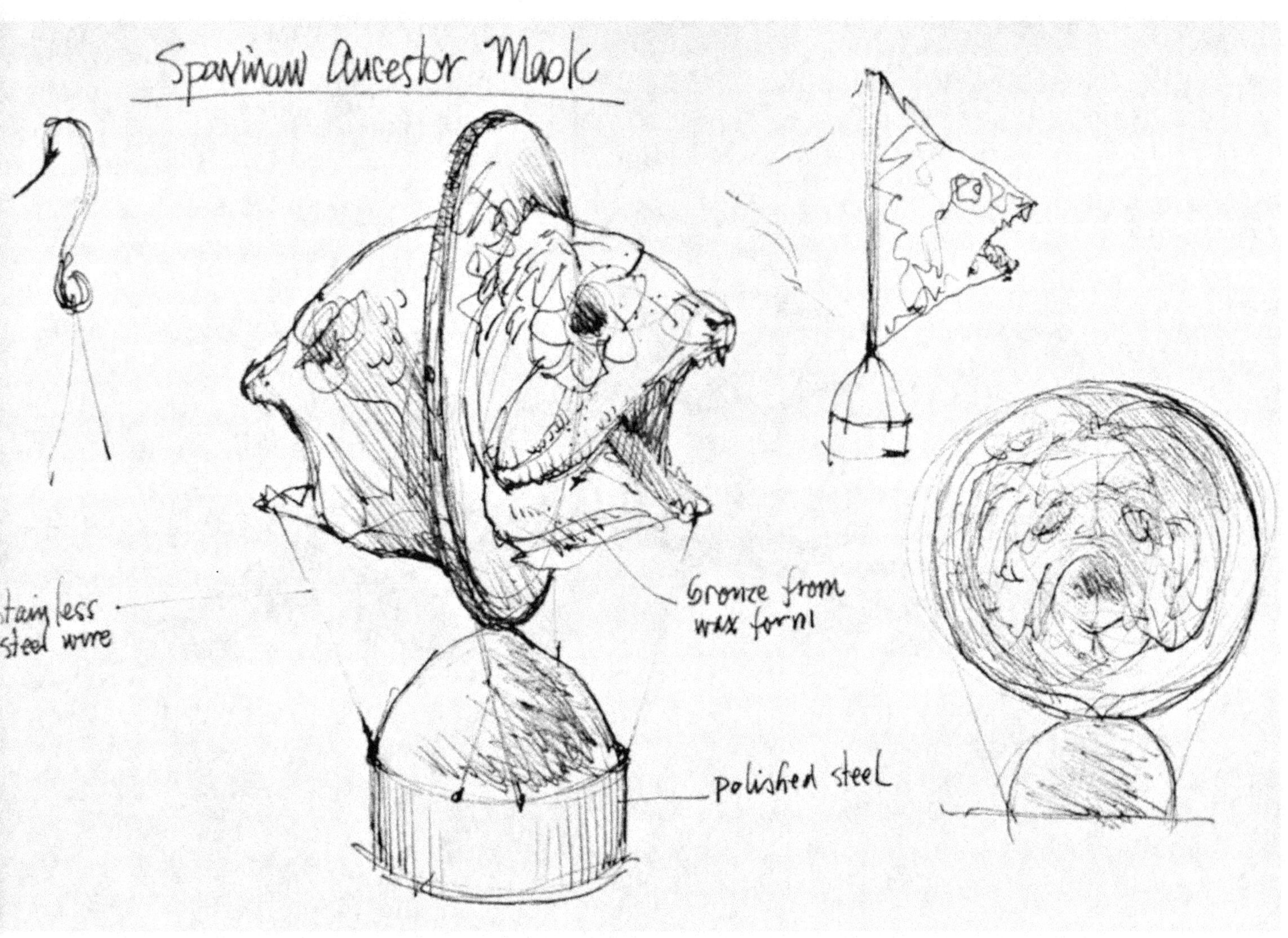

Spaulman Ancestor Mask
stainless steel wire
Bronze from wax form
polished steel

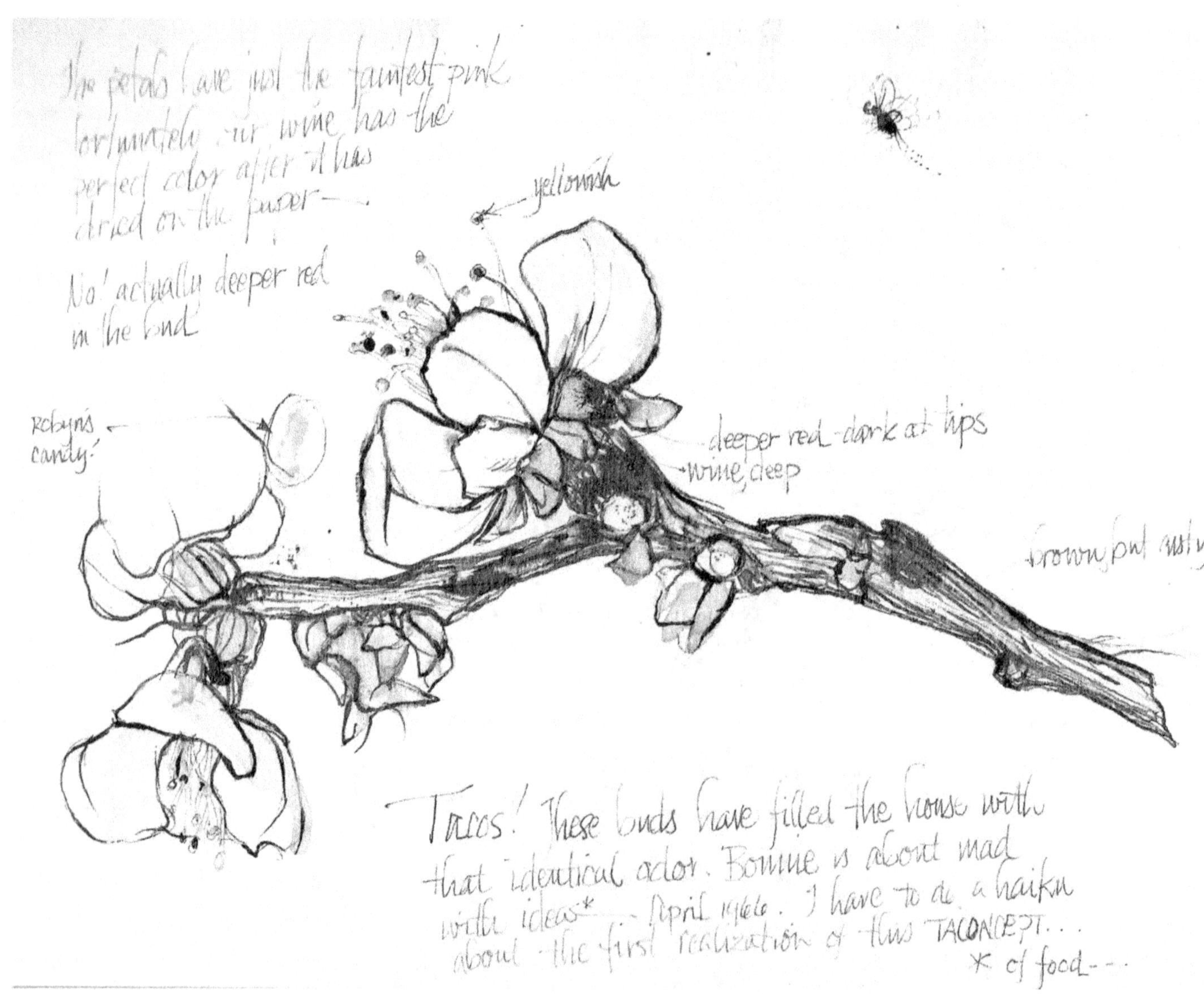

The petals have just the faintest pink.
fortunately our wine has the
perfect color after it has
dried on the paper —

No! actually deeper red
in the bud

robyn's candy!

yellowish

deeper red - dark at tips
wine, deep

brown, but ashy

Tacos! These buds have filled the house with
that identical odor. Bonnie is about mad
with ideas* — April 1966. I have to do a haiku
about the first realization of this TACONCEPT...
* of food — — —

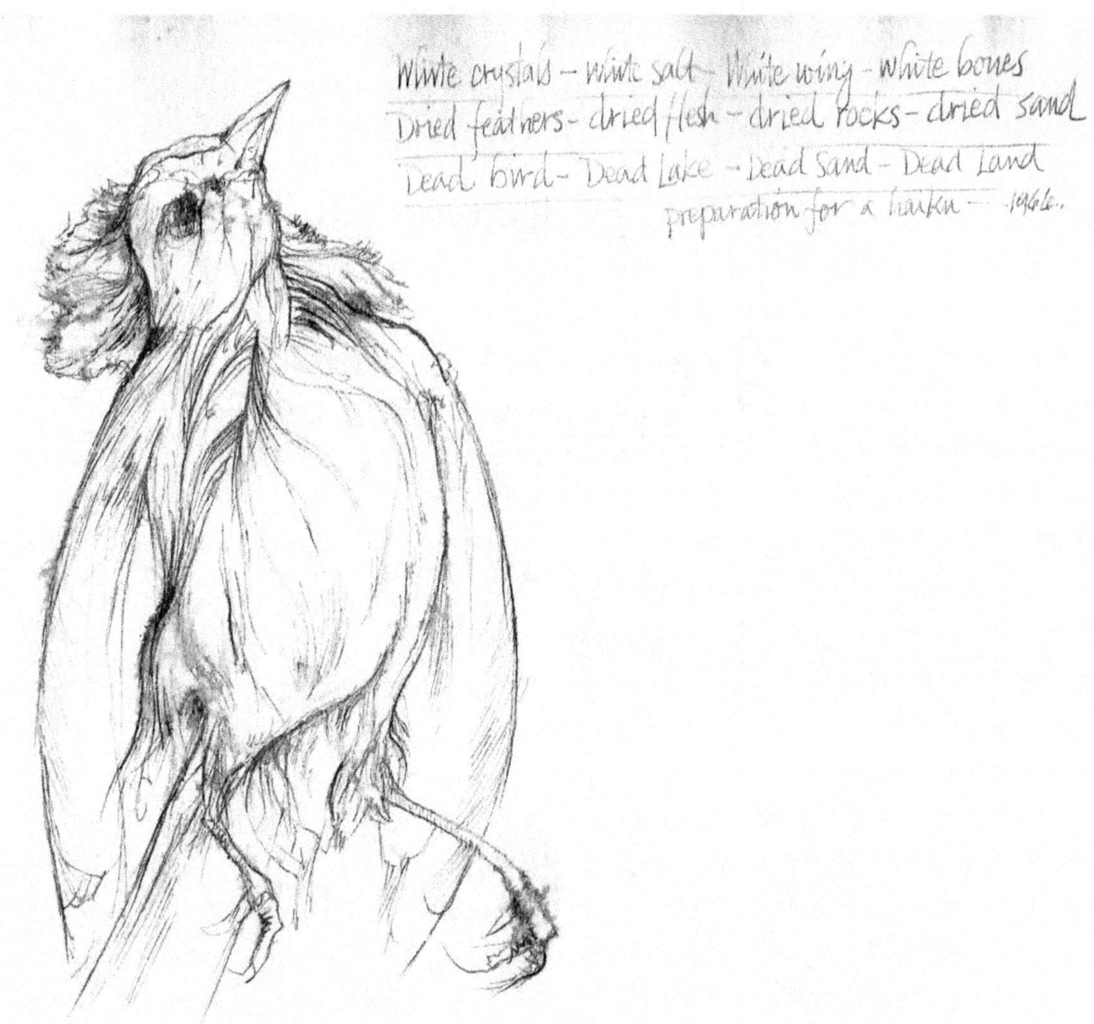

White crystals — white salt — White wing — white bones
Dried feathers — dried flesh — dried rocks — dried sand
Dead bird — Dead Lake — Dead Sand — Dead Land
preparation for a haiku — 1966.

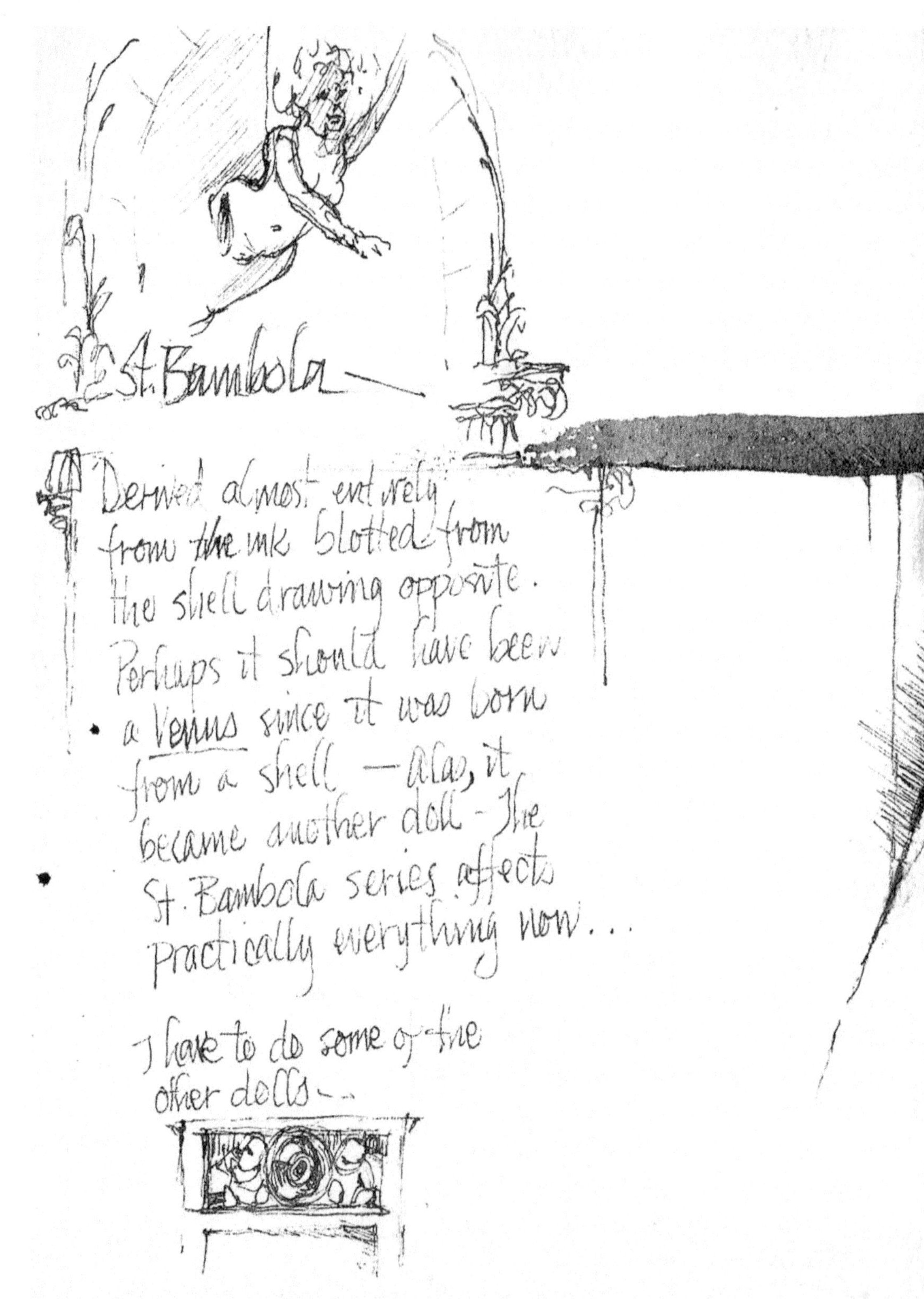

Derived almost entirely
from the ink blotted from
the shell drawing opposite.
Perhaps it should have been
a Venus since it was born
from a shell — Alas, it
became another doll — The
St. Bambola series affects
practically everything now...

I have to do some of the
other dolls —

BOOK 3 drawings from 1967

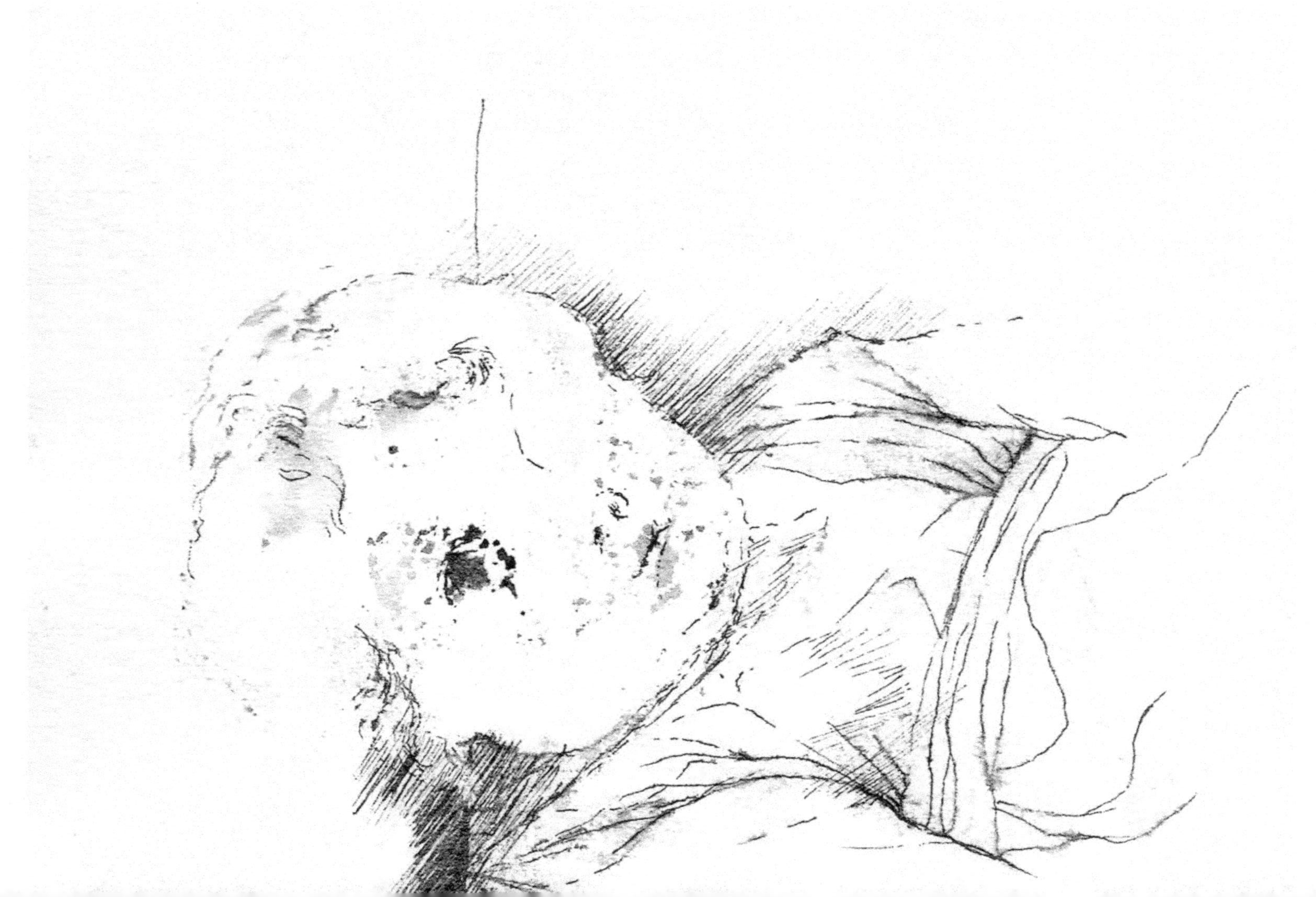

black
yellow ochre
black tips
Red

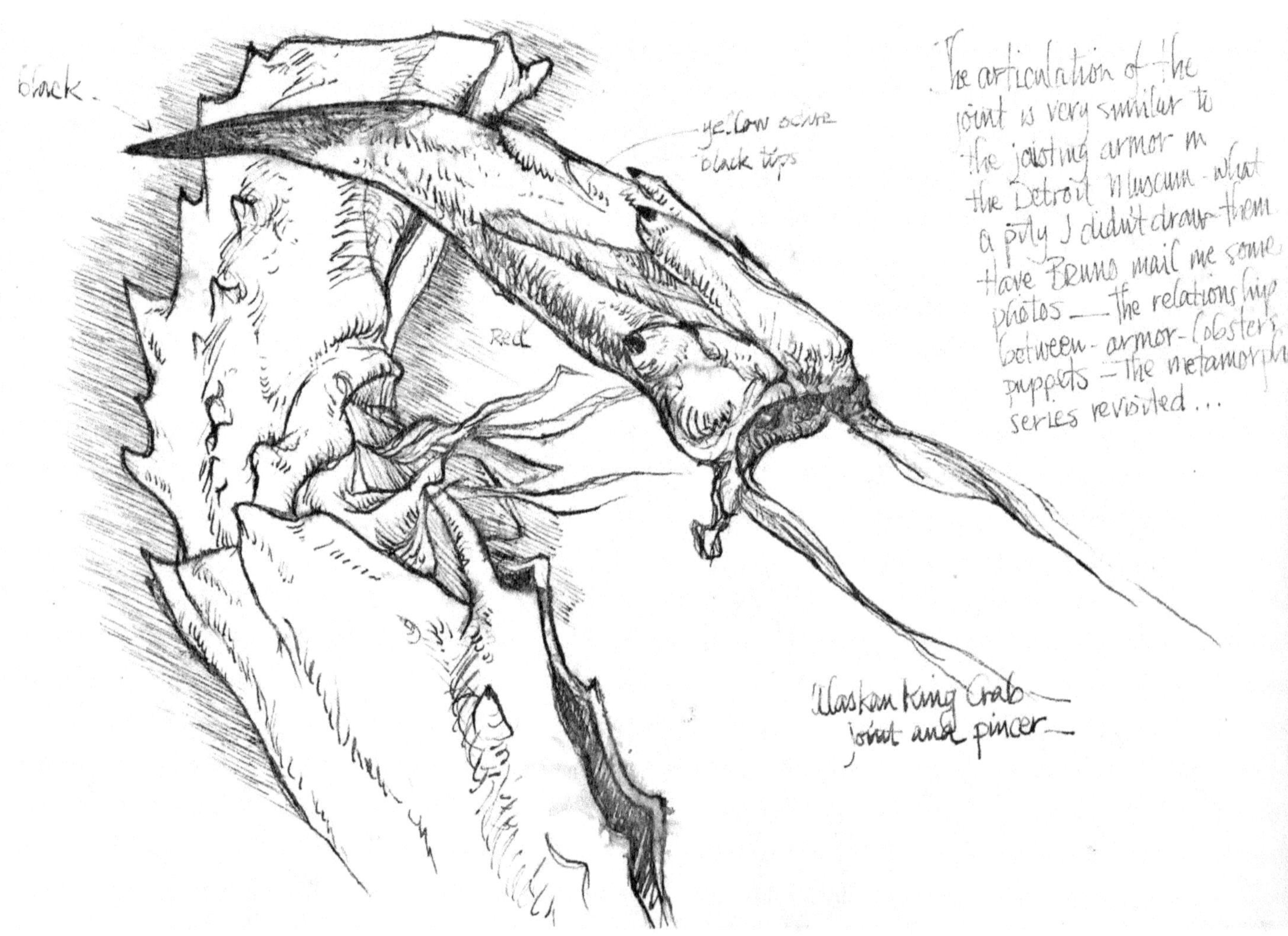

The articulation of the
joint is very similar to
the jousting armor in
the Detroit Museum - what
a pity I didn't draw them.
- Have Bruno mail me some
photos —— The relationship
between - armor - lobster;
puppets — The metamorphic
series revisited …
Alaskan King Crab
joint and pincer

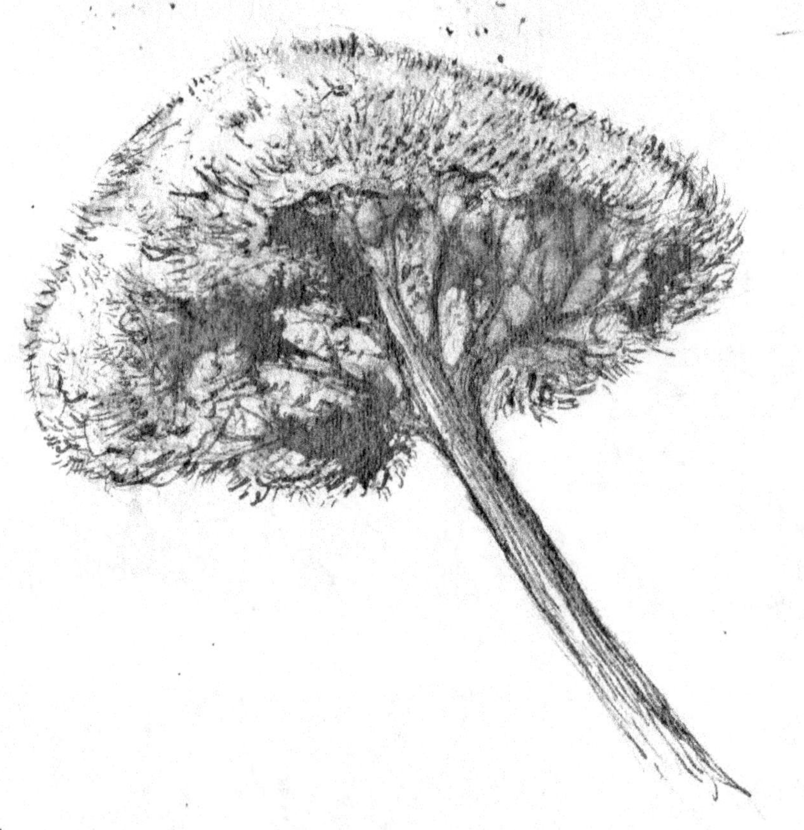

This strange weed — almost as
if it were a tiny Roman pine.

Along the Appian Way or in the
Villa Borghese long rows of these
pines — while here in Utah
this weed stands in long rows
on the architecture students'
model ——— as the properly
scaled tree.

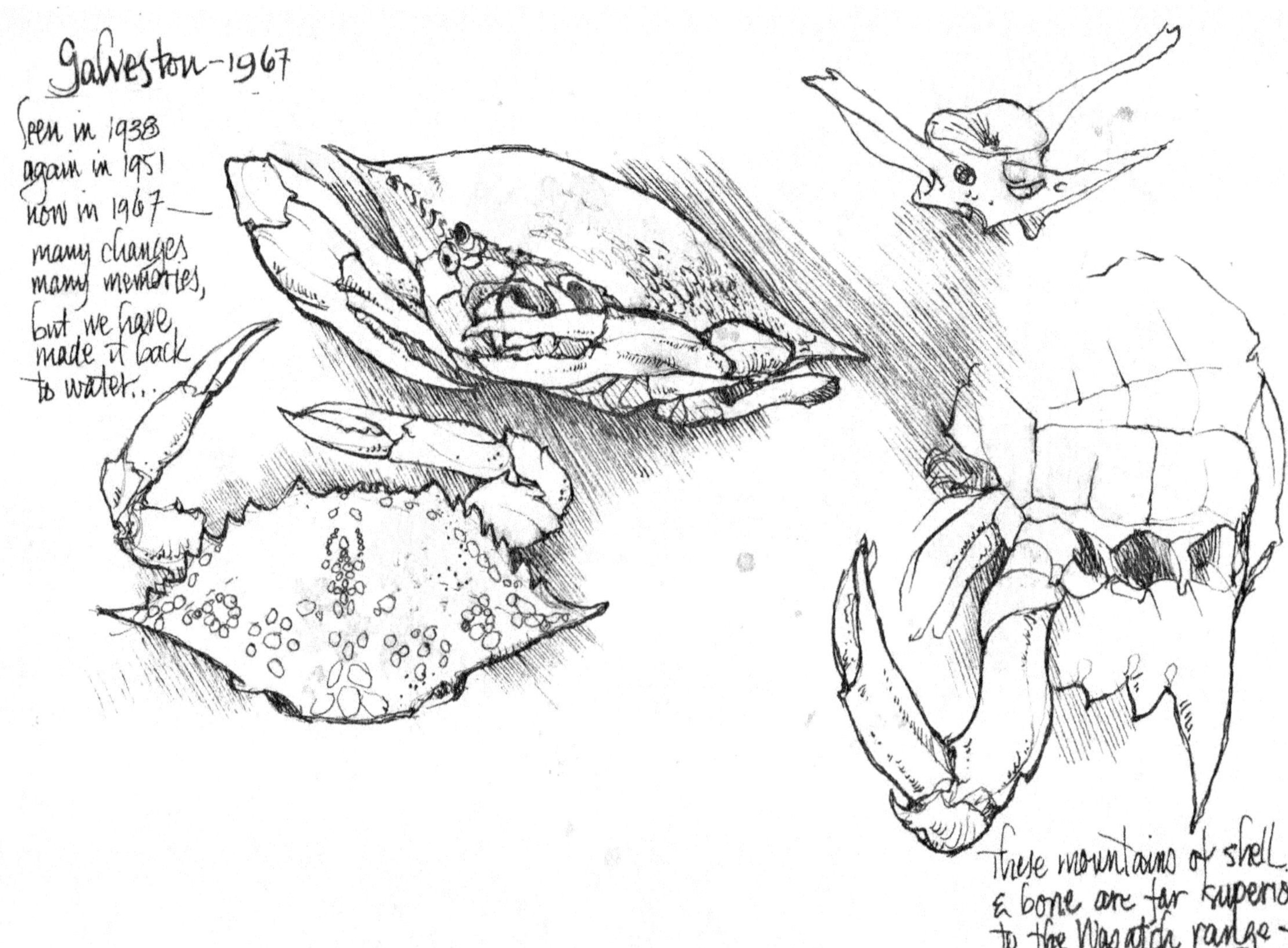

Galveston-1967

Seen in 1938
again in 1951
now in 1967—
many changes
many memories,
but we have
made it back
to water...

These mountains of shell
& bone are far superior
to the Wasatch range—

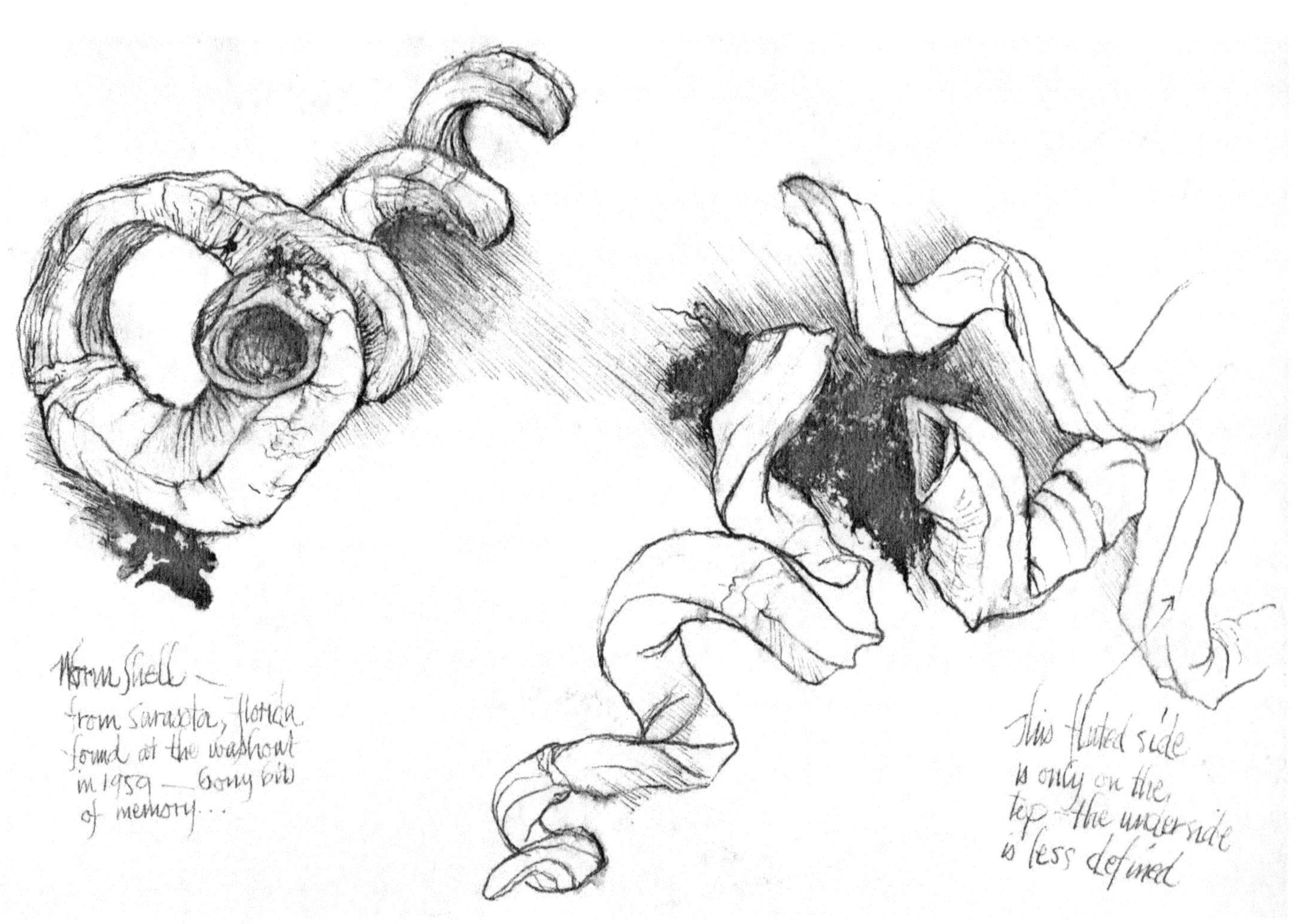

Worm Shell —
from Sarasota, Florida
found at the washout
in 1959 — bony bits
of memory...
This fluted side
is only on the
top — the underside
is less defined

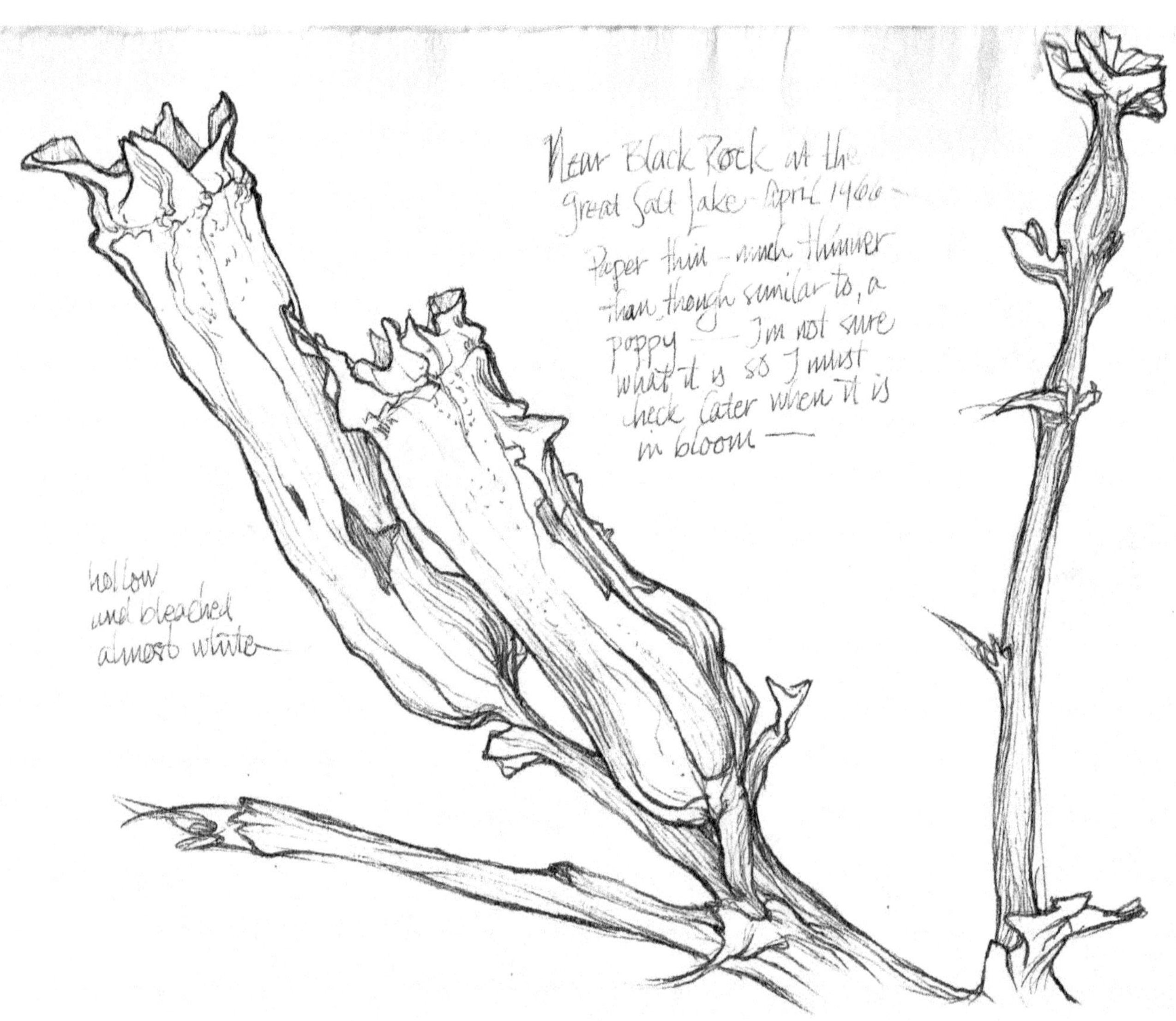

Near Black Rock at the
Great Salt Lake - April 1966 -

Paper thin - much thinner
than though similar to, a
poppy ——— I'm not sure
what it is so I must
check later when it is
in bloom ——

hollow
and bleached
almost white ——

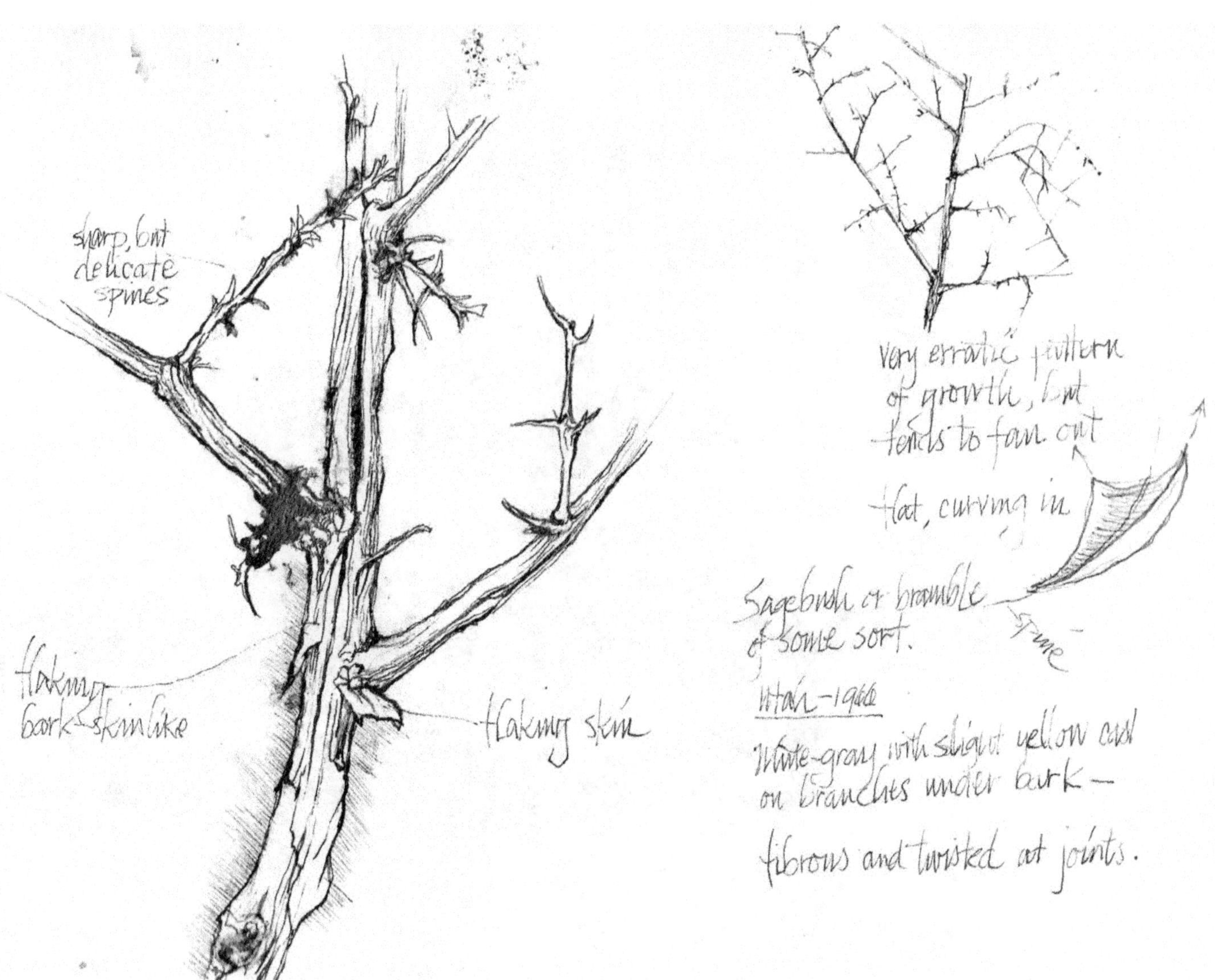

sharp, but delicate spines
Flaking bark skin like
Flaking skin
Very erratic pattern of growth, but tends to fan out
flat, curving in
Sagebrush or bramble of some sort.
Utah — 1966
White-gray with slight yellow cast on branches under bark —
fibrous and twisted at joints.
spine

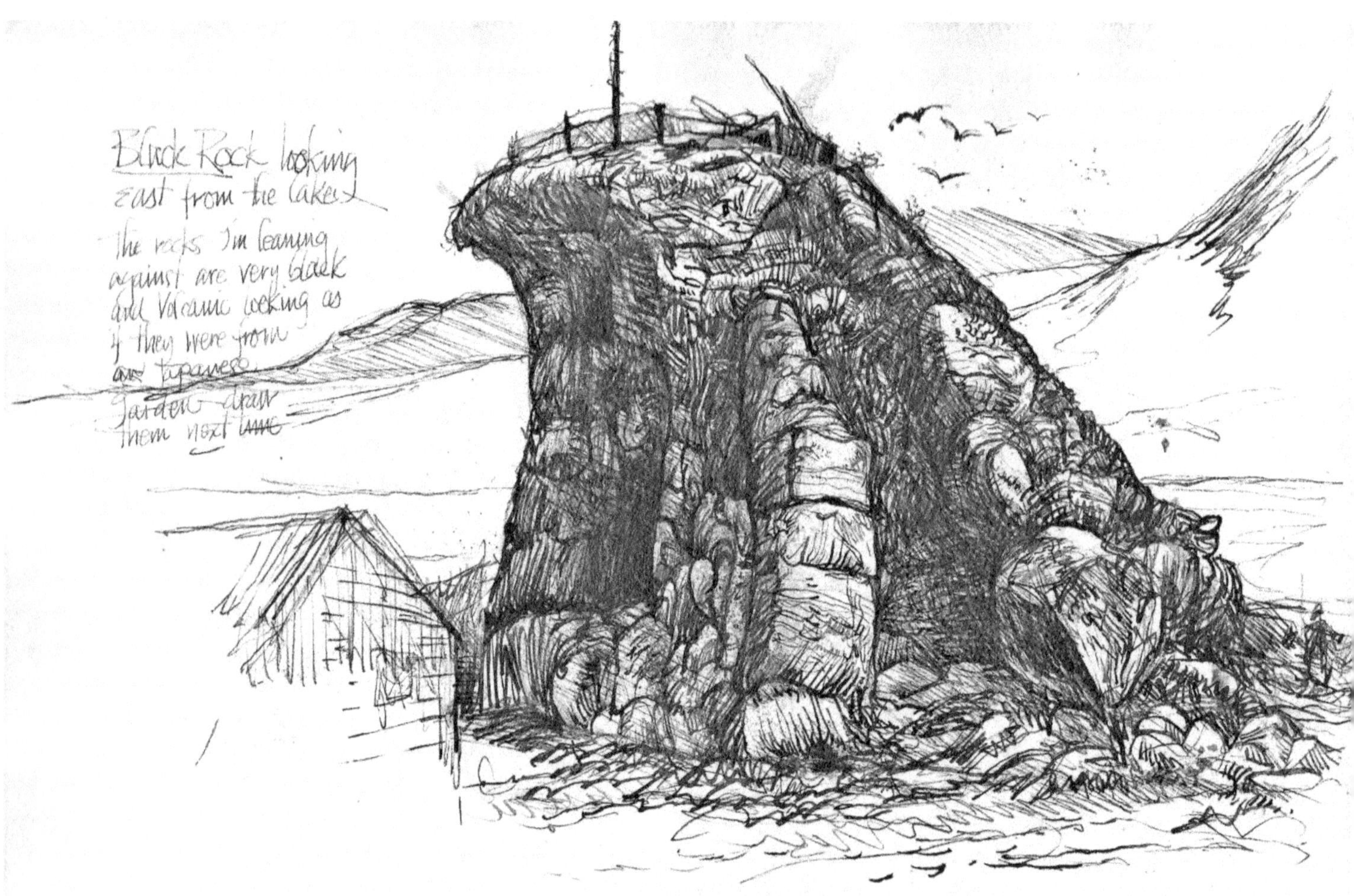

Black Rock looking
east from the lake.
the rocks I'm leaning
against are very black
and Volcanic looking as
if they were from
our Japanese
Garden draw
them next time

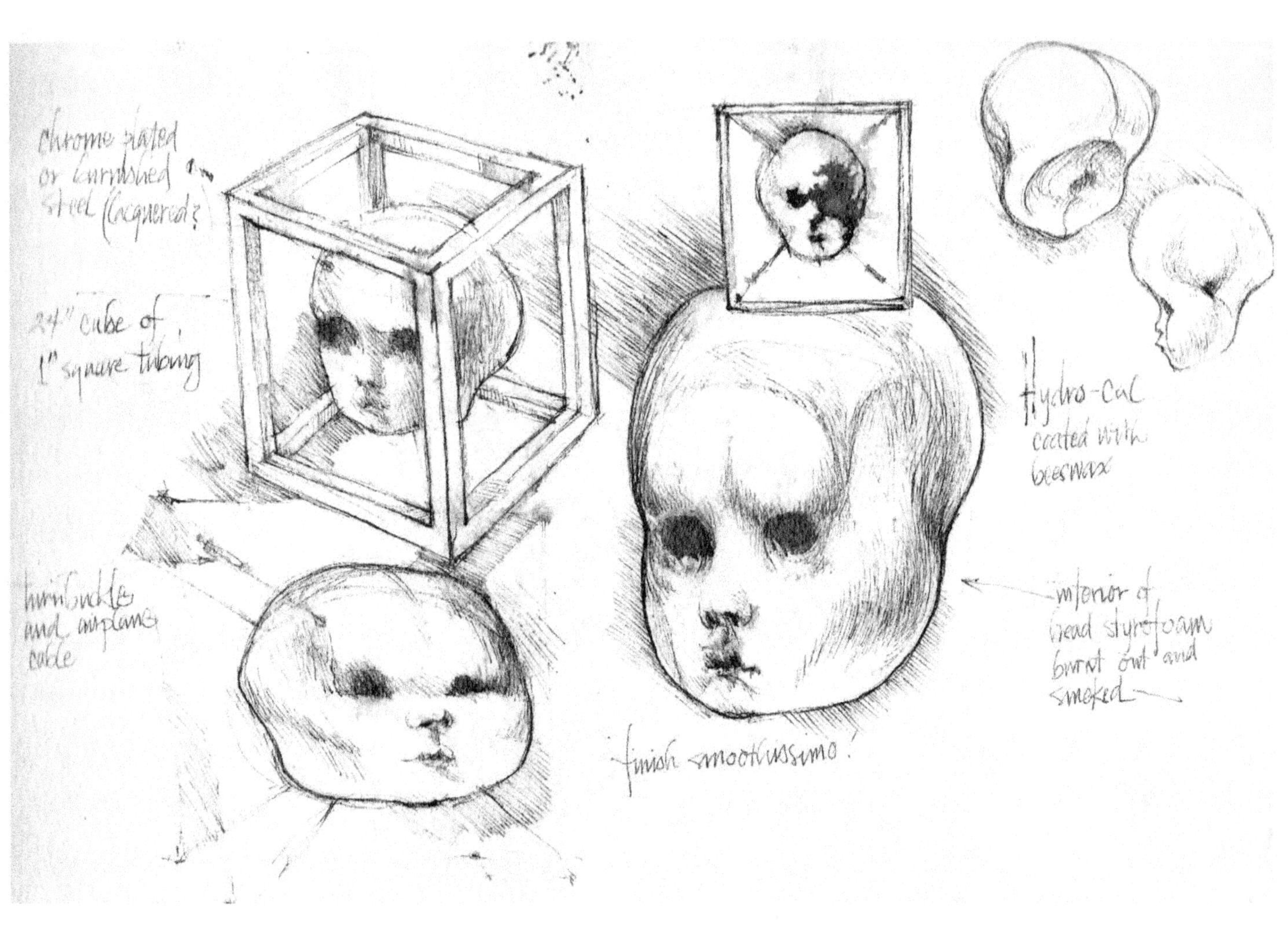

chrome plated
or burnished
steel (lacquered?)

24" cube of
1" square tubing

turnbuckles
and airplane
cable

Hydro-cal
coated with
beeswax

interior of
head styrofoam
burnt out and
smoked

finish smoothissimo!

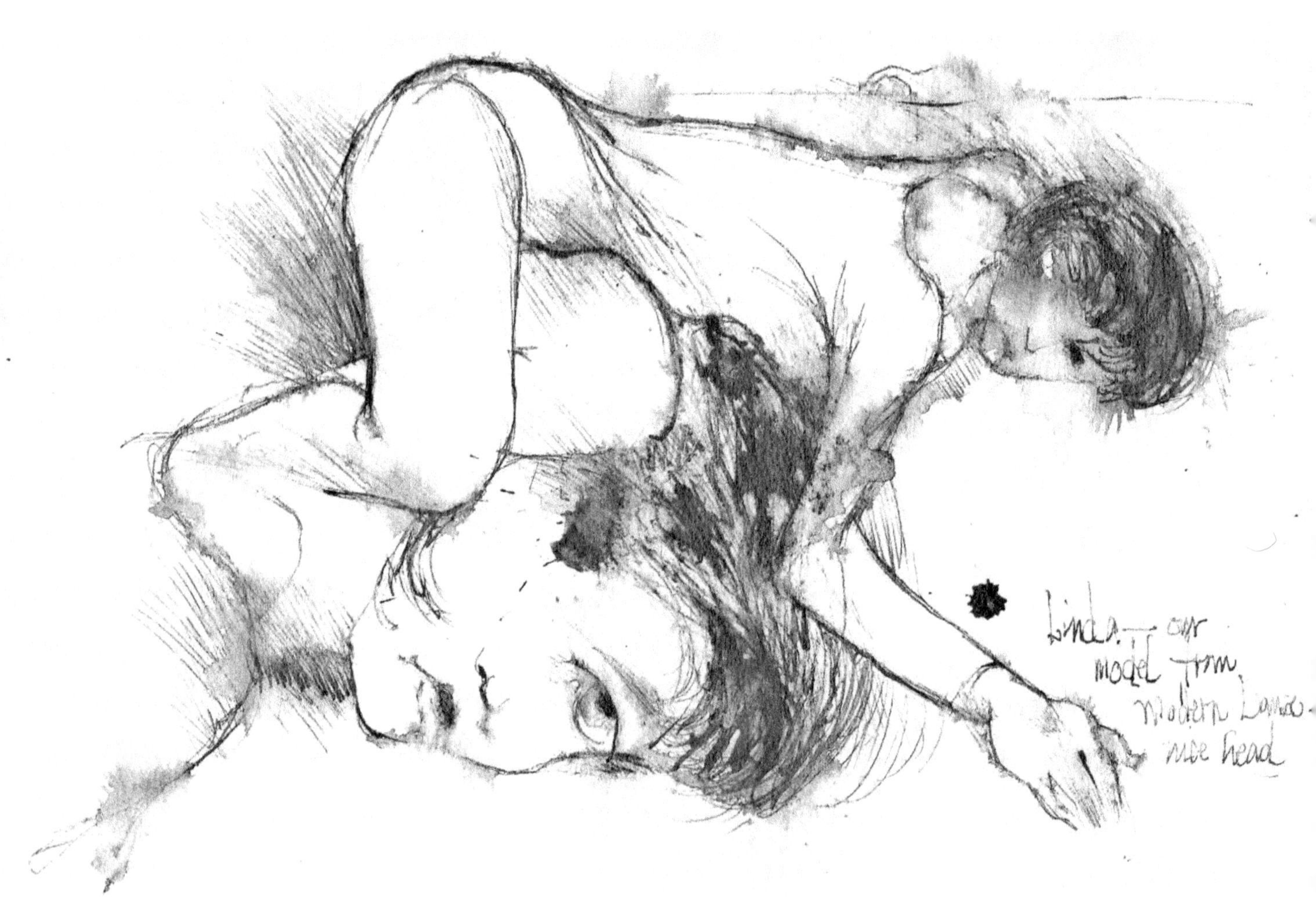

Linda — our
model from
modern Lang
nice head

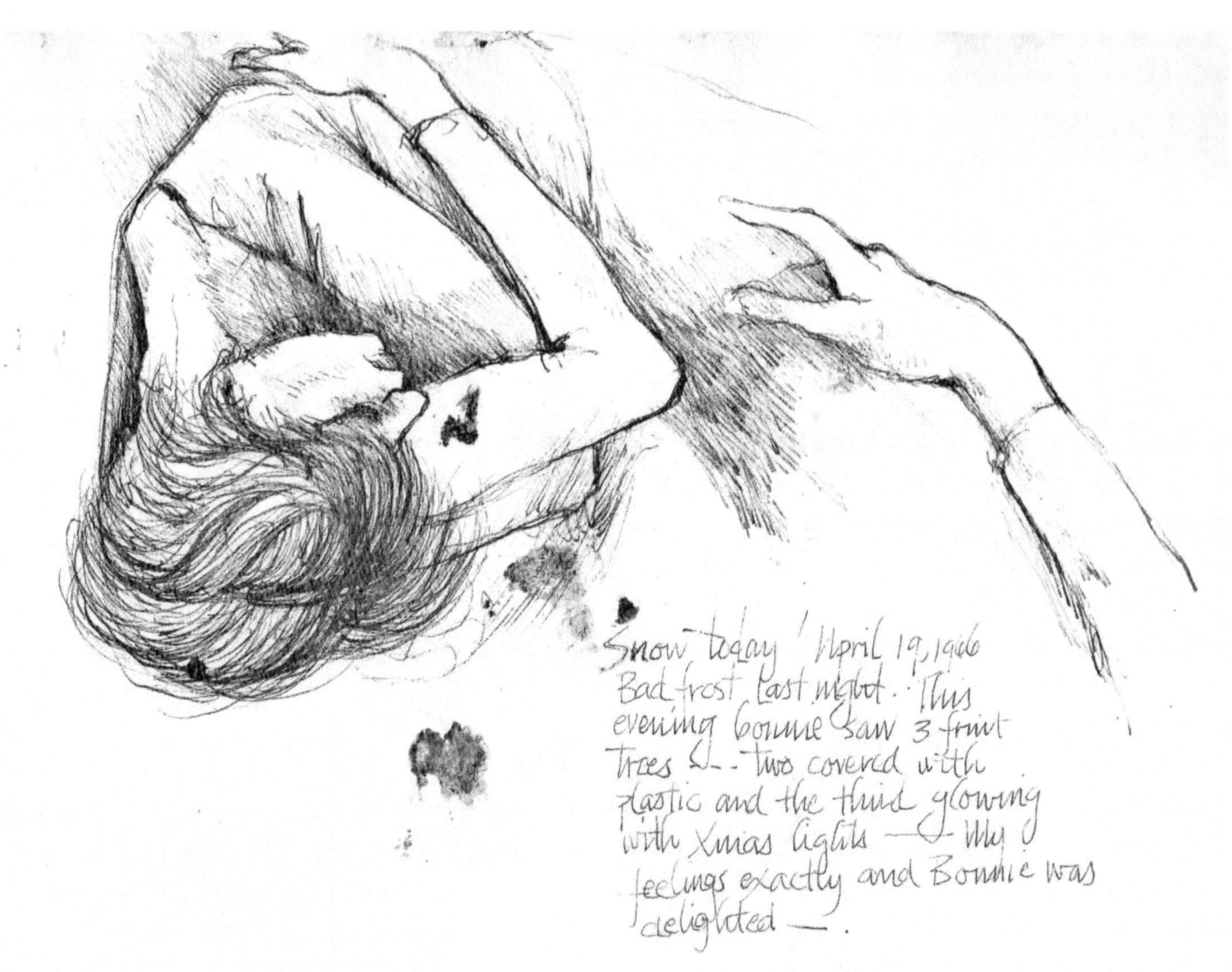

Snow today ' April 19, 1966
Bad frost last night. This
evening Bonnie saw 3 fruit
trees 2 — two covered with
plastic and the third glowing
with Xmas lights — My
feelings exactly and Bonnie was
delighted — .

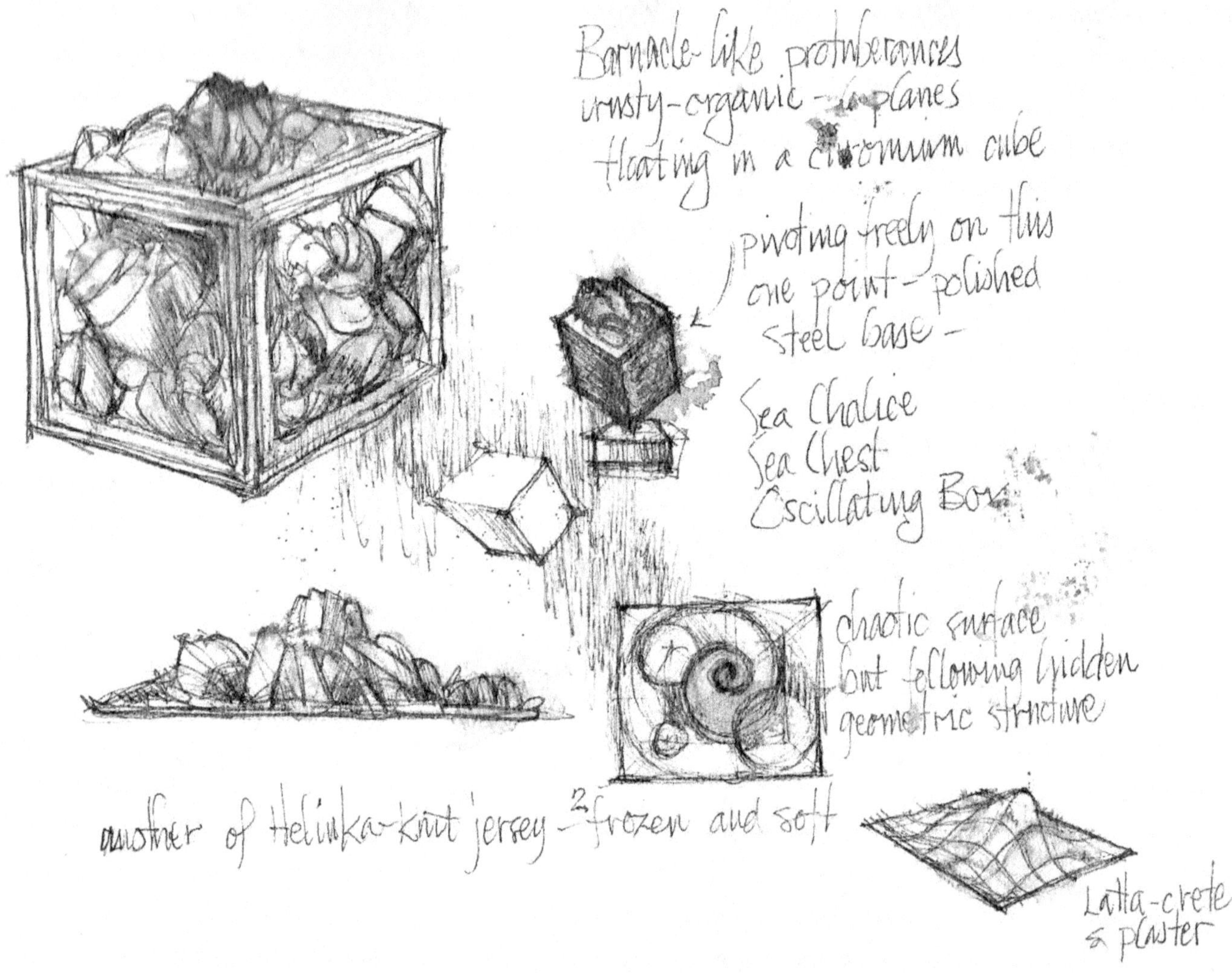

Barnacle-like protuberances
crusty-organic- planes
floating in a chromium cube

pivoting freely on this
one point - polished
steel base -

Sea Chalice
Sea Chest
Oscillating Box

chaotic surface
but following hidden
geometric structure

another of Helinka-knit jersey - frozen and soft

Latta-crete
& plaster

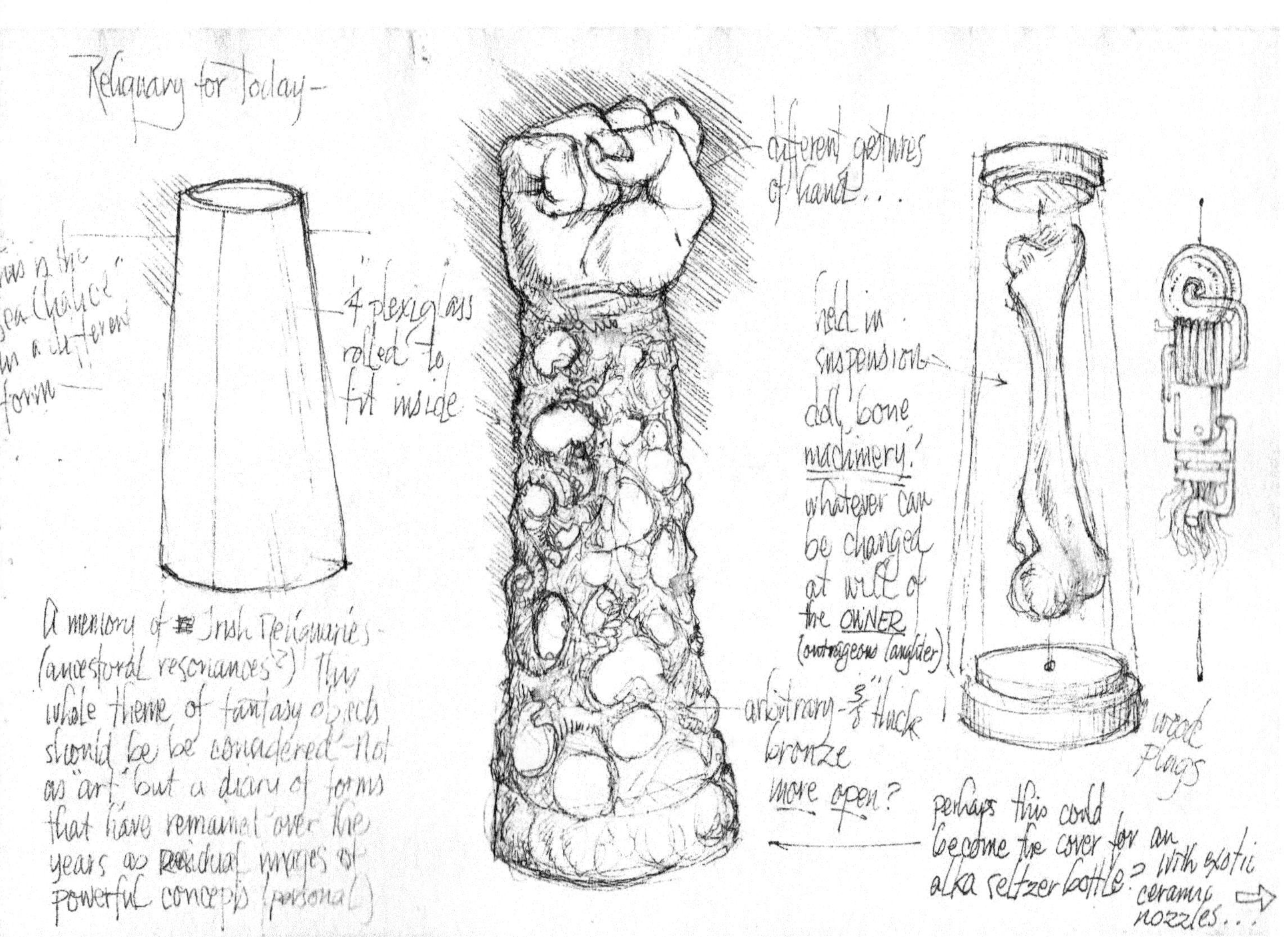

Reliquary for today—
as in the "sea Chalice" in a different form—
4" plexiglass rolled to fit inside
A memory of Irish Reliquaries (ancestoral resonances?) This whole theme of fantasy objects should be be considered—not as "art" but a diary of forms that have remained over the years as Residual images of powerful concepts (personal)
different gestures of hand . . .
held in suspension— doll, bone, machinery! whatever can be changed at will of the OWNER (outrageous laughter)
arbitrary—⅜" thick bronze more open?
wood plugs
Perhaps this could become the cover for an alka seltzer bottle? with exotic ceramic nozzles . . .

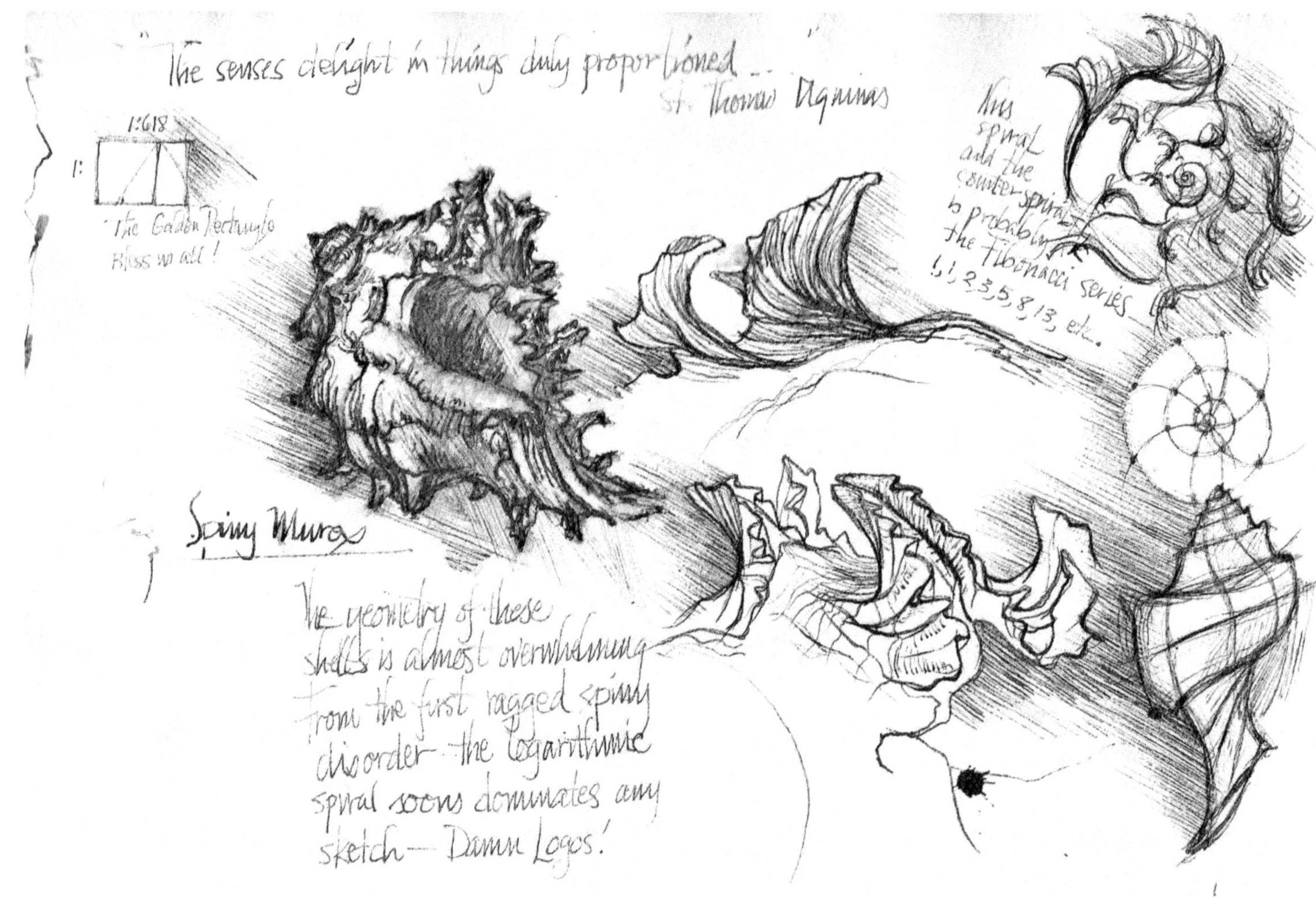

"The senses delight in things duly proportioned..."
St. Thomas Aquinas

1:618
1:
The Golden Rectangle
Bliss to all!

This spiral and the counter spiral is probably the Fibonacci series 1, 1, 2, 3, 5, 8, 13, etc.

Spiny Murex

The geometry of these shells is almost overwhelming from the first ragged spiny disorder the logarithmic spiral soon dominates any sketch — Damn Logos!

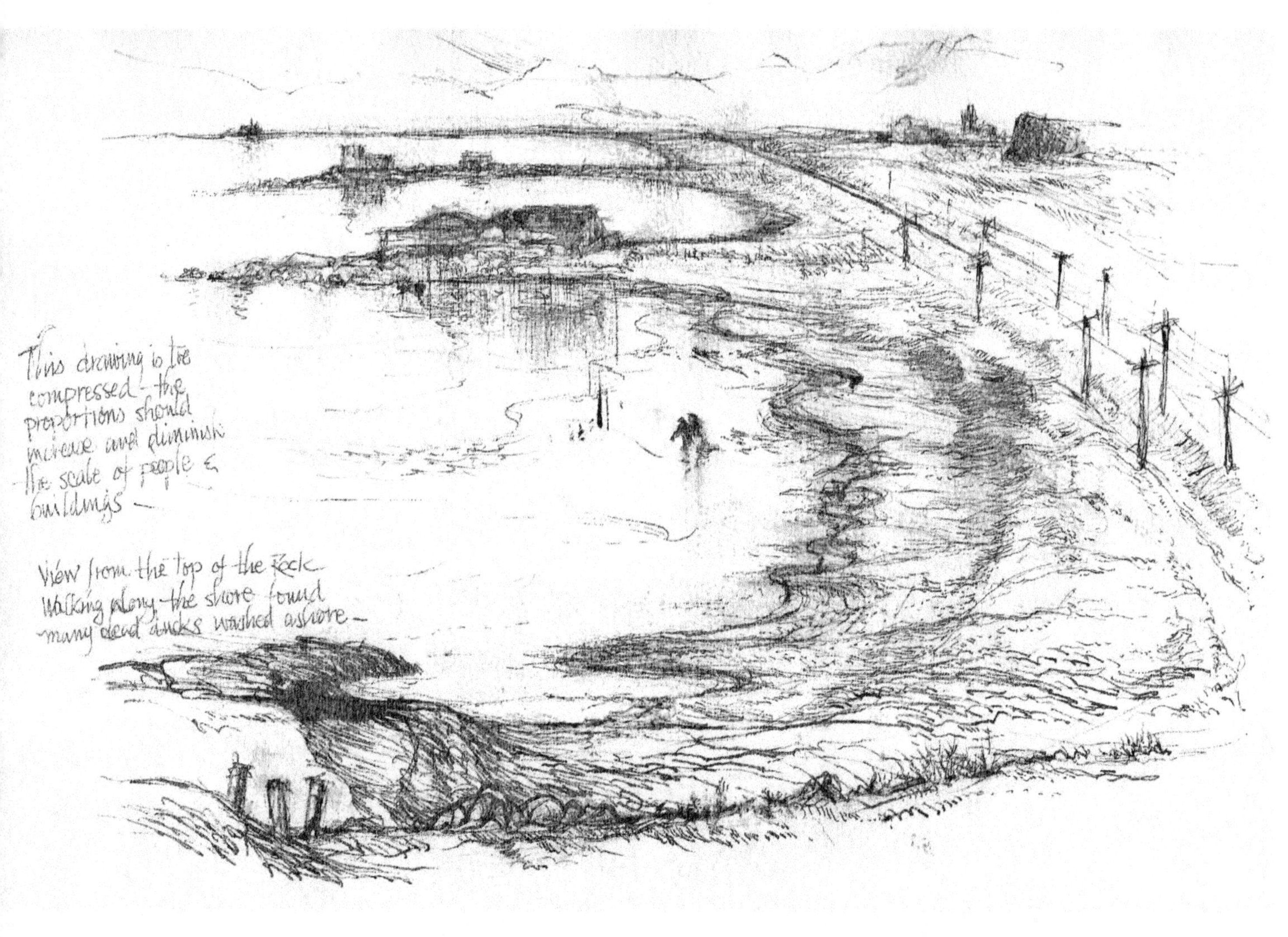

This drawing is too
compressed – the
proportions should
increase and diminish
the scale of people &
buildings –

View from the top of the Rock
Walking along the shore found
many dead ducks washed ashore –

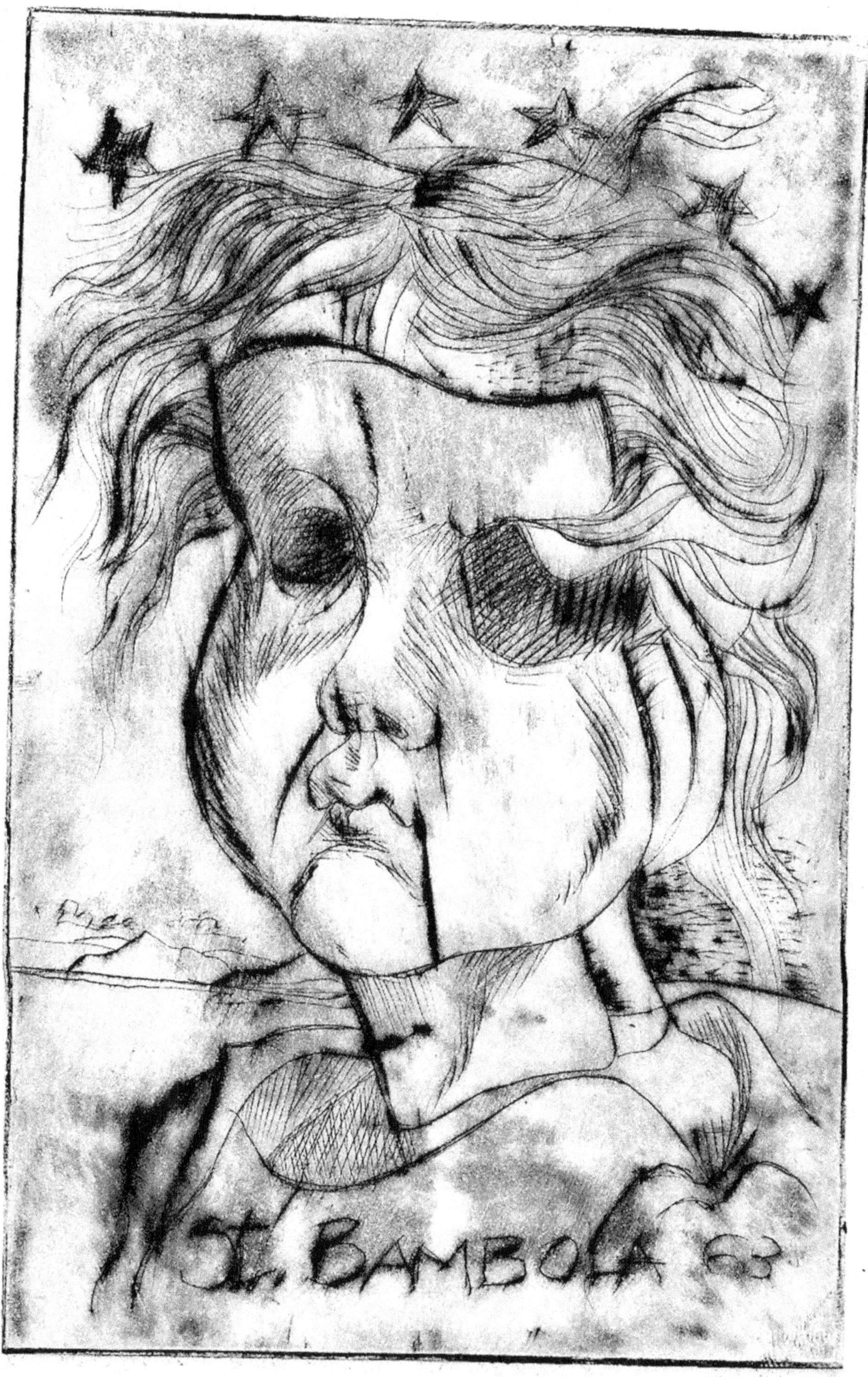

I. BAMBOLA 68

A Note of Levity after so much Soul-searching —
Nostalgia like guests and fish shouldn't be
kept too long — Boo! Bad! — The dredging of memory
should only function if it serves to jog the archetypal
crevices of the "reptilian brain...."

tornado

My reptilian
brain stem
refuses to enter
into my cortical
problem —

← BLOT

Between the
spontaneous
thoughts and
its recording
is a time lag
that blunt the
multi-layered
aspect of what
I want to write.
I may have to
improvise a Joycean
types of invention
to create a shorthand
for myself.

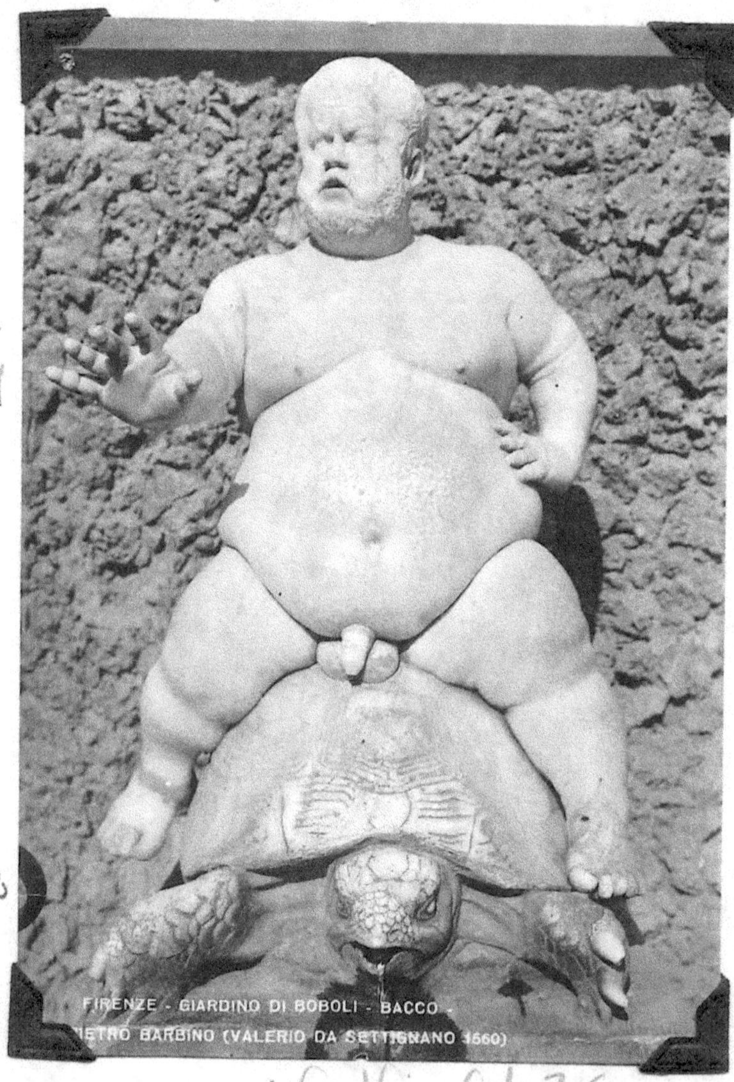

Why this photo? (CHECK ONE)
☐ Looks like Camblin with a beard
☐ Looks like Camblin with a penis
☐ Looks like Camblin on a turtle

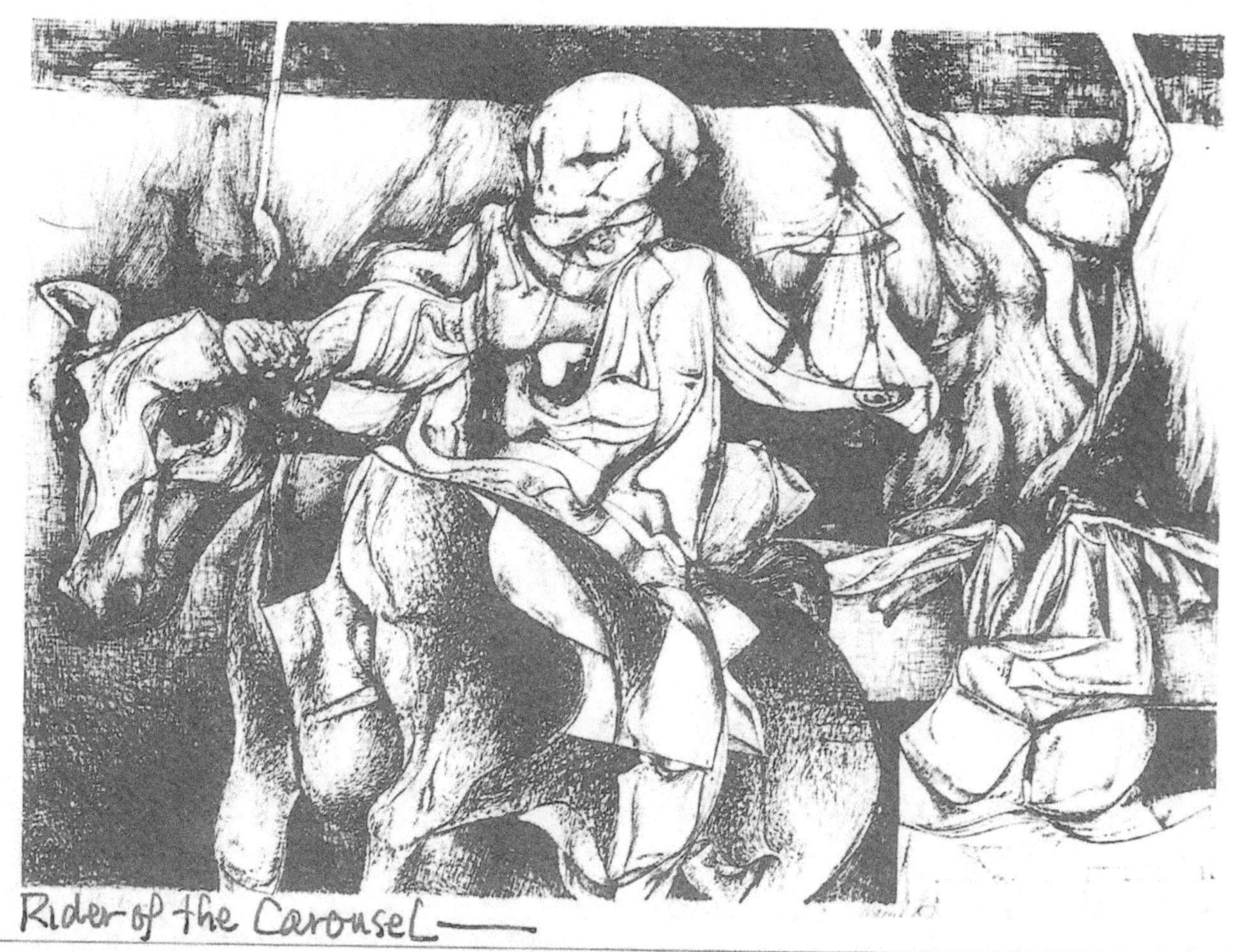

Rider of the Carousel———

Carousel of Four was the first — a large pen & ink collage
but it started the drawings that have pre occupied me
for the last 10 years. It was related to the Four Horsemen
of the Apocalypse (sp?)
     Apocalypse (hell with it!) the Wheel of Life a minor
disagreement with Keronacs' Dharma Bums and an
enchantment with Laotse & Zen... I felt at the time
I was right — I still do, but now there is room more
than <u>one</u> opinion...
If I try to write all of the related random thoughts
it will take forever.

Too manys <u>I</u>'s

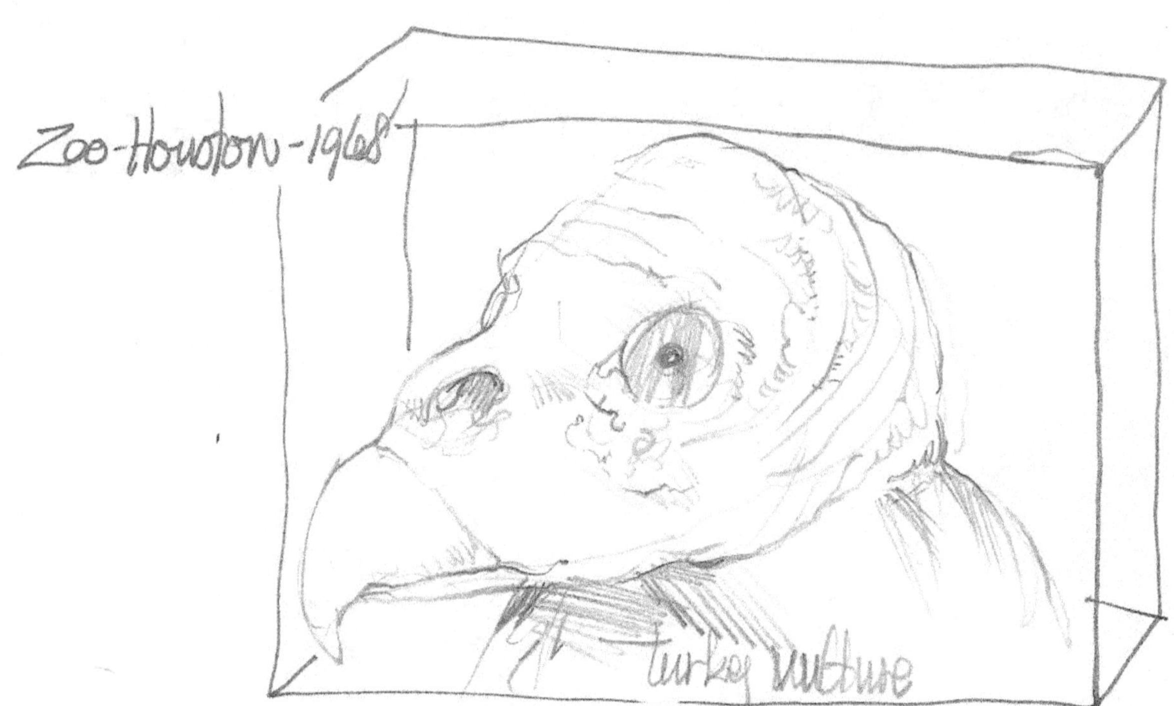

Talons, claws — clinging rather
tearing — Beaks = phallic?

Bones — joints — articulation
This reocurrs over and over
notes in the other sketchbook.

joining·function

exo-skeleton
more emotional shape hard-soft
than our hidden one.

⌐ ...put some back-bone in it
⌐ ...he has a hard-on
⌐ ...Adams rib
⌐ ...pirate's flag

I'll have to do it
another day — I still
have my hang-up of
drawing in front of
others ——— and the
~~zoo~~ zoo was filled
with millions of
kids on the end-of-
school picnics

Hawks eagles, bats
reptiles

feet and beaks and eyes.

Violence — stillness
beautiful form-ugly reputation
symbolic of darkness

Note written to myself in <u>1966</u> after finding a dead
bird at the edge of the <u>Great Salt Lake</u> in Utah.

A phoenix frozen in a
salty shell unable to
burn itself to new life.
Trapped in that chrysalis
of soda-sand — Baked, not
burned by desert dryness.
It waits with its eternal
mineral egg for the hatching
fire —

When each time comes - When
it is said and the meaning
revealed we find it is an
empty rib cage full of sand.
We were not deceived, the
living was the meaning. Those
salty wings - a residue for
those left behind to ponder
and fret about at the end —

It all folds back into
itself some 80 billion
years from now. The
bird and I will sit and
wait for that magnificent
pulse ——

Notes on the drawing
<u>White Gull -1967</u>

Bone white broken out from
Ribbed feather salt wound —
Gull death - salty flutter of
crusty wings
Clad heart pounds the sand
lung

Dry taste of salt on feathers

Pencil marks around the lifeless
form giving it another life
or stopping it from continuing
decay

Rib-cage - Hollow and rigid feathers
making a gray drawing on the
wall - Shadows with more
color and life than these
few bones —

Why does this poor bird
move me to record its fate?
The bird, its death or just
its shape —

That shape seen so
many times in all
Kind of dead and
dying things —

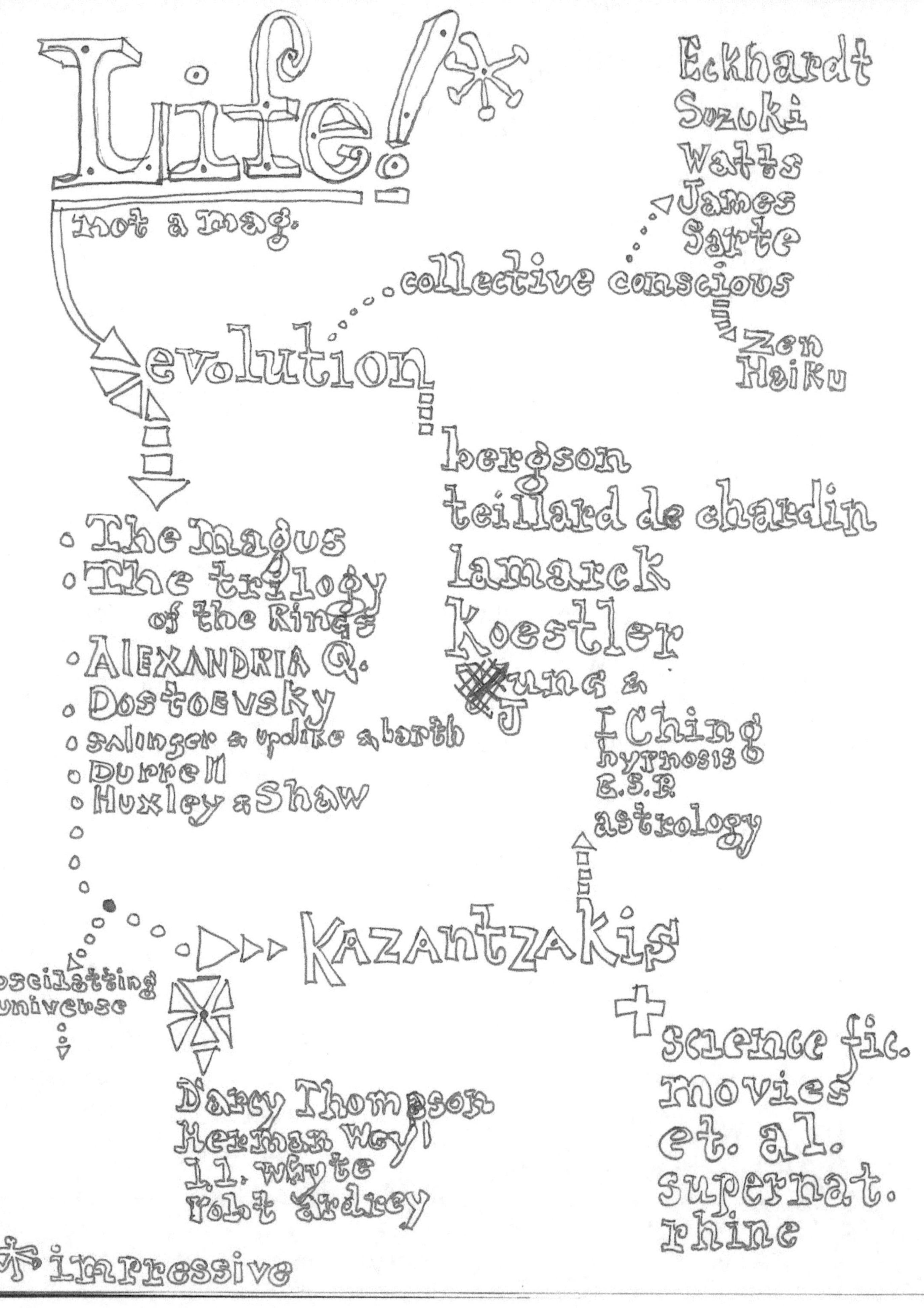

Life! /X
not a mag.
evolution
collective conscious
Eckhardt
Suzuki
Watts
James
Sarte
Zen
Haiku
bergson
teillard de chardin
lamarck
Koestler
Jung &
I Ching
hypnosis
E.S.P.
astrology
The Magus
The trilogy
of the Rings
Alexandria Q.
Dostoevsky
salinger & updike & barth
Durrell
Huxley & Shaw
oscillating
universe
Kazantzakis
+
science fic.
movies
et. al.
supernat.
rhine
D'arcy Thompson
Herman Weyl
L.L. whyte
Rob't Ardrey
impressive

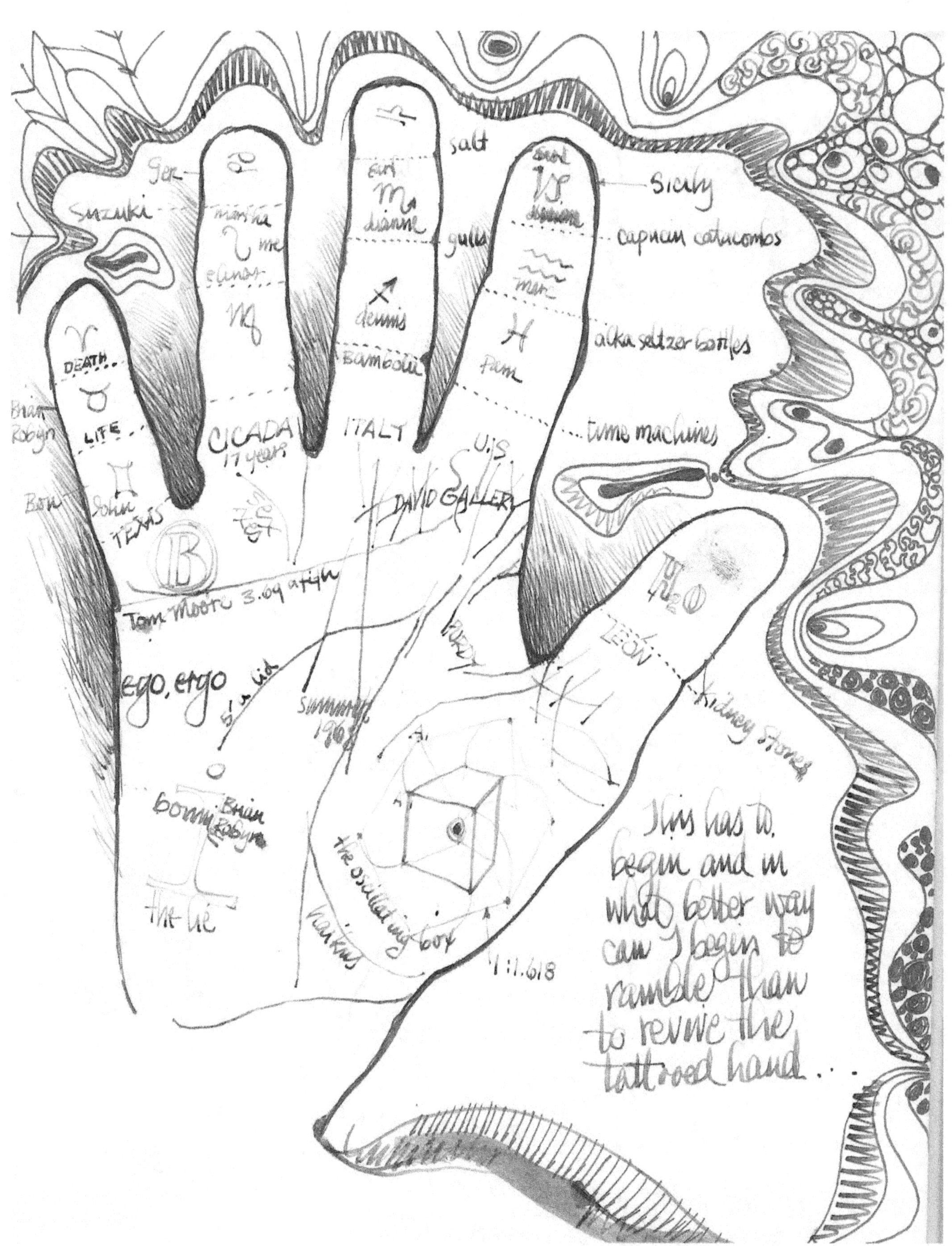

Ger-
Suzuki
Brian
Robyn
Born John
TEXAS
ego, ergo
bonn Brian Robyn
The tie
Tom Moore 3.69 a 74u
CICADA
17 years
ITALY
salt
earl
Ma
dianne
dennis
Bamboo
DAVID GALLERY
U.S.
summer
1967
the oscillating my boy
hawking
1:1.618
sol
US
gulla
man
Pam
Sicily
capuchin catacombs
alka seltzer bottles
time machines
DEATH
LIFE
John
H₂O
LEON
kidney stones
This has to
begin and in
what better way
can I begin to
ramble than
to revive the
tattooed hand...

<u>Ecology of Art</u> or (try not to, ^{WRITE} while inebriated)
"That's an interesting
idea — I'm keep telling my students to "Do your own
thing" — Know thyself — etc. But I never thought
about using the example of <u>eco</u>logy and the people
that do study it — One can hear many valid
reasons that an artist should be <u>this</u> or <u>that</u>,
Why he should be involved socially — politically or
with religious attitudes and some artists should,
but rather, than judge why not assume that in really
trying to do his thing it may have something to do
with <u>our</u> balance of nature — <u>Some may serve</u>
<u>who only seem to indulge themselves</u>. Once upset,
this balance can wreak havoc — man is the
worst offender in changing his physical world —
maybe the artists are some of few that are
fighting for existence when everything around
us is wishing us to be "<u>in</u>" — "<u>for</u>" or "<u>about</u>"
And yet he is just <u>being</u> — not in conflict — not
destroying — trying to <u>be</u> in a world gone very
wrong — and he may have no effect what-so-
ever and eventually becomes extinct...

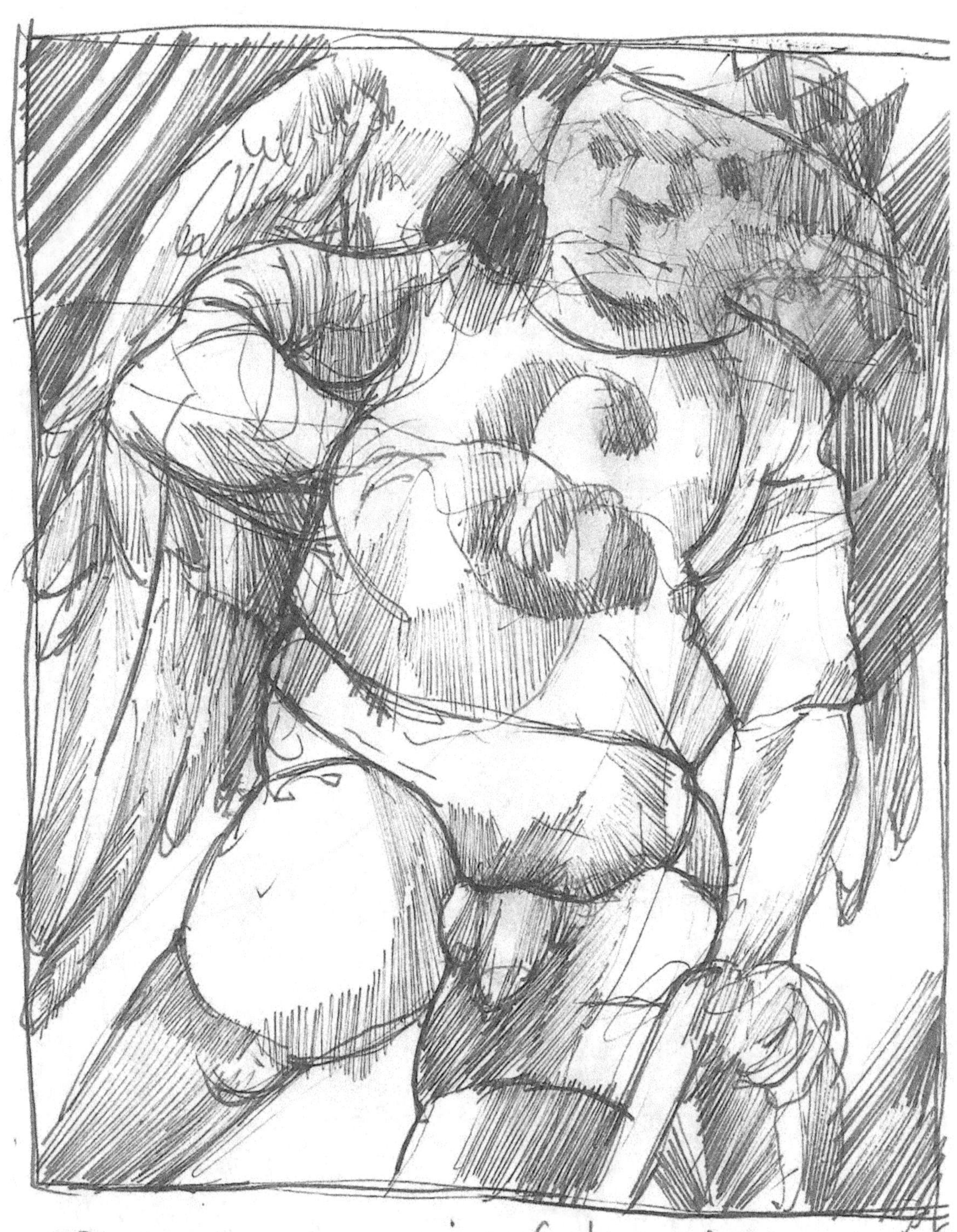

Shades of 1950 · coming back as the avenging angel whispering words of seduction concerning work —even Time machines are better than this. Find something to draw from . . . .

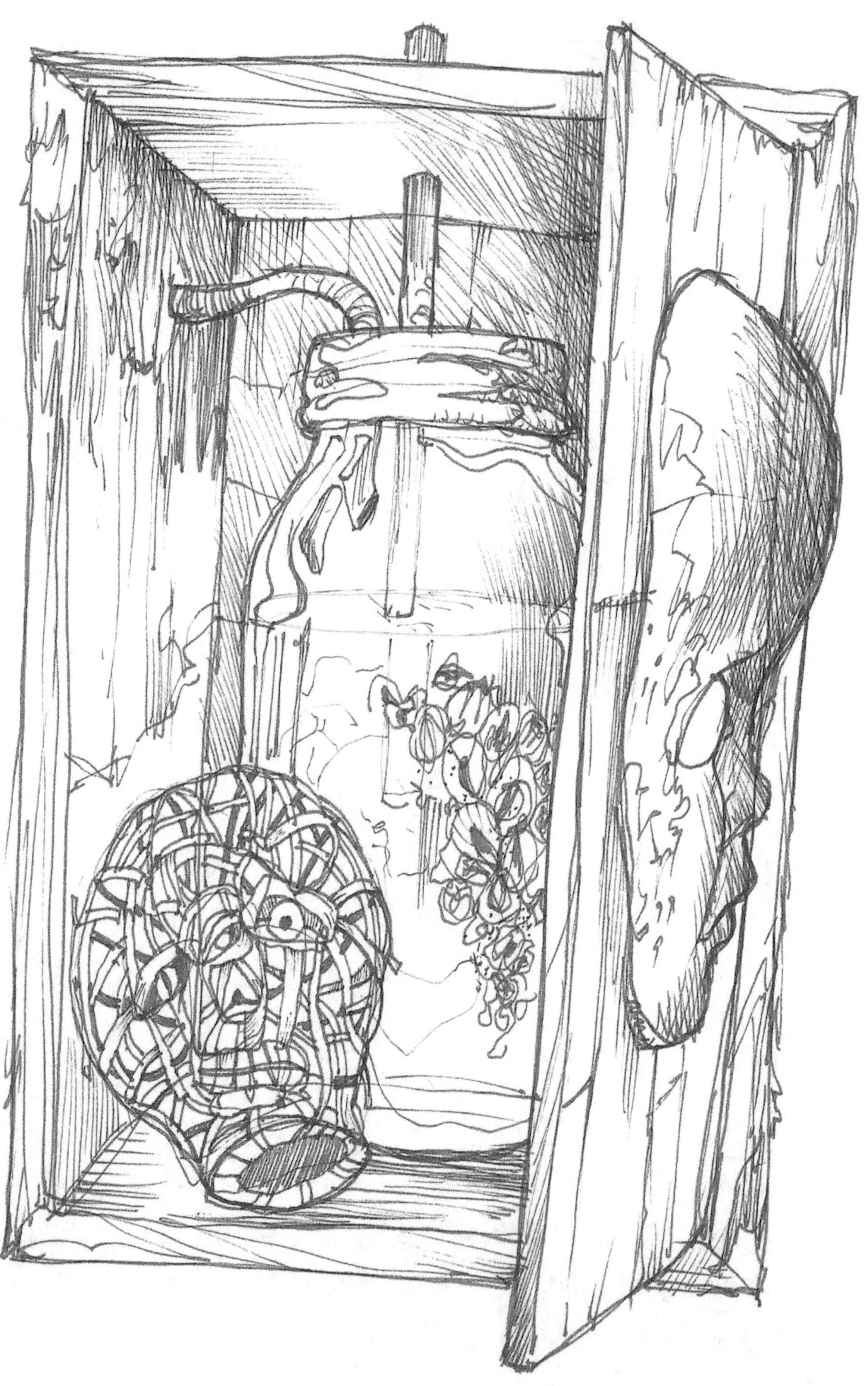

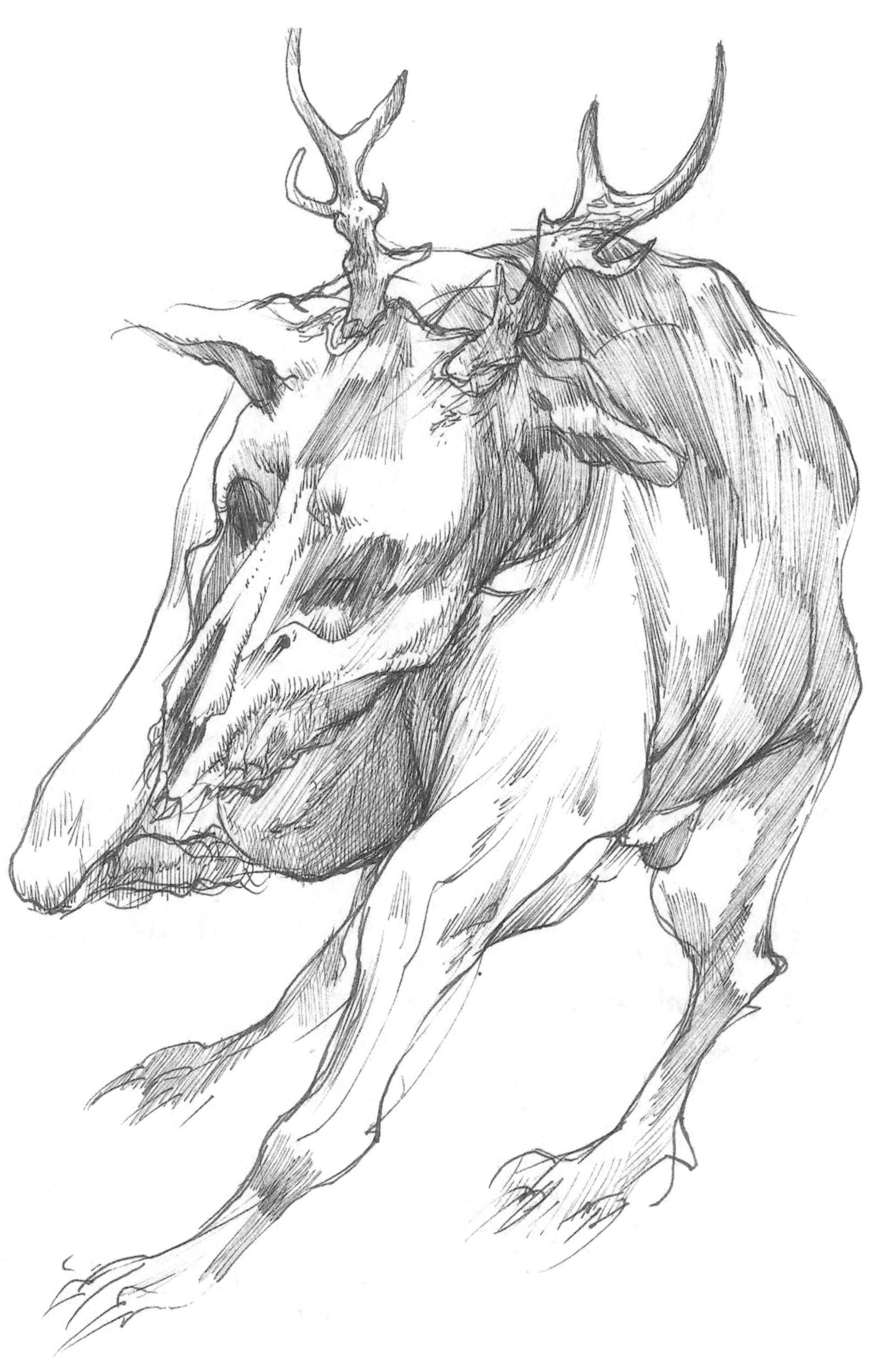

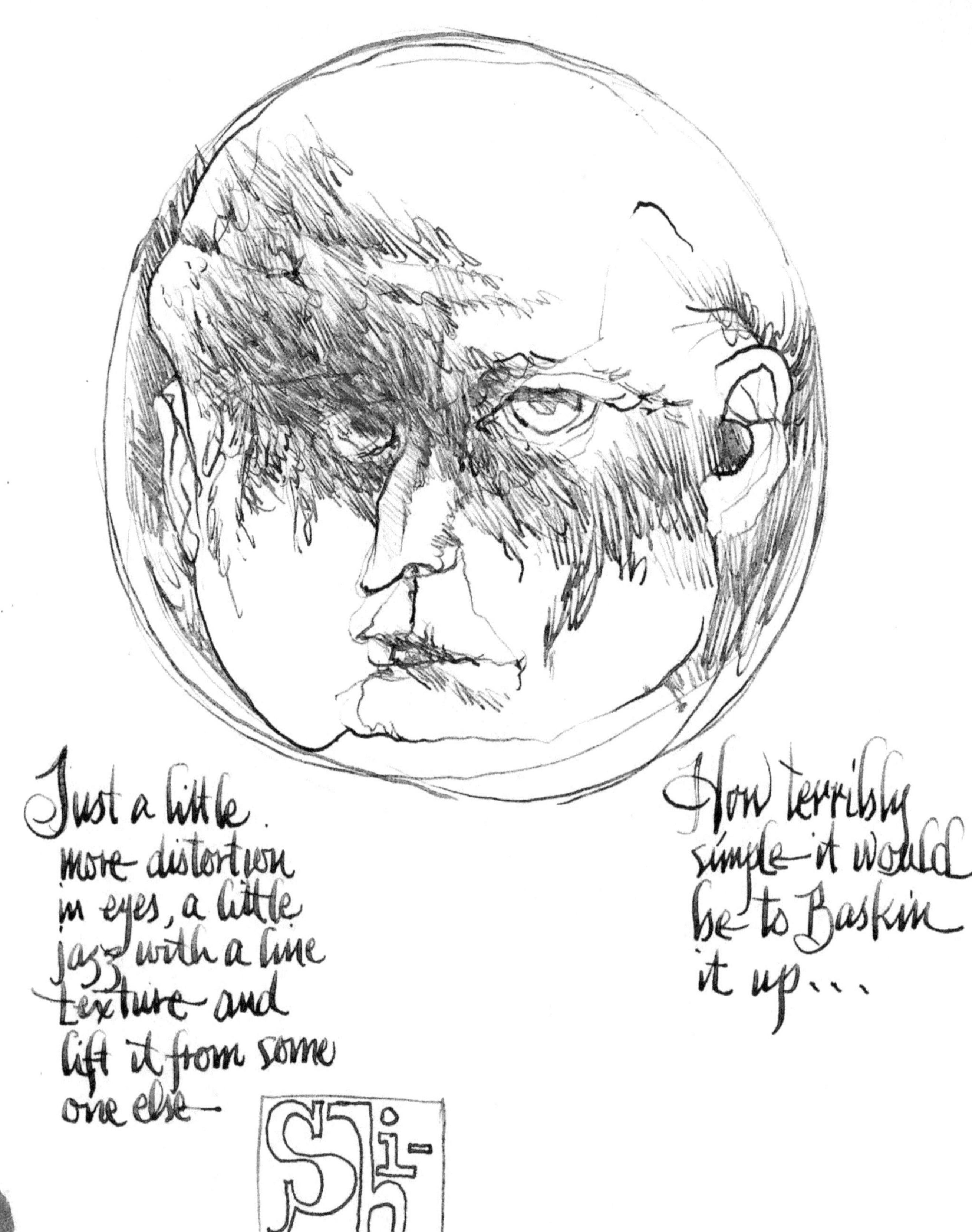

Just a little
more distortion
in eyes, a little
jazz with a line
texture and
lift it from some
one else —

How terribly
simple it would
be to Baskin
it up...

Shit

...still it's his thing
and the idea's
not that bad...

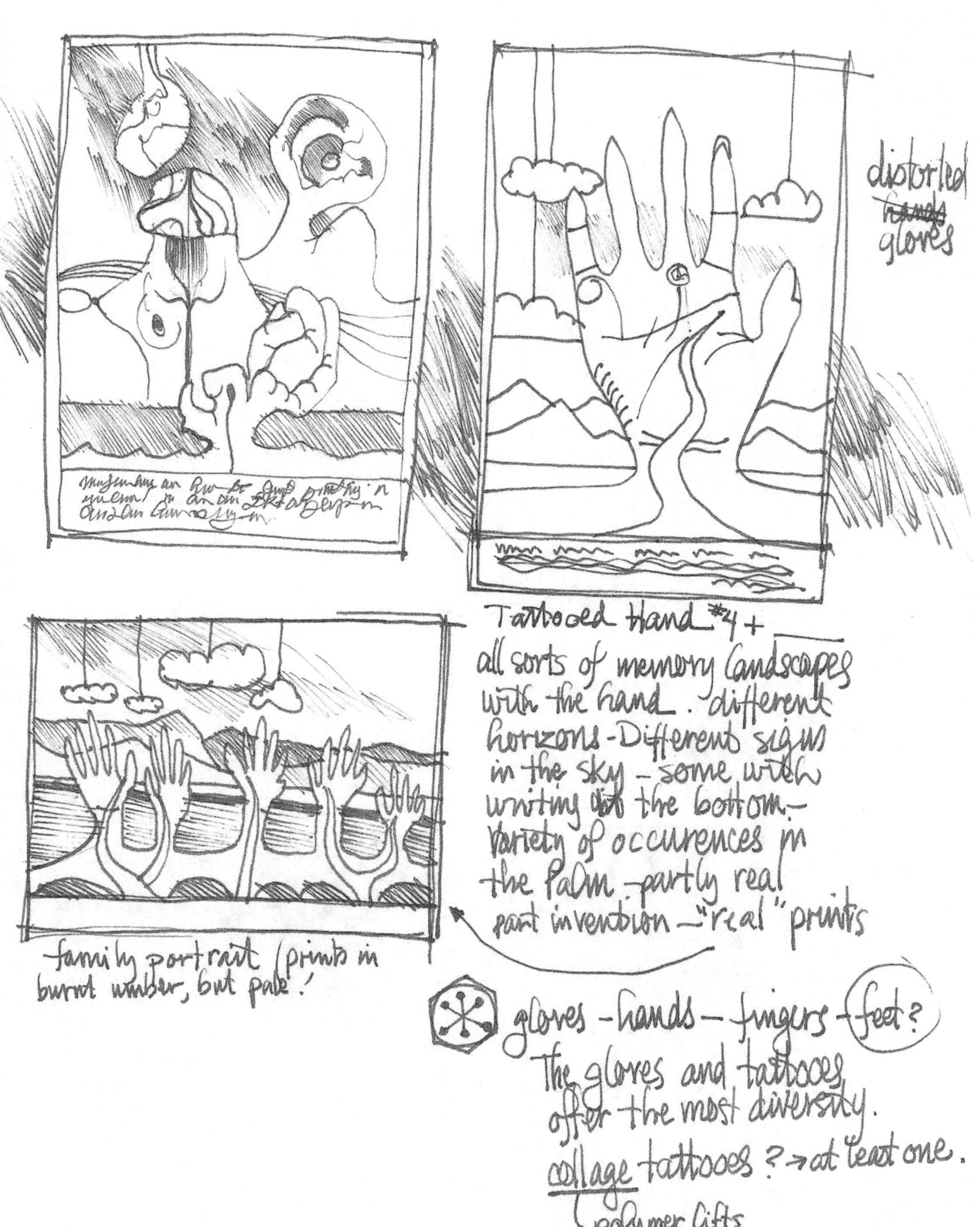

distorted
gloves

family portrait (prints in
burnt umber, but pale!)

Tattooed Hand #4 + ___
all sorts of memory landscapes
with the hand. different
horizons - Different signs
in the sky - some with
writing at the bottom -
variety of occurences in
the palm. partly real
part invention - "real" prints

gloves - hands - fingers - feet?
The gloves and tattooes
offer the most diversity.
collage tattooes? → at least one.
polymer lifts

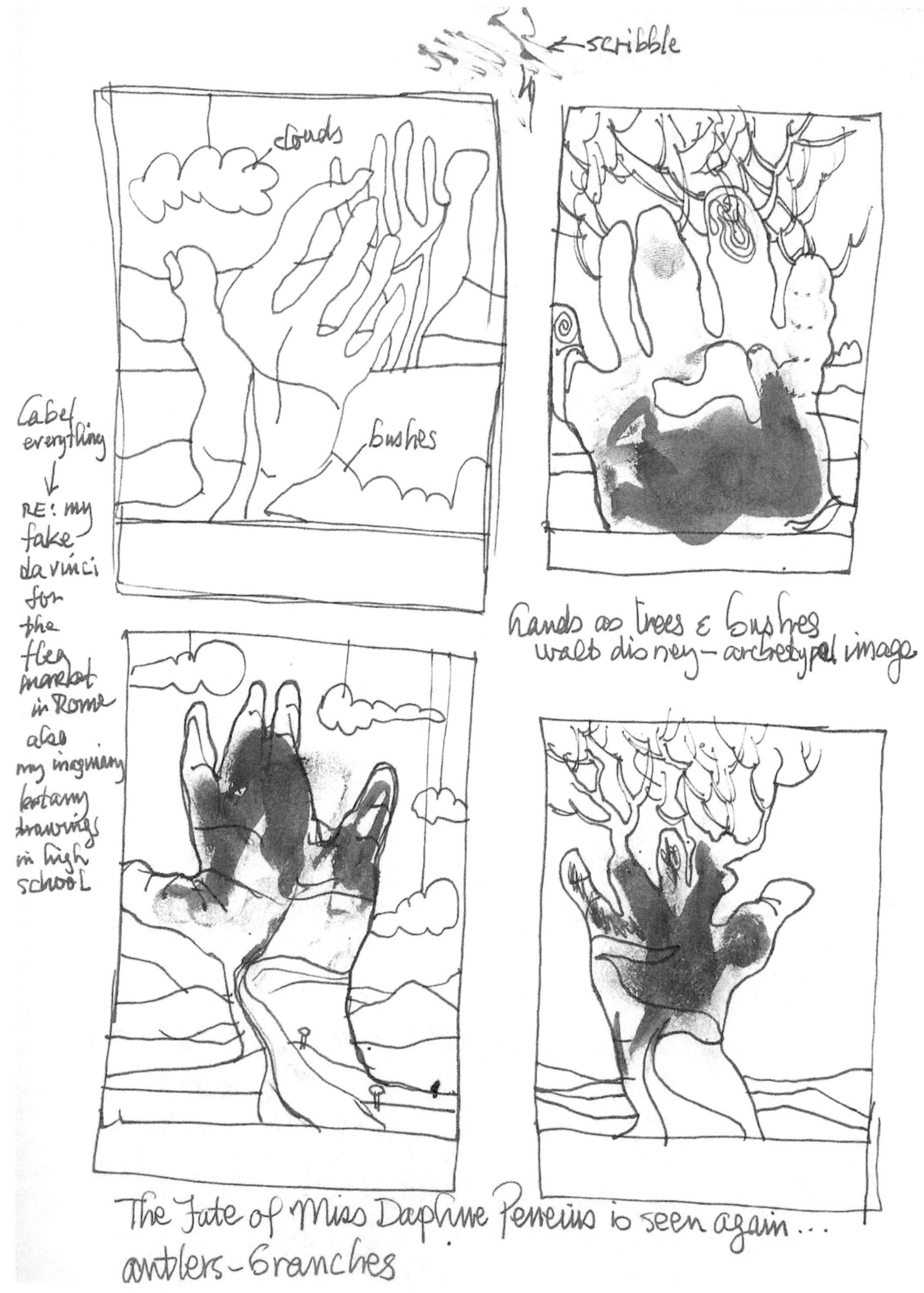

scribble
clouds
bushes
Label everything
↓
RE: my
fake
da vinci
for
the
flea
market
in Rome
also
my imaginary
botany
drawings
in high
school
Hands as trees & bushes
walt disney — archetypal image
The Fate of Miss Daphne Peneius is seen again...
antlers — branches

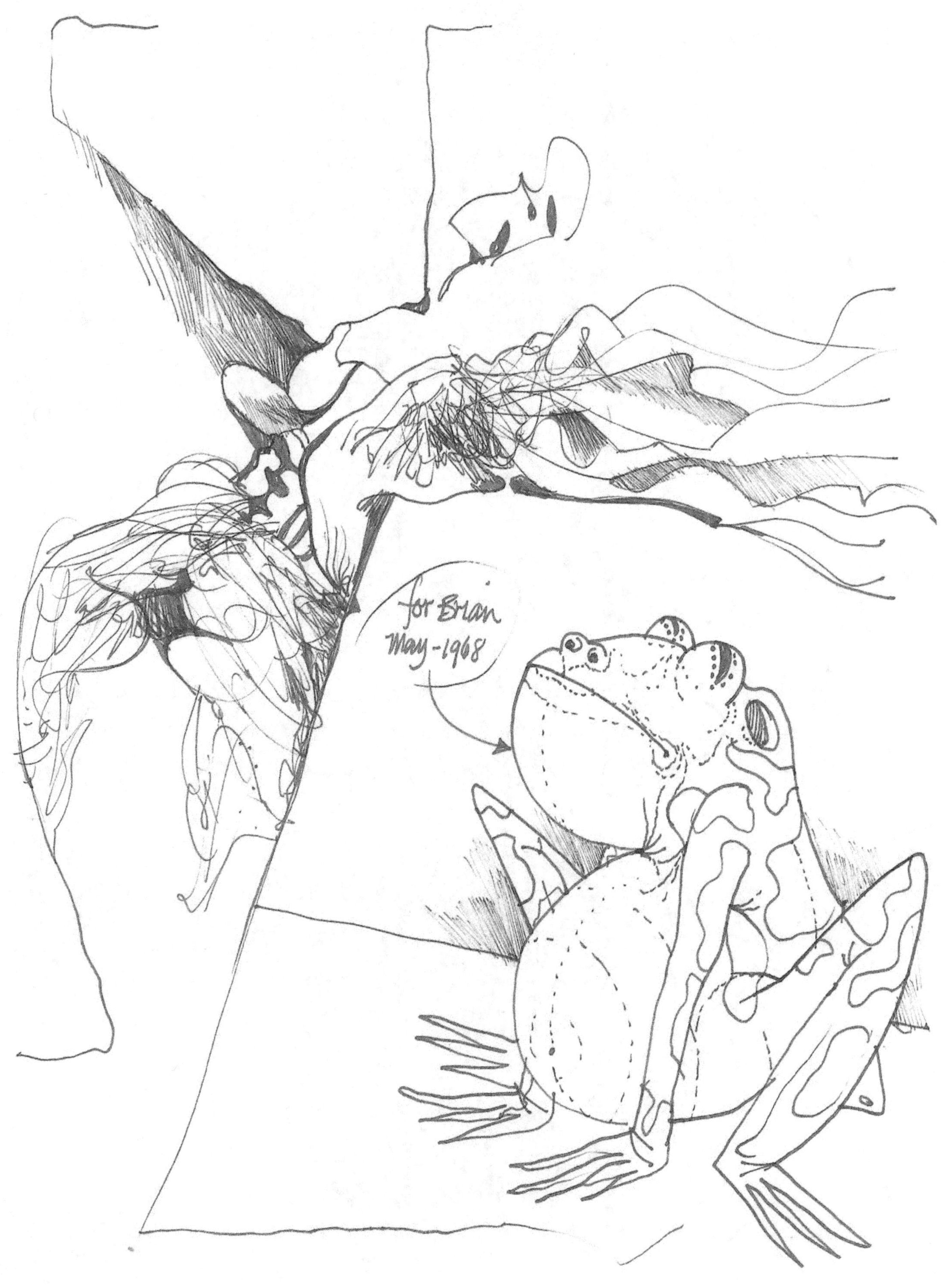

for Brian
May - 1968

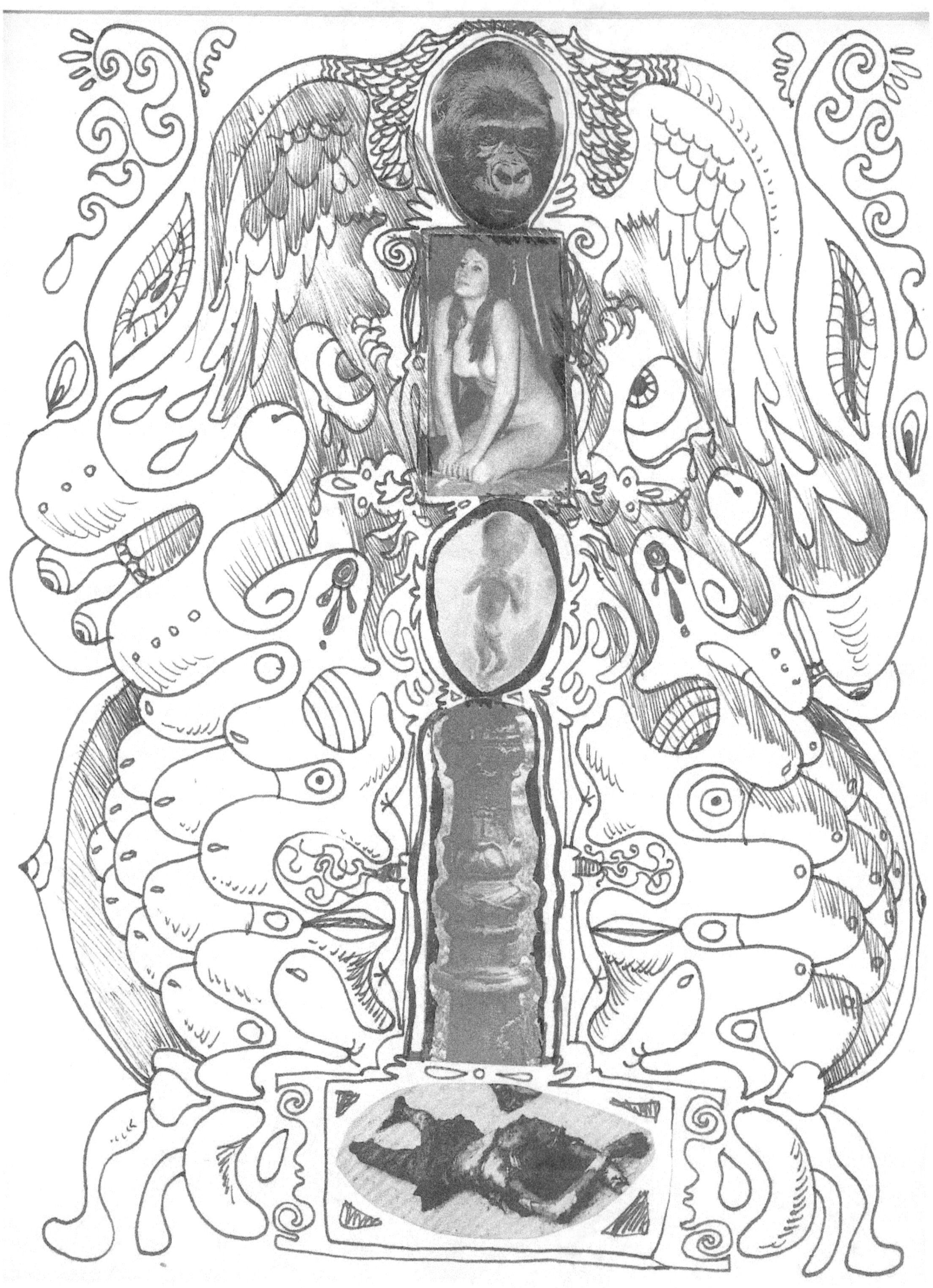

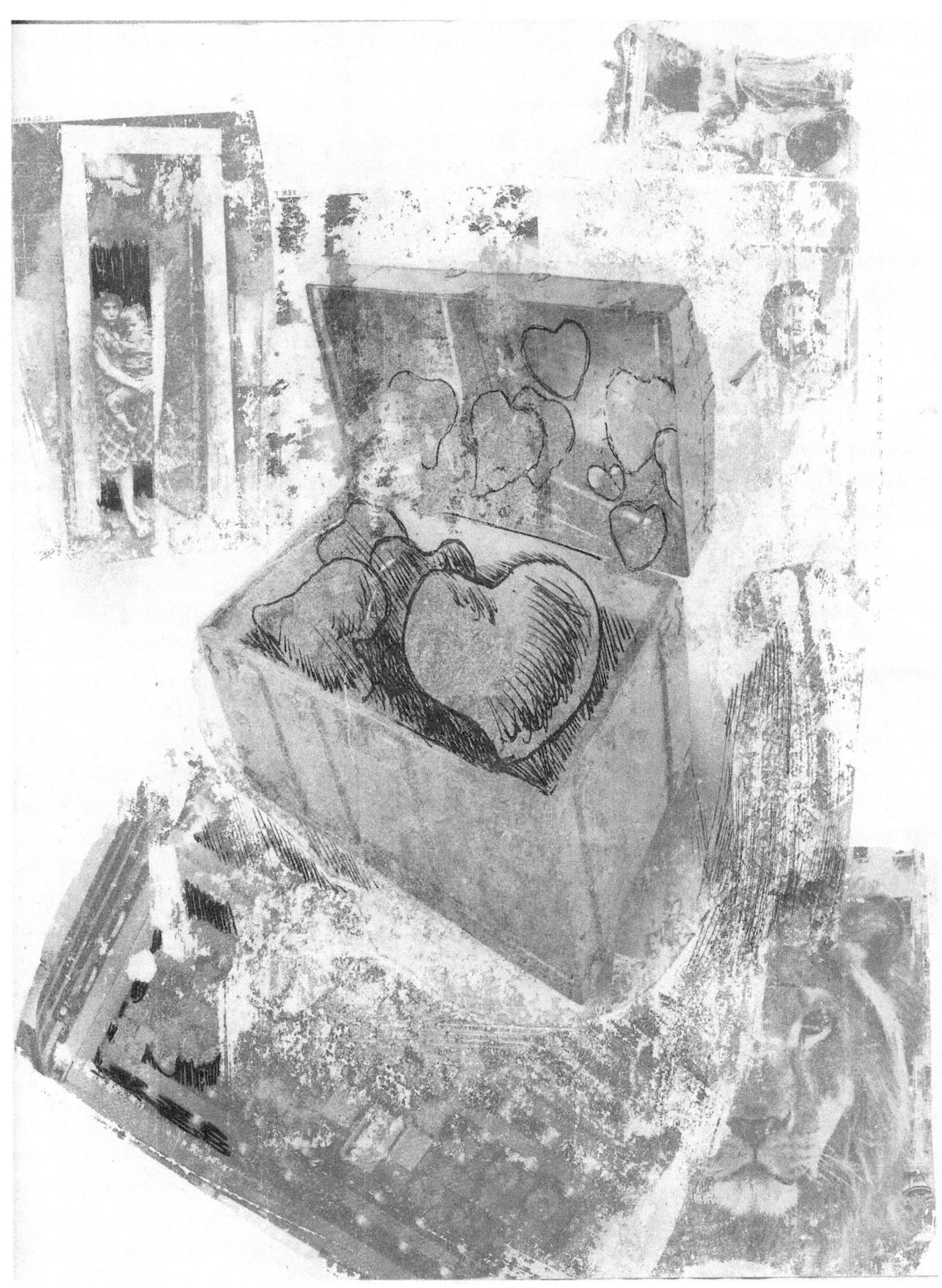

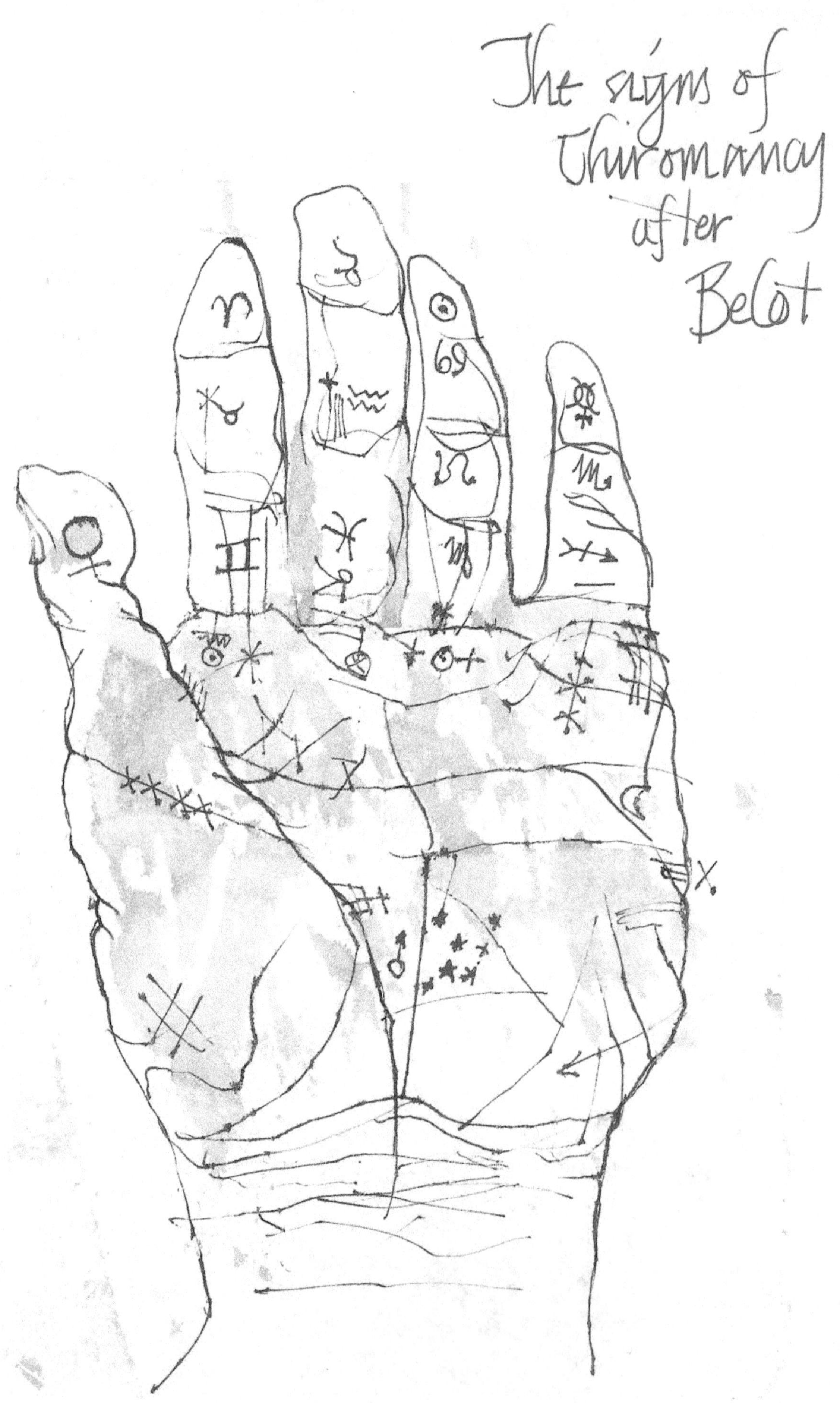
The signs of
Chiromancy
after
Belot

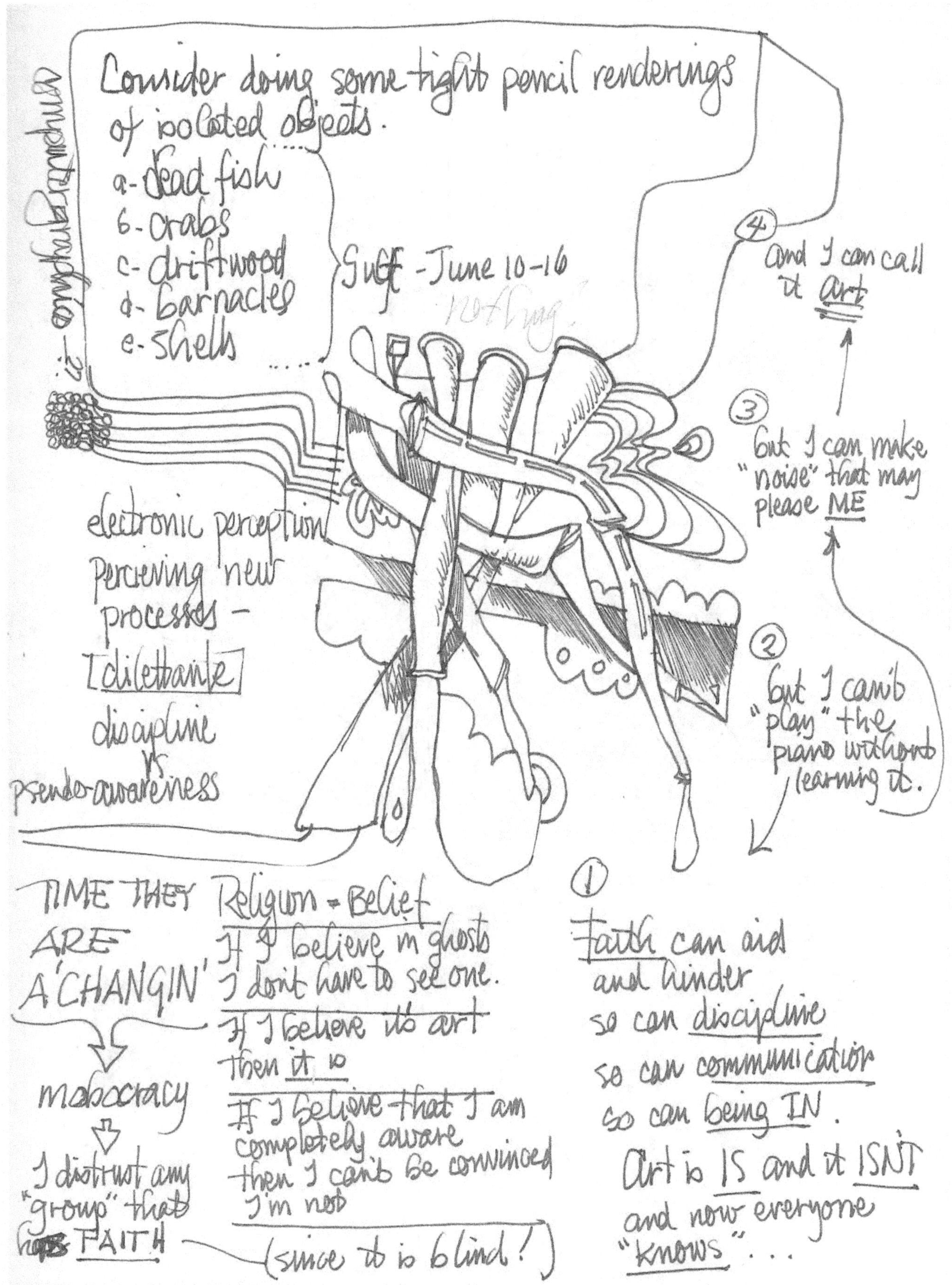
... omphalobranchia ...

Consider doing some tight pencil renderings
of isolated objects.
a- dead fish
b- crabs
c- driftwood
d- barnacles
e- shells

Gulf - June 10-16
nothing.

electronic perception
Percieving "new"
processes -
[dilettante]
discipline
vs
pseudo-awareness

④ and I can call
it art

③ but I can make
"noise" that may
please ME

② but I can't
"play" the
piano without
learning it.

TIME THEY
ARE
A 'CHANGIN'

mobocracy

I distrust any
"group" that
has FAITH

Religion = Belief
If I believe in ghosts
I don't have to see one.

If I believe its art
then it is

If I believe that I am
completely aware
then I can't be convinced
I'm not

(since it is blind!)

① Faith can aid
and hinder
so can discipline
so can communication
so can being IN.

Art is IS and it ISN'T
and now everyone
"knows"...

FUNK '68

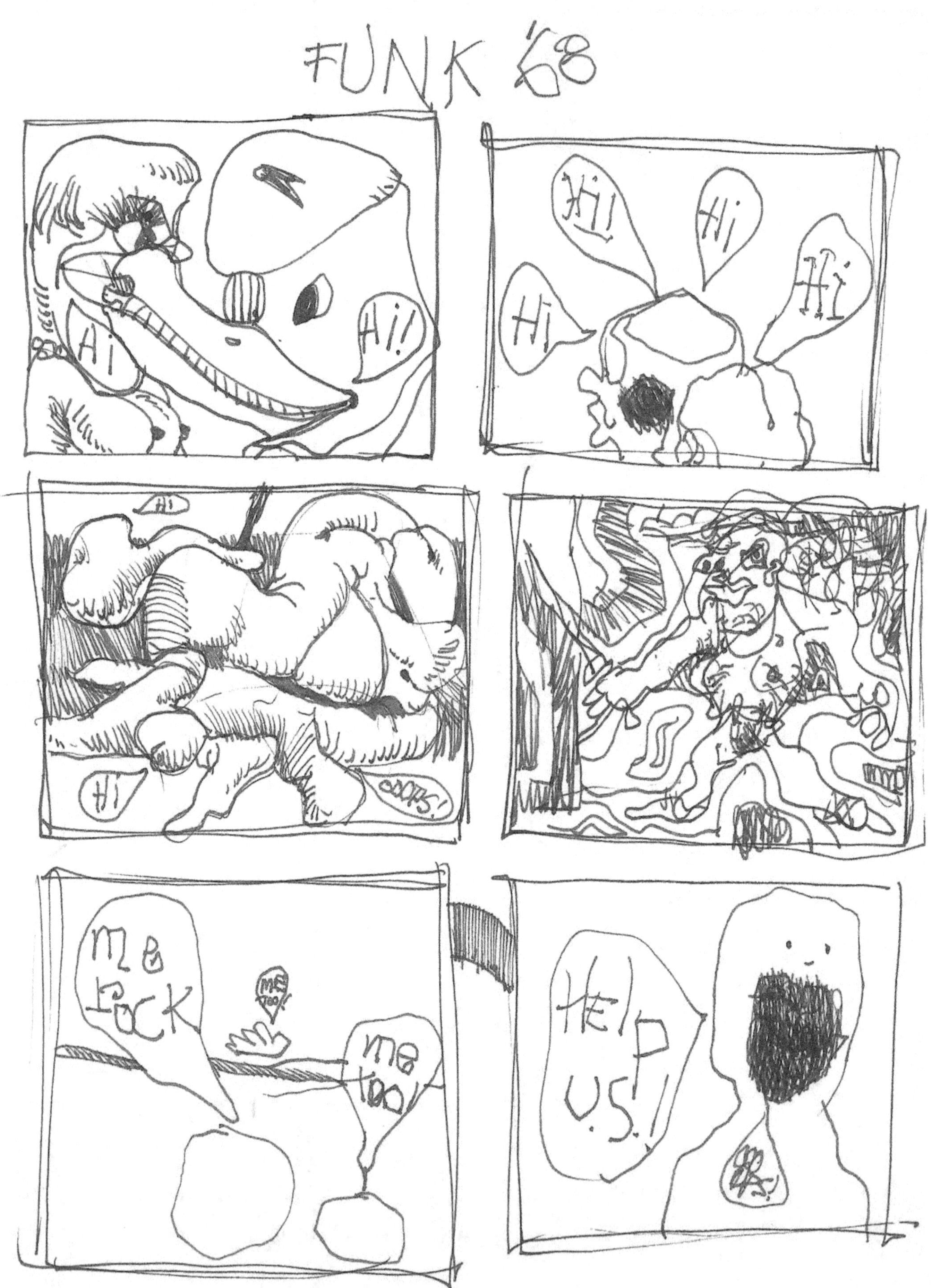

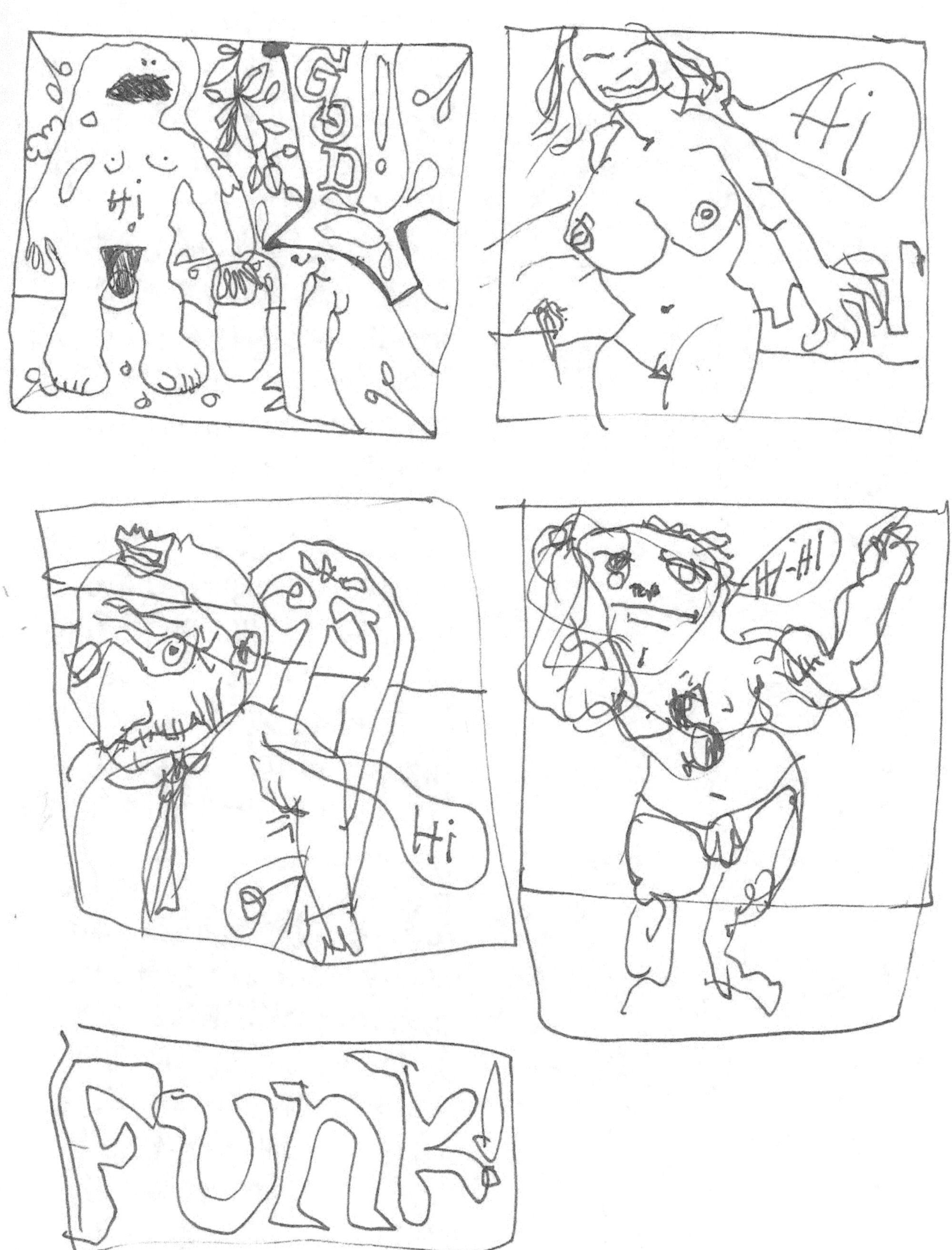

GOD!
PUNK
Hi
Hi
Hi
HI-HI
S

The images dissolve and shift. Content become a meaningless stream of Past and Future; The Wheel circles, the Locust sings for a short time.... The will to believe and hold the chaos in check begins to tickle and scratch. Juggling one, dropping another—holding 80 billion dust-motes and pouring them into a logic bottle is tiring work.—To follow a simpler, but harder, Way erases all the drawings that one feels that he must make—The goal is a mirage, but yet it captures pieces from time to time, of what it is really... Drawing on a frosted window, the water-finger eyes in a balloon-face allow a hazy look out into space—then it fogs over and another pattern takes its place— I can see that captured truth in other work of other people, but mine seems always to be close, but never yet stands completely free of me except so very-few pieces—And their freedom frightens me....

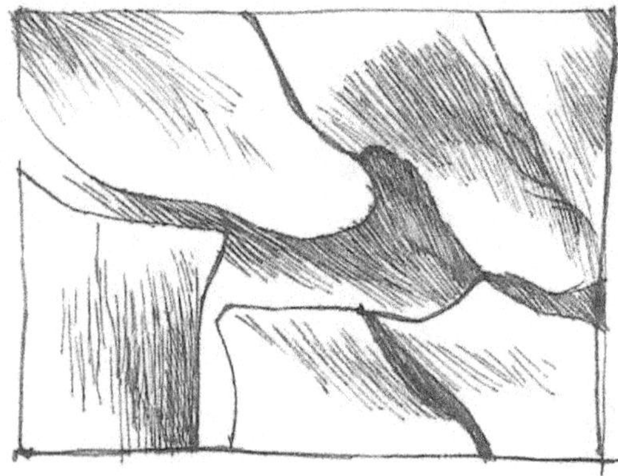

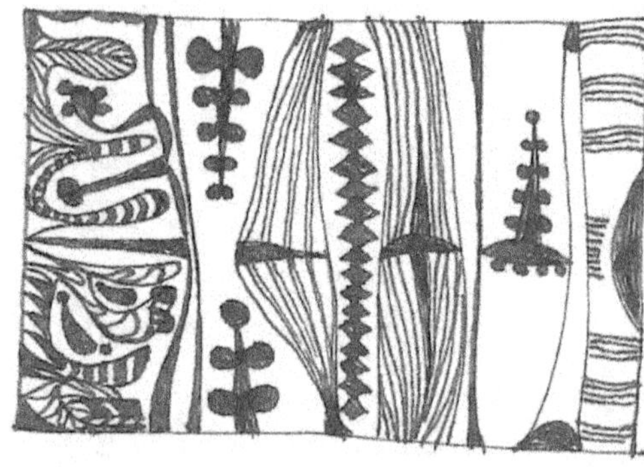

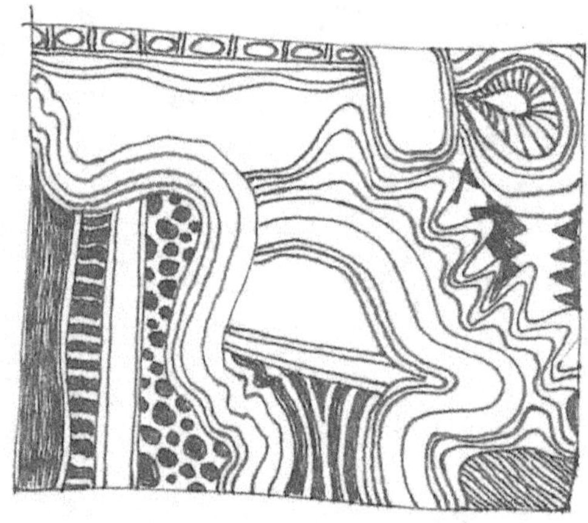

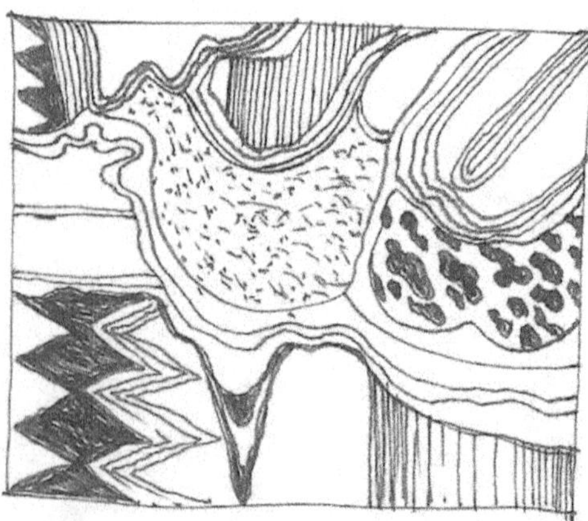

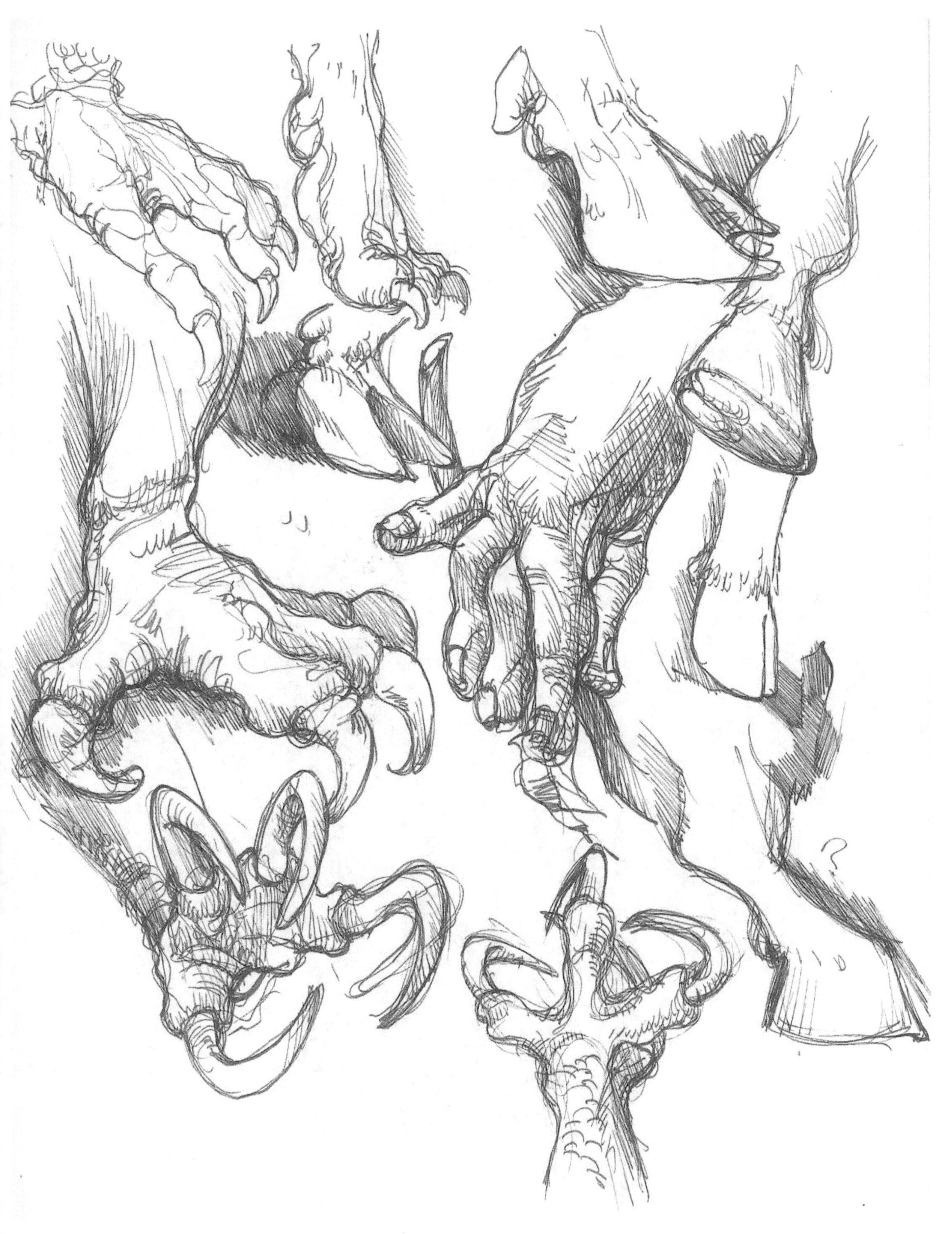

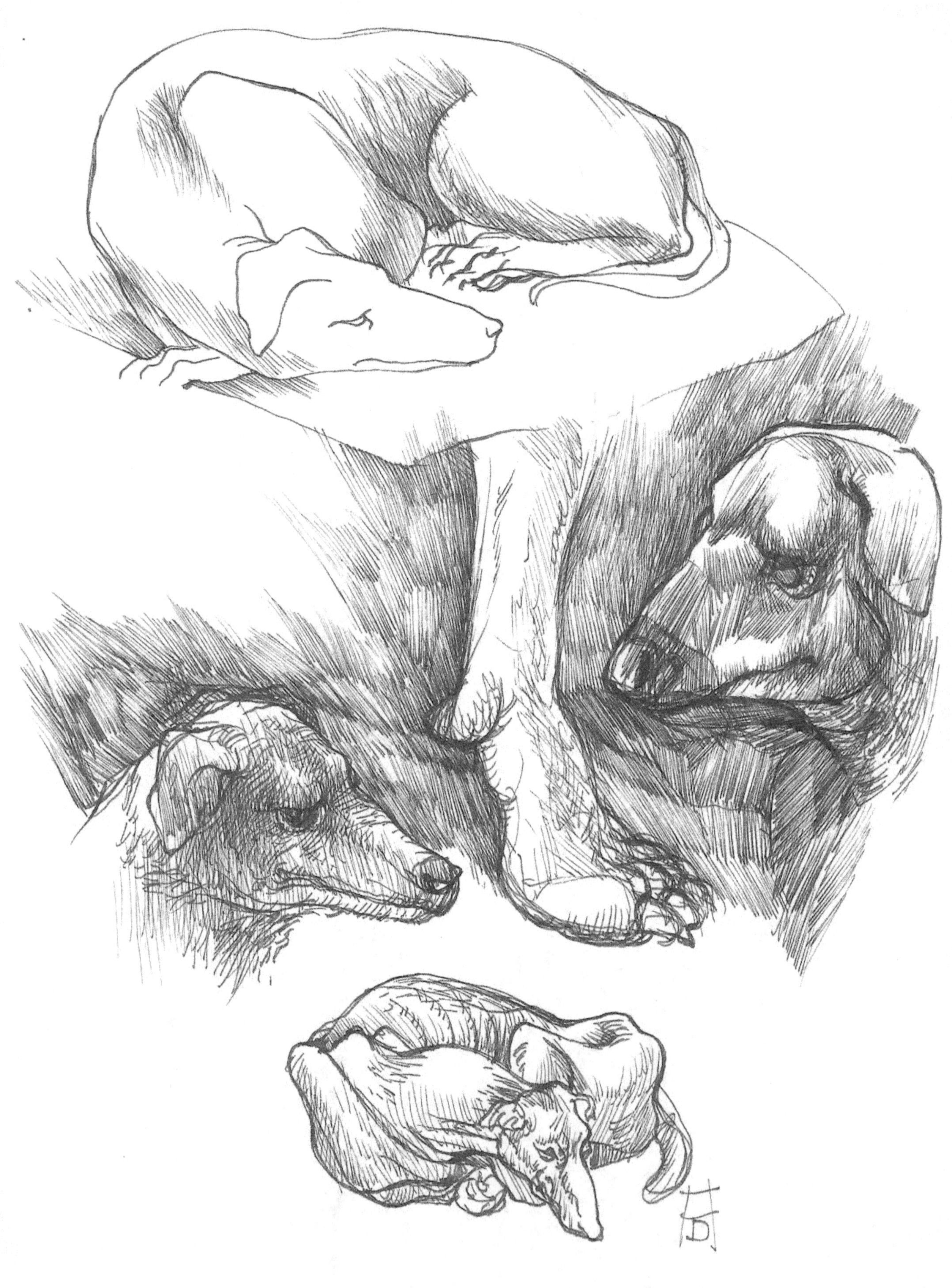

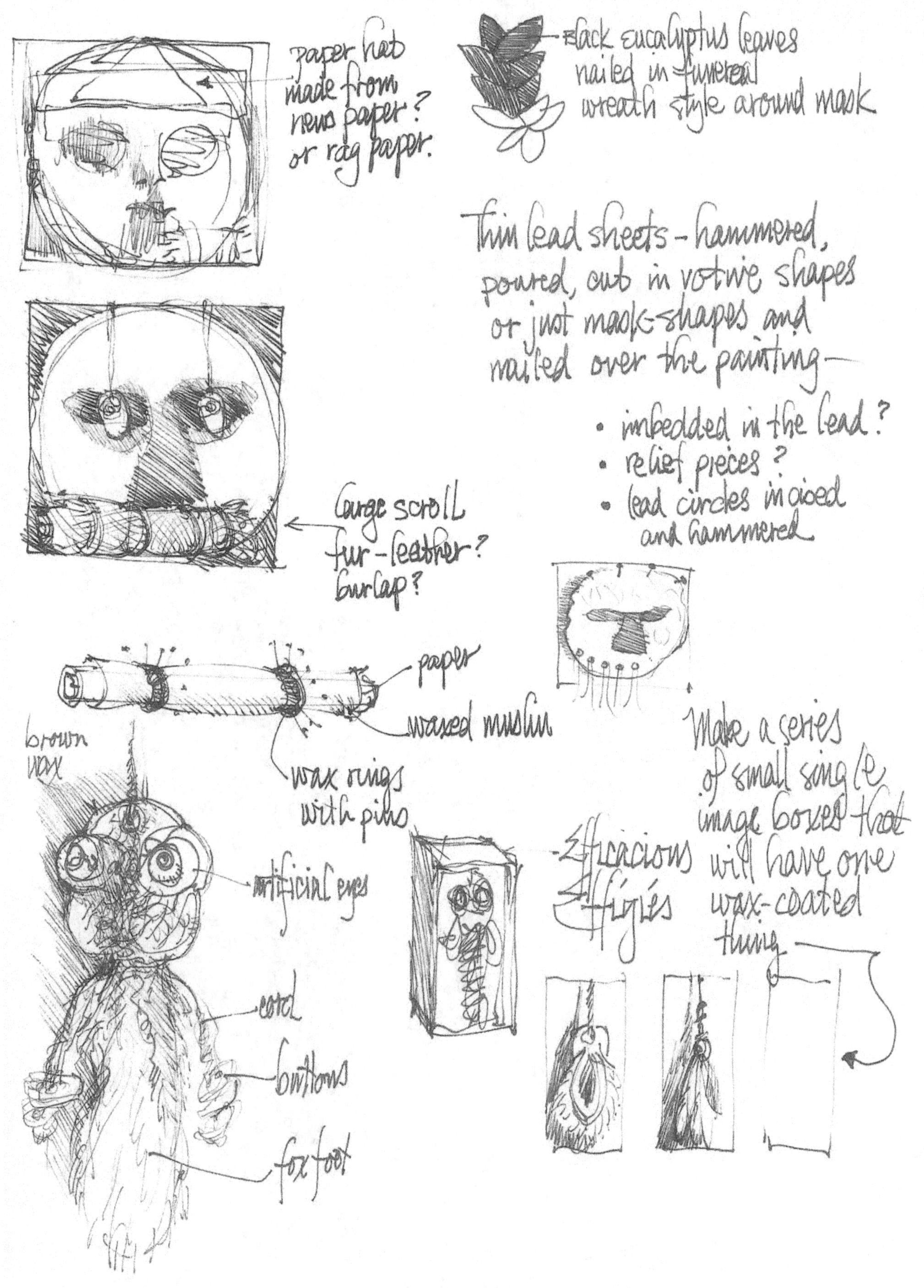

paper hat made from news paper? or rag paper.

Black eucalyptus leaves nailed in funereal wreath style around mask

Thin lead sheets - hammered, poured, cut in votive shapes or just mask-shapes and nailed over the painting —

• imbedded in the lead ?
• relief pieces ?
• lead circles incised and hammered.

Large scroll fur - feather? burlap?

paper

waxed muslin

wax rings with pins

brown wax

artificial eyes

cord

buttons

fox foot

Make a series of small single image boxes that will have one wax-coated thing

Efficacious Effigies

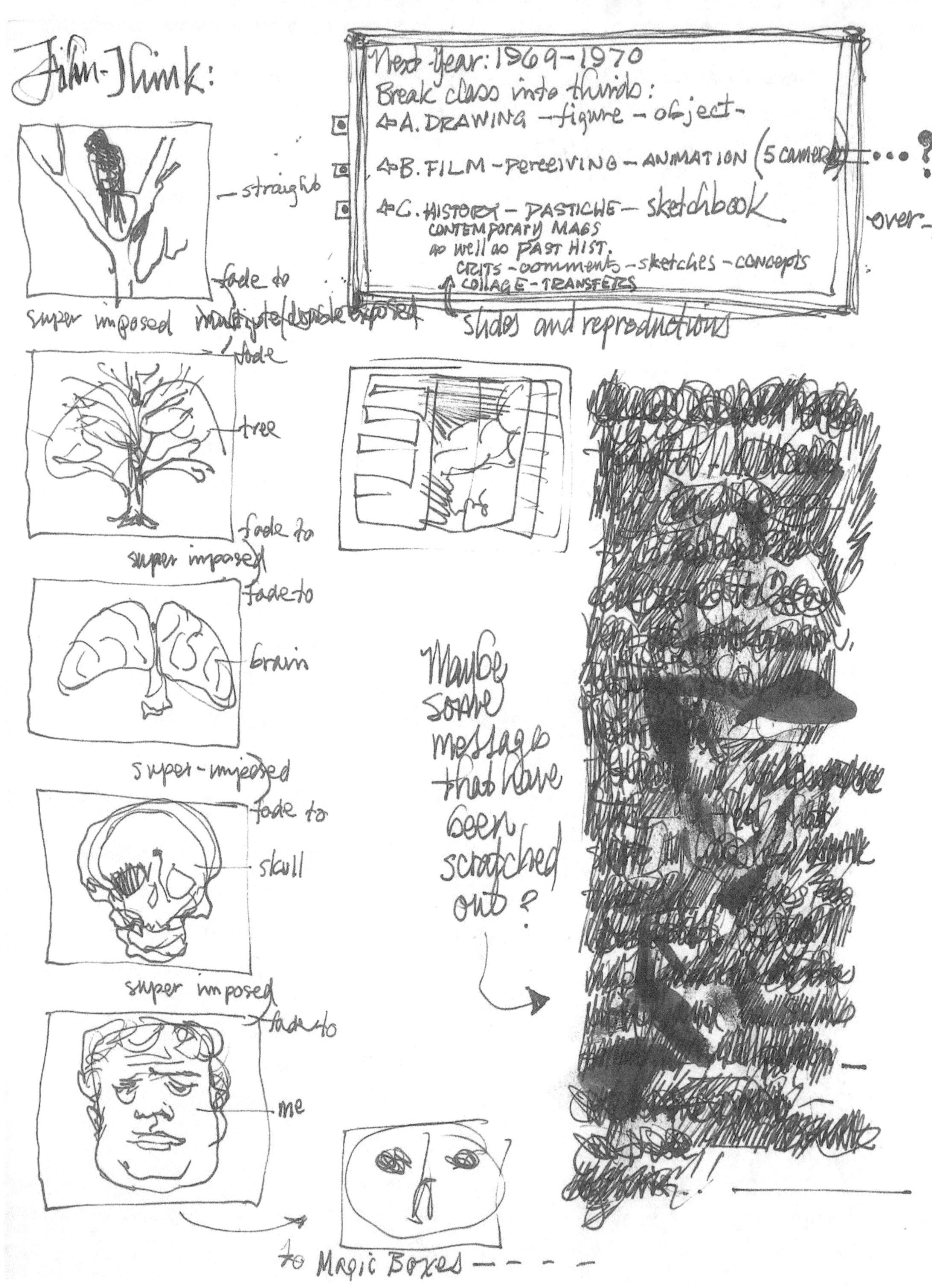
John - Think:

— straight

fade to
super imposed multiple/double exposed
fade

tree

fade to
super imposed
fade to

brain

super-imposed
fade to
skull

super imposed
fade to

me

to MAGIC BOXES — — — —

Next Year: 1969-1970
Break class into thirds:
A. DRAWING — figure — object —
B. FILM — perceiving — ANIMATION (5 CAMERA) — ... ?
C. HISTORY — PASTICHE — sketchbook
   CONTEMPORARY MAGS
   as well as PAST HIST.
   CRITS — comments — sketches — concepts
   COLLAGE — TRANSFERS
over →
Slides and reproductions

Maybe
some
message
that have
been
scratched
out ?

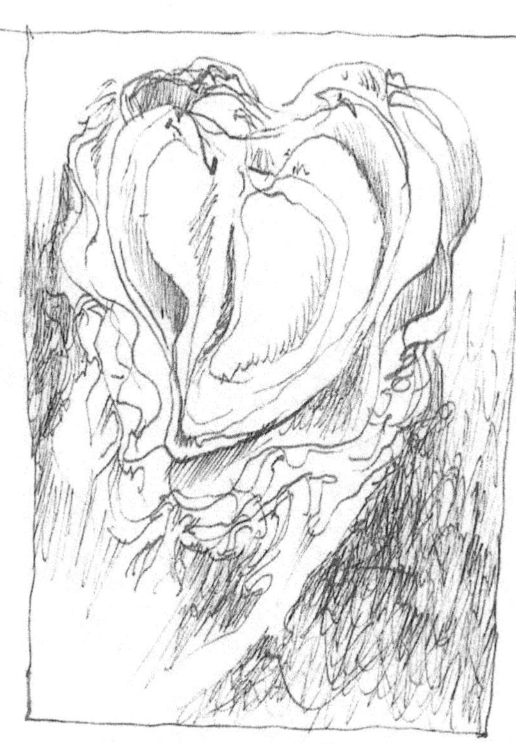

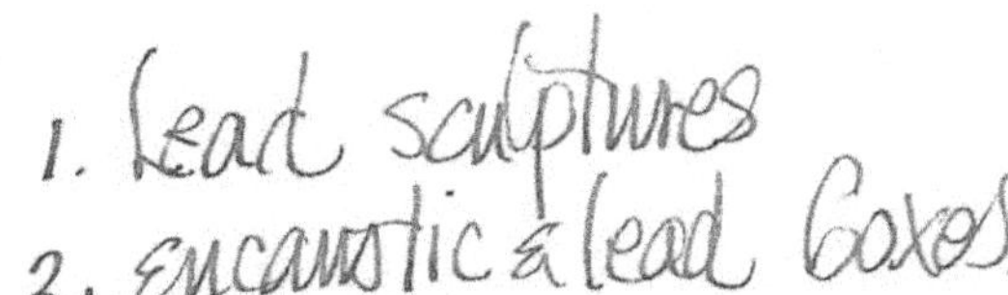

1. Lead sculptures
2. Encaustic & lead Boxes

3. Drawings after lead pieces

4. New series of drawings
   that are object oriented
   Get an object from
   different people
   and "groove" on it.

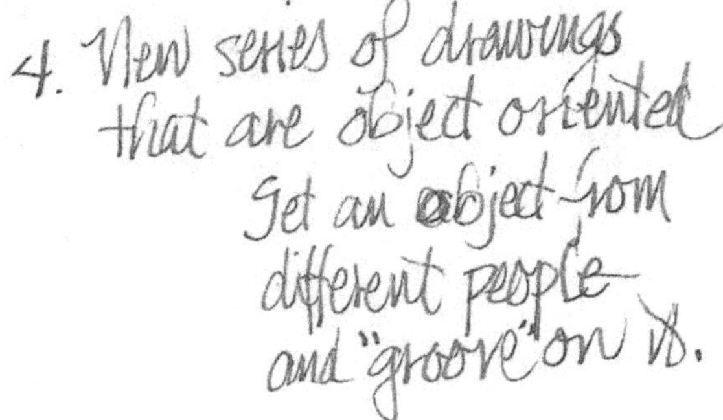

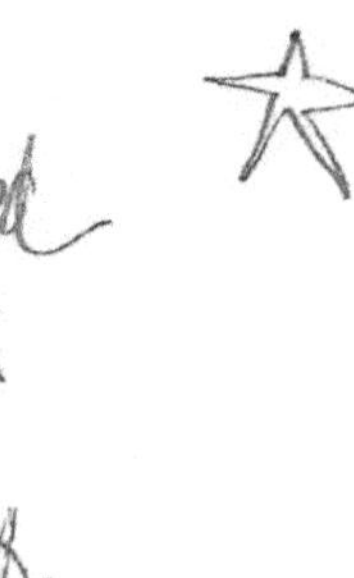

5 Start some more writing
  for new "mythology" drawings —

  Maybe a book?
           Many drawings - few words

6. Try some landscape and
   "organic" drawings

7. I need to do some completely
   "unaware" drawings - where I
   can make just marks.
   This is most likely an outgrowth
   of the class projects...

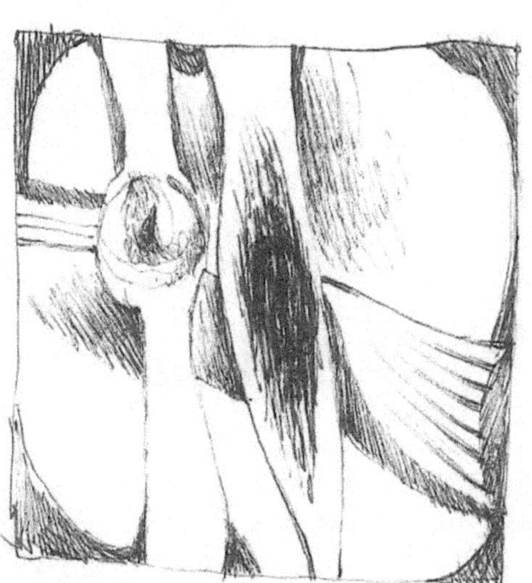

The need for content — how
to turn myself on and not
be concerned with NOW — I
have to get my WU-SHIH
back ...

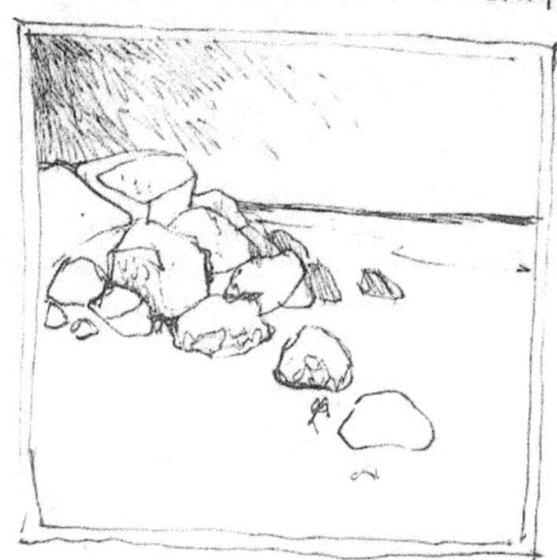

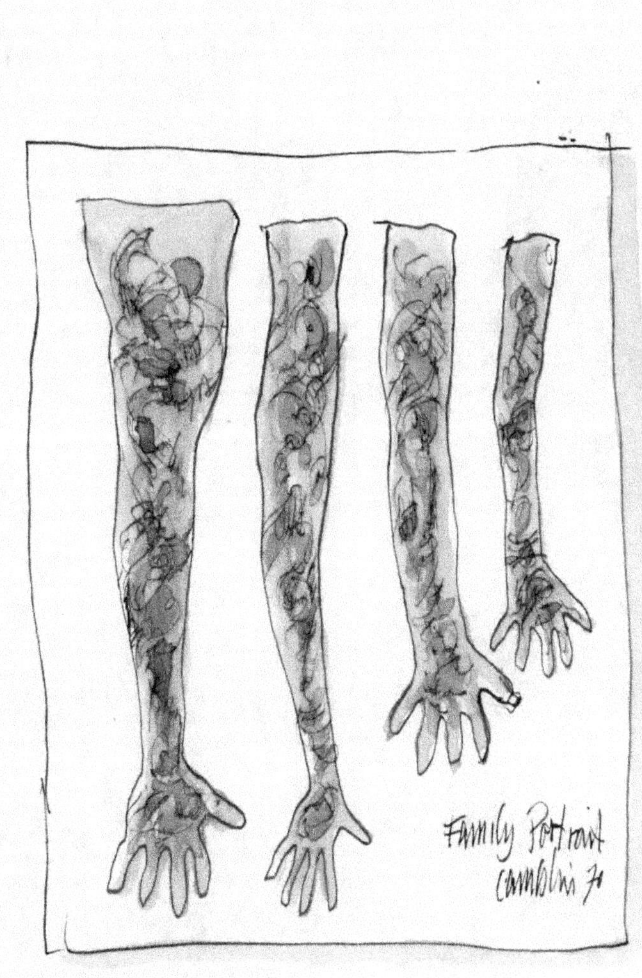

Family Portrait can take each member
of their family and do a montage of
events depicted by symbolic tattooes.

The traditional tattooes seem to be,
hearts, arrows, ribbons, roses, birds
(predatory and song) knives and
panthers — plno skulls and flags...

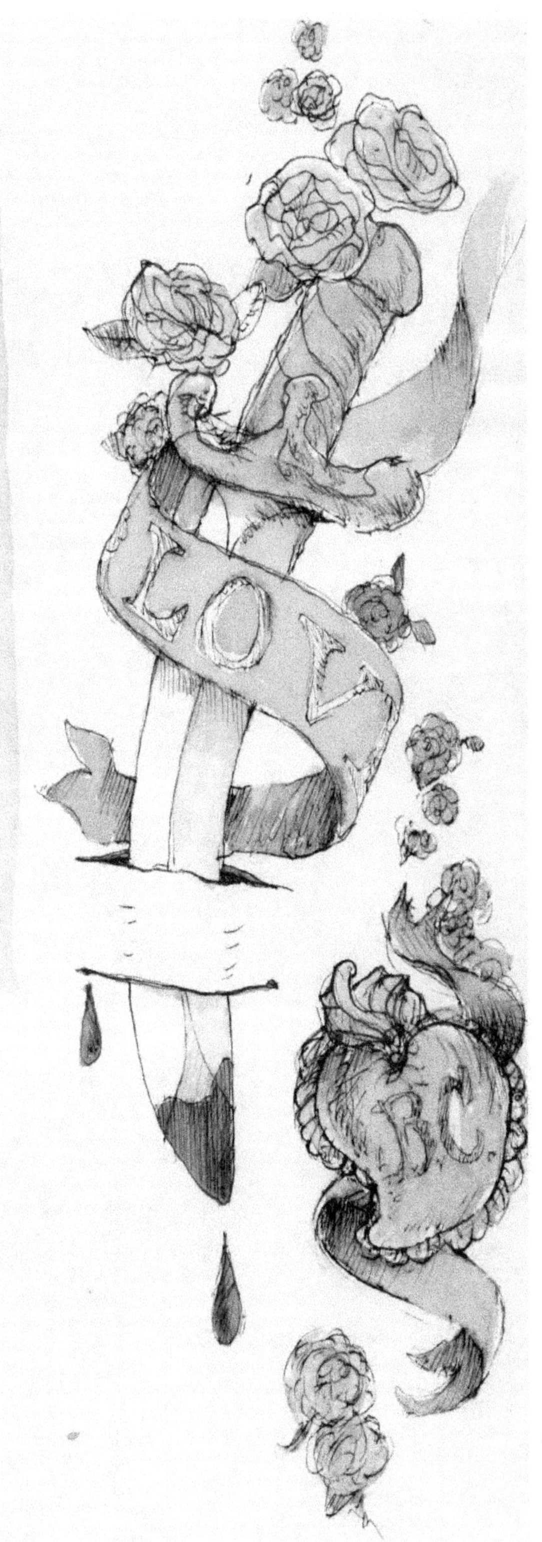

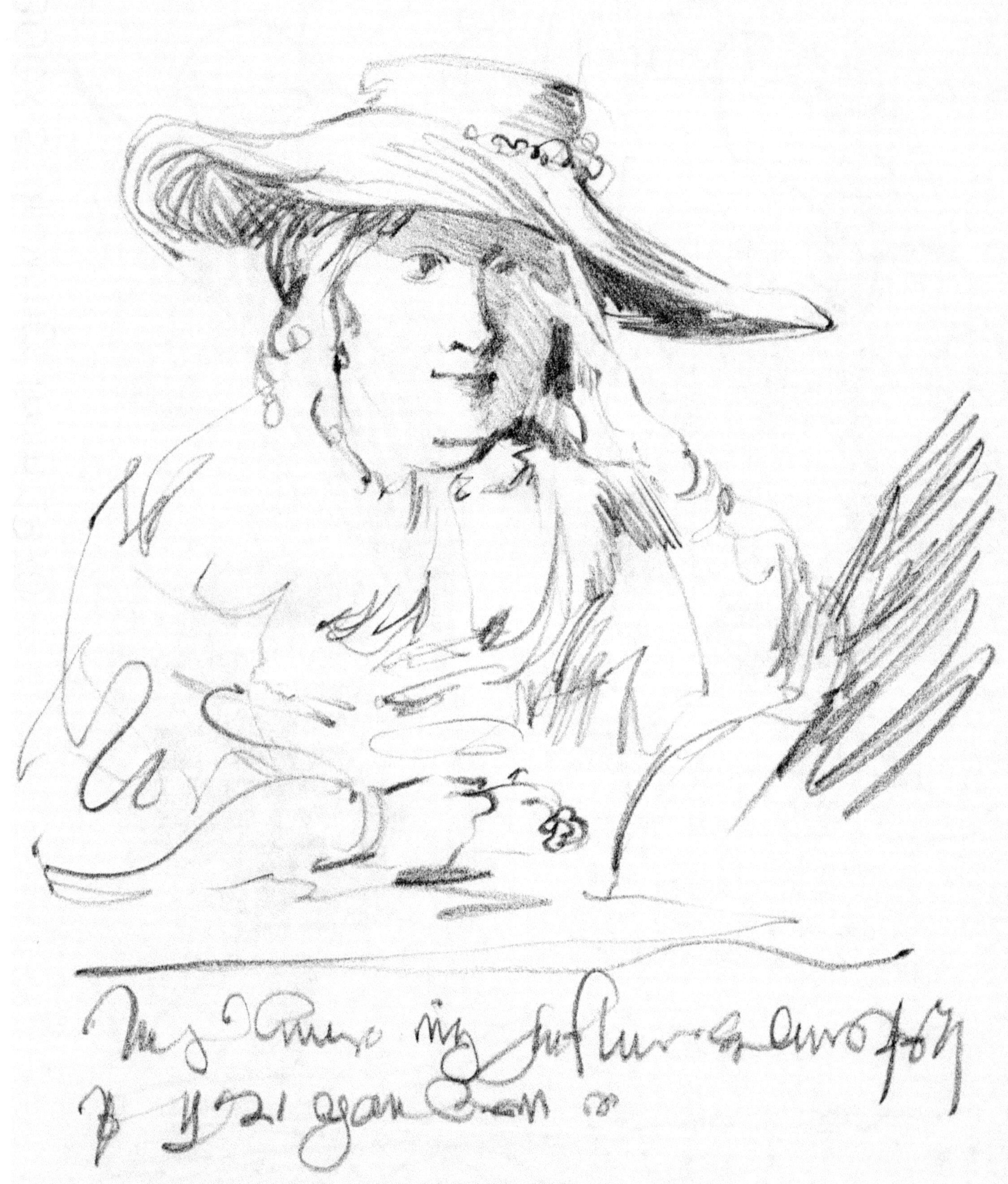

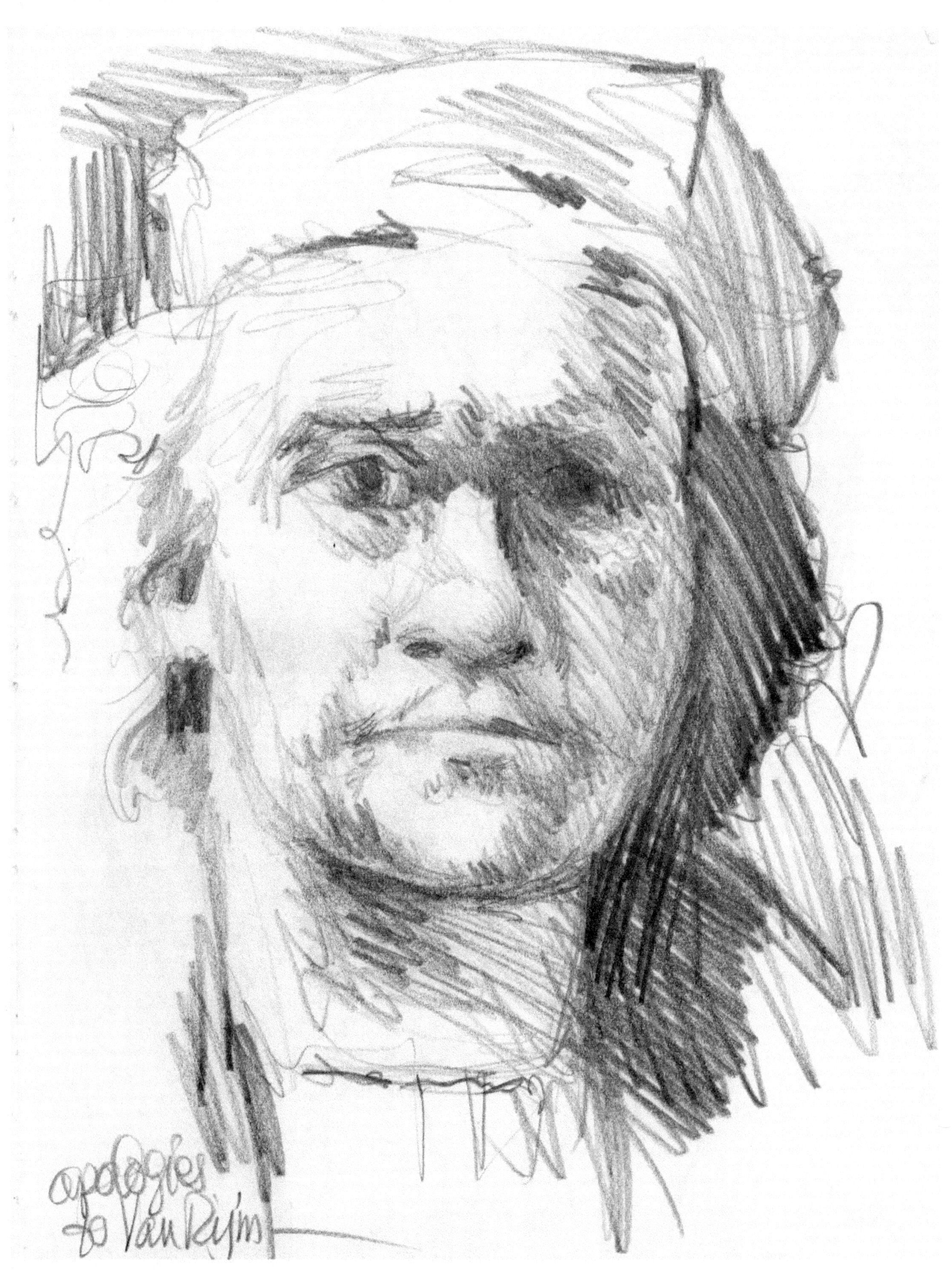
apologies
to Van Rijn

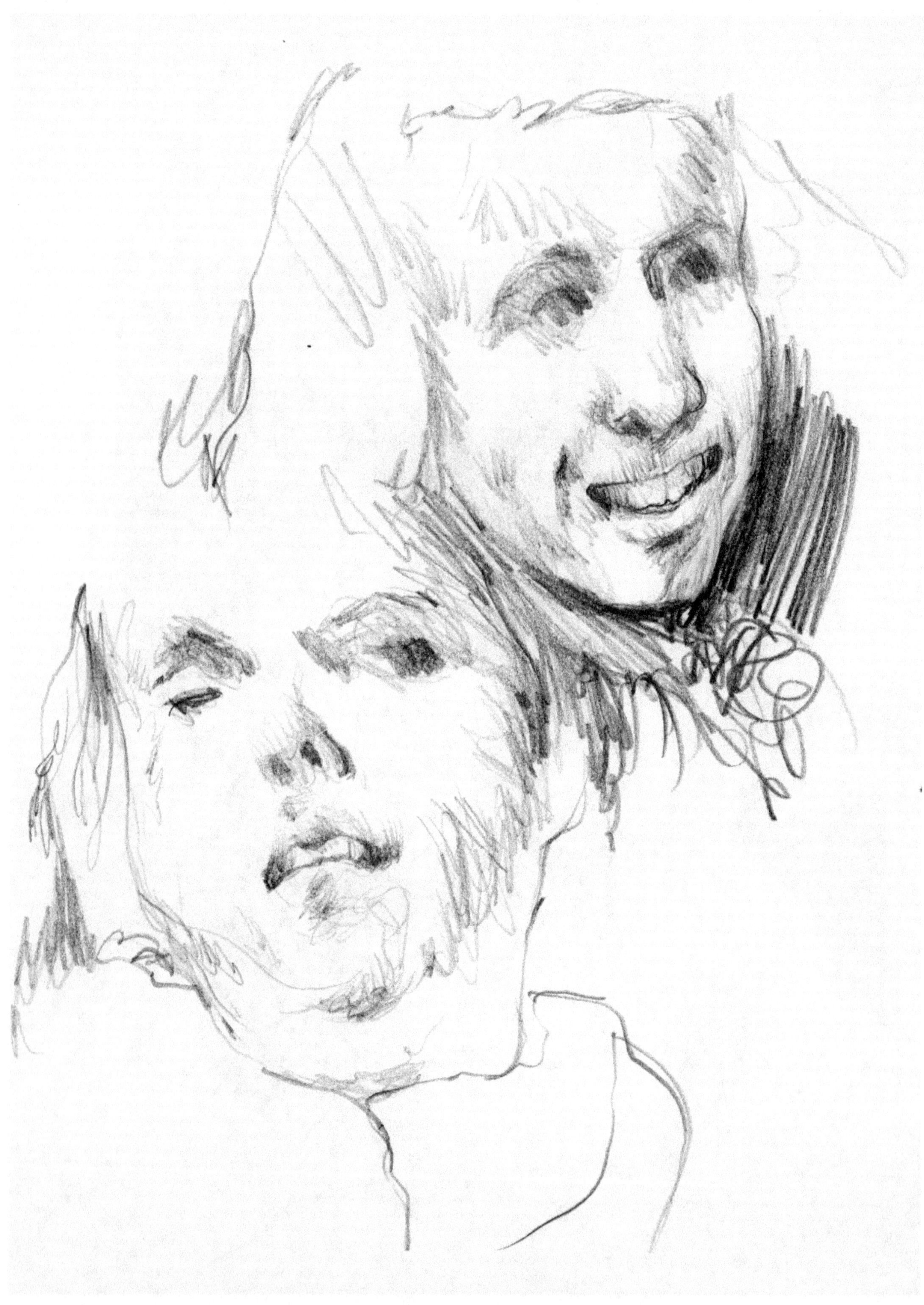

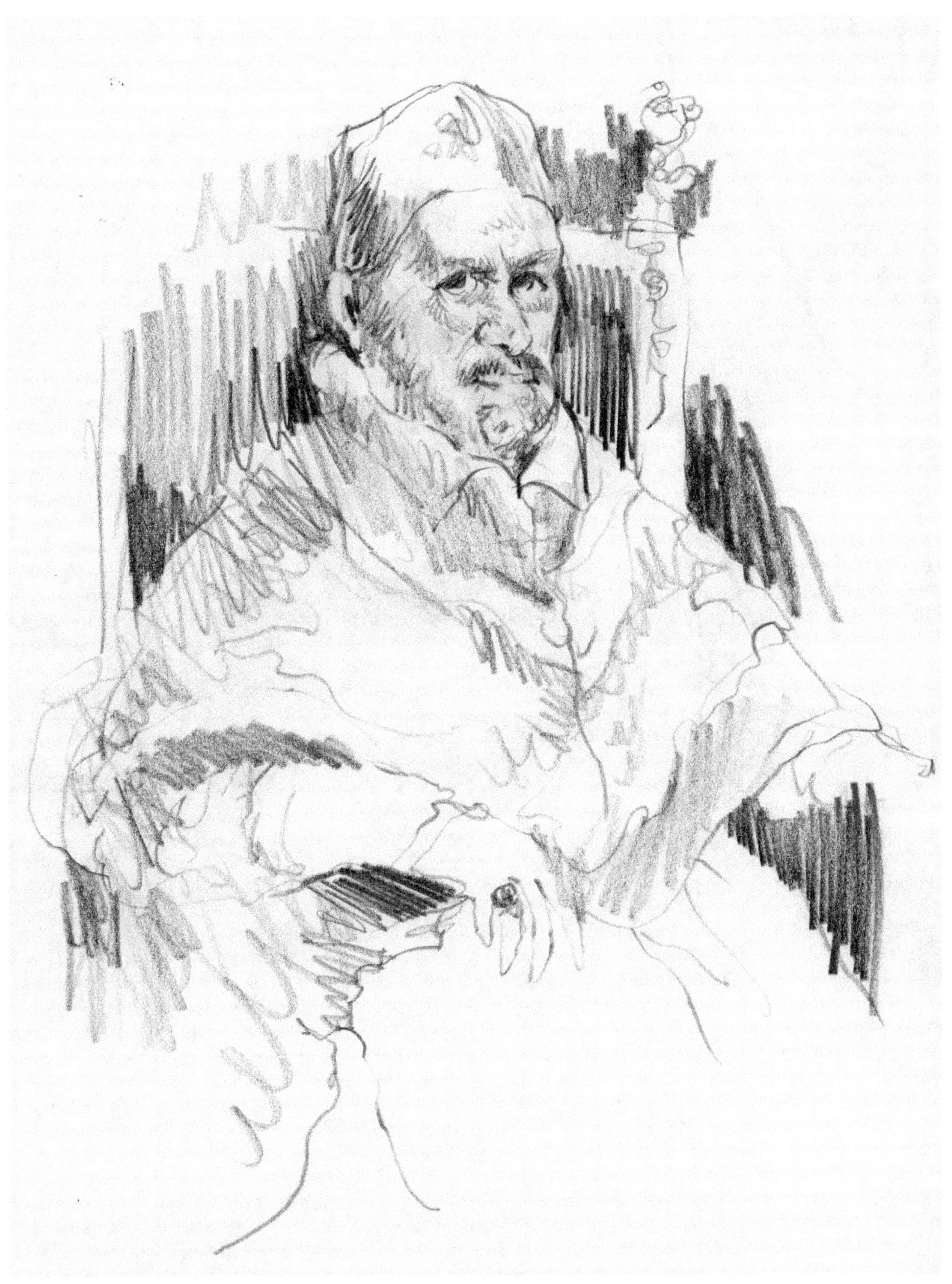

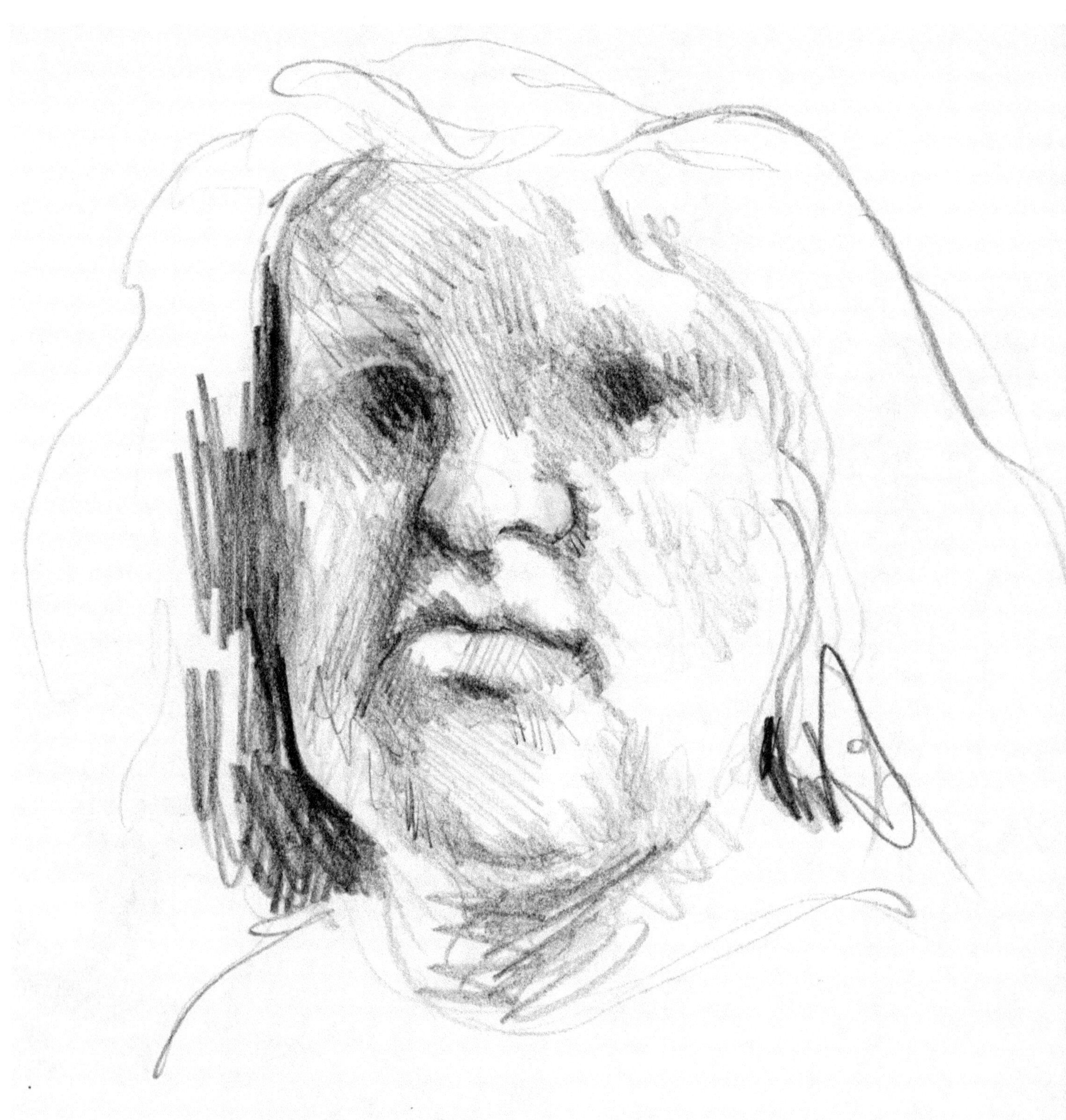

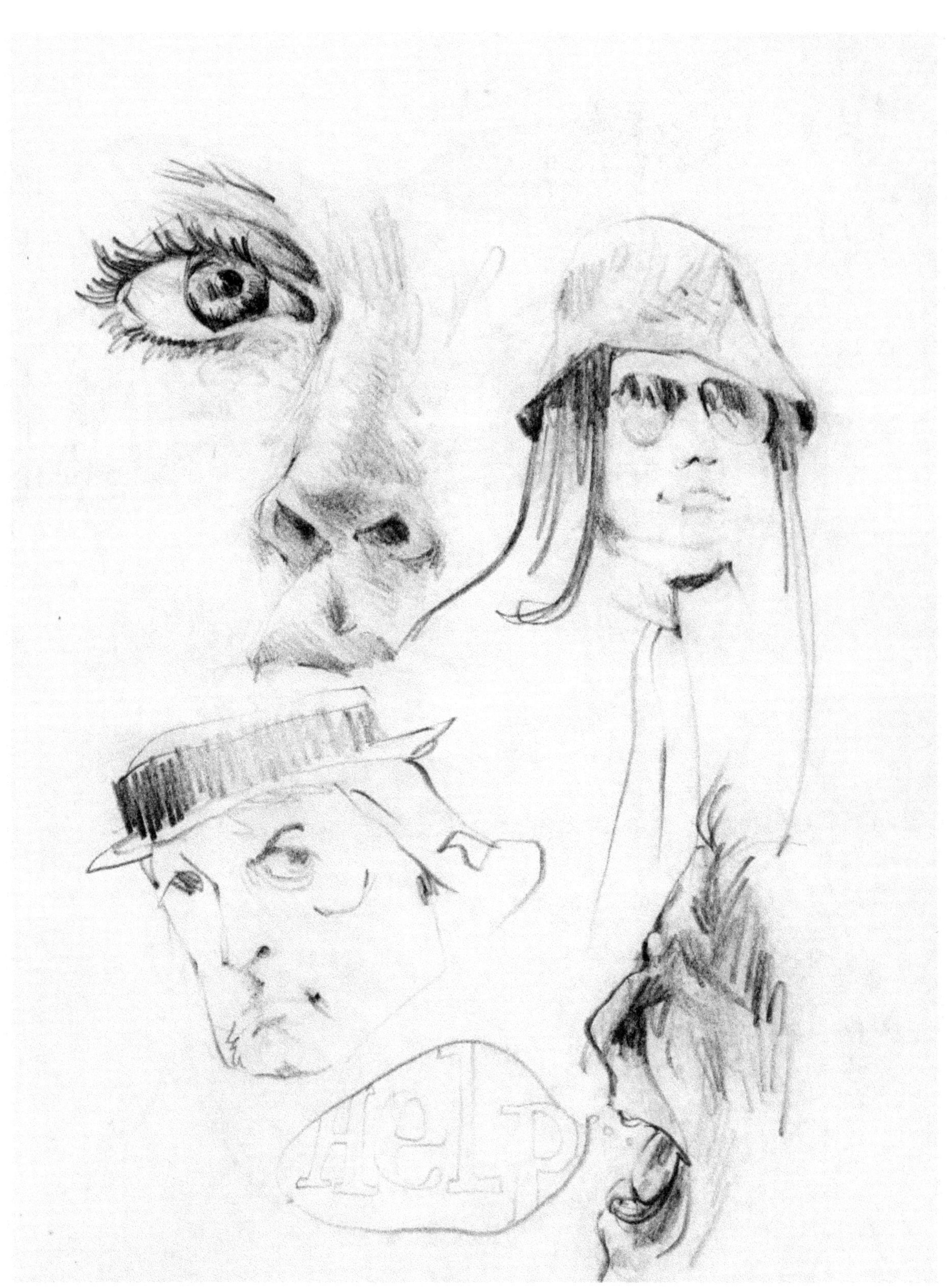
HELP

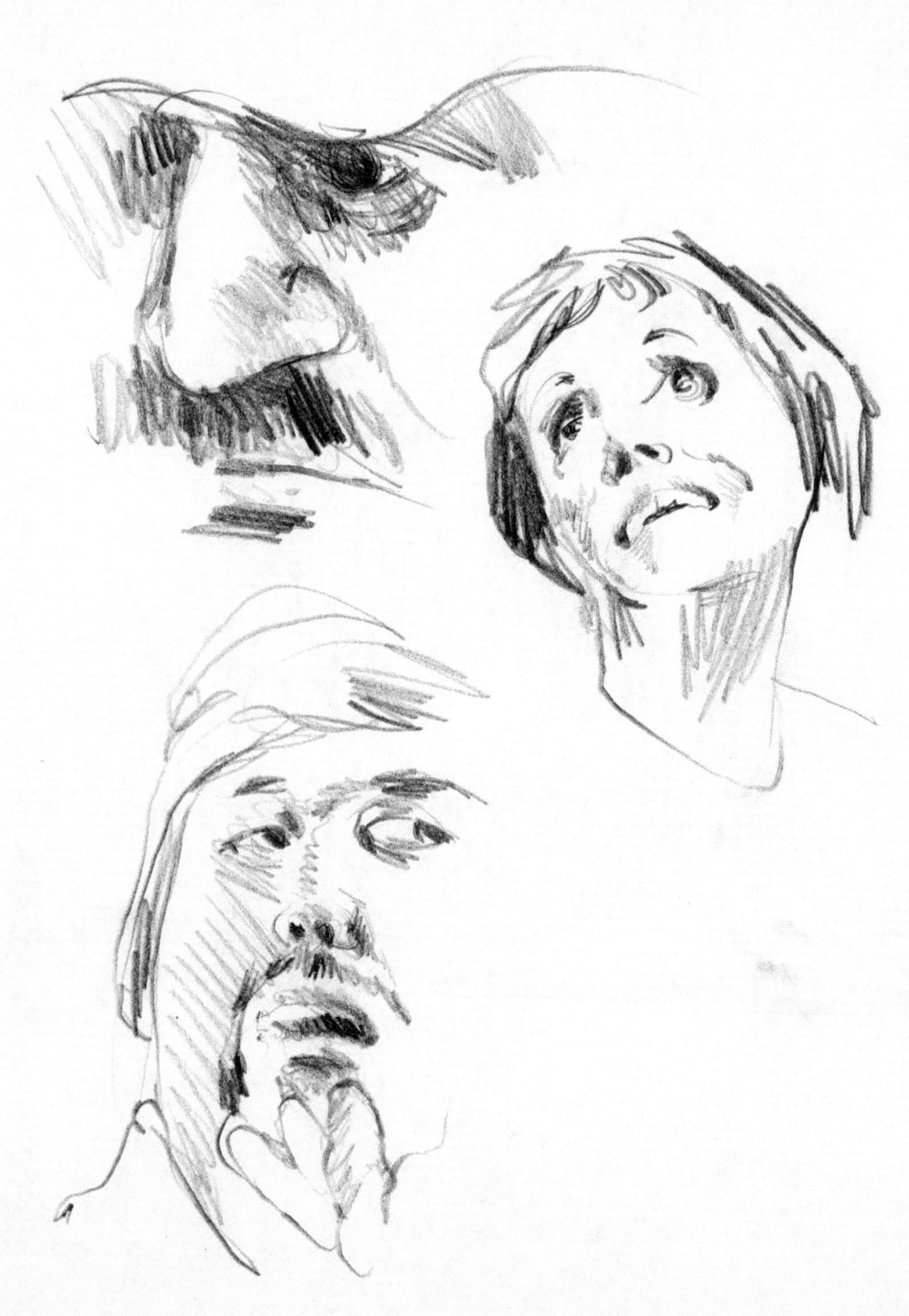

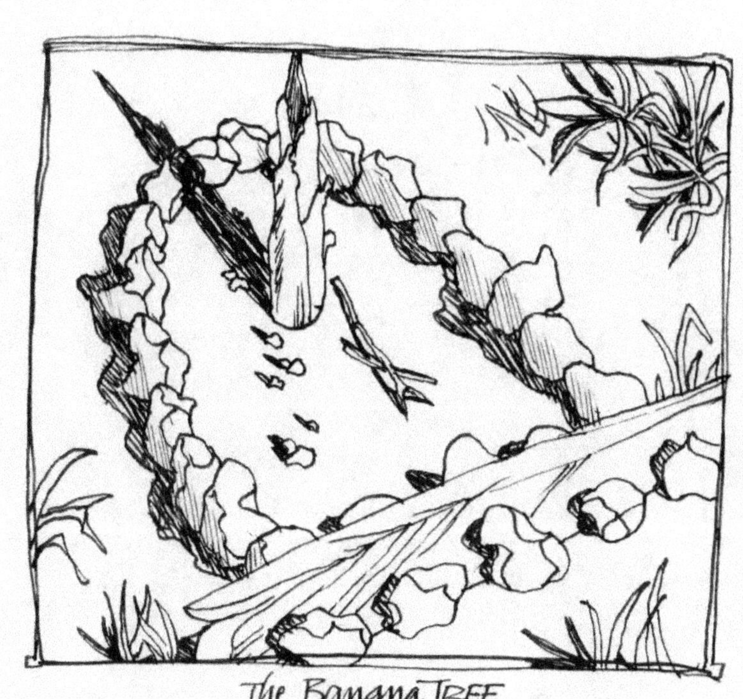

The Banana TREE

Childrens Tree
The Banana Shrine

The funk composition is
intriguing after my
"classical" period —
drawing on the site
has never appealed to
me — so maybe the
photographs will help —

Working directly from photographs
try and develop that line from
years ago avoiding the Vespignani
touch — perhaps wax resist in
some areas.
Watercolor washes and try to
not get into Wiley's bag —
You cannot be unaware of
other artists — people are always
showing you things — and
damn often they _are_
where you _were_ going —

I need to find another mythology to invent — I find it harder
all the time to sit down and turn out some drawings that
will be part of the production — St. Bumbola — scarecrows — etc.

Keep Looking and drawing —

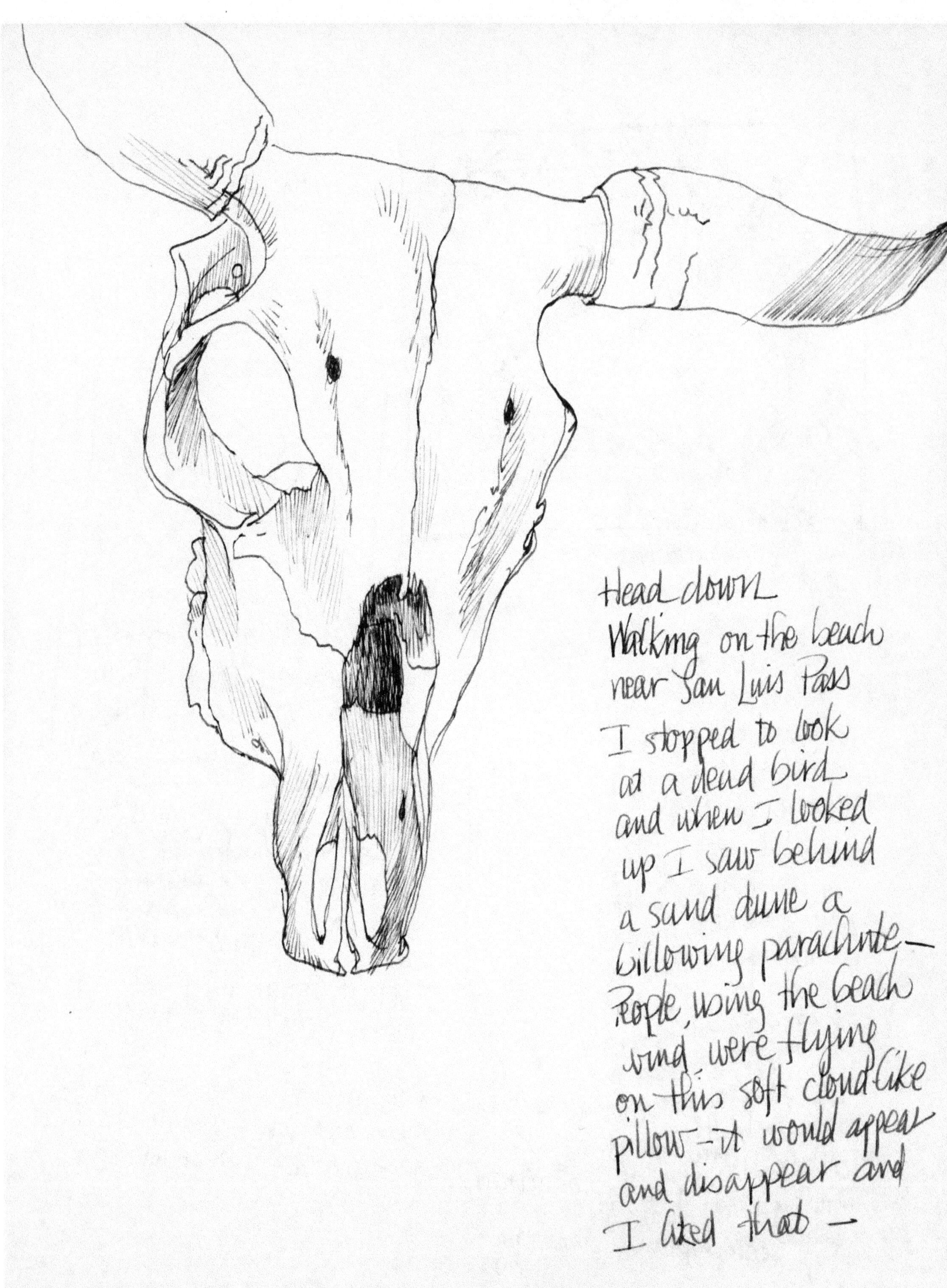

Head down
Walking on the beach
near San Luis Pass
I stopped to look
at a dead bird
and when I looked
up I saw behind
a sand dune a
billowing parachute—
People, using the beach
wind, were flying
on this soft cloud-like
pillow—it would appear
and disappear and
I liked that —

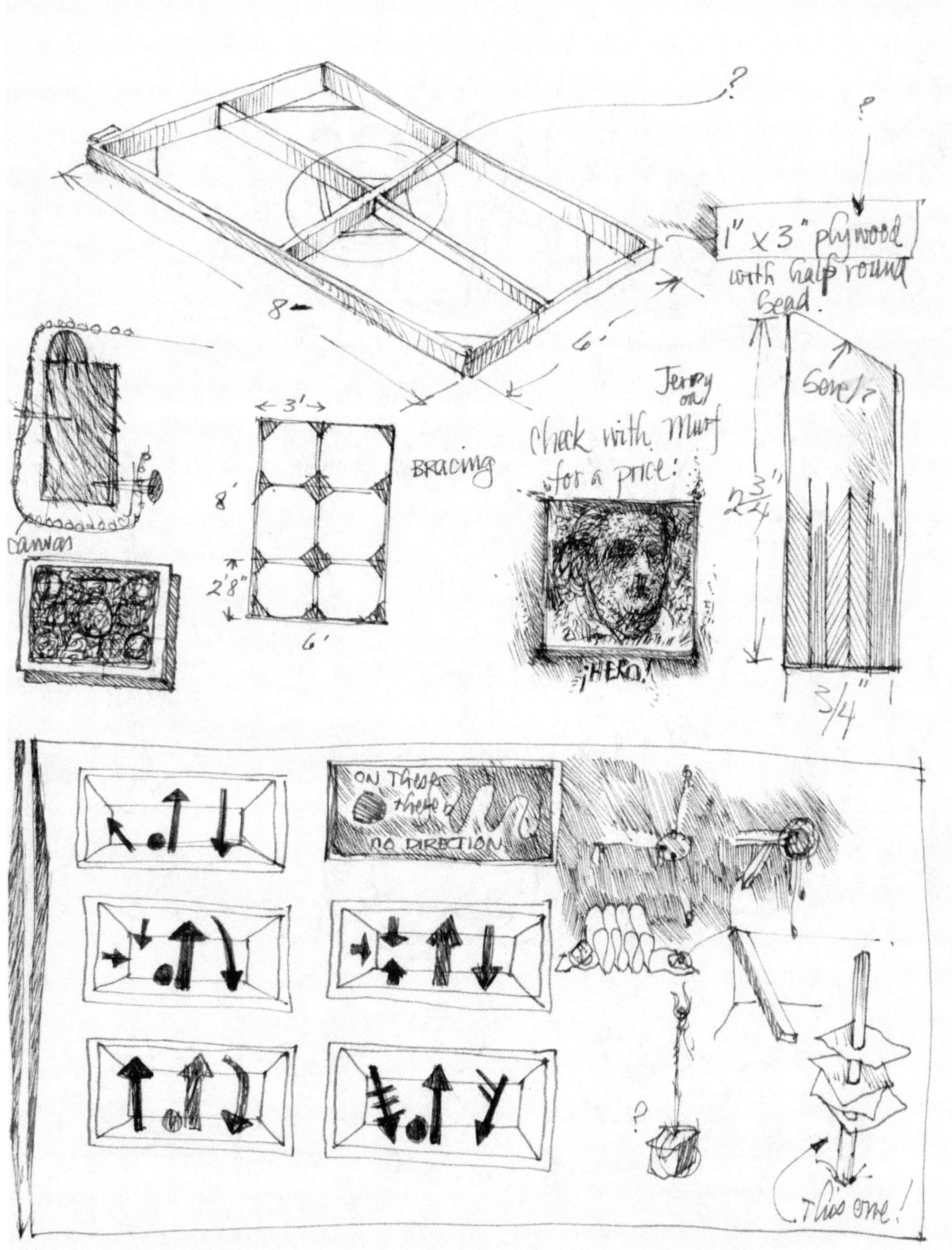

1" x 3" plywood with half round bead.
8'
6'
canvas
3'
8'
2'8"
6'
bracing
Jerry on
Check with Murf for a price.
¡HERO!
Sore/?
2 3/4"
3/4"
ON THERE there is NO DIRECTION
?
This one!

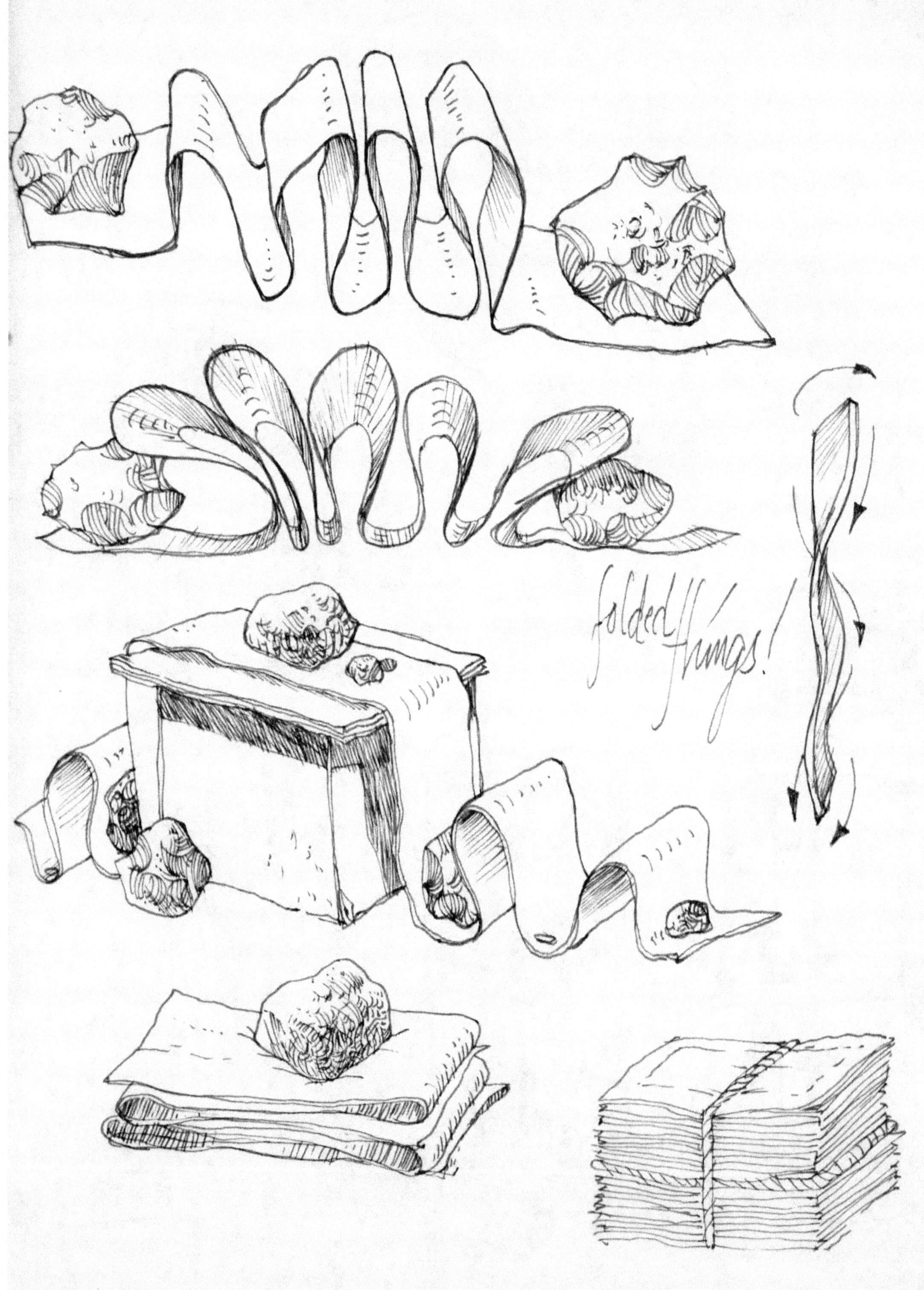

folded things!

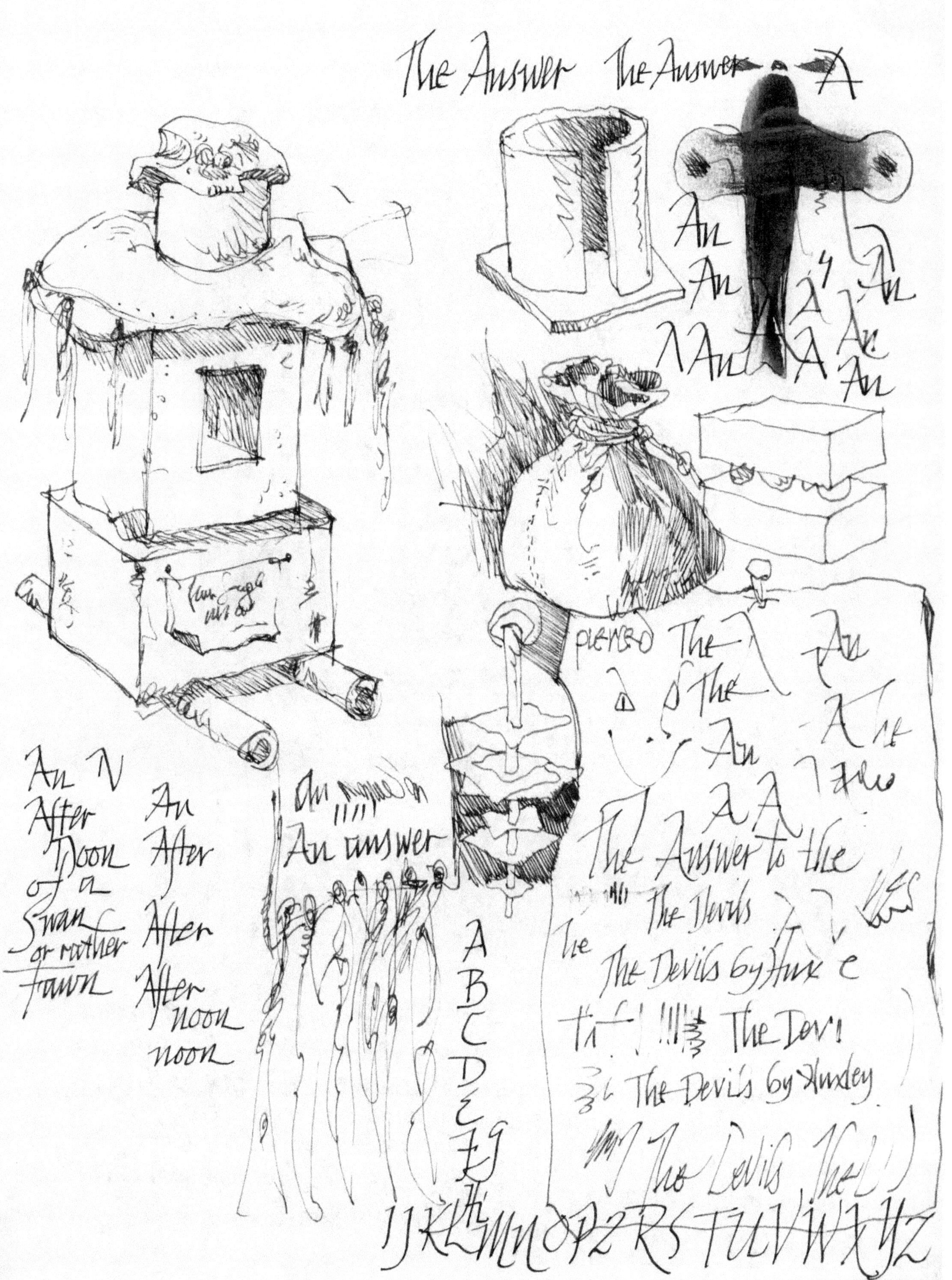

The Answer   The Answer   A
An
An
An answer
An answer
An
After
noon
of a
Swan
or rather
Fawn
An
After
After
After
noon
noon
A B C D E F G H I J K L M N O P Q R S T U V W X Y Z
The Answer to the
The Devils
The Devils by Huxle e
The Dev'l
The Devils by Huxley
The Devils The

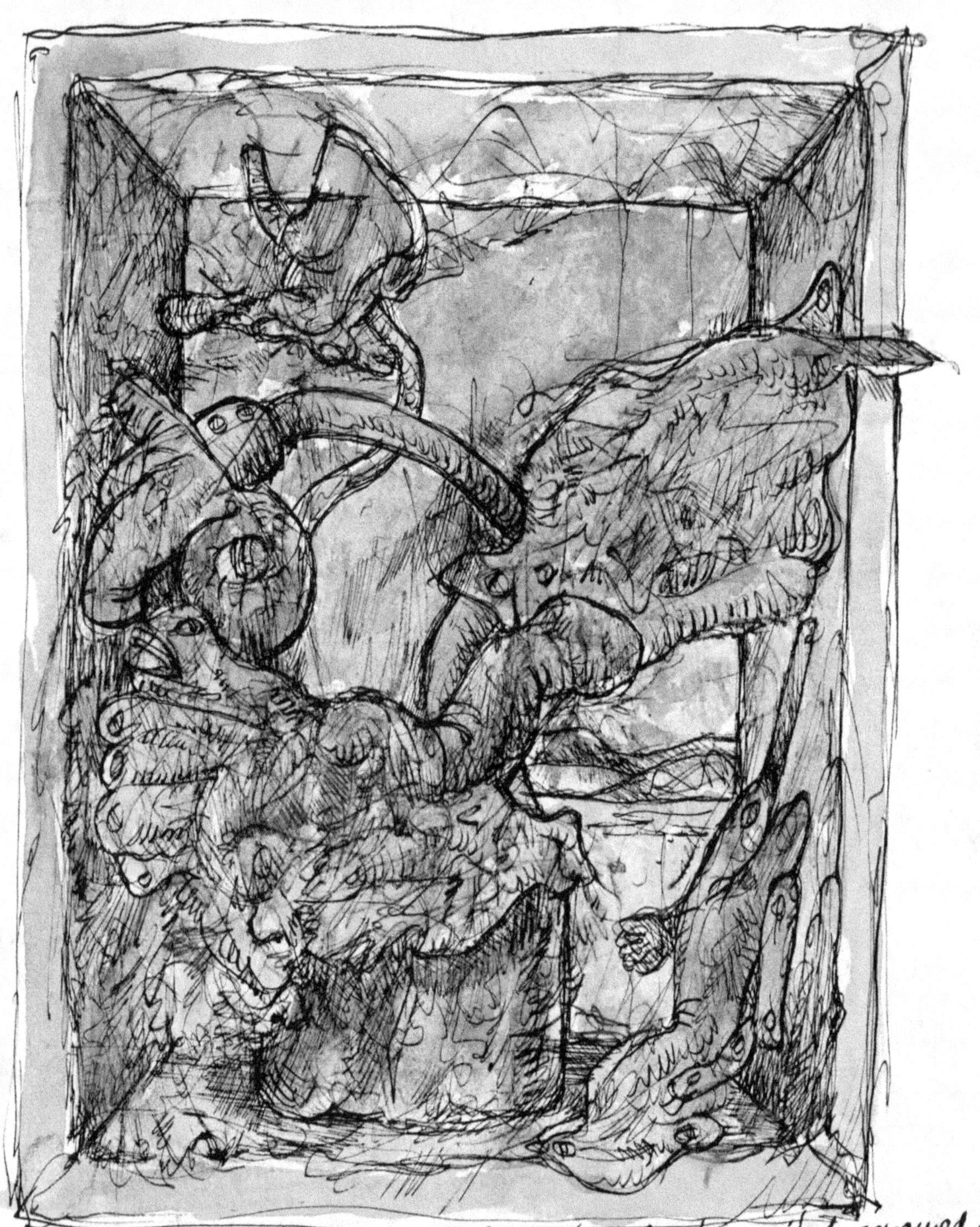

Fluid bearing tubes going where?/ all objects nailed, screwed, pierced, immobilized — Can things still change — Are these boxes the chrysalis stage of the Larvae? the non-understanding of the caterpillar of his next phase — Metamorphosis drawings were positive, are these negative? — Is it ending? What are the implications in tubes, jars, rocks, cracks, pipes, valves — is this my own mortality?

Is TROT·LINE FISHING the reminiscence before death . . . .

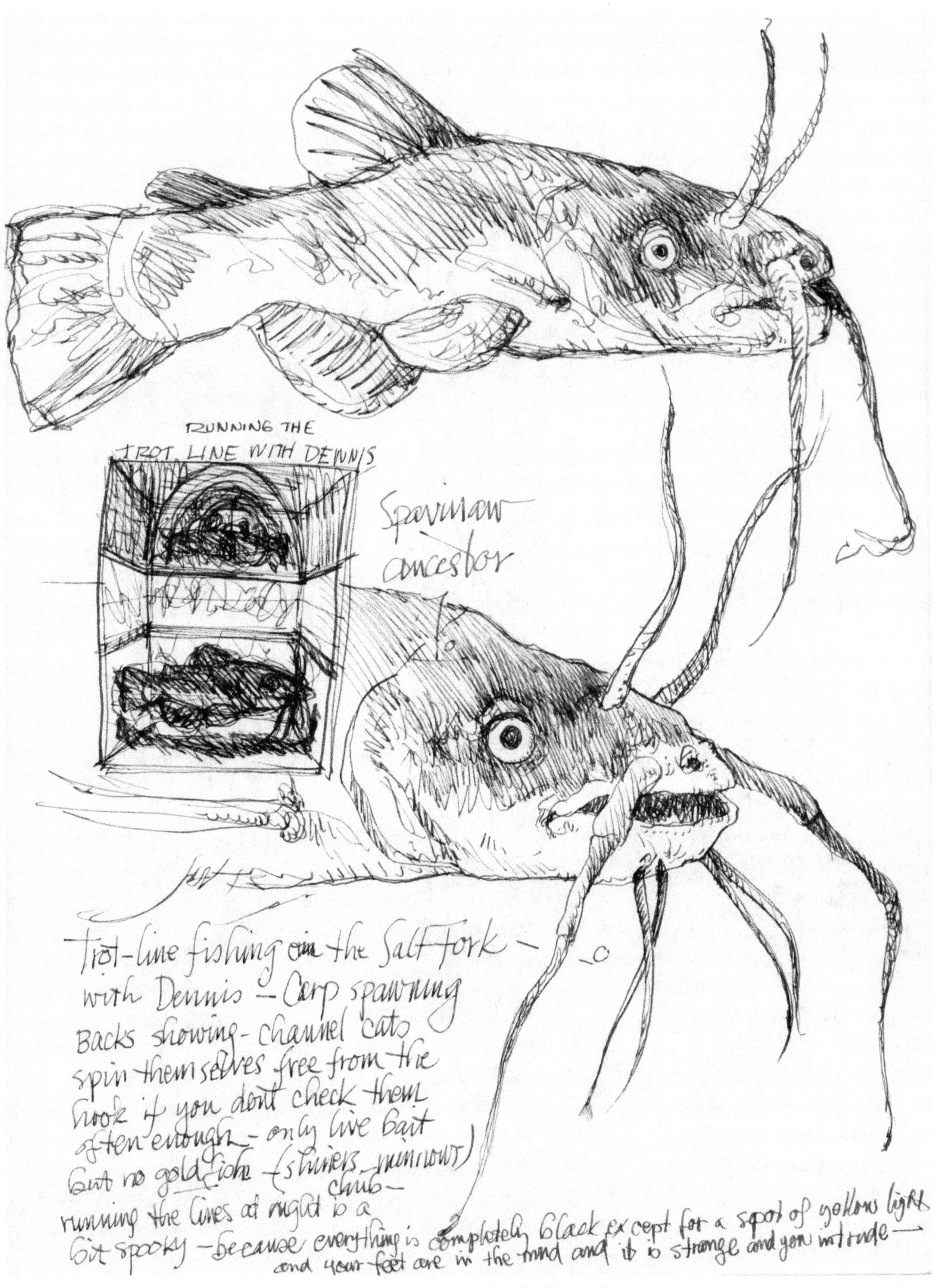

Trot-line fishing on the Salt Fork —
with Dennis — Carp spawning
Backs showing - channel cats
spin themselves free from the
hook if you dont check them
often enough - only live bait
but no goldfish (shiners, minnows)
chub —
running the lines at night is a
bit spooky —because everything is completely black except for a spot of yellow light
and your feet are in the mud and it is strange and you intrude—

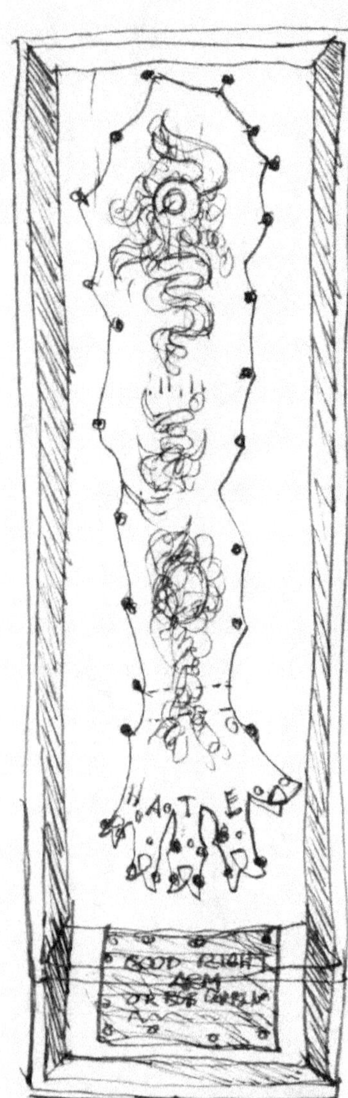

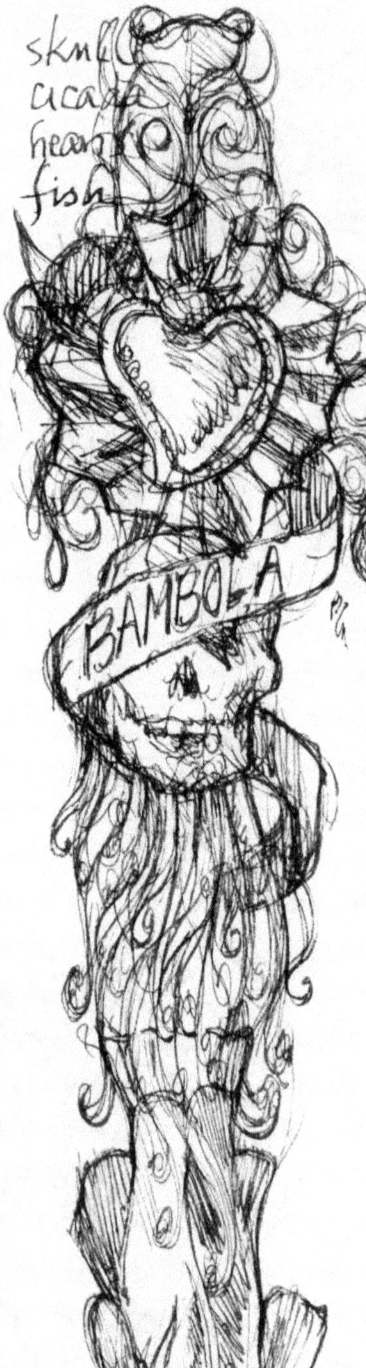

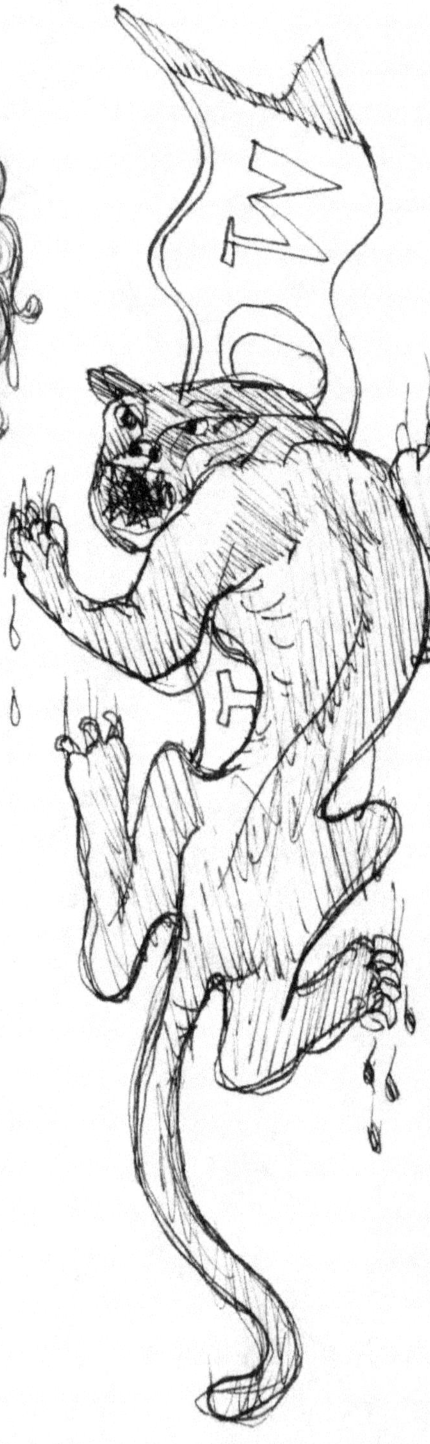

skull
cicada
heart
fish

BOB'S GOOD RIGHT ARM

The first time I did not get a tattoo was
in Ponca City. In the ninth grade
or with needle and ink the brave
wrote names on arms and legs...
The second time I wasn't tattooed
was in Lawton, Oklahoma. Ralph
and Chuck got Wayne drunk and
had both of his arms tattooed
from elbow to shoulder... The
third time I passed up a tattoo
was in San Francisco where
I watched a girl have a bluebird
put on each breast... now
I am busy doing designs for the
fourth time I will not be tattooed.
But Bonnie has always been
my good right arm....

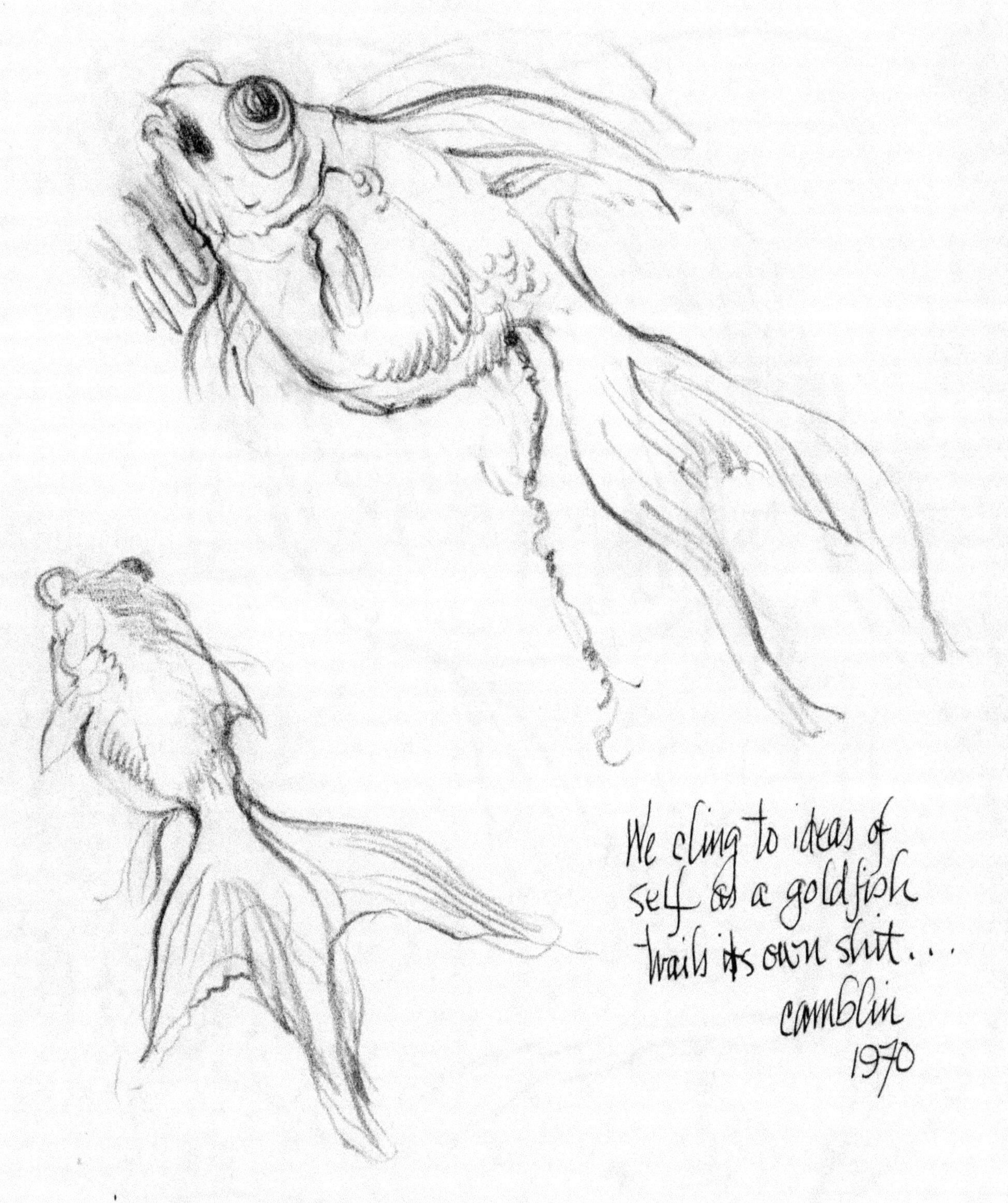

We cling to ideas of
self as a goldfish
trails its own shit...
camblin
1970

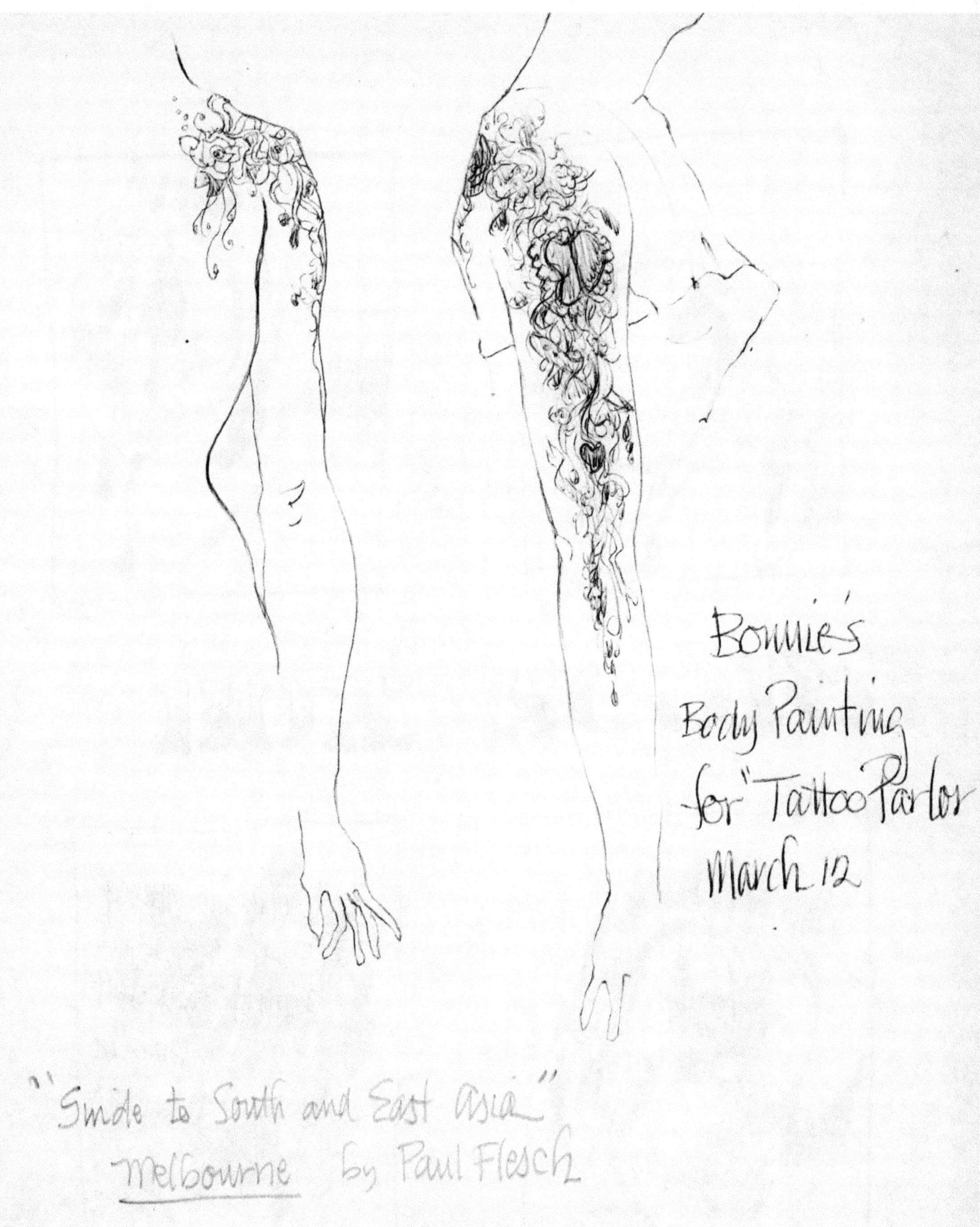

Bonnie's
Body Painting
for "Tattoo Parlos"
March 12

"Smile to South and East Asia"
Melbourne   by Paul Flesch

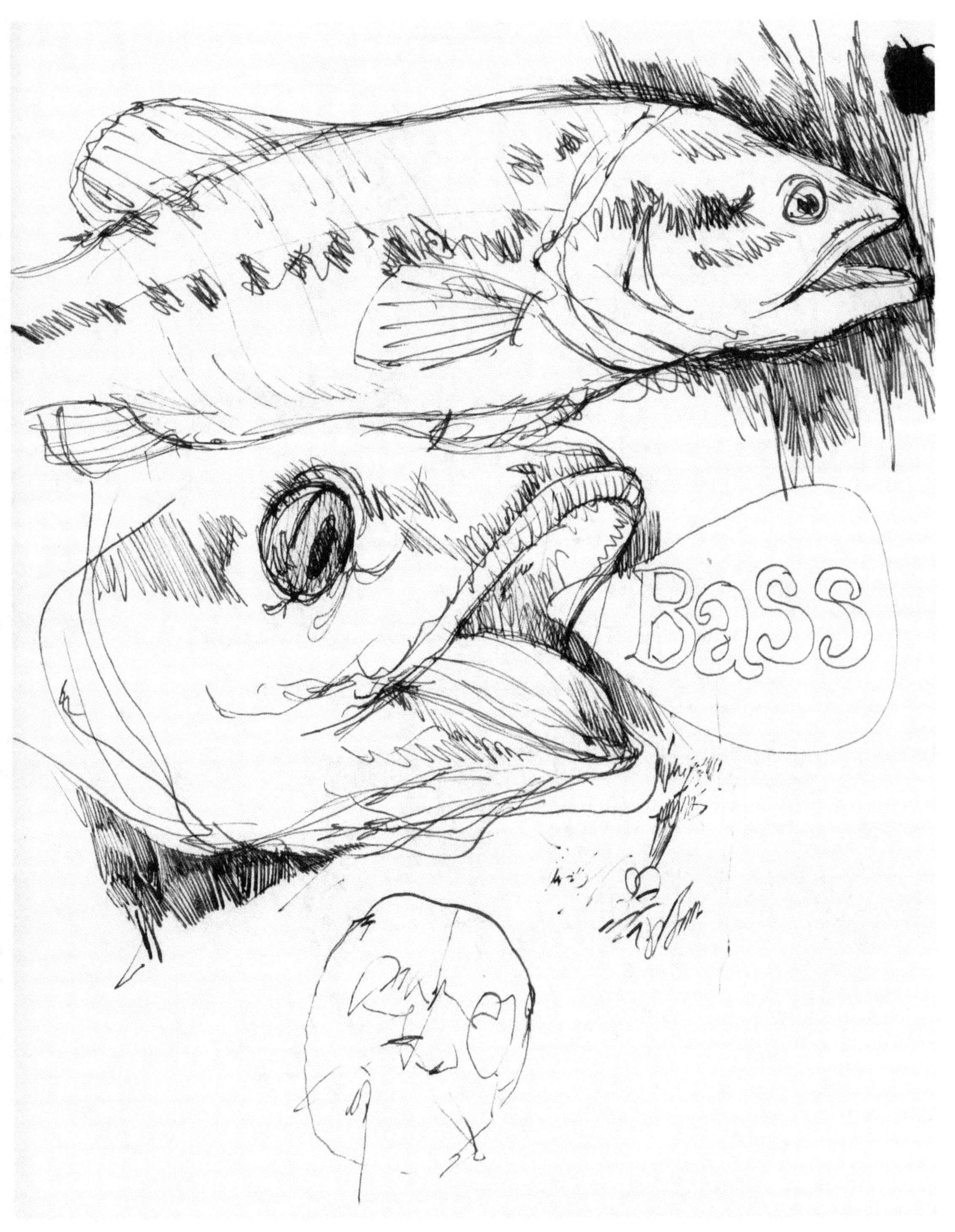

Bass

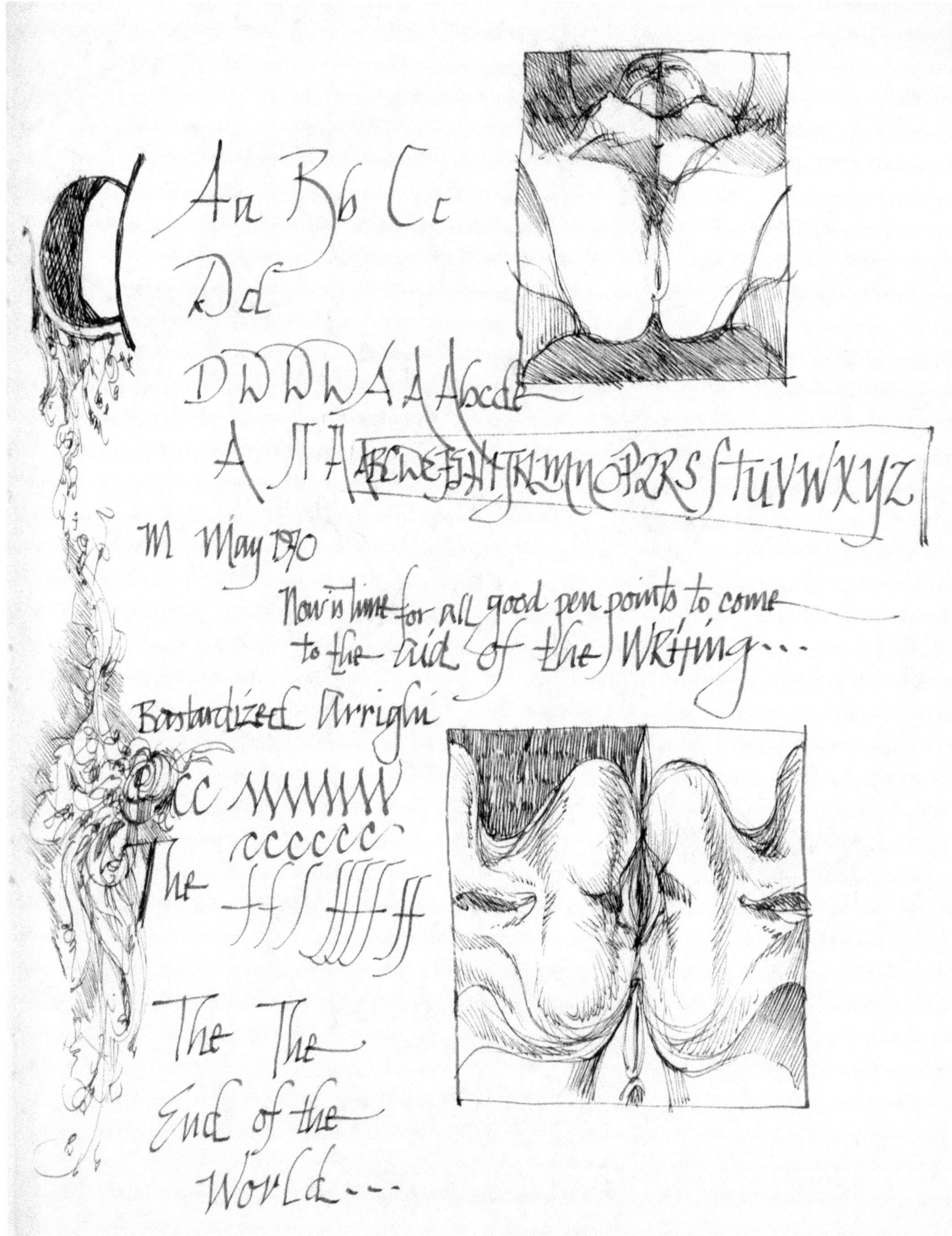
Aa Bb Cc
Dd
ABCDEFGHIJKLMNOPQRSTUVWXYZ
M May 1970
Now is time for all good pen points to come
to the aid of the Writing...
Bastardized Arrighi
The
The The
End of the
World...

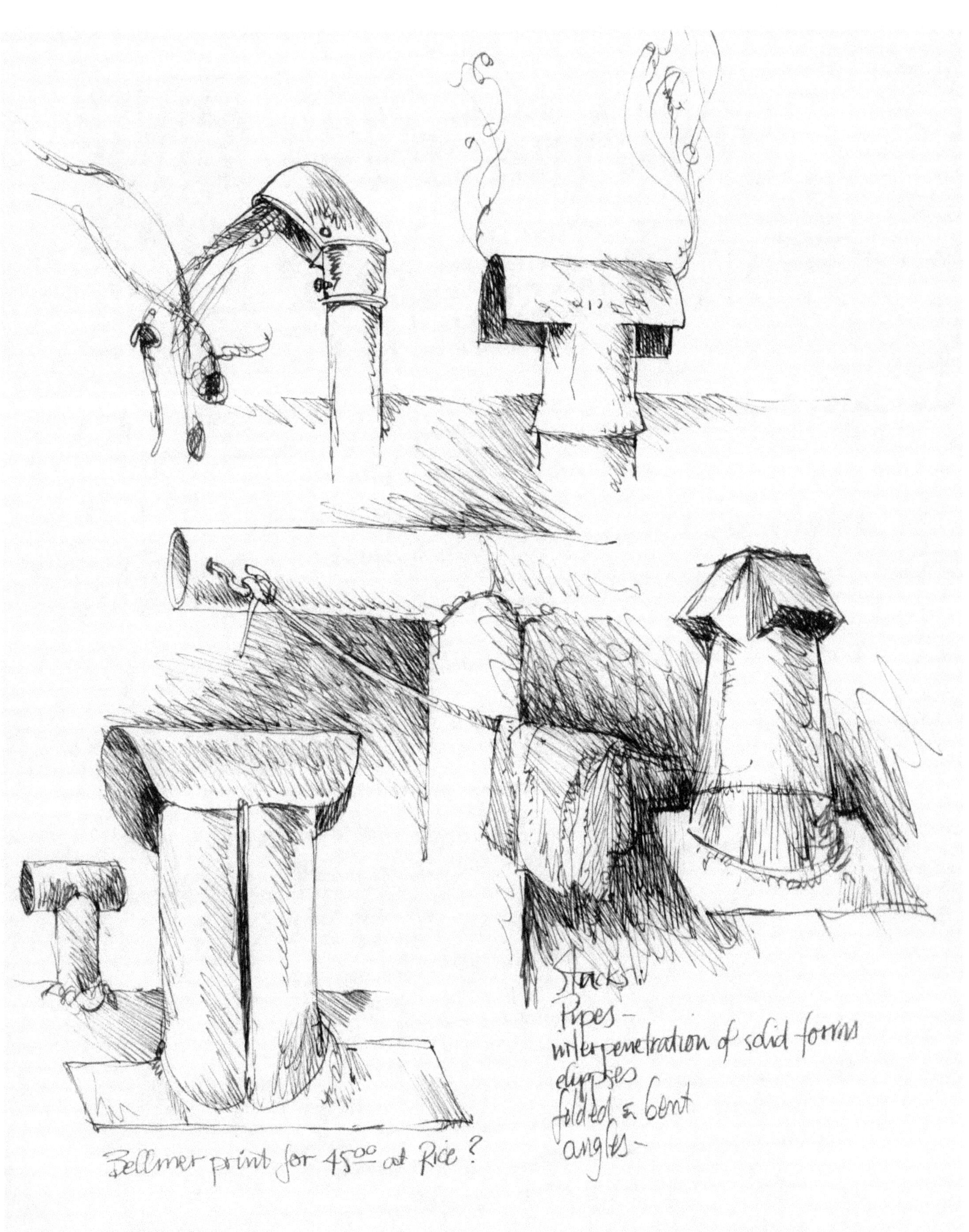
Stacks:
Pipes —
interpenetration of solid forms
ellipses
folded & bent
angles —
Bellmer print for 45⁰⁰ at Rice?

BOOK 6 drawings from 1971

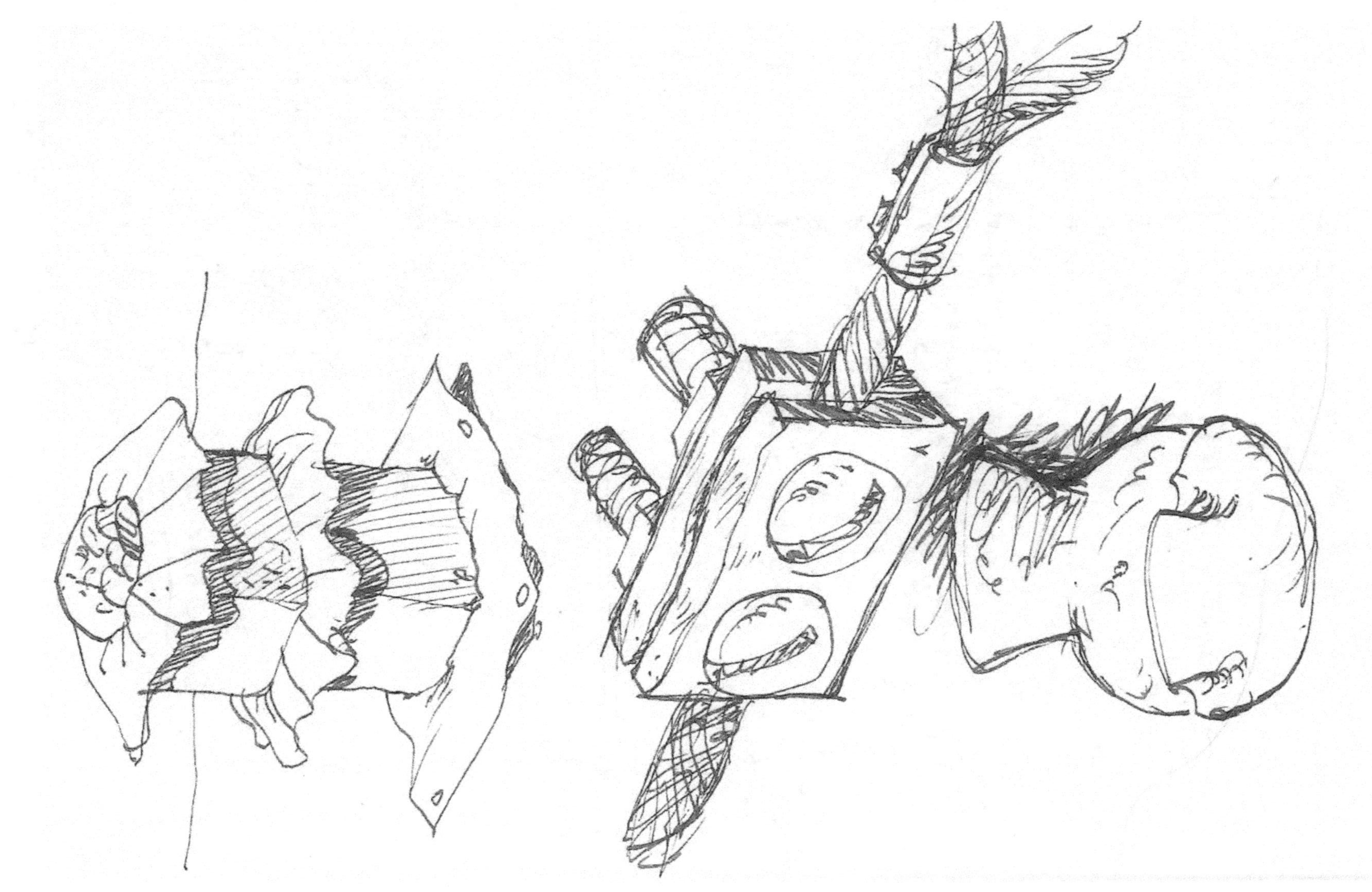

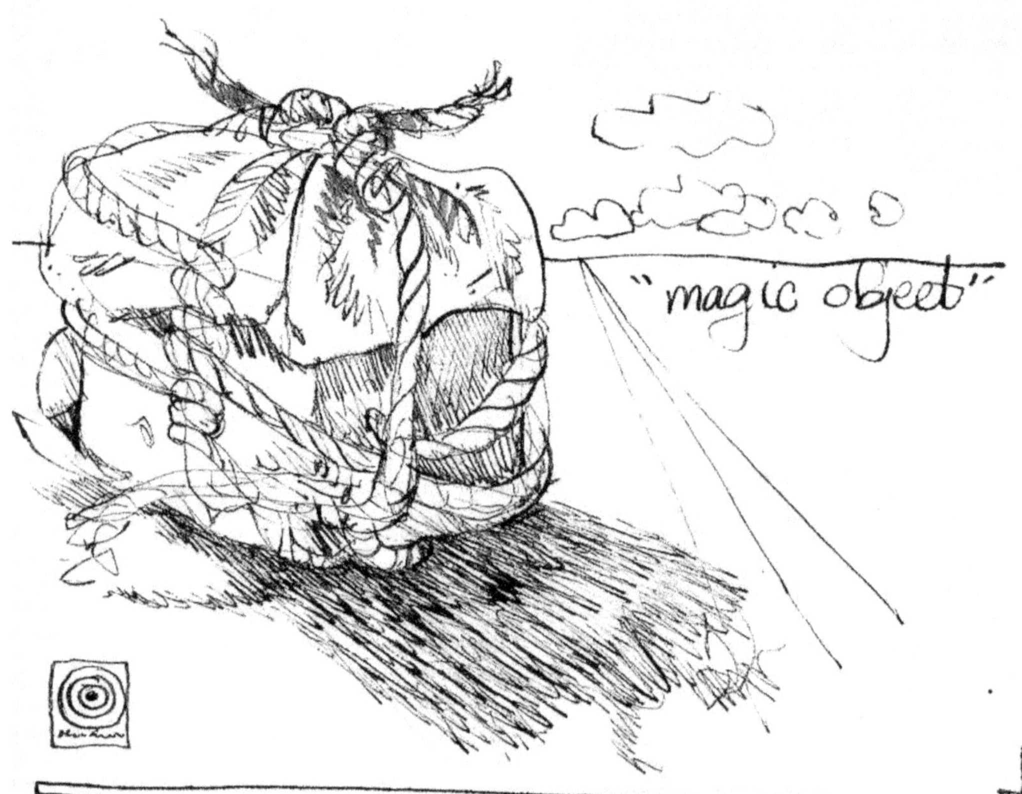

This semester was a 'fiasco' - I think
I expected too much from this bunch of
"intellectual" cripples - They will never get what
I mean since I tried to TEACH - a sad mistake
on both sides - They are unable to try and I
tried to hard to show them my "precious" seashell.
Unless people come looking then it is a waste
of time to offer __ I shall have to rethink
my position - O'Neil is too structured and
trains hands ___ But they need that discipline
Tate is unstructured __ and it borders on
fun and games ___ But RICE students need that
point of view very much ___ What do I offer
at this point? Very little __ I never trained
just for mechanical skill and I can't be
totally permissive and wax enthusiastic over
sophomore enthusiasm - If they don't turn
me on I can't feedback anything — Maybe
If is time to quit — Don't be a martyr, camblin!

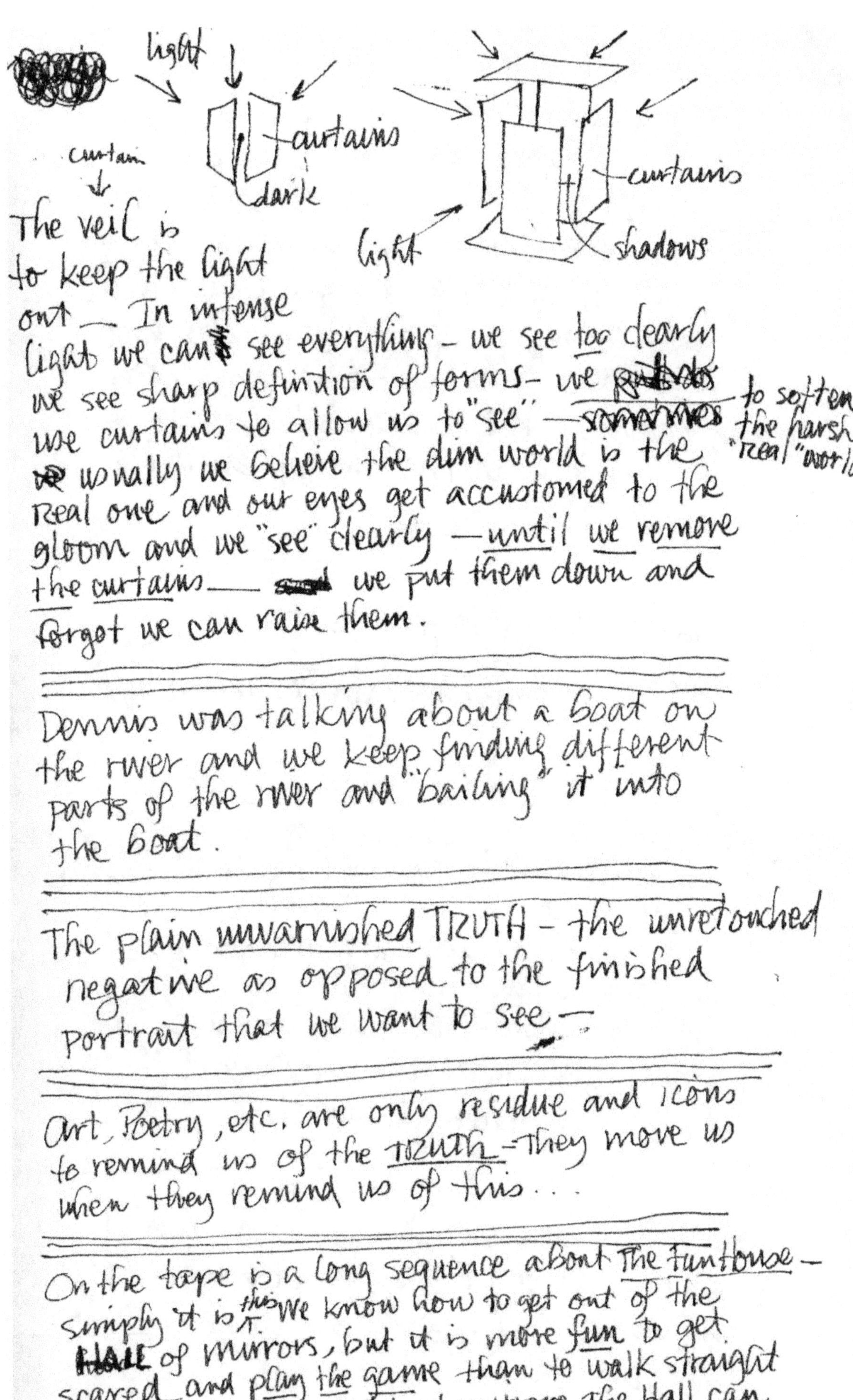

The veil is
to keep the light
out — In intense
light we can't see everything — we see too clearly
we see sharp definition of forms — we
use curtains to allow us to "see" — sometimes to soften
the harsh
usually we believe the dim world is the "real" world
real one and our eyes get accustomed to the
gloom and we "see" clearly — until we remove
the curtains — we put them down and
forgot we can raise them.

Dennis was talking about a boat on
the river and we keep finding different
parts of the river and "bailing" it into
the boat.

The plain unvarnished TRUTH — the unretouched
negative as opposed to the finished
portrait that we want to see —

Art, Poetry, etc. are only residue and icons
to remind us of the TRUTH — they move us
when they remind us of this . . .

On the tape is a long sequence about the Fun House —
simply it is this we know how to get out of the
HALL of mirrors, but it is more fun to get
scared and play the game than to walk straight
through. The better quality of mirrors, the Hall can

"fool" you easier but we still "know" it is a
FUN HOUSE now matter how scary and we can
quit when we wish and "find" our way out.
The REAL world is just this and nothing else
if you don't believe it then you are still "playing"
the game in FUN HOUSE and bumping into the
mirrors and scaring yourself. No matter how
REAL the game seems —— one only needs
to really laugh — not a laugh of bravado ~~but~~
~~not~~ but the one from the gut of enjoying
the game ——

"...We have nothing to fear, but fear
ourself"
                        camblin — sunday Feb 28, 1971
                                3:00 a.m.

To know how good _it_ is you have to stop _it_
and do something else — and then that becomes
good to and so to realize its "goodness" you
have to do something else — and the faster you
keep _moving_ you find that there is no
separation and you — "Eat when you are
hungry and sleep when you are tired" —
and that is all there is to it ——

When Zen monks say that we are _always_
the Buddha but we keep forgetting it most
of the time — I _knew_ ~~that~~, but ~~I~~ now I
know it . . .

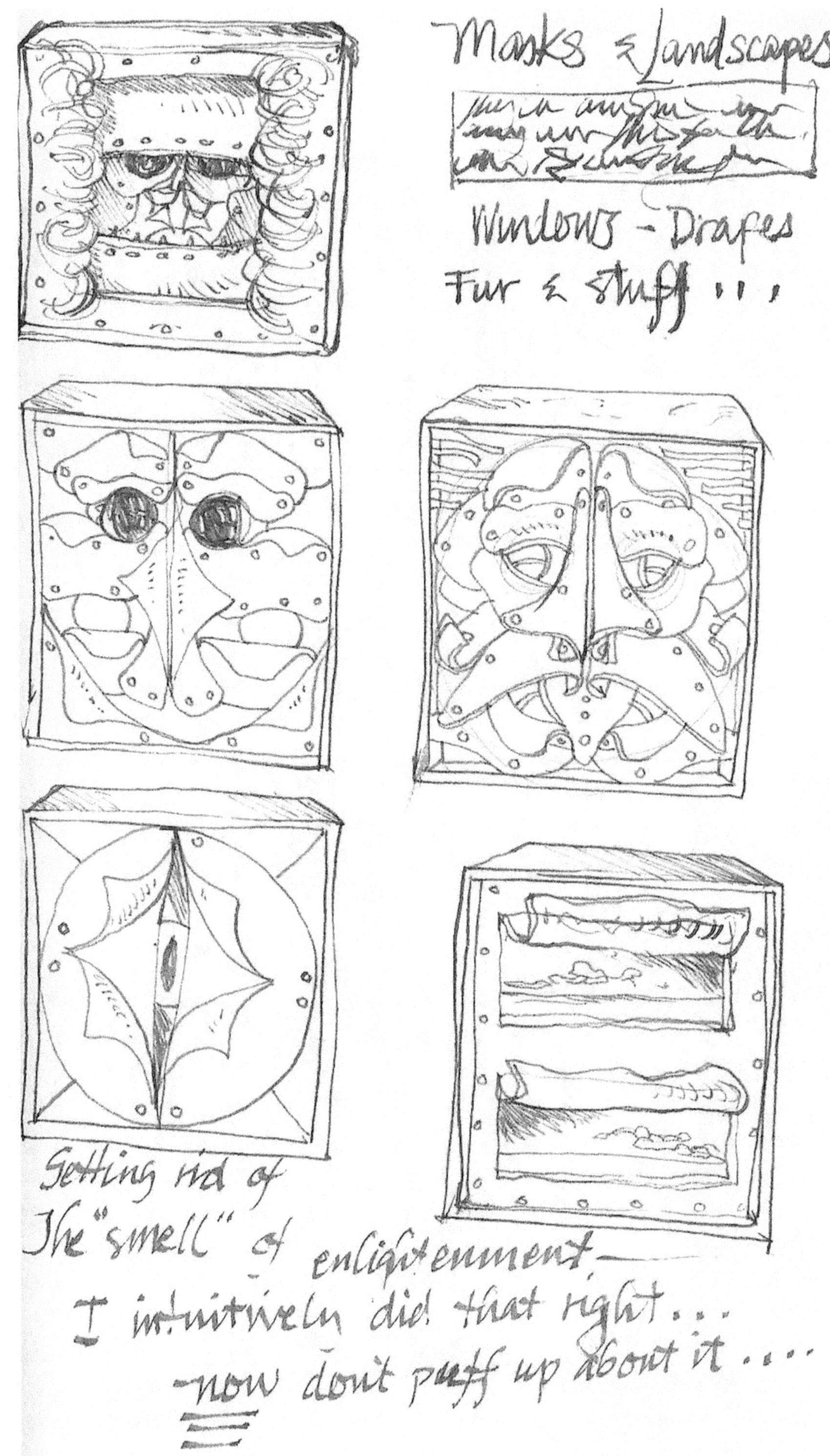

Masks & Landscapes
Windows - Drapes
Fur & stuff · · ,
Getting rid of
The "smell" of enlightenment —
I intuitively did that right...
— now don't puff up about it....

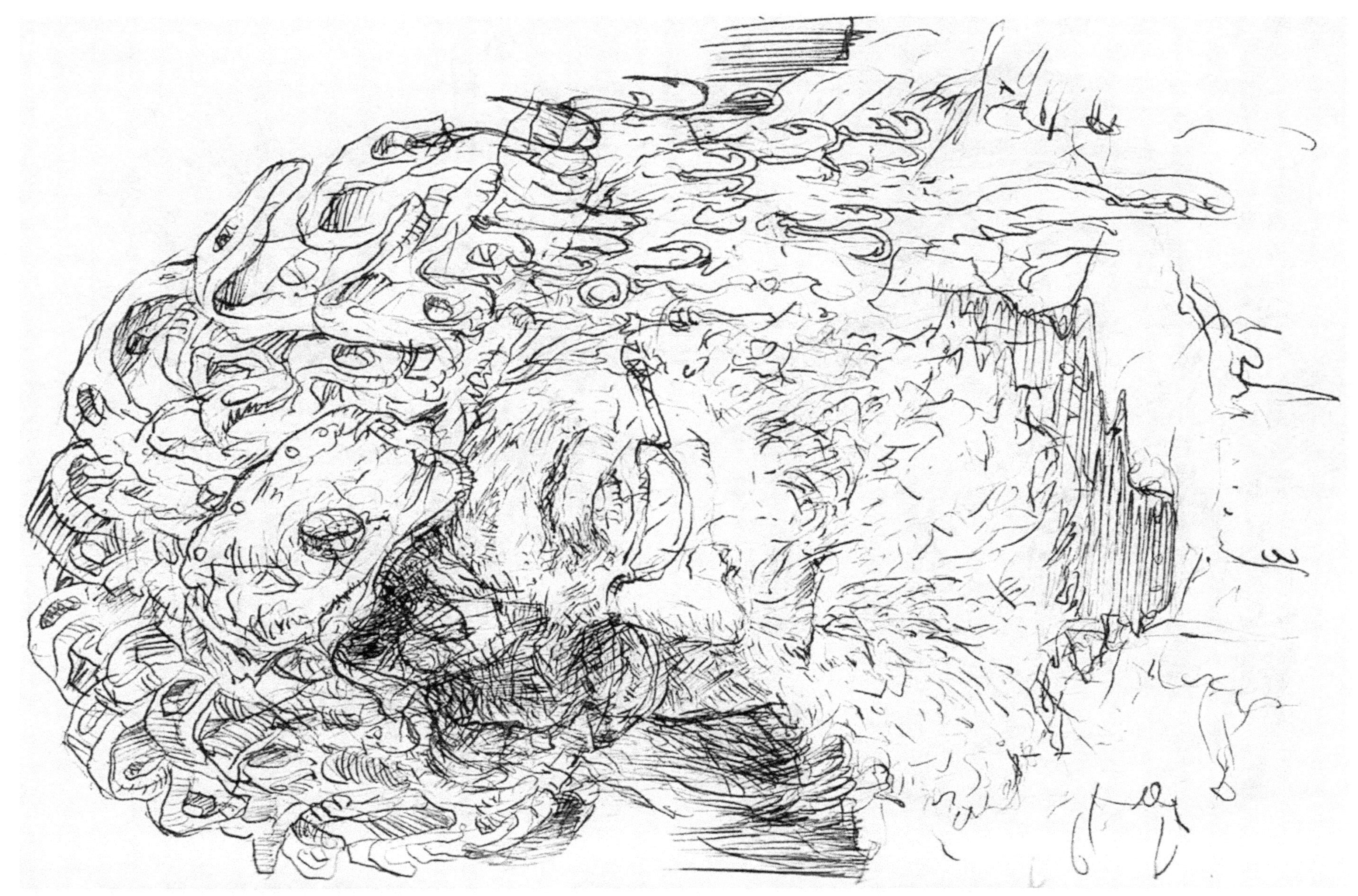

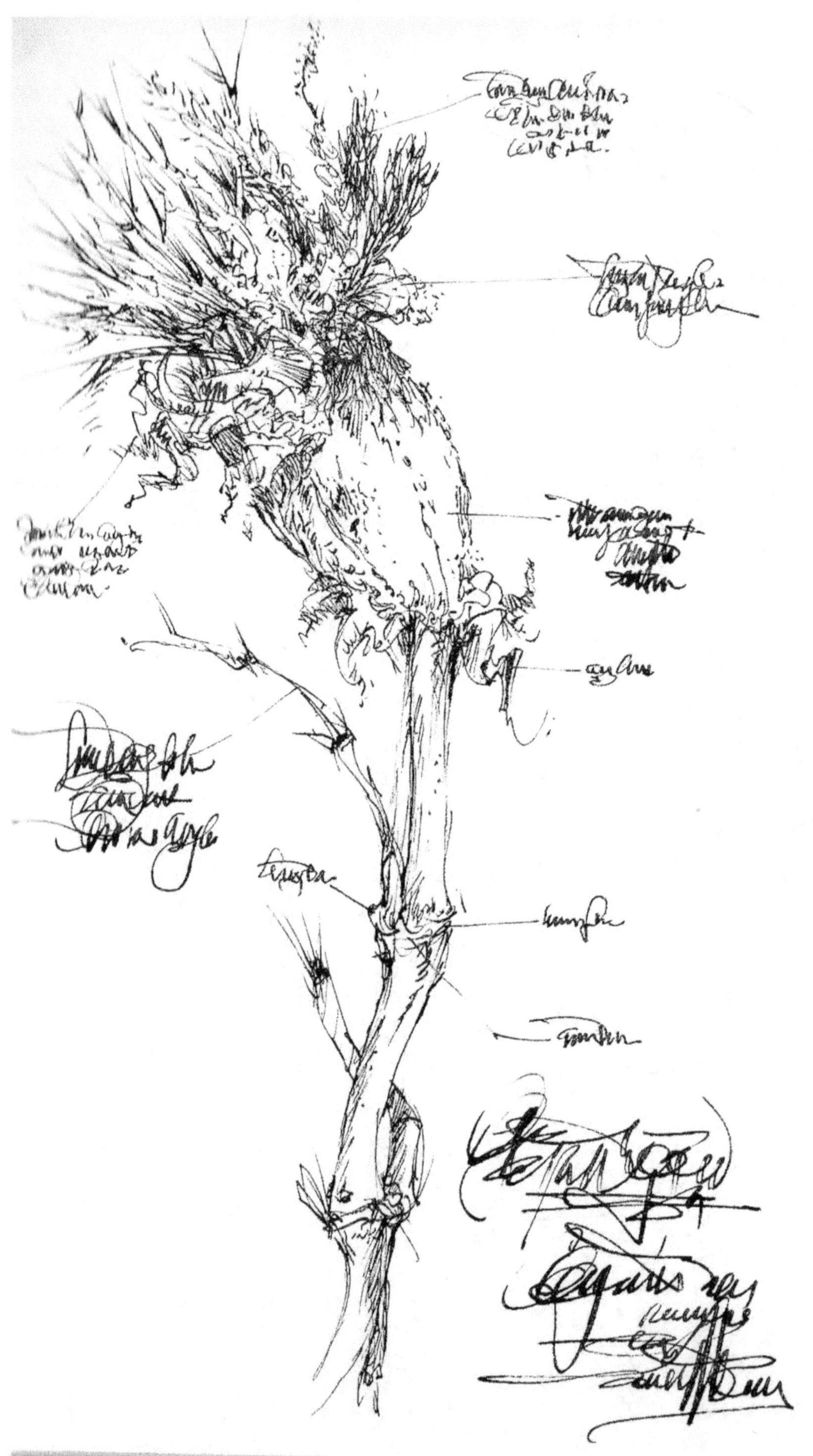

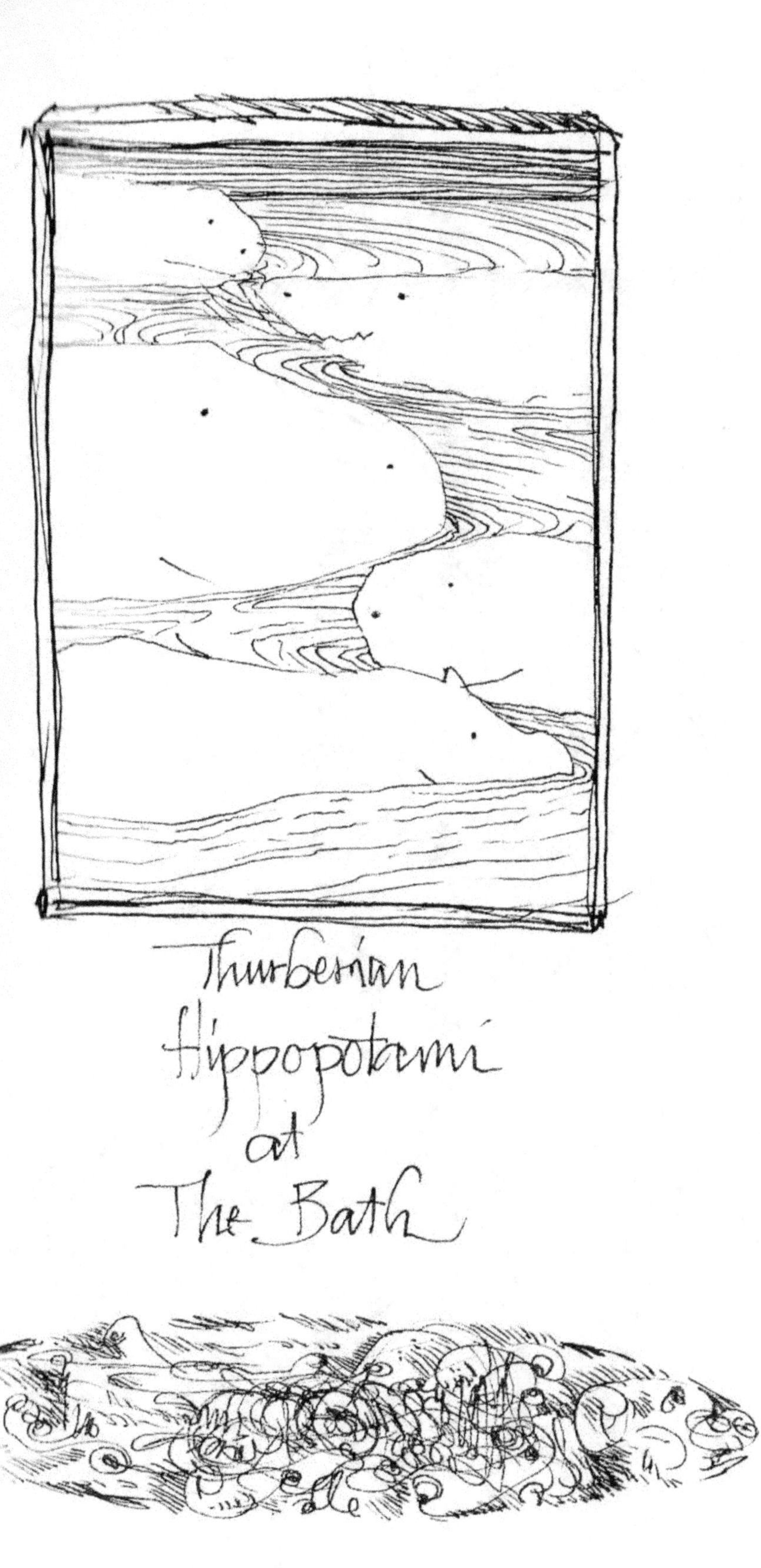

Thurberian
Hippopotami
at
The Bath

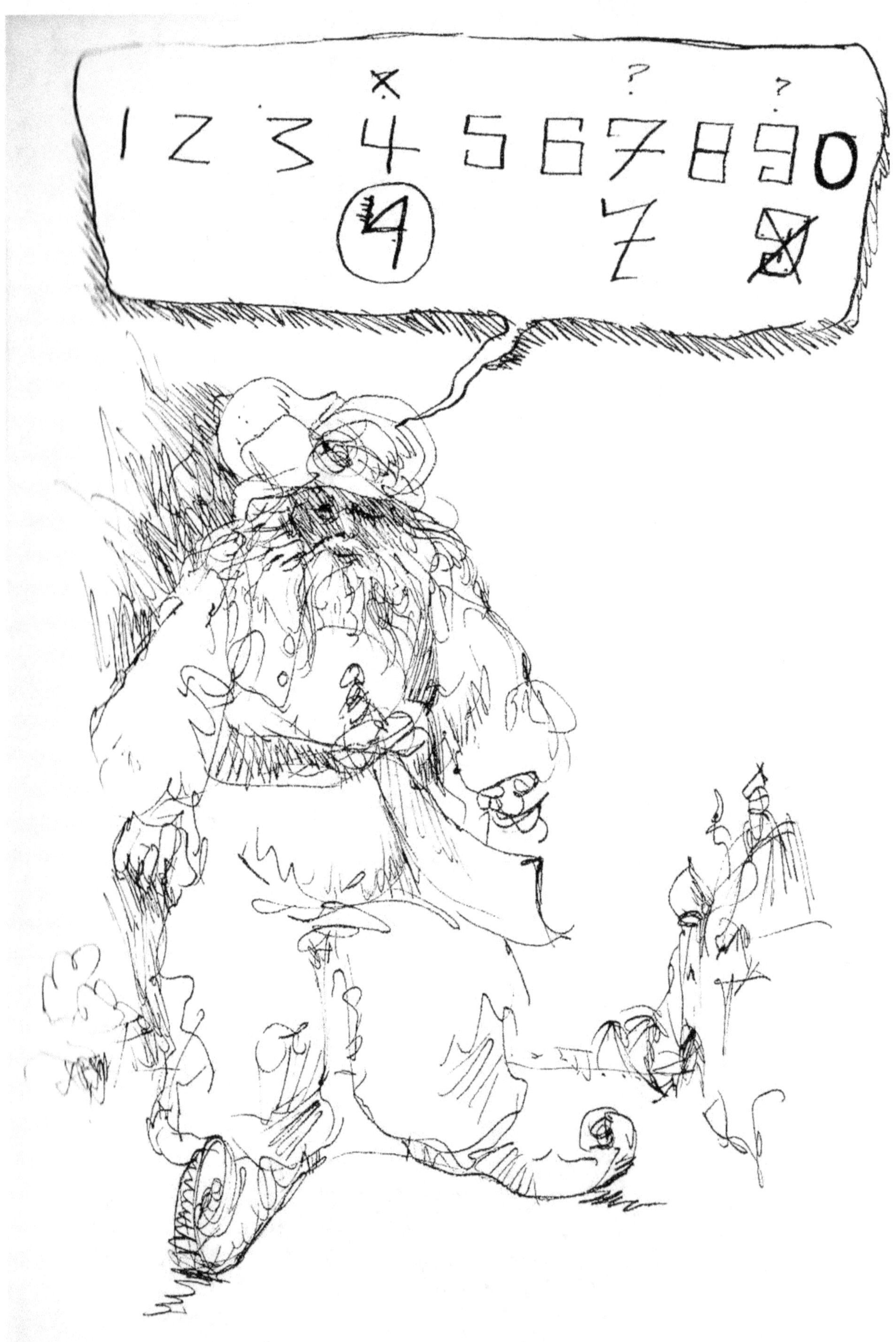

1 2 3 4 5 6 7 8 9 0
4

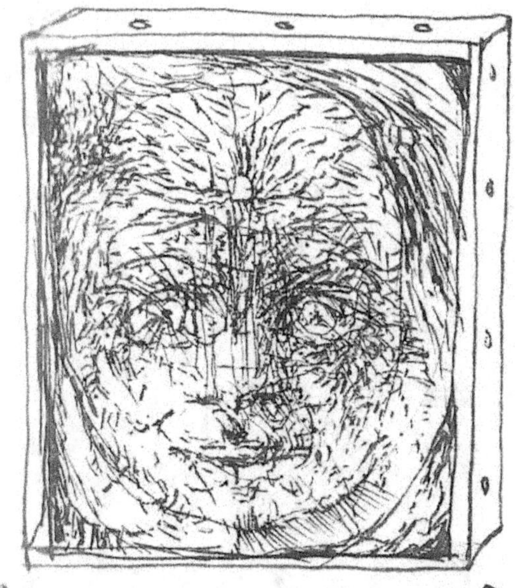

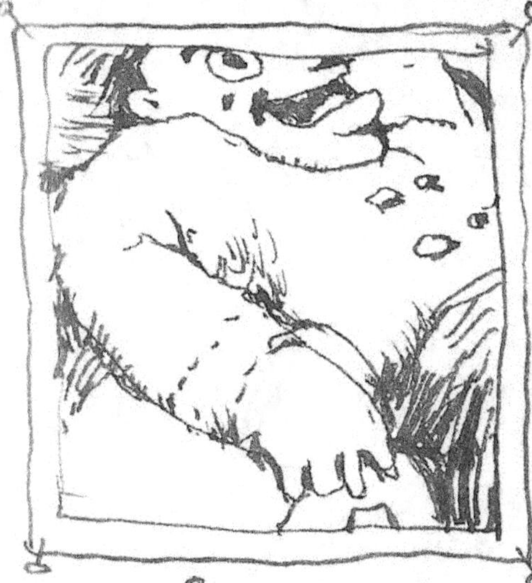

Snakeskins!
as a magic object
symbol of something
transformed...

Pictures as snakeskins
of the artist—left
behind... a bit of
magic... partially
effective... cures
anything.. Snakeskins
to be followed...
getting closer to the
searching worm...
My God, how transcendent,
how pompous! A
much better way to
say it...

When understood—
all Truth is funny.
Everything is funny.
Only because we
have been so serious
about It. It makes
us laugh to really
understand—Yeah,
of course, wow!,
I get it, Yeah...

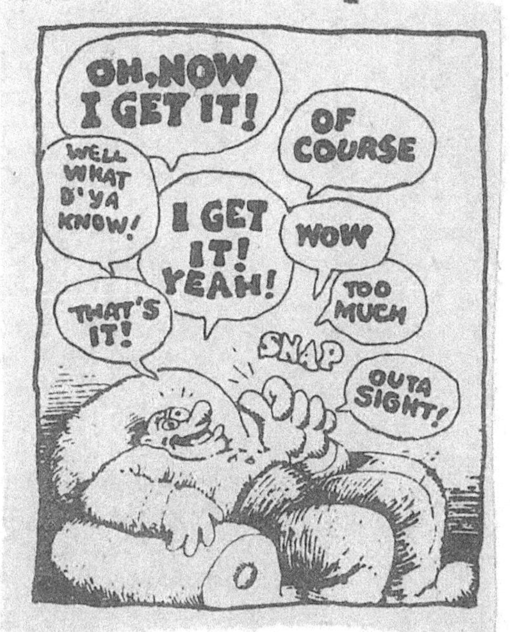

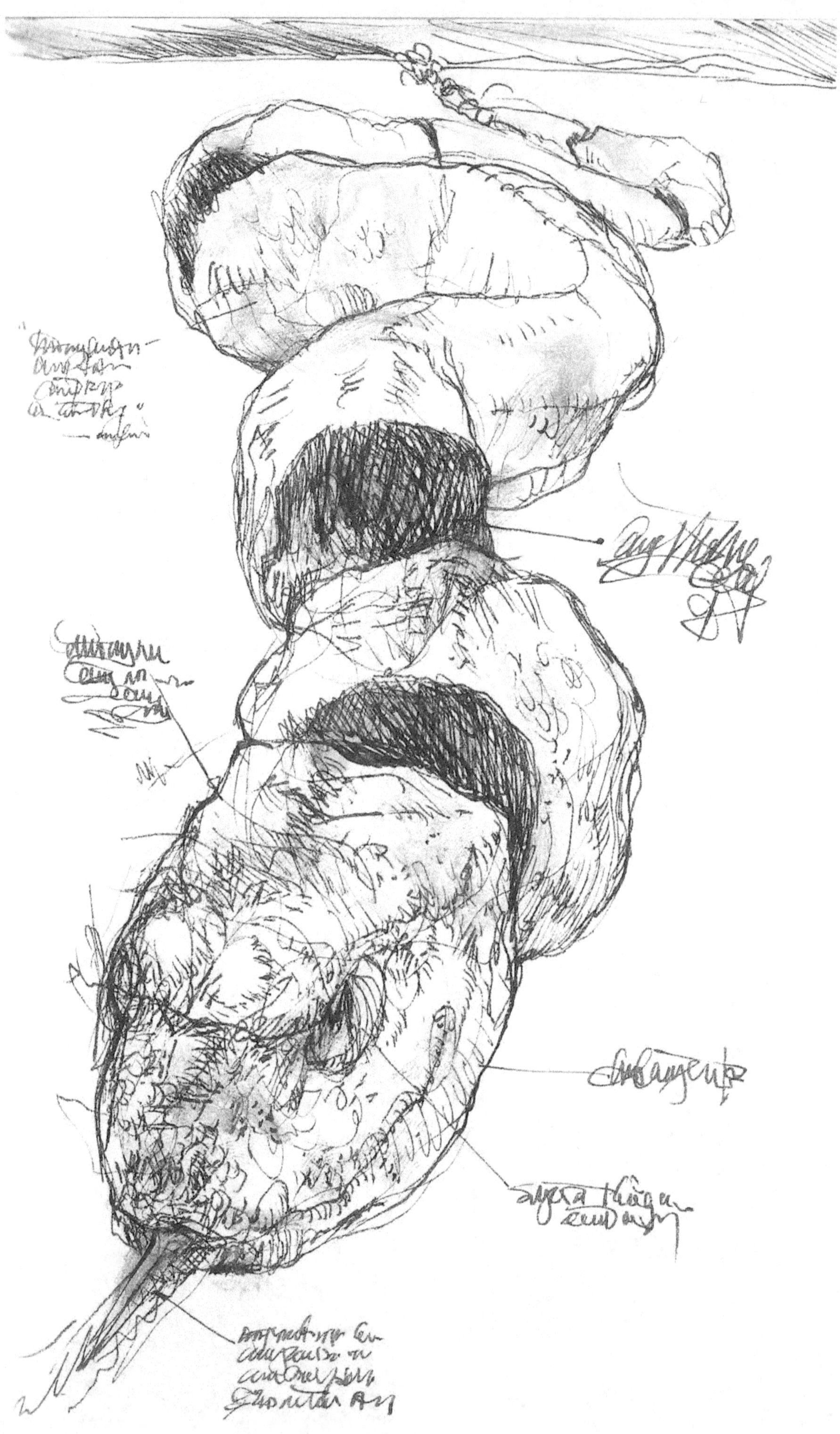

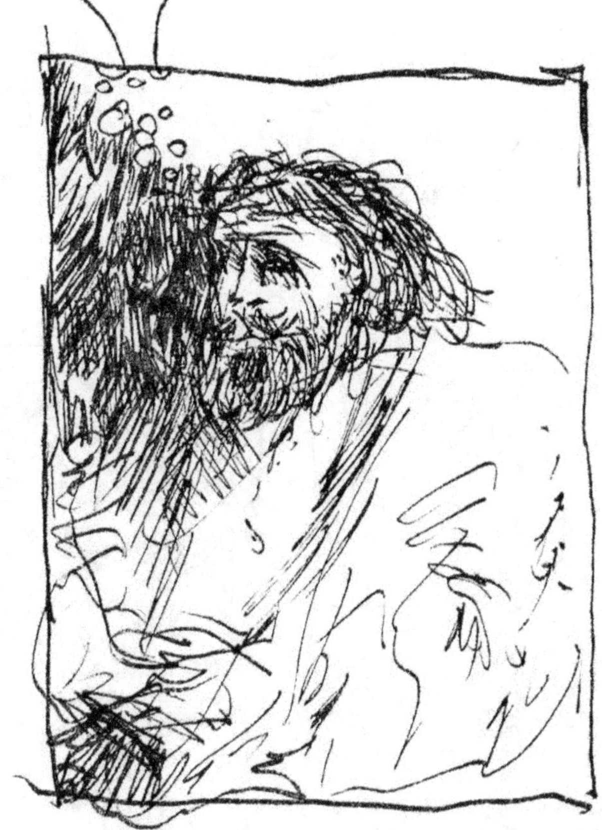

... I have over-reacted again and confused all the issues - The simplest solution would be for me to avoid faculty meetings — It is unlikely that everyone is as dumb as they act — or as capricious, so my megalomania must be kept in check — Historians love "artistic madness" when it isn't alive and well and attending meetings —

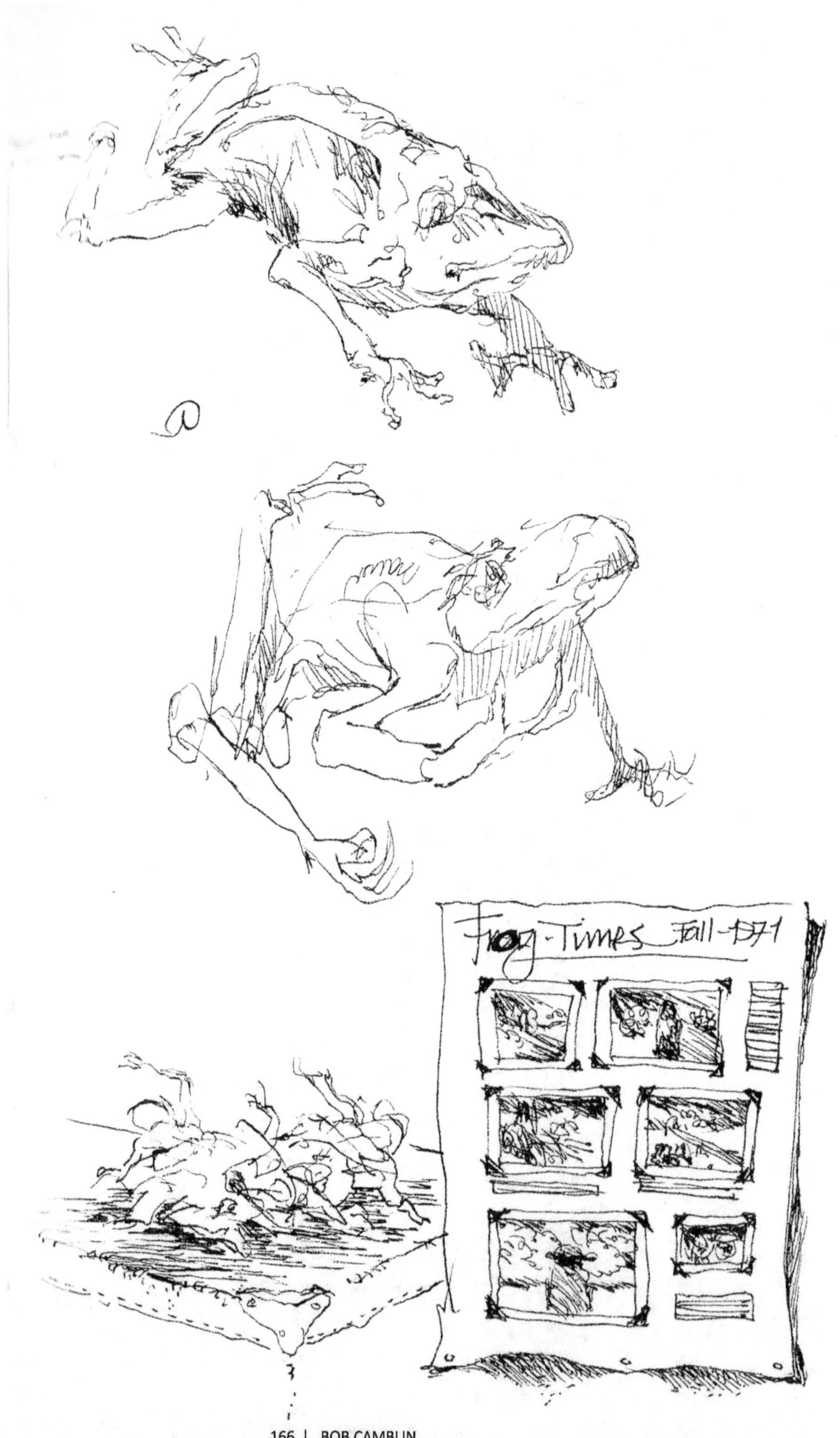

Frog-Times Fall-1971

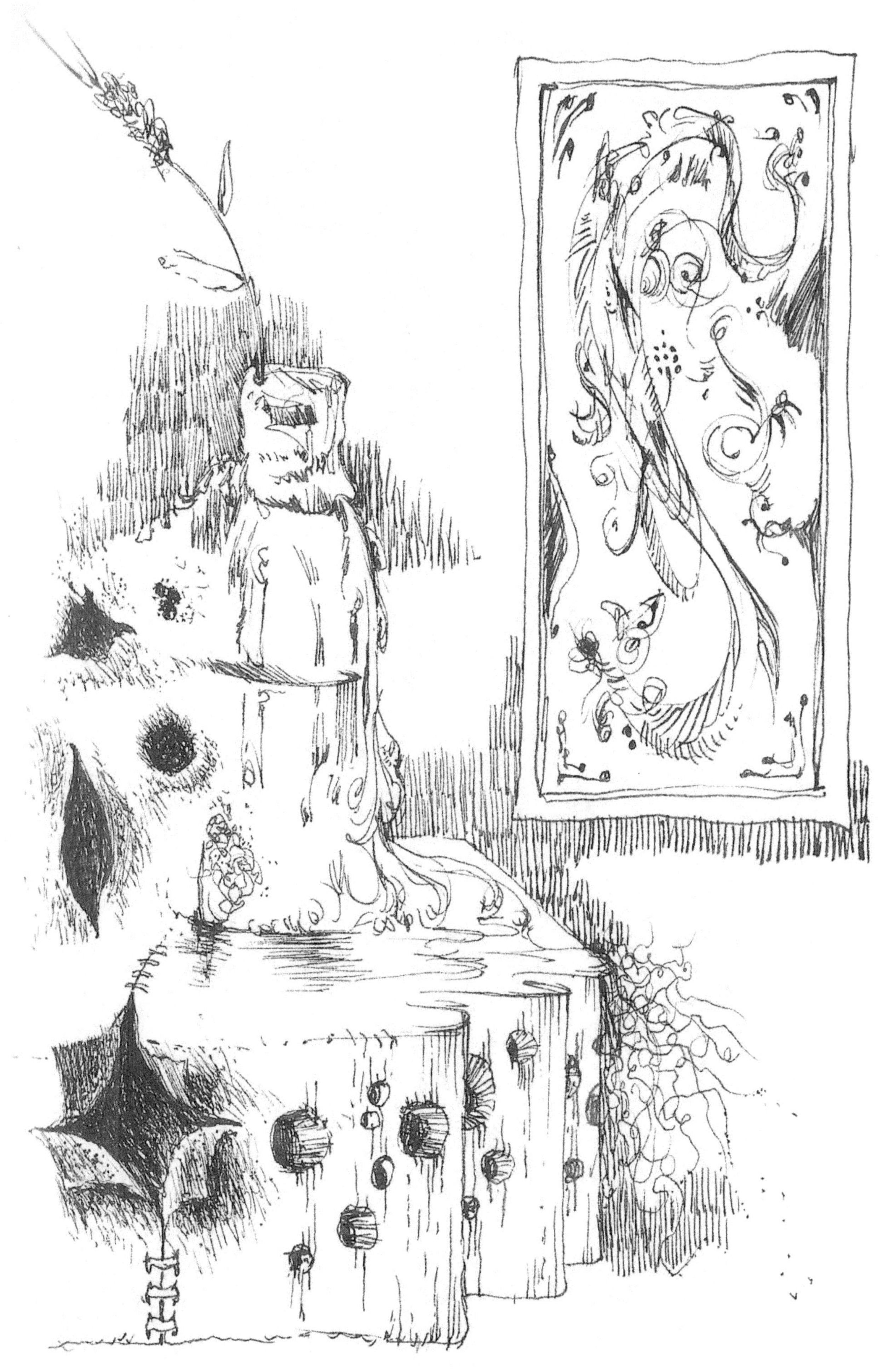

manuscript
gothic church }

Leonardo
Renaissance }

Baroque }
Rubens }

ROCOCO
Nᵉ CLASSIC

ACADEMY
'859 Impressionism - seurat
'907 cubism
'874 symbolist - surreal
art nouveau excess
'920 bauhaus - classic
'950 international style
'959 Neo - Romantic
'960
'970

ROMANTIC — pendulum swing
CLASSIC

INTUITION }
LOGIC } BALANCE

no slice of life in reality — History
makes slice
                neo
pop art, dada,

MICRO - MACRO - TECH.

nov-9-18
?

Show slides
of history

ZEITGEIST { TECH.
WRITING
GRAPHICS - ARCH
SCIENCE - ART

Art as future
Art as non-commerce

1 ART - EXPERIENCE
2 AVANT GARDE
3 CONTEMPORARY
4 CLICHE   seen as
5 KITSCH   seen as

TIME APPROX

ROTATING
TRAPEZOID
as the theme.

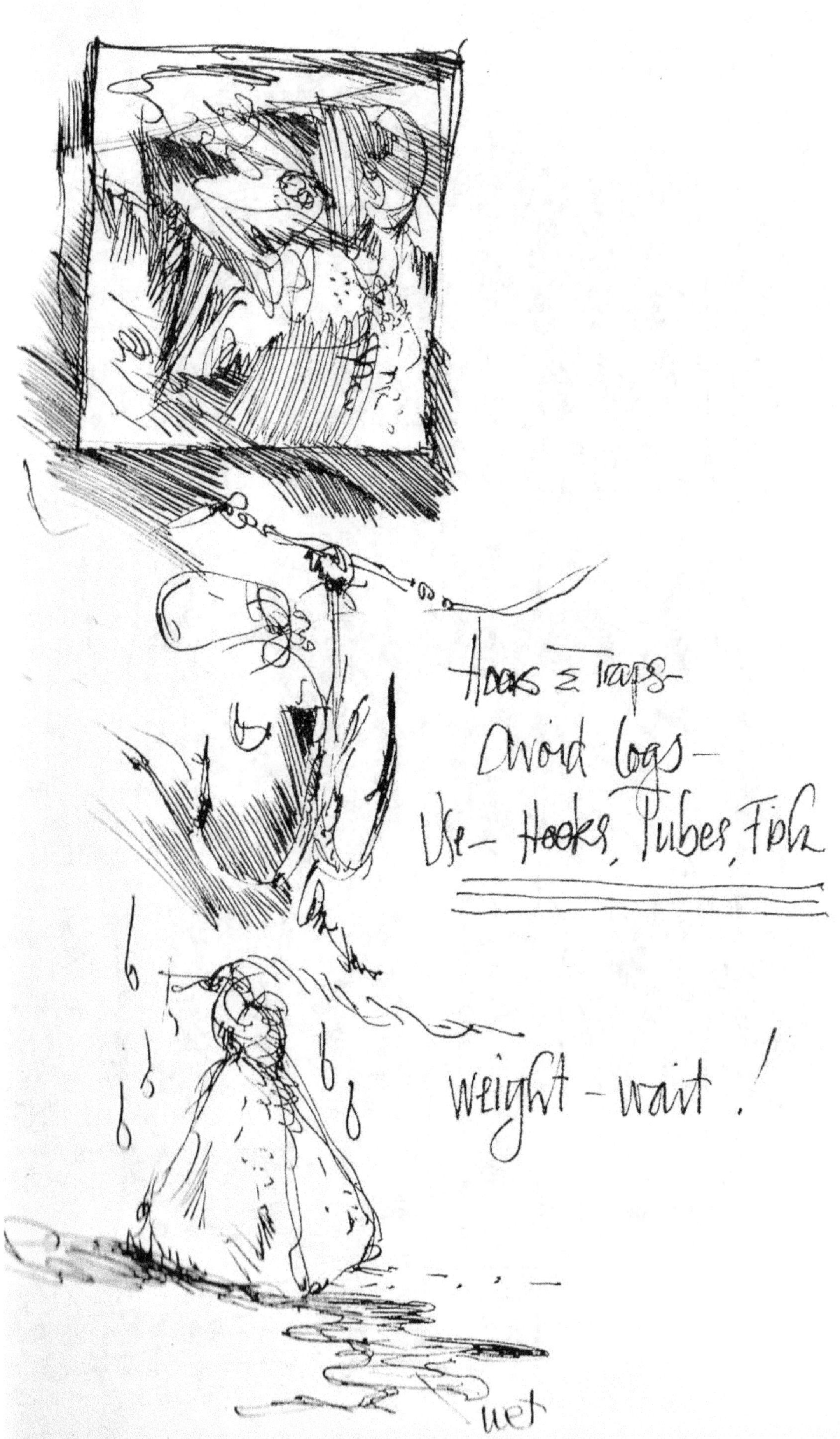

Hooks & Traps
Avoid logs —
Use — Hooks, Tubes, Fish
weight — wait . !
net

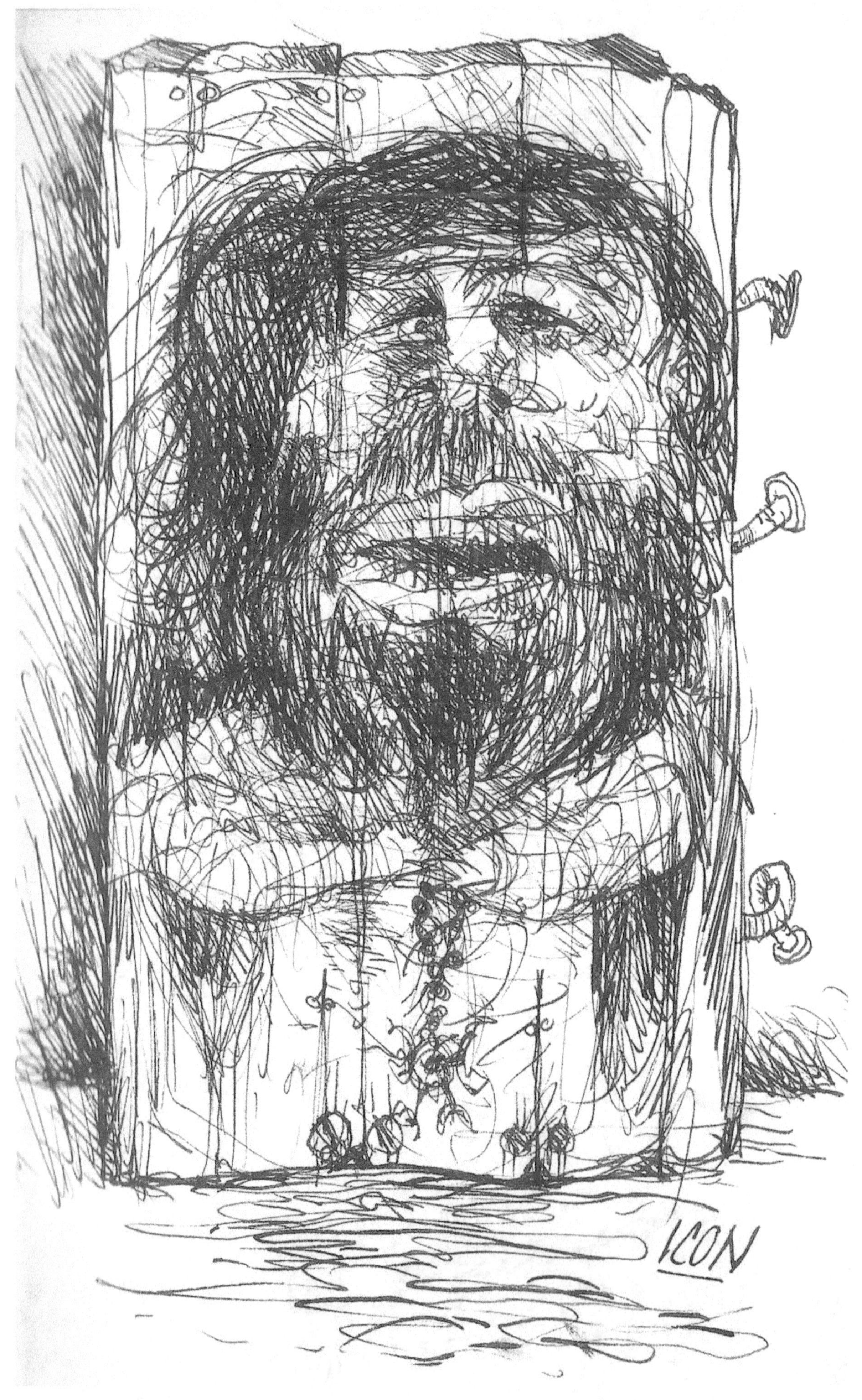

ICON

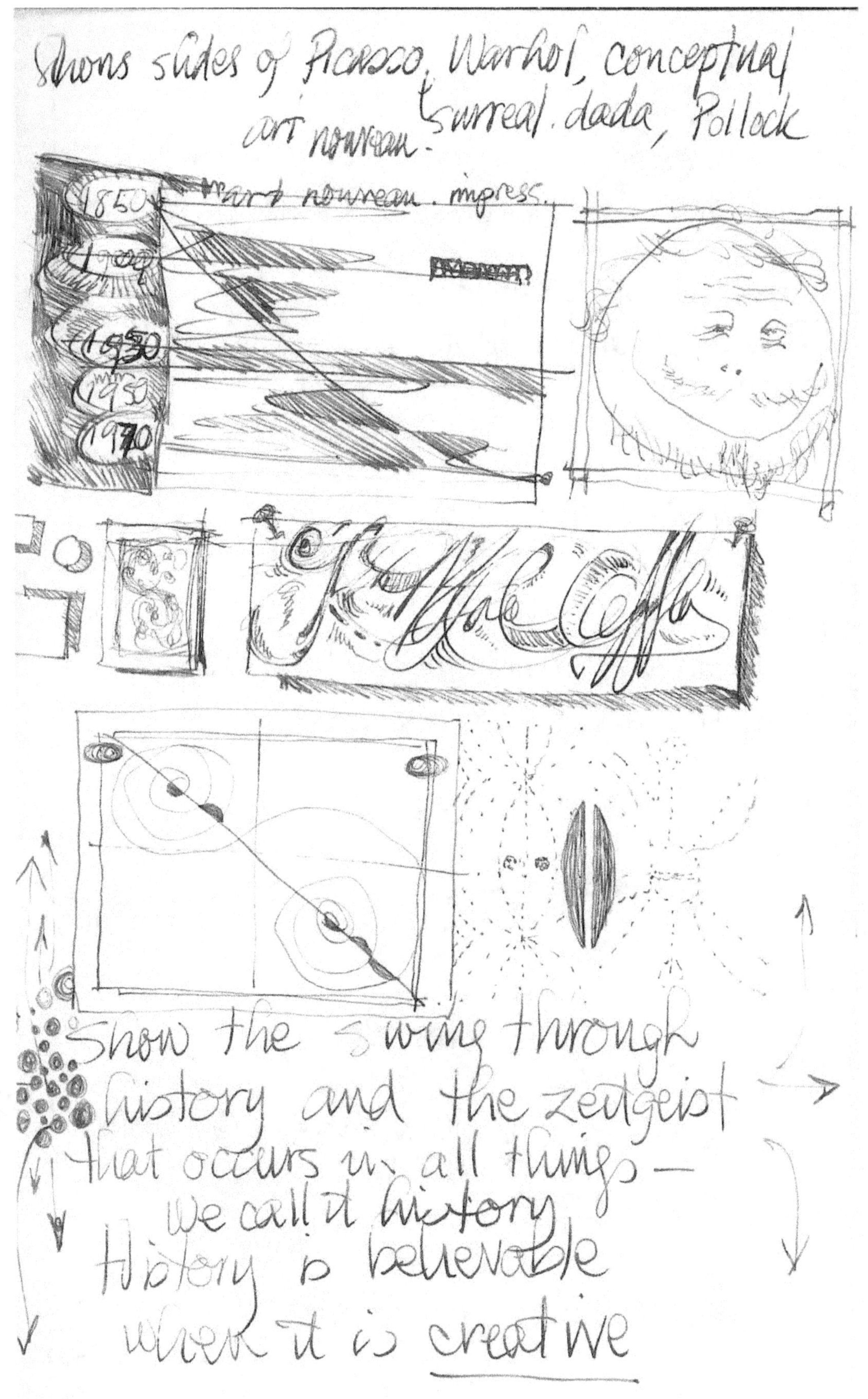

Shows slides of Picasso, Warhol, conceptual
art nouveau. Surreal. dada, Pollock
art nouveau. impress.
1850
1900
1950
1950
1970
show the swing through
history and the zeitgeist
that occurs in all things —
we call it history
History is believable
when it is creative

Process:

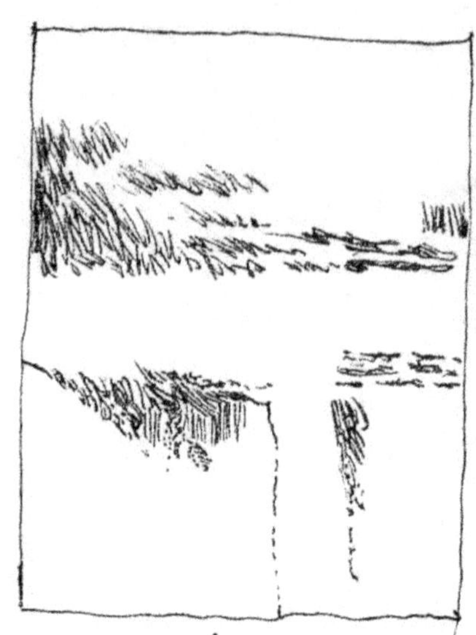

Process is not technique...
Process is not art, but
art in the process of
becoming...
It is not art when it is finished —

Much of the "conceptual" work uses building
materials as invisible tools. Technology creates
new still lifes —

Primitive, Religious, Shrines

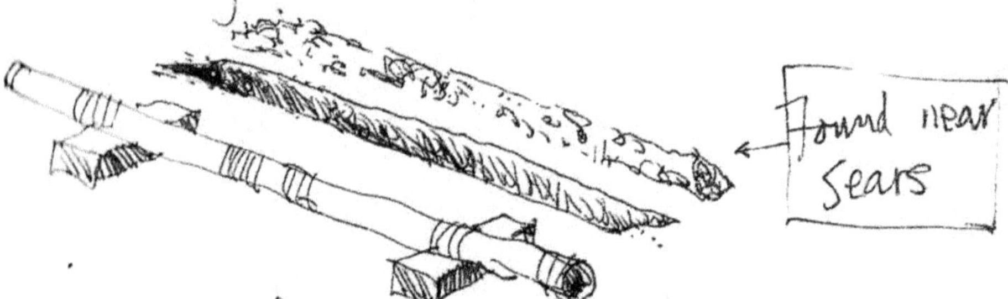

Must get on the
bike and find some more shrines (unknown, unseen)

~~Shrine is one focus~~
Shrines are only one kind of focus —
What else is "direct pointing" — at the moon
                                not the finger...
If traps & shrines
are combined — What?
; Build some traps and find some shrines !

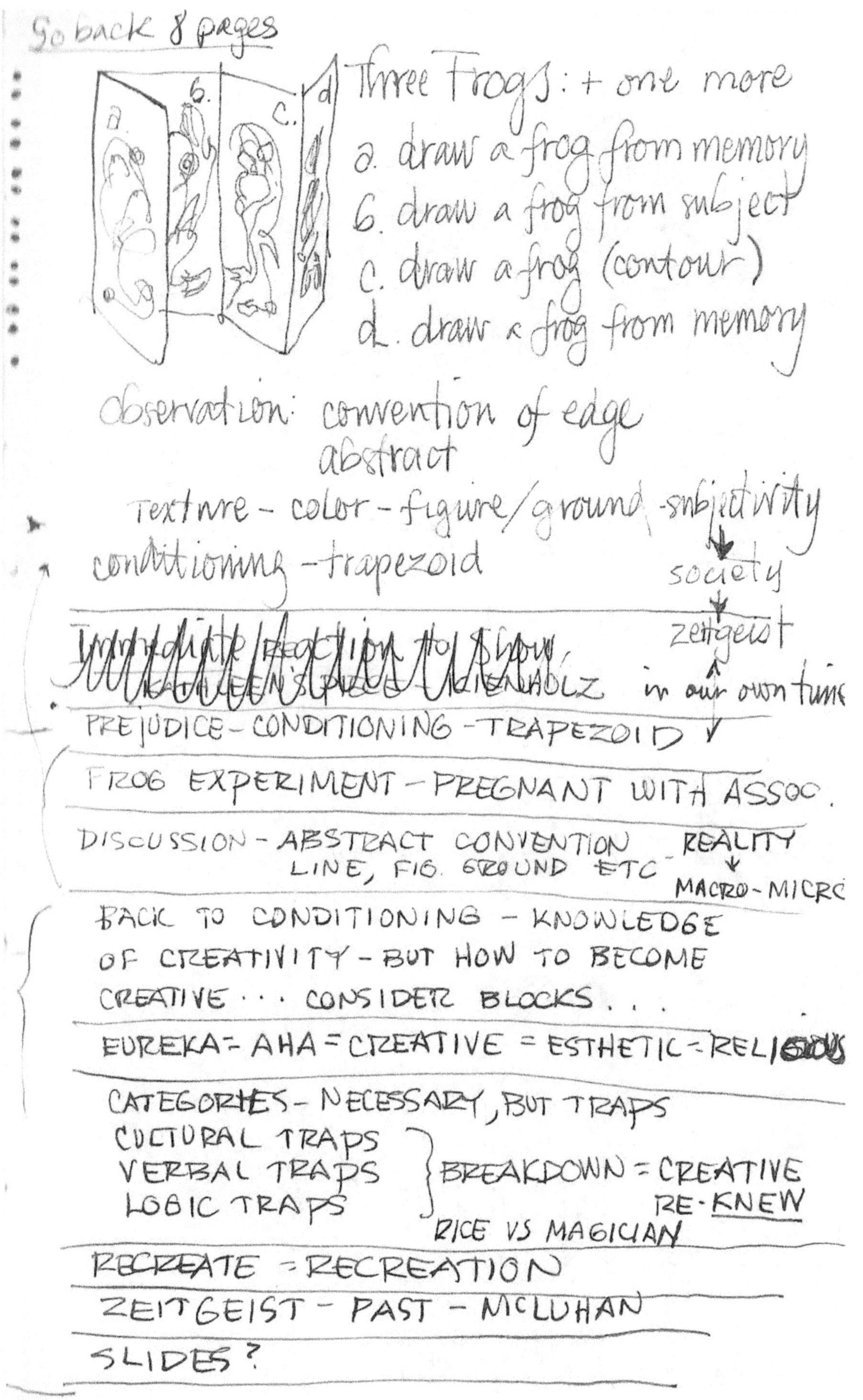

Three Frogs: + one more

a. draw a frog from memory
b. draw a frog from subject
c. draw a frog (contour)
d. draw a frog from memory

observation: convention of edge
          abstract
  Texture – color – figure/ground – subjectivity
conditioning – trapezoid   society
                               zeitgeist

~~Immediate Action to show~~ ~~SPACE~~ in our own time

PREJUDICE – CONDITIONING – TRAPEZOID

FROG EXPERIMENT – PREGNANT WITH ASSOC.

DISCUSSION – ABSTRACT CONVENTION   REALITY
      LINE, FIG. GROUND ETC   MACRO – MICRO

BACK TO CONDITIONING – KNOWLEDGE
OF CREATIVITY – BUT HOW TO BECOME
CREATIVE · · · CONSIDER BLOCKS · · ·

EUREKA = AHA = CREATIVE = ESTHETIC – RELIGIOUS

CATEGORIES – NECESSARY, BUT TRAPS
  CULTURAL TRAPS
  VERBAL TRAPS   } BREAKDOWN = CREATIVE
  LOGIC TRAPS   RE-KNEW
          RICE VS MAGICIAN

RECREATE = RECREATION

ZEITGEIST – PAST – McLUHAN

SLIDES ?

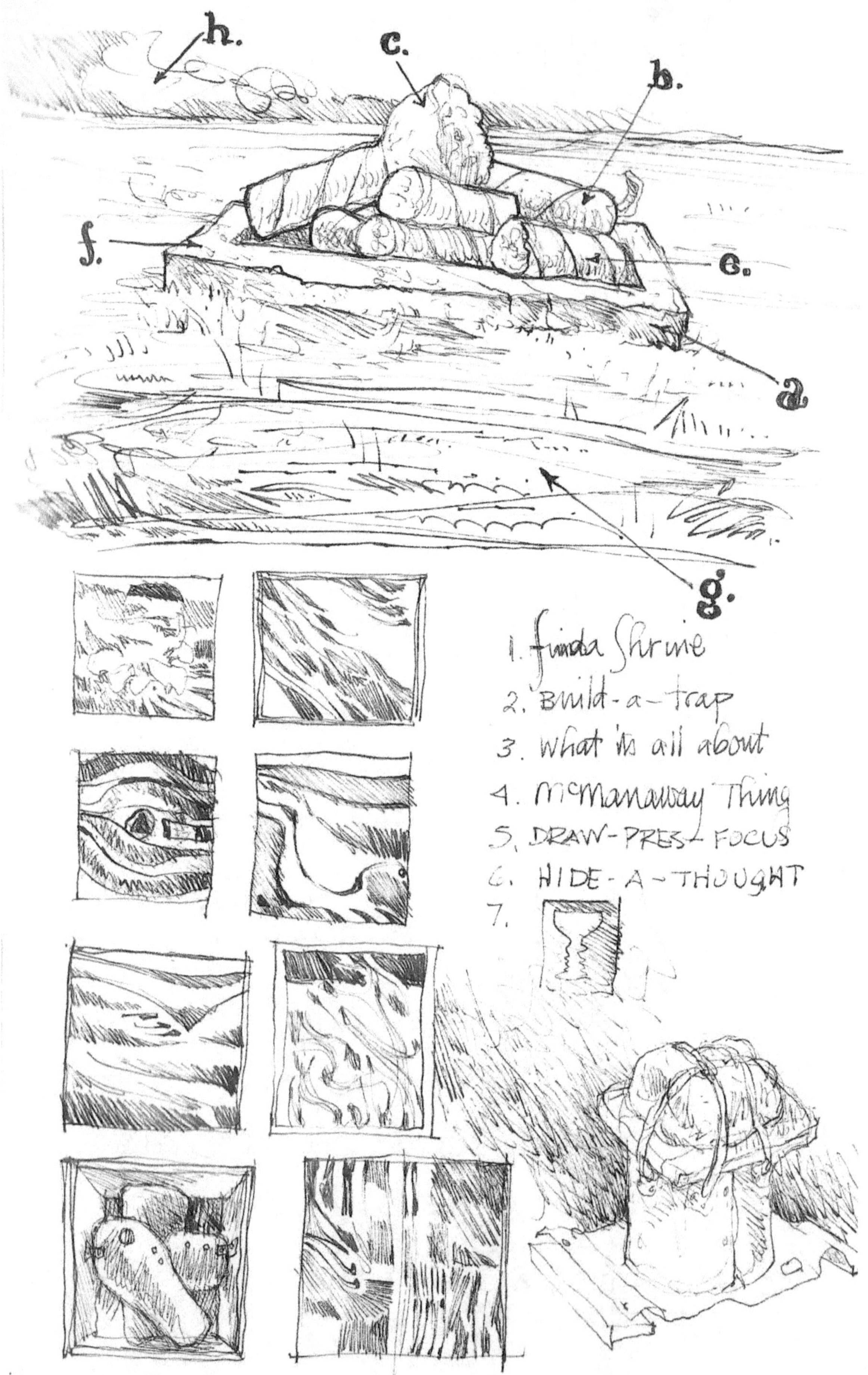

h.
c.
b.
f.
e.
a.
g.
1. finda Shrine
2. Build-a-trap
3. what its all about
4. McManaway Thing
5. DRAW-PRES-FOCUS
6. HIDE-A-THOUGHT
7.

"Dick, Dick, see the dog."
"Yes, Earl, "tell Jim to look."
"Jim, Jim, do you see the
brown dog with no head."
"Yes, Dick, I shall tell
Pat, Jack, ~~Richard~~ and Joe
to come and see. It
is a fine dog. ".
"What are you going to
do with the brown dog,
Dick?"
"Let's give it to Bob he
likes things like that".
"Yes, Yes," said Earl, Jim,
Joe, Richard, ~~and Pat~~.
and Jack

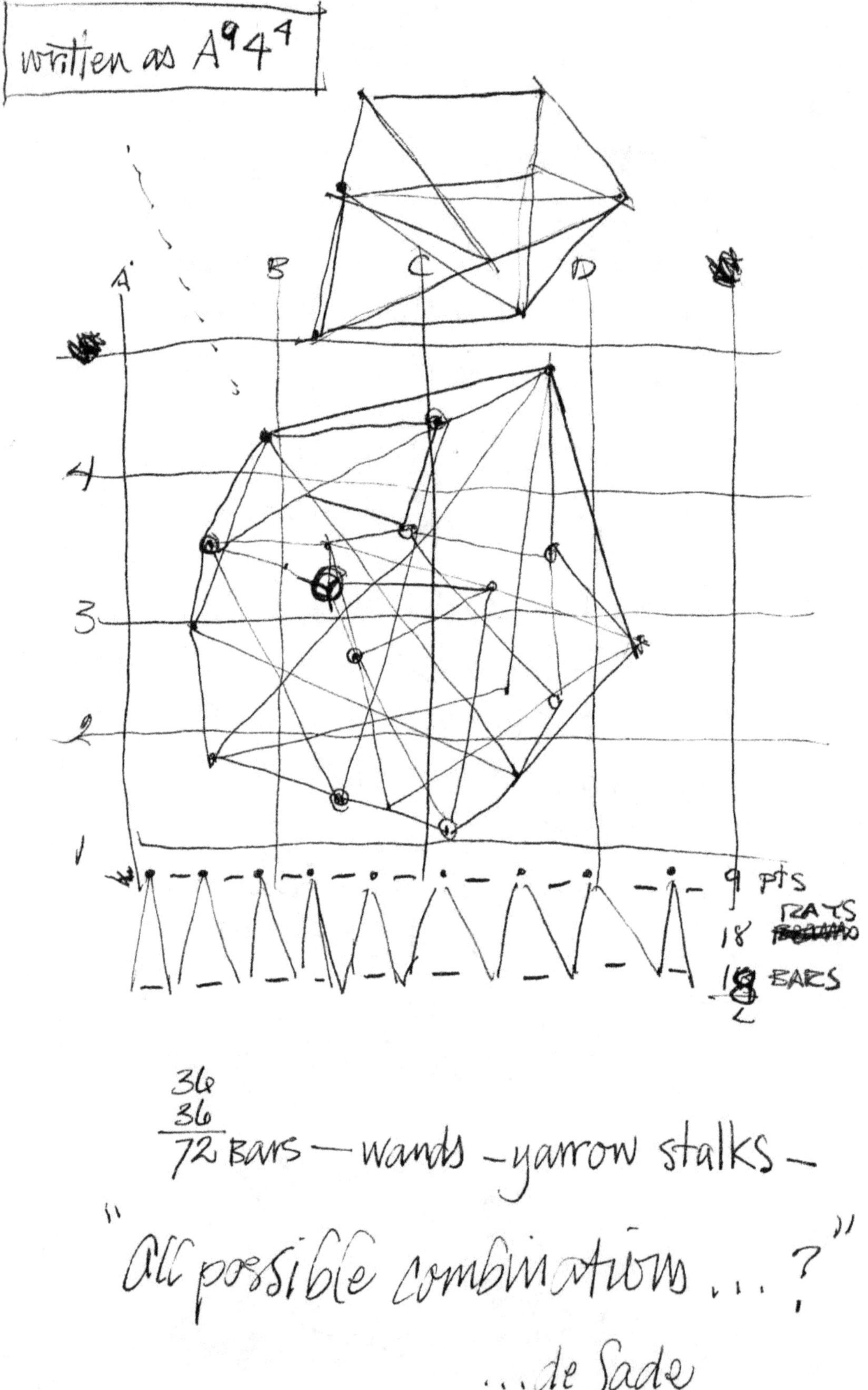

36
36
—
72 BARS — wands — yarrow stalks —

"All possible combinations … ?"

… de Sade

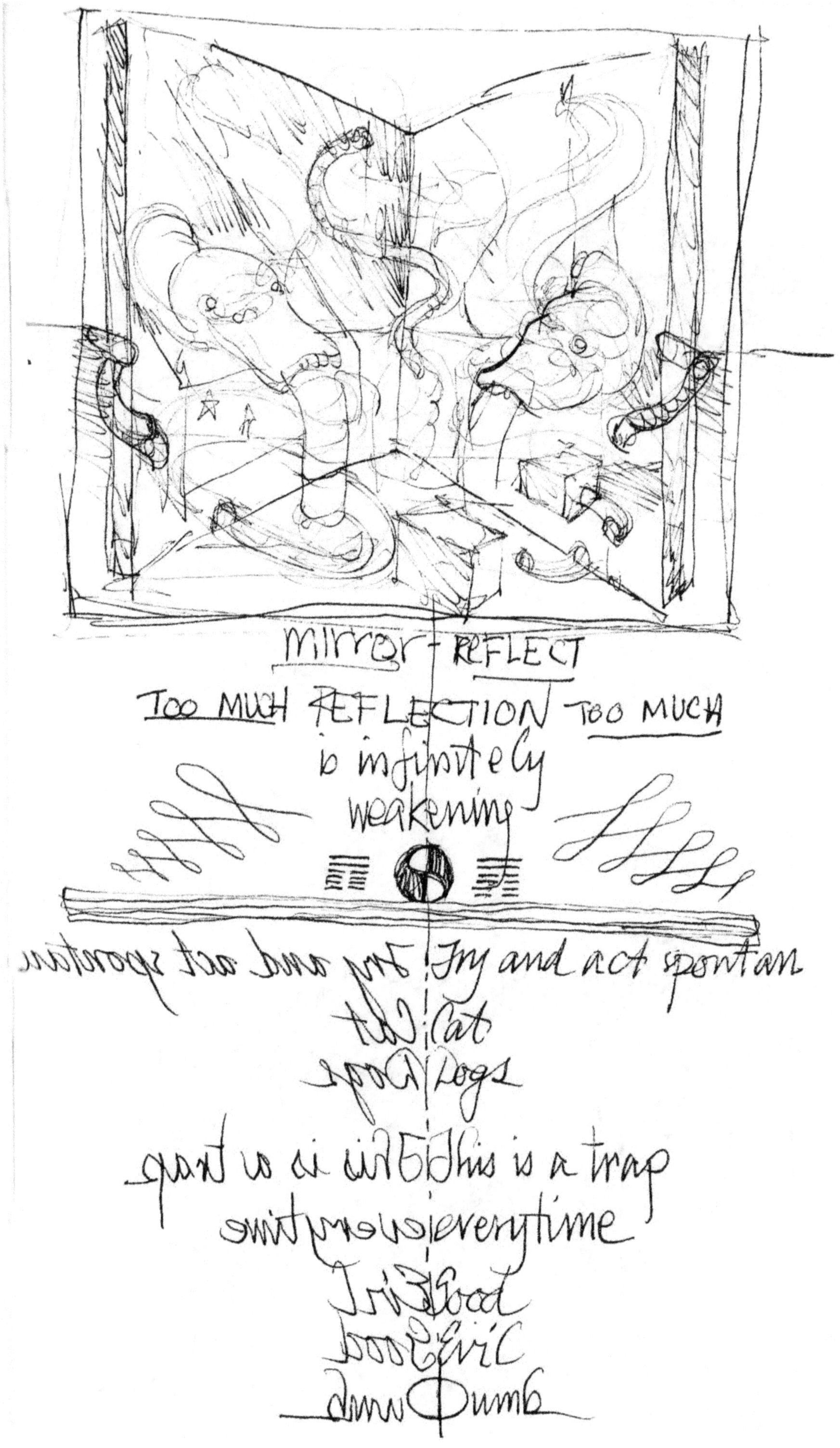

mirror-REFLECT
TOO MUCH REFLECTION TOO MUCH
is infinitely
weakening

Tate's Secret Sign Art:

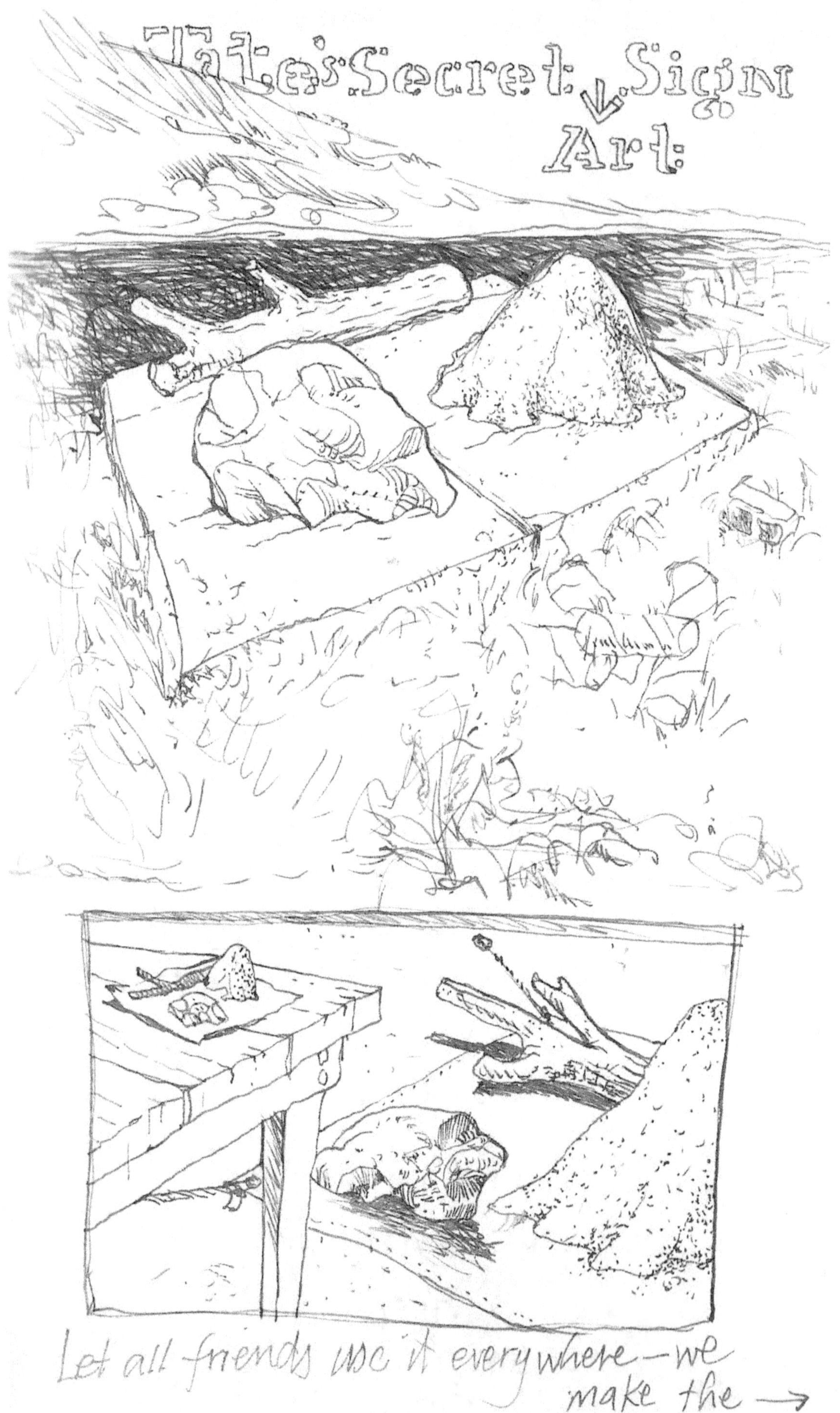

Let all friends use it everywhere—we make the →

I saw Mr. Peanut on the streets of Tulsa, Oklahoma in 1936 (in the winter...

Earl Staley always wanted to see an Oscar Niemeyer Wiener Truck, but never did until after he was married in 1959.

Betty Staley saw Popeye eat a can of spinach (and the can, too) at a theater in Bristol, Virginia in 1945

Bonnie Camblin saw

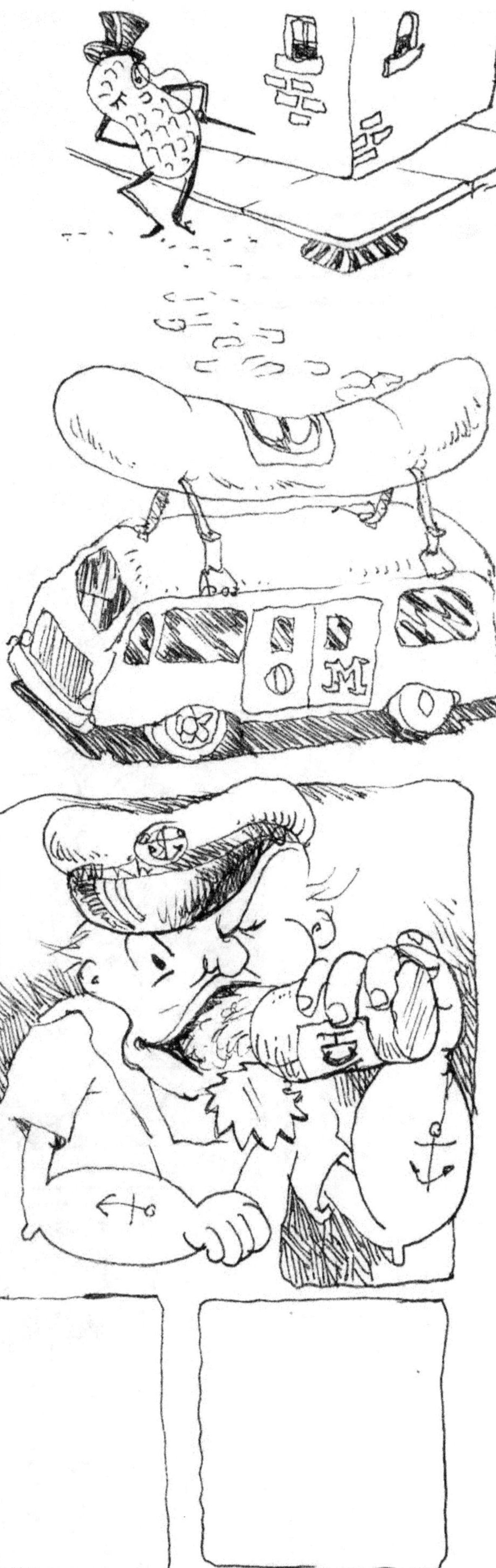

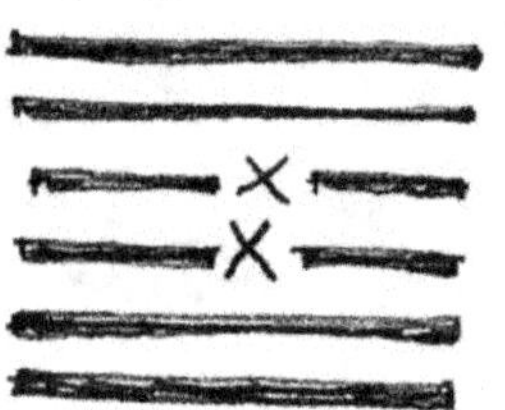

This is the same hexagram thrown last week at the end of the battle...

Dec 14, 1971
Shaw - Albuquerque
Camblin - Houston

CHUNG FU - Inner Truth

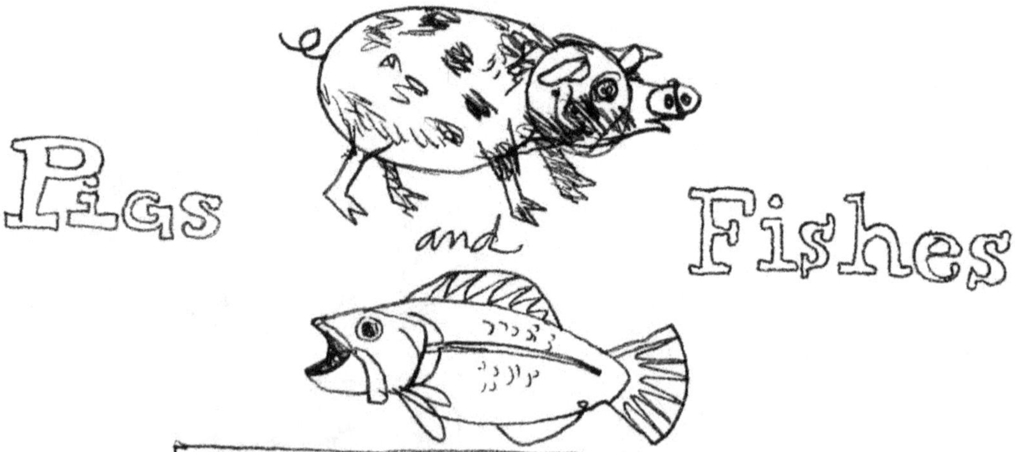

Pigs and Fishes

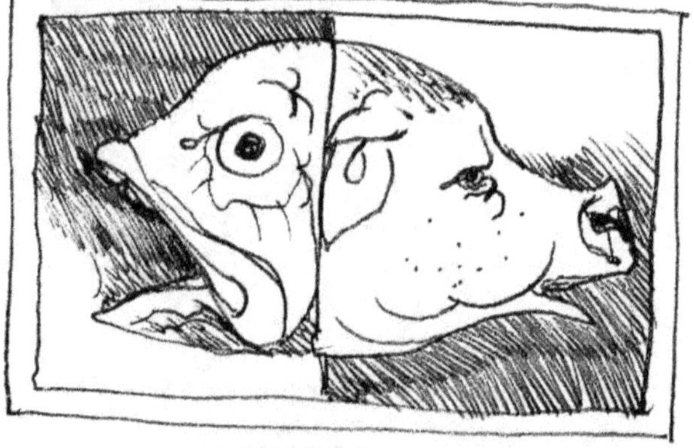

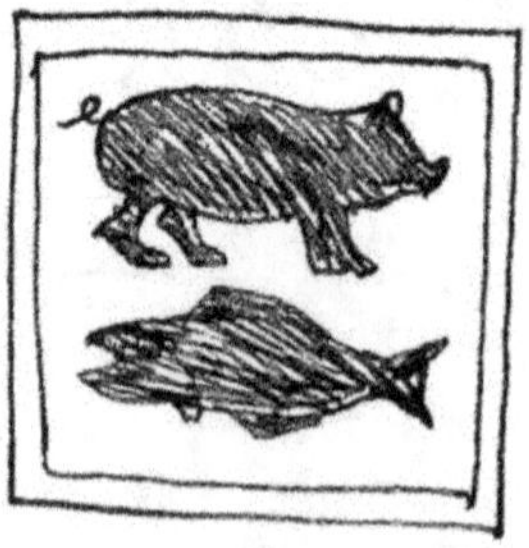

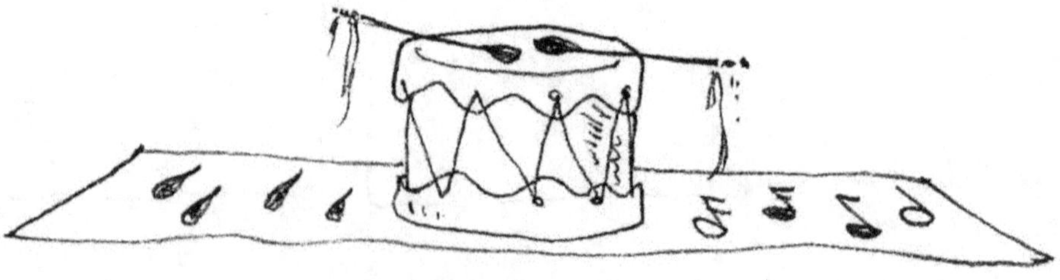

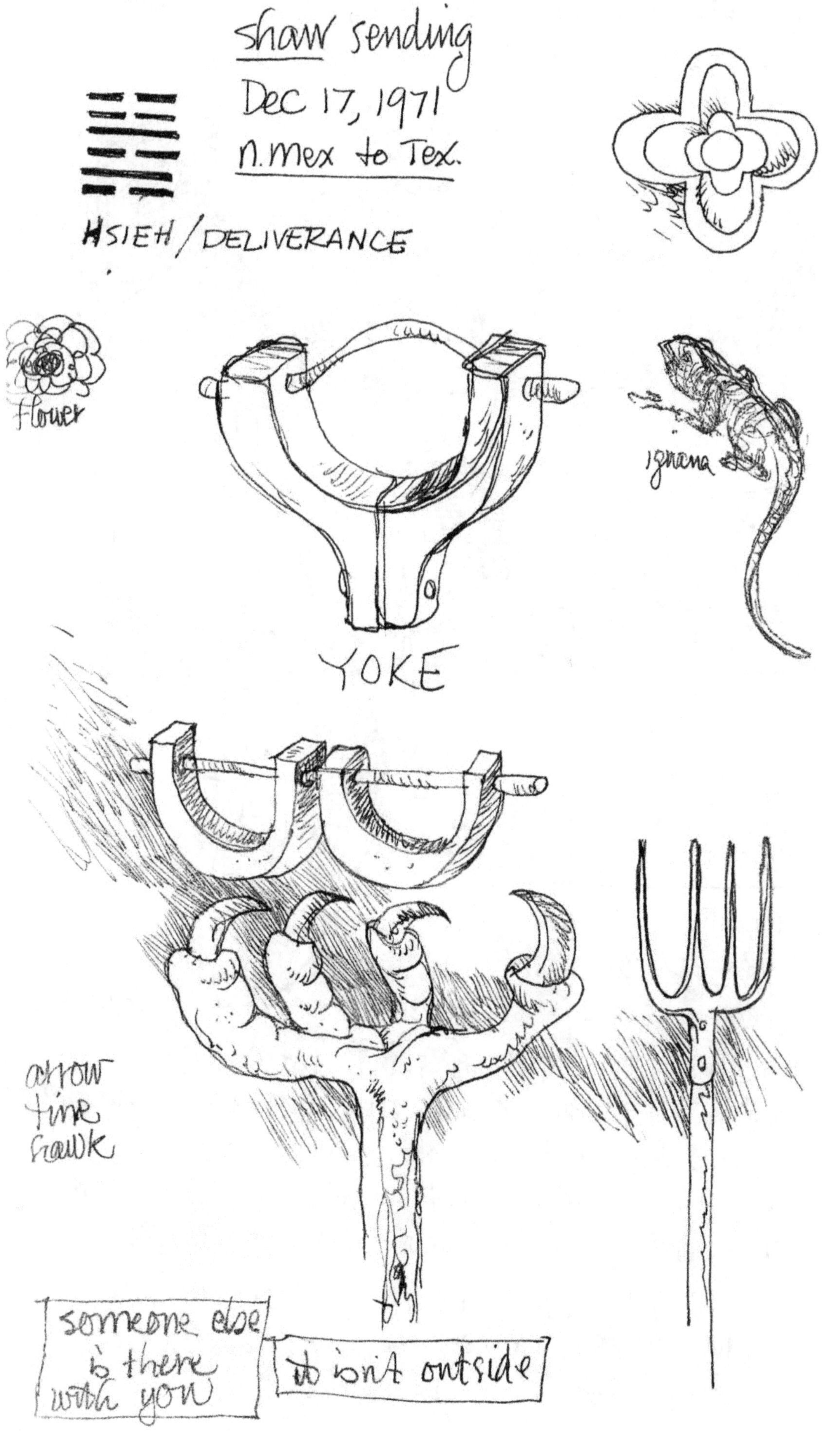

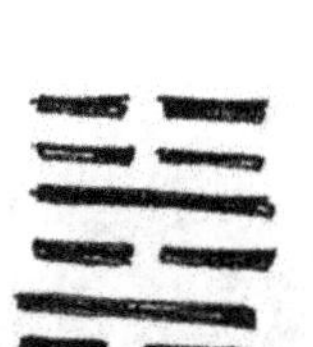

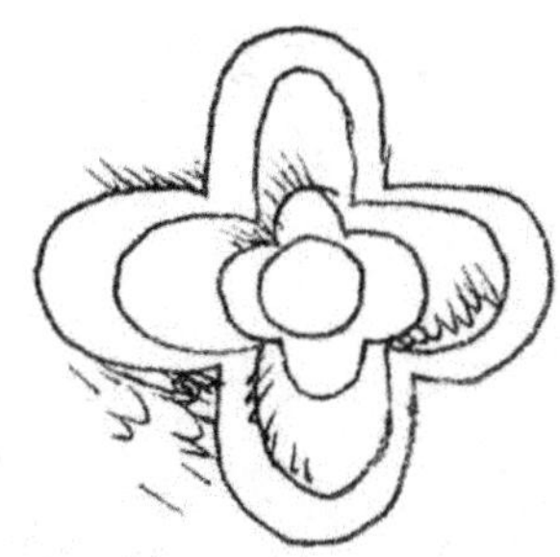

flower

YOKE

iguana

arrow
time
hawk

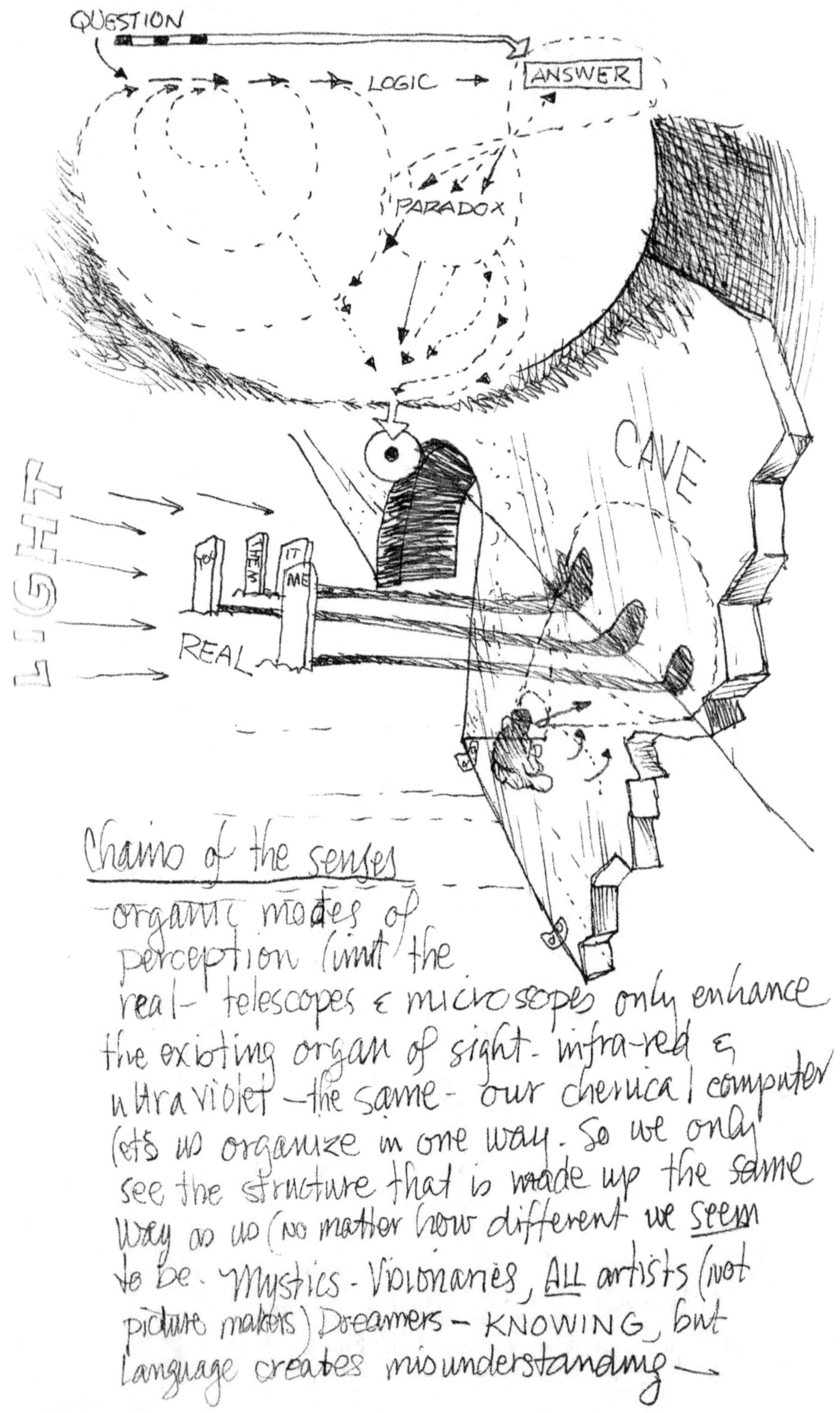

Chaos of the senses
- organic modes of
perception limit the
real - telescopes & microscopes only enhance
the existing organ of sight. infra-red &
ultra violet - the same - our chemical computer
lets us organize in one way. So we only
see the structure that is made up the same
way as us (no matter how different we seem
to be. Mystics - Visionaries, ALL artists (not
picture makers) Dreamers - KNOWING, but
language creates misunderstanding -

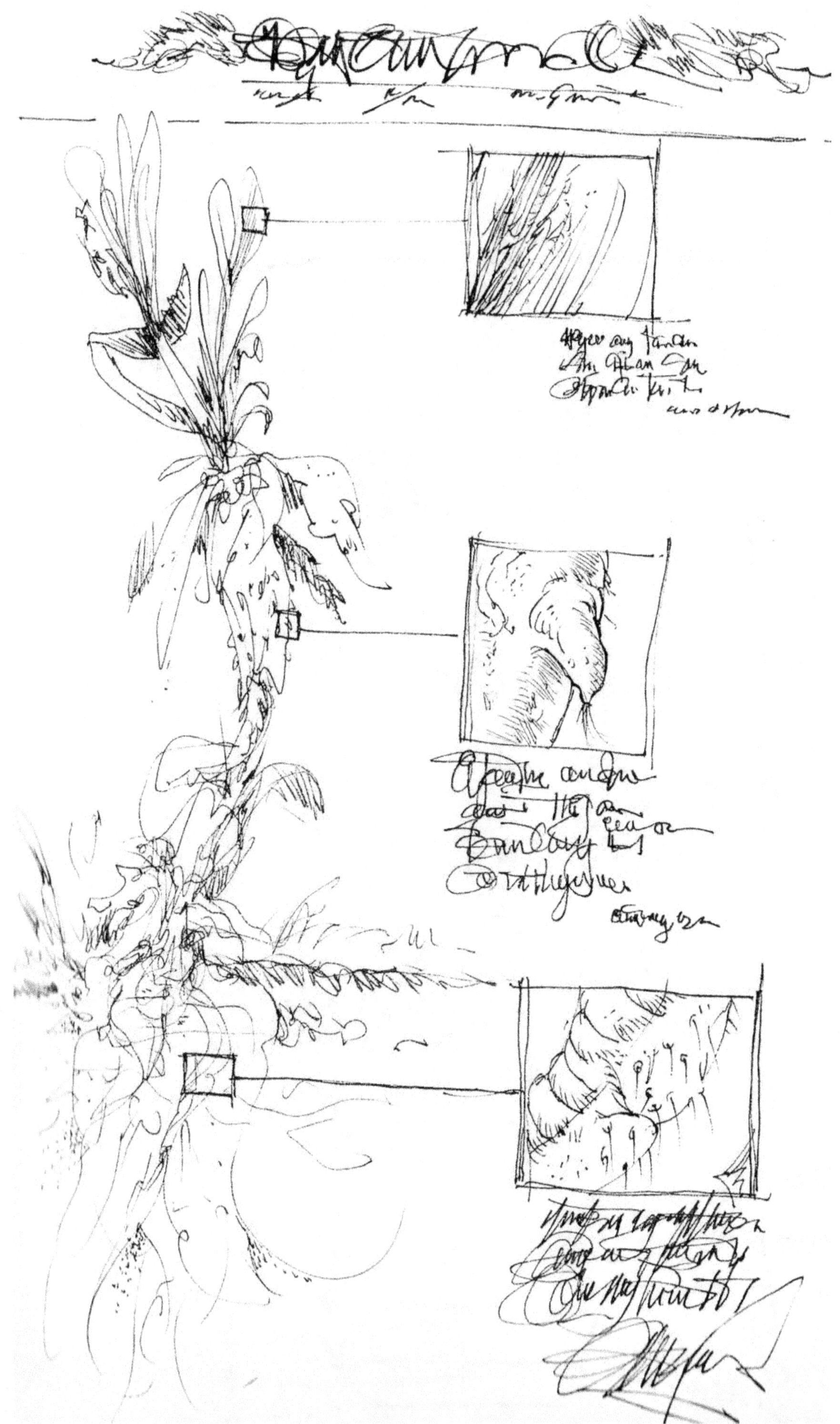

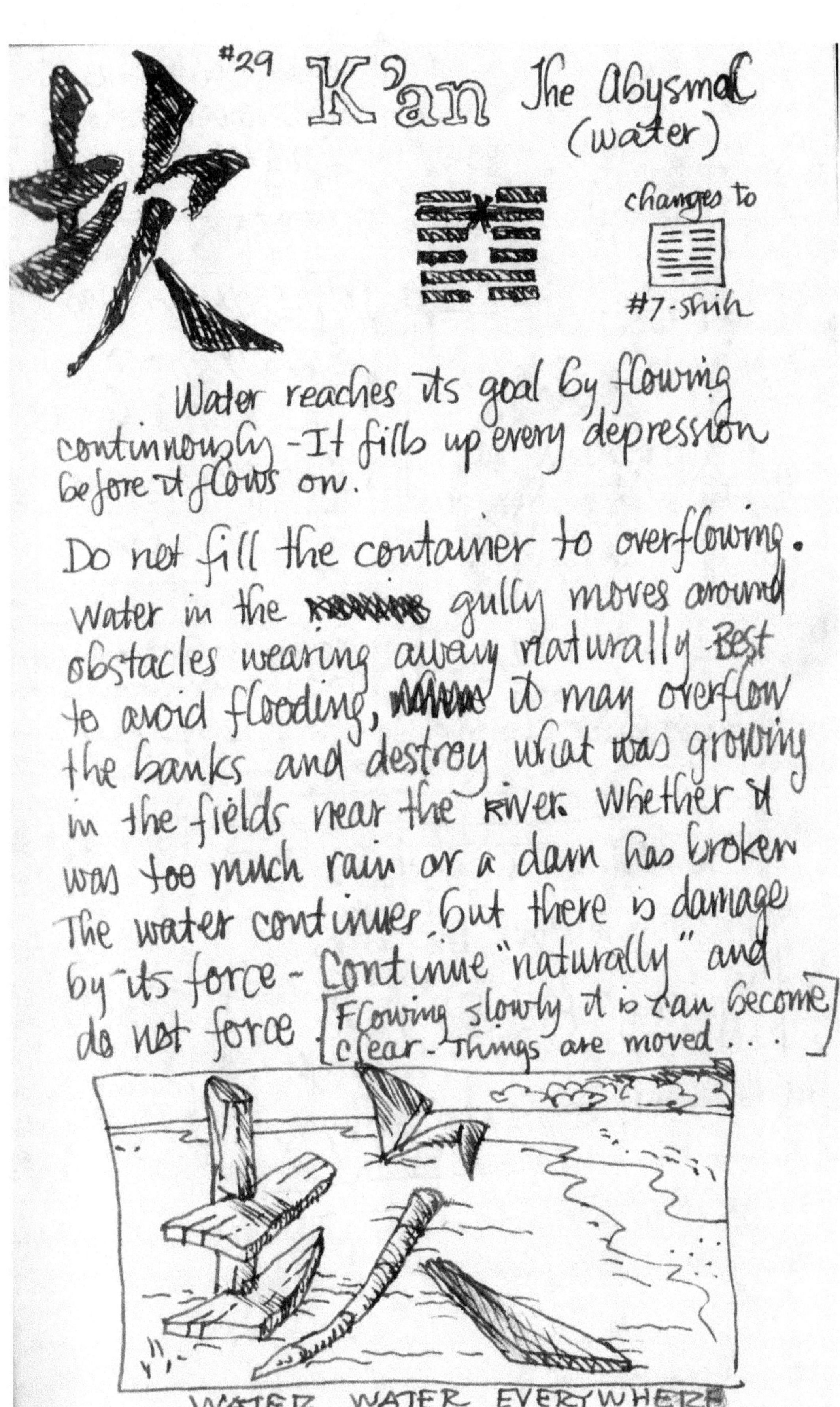

Water reaches its goal by flowing continuously – It fills up every depression before it flows on.

Do not fill the container to overflowing. Water in the ~~xxxxx~~ gully moves around obstacles wearing away naturally – Best to avoid flooding, ~~xxxx~~ it may overflow the banks and destroy what was growing in the fields near the river. Whether it was too much rain or a dam has broken the water continues, but there is damage by its force – Continue "naturally" and do not force. [Flowing slowly it is can become clear – Things are moved . . .]

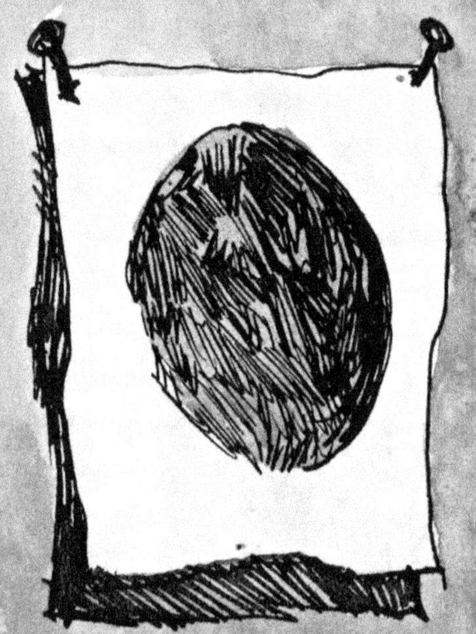

To find the power that is no power.
To do the work that is not work.
To laugh the true laugh.

BENDING IS NOT BOWING

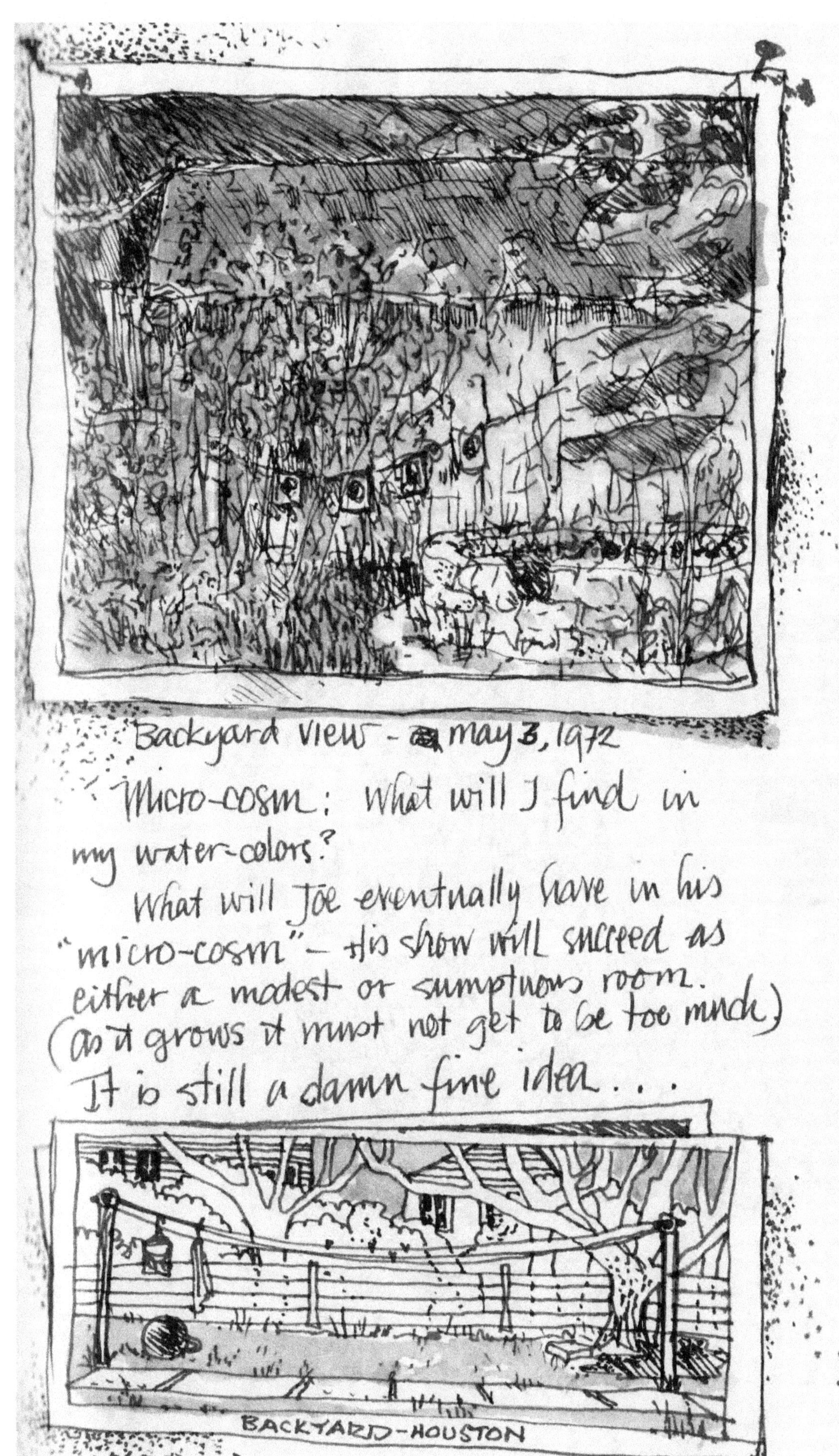

Backyard view - May 3, 1972

Micro-cosm: What will I find in my water-colors?

What will Joe eventually have in his "micro-cosm" — His show will succeed as either a modest or sumptuous room. (as it grows it must not get to be too much) It is still a damn fine idea . . .

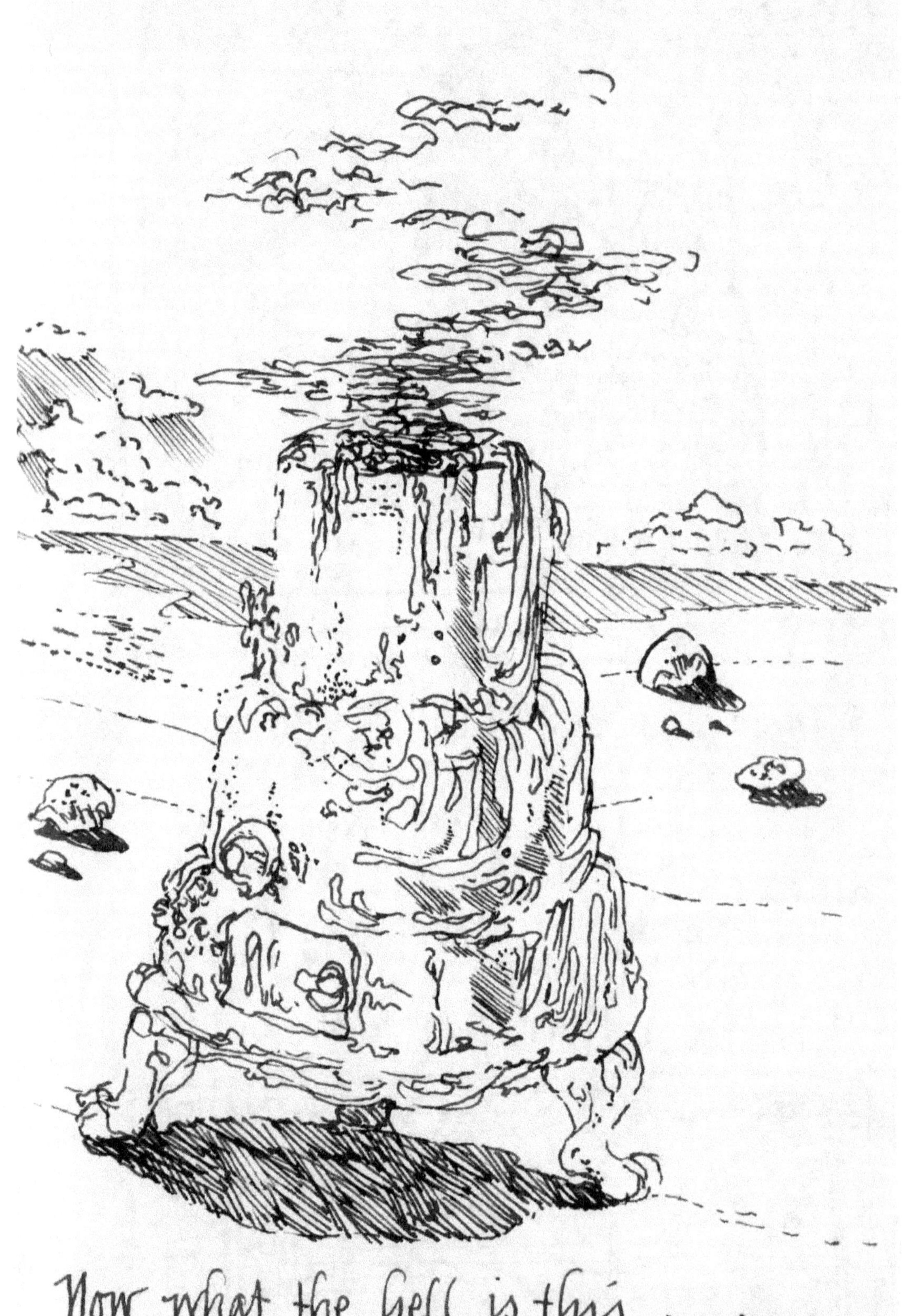

Now, what the hell is this . . .

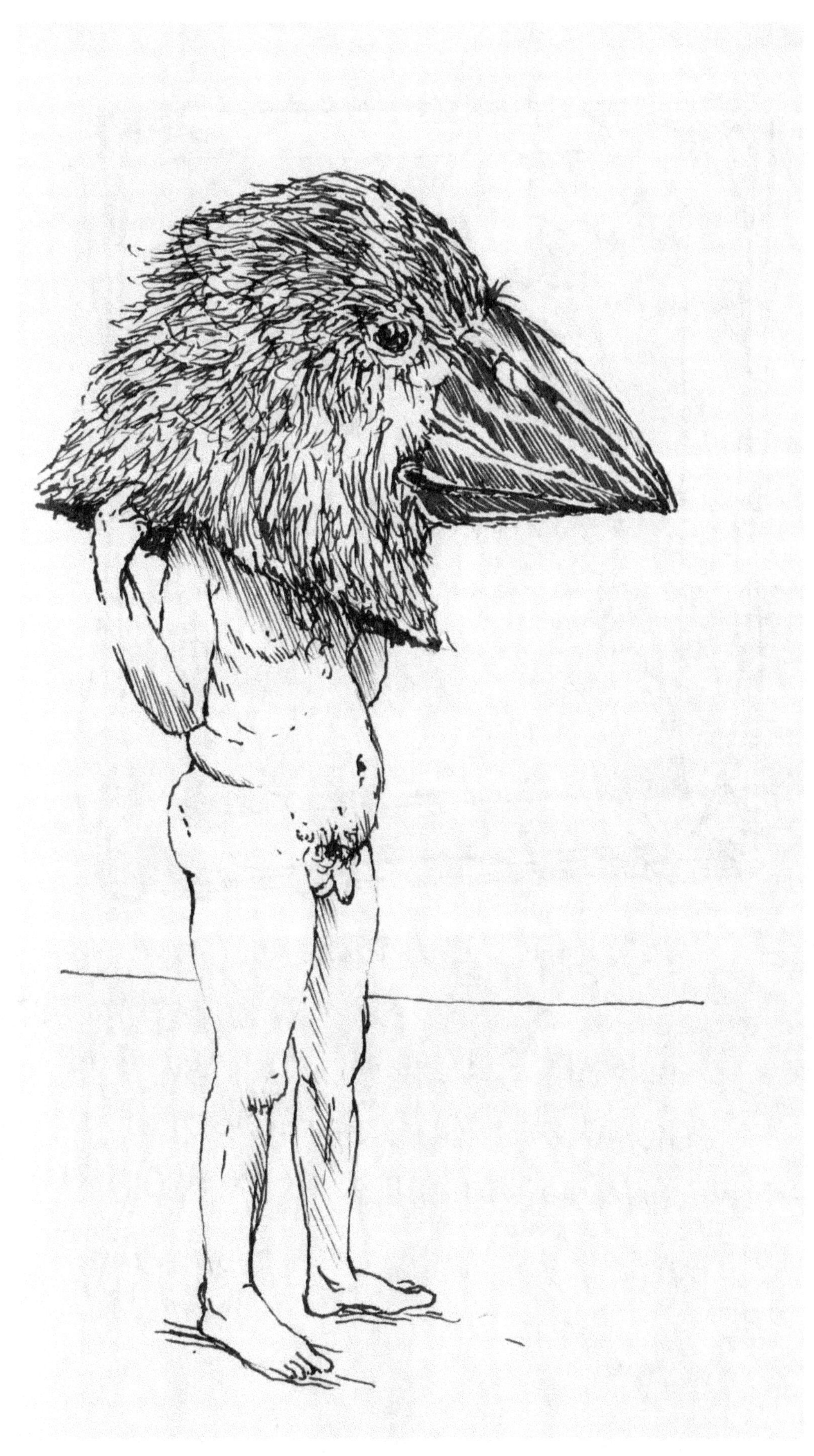

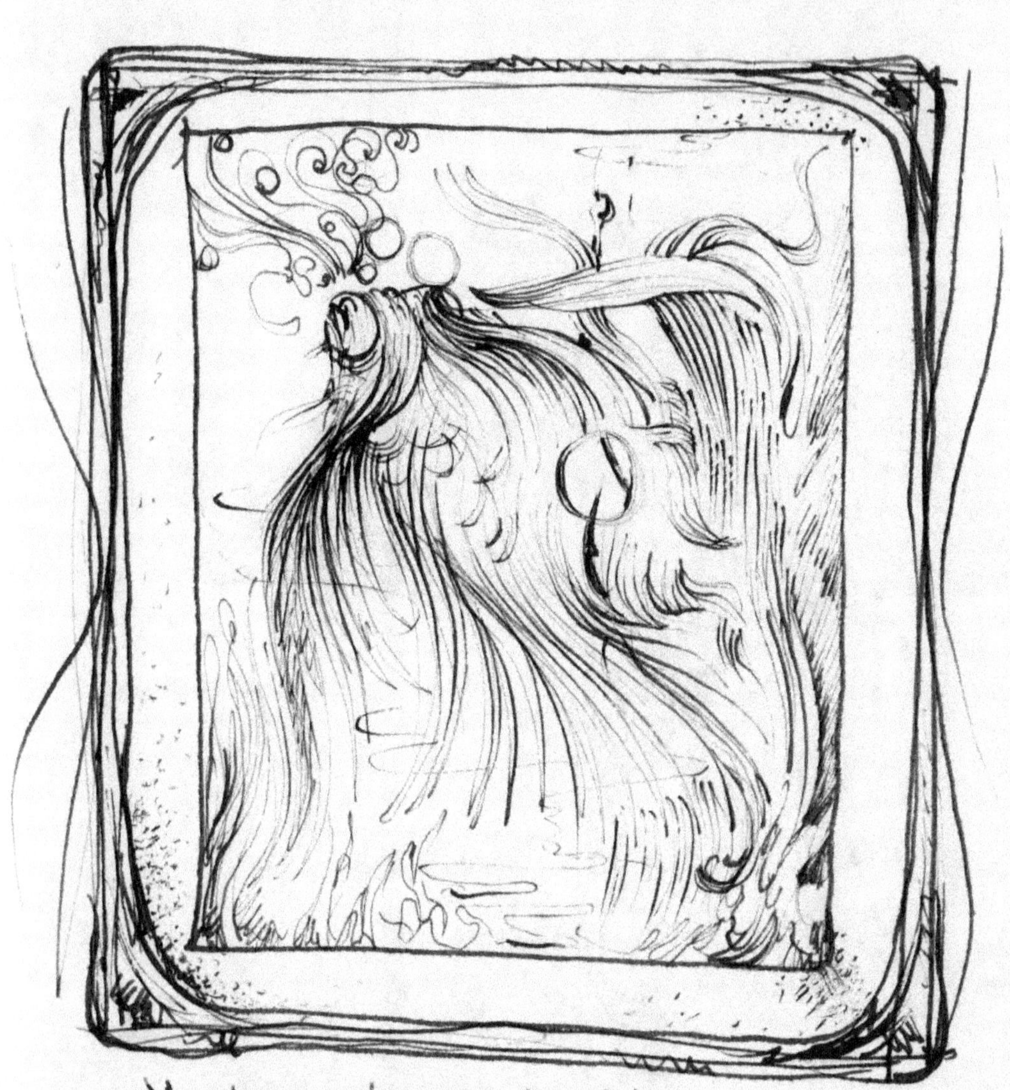

"How strange to think of giving up
all ambition!
Suddenly I see with such clear eyes
The white flake of snow
That has just fallen in the horse's mane!"

Robert Bly
— Naked Poetry

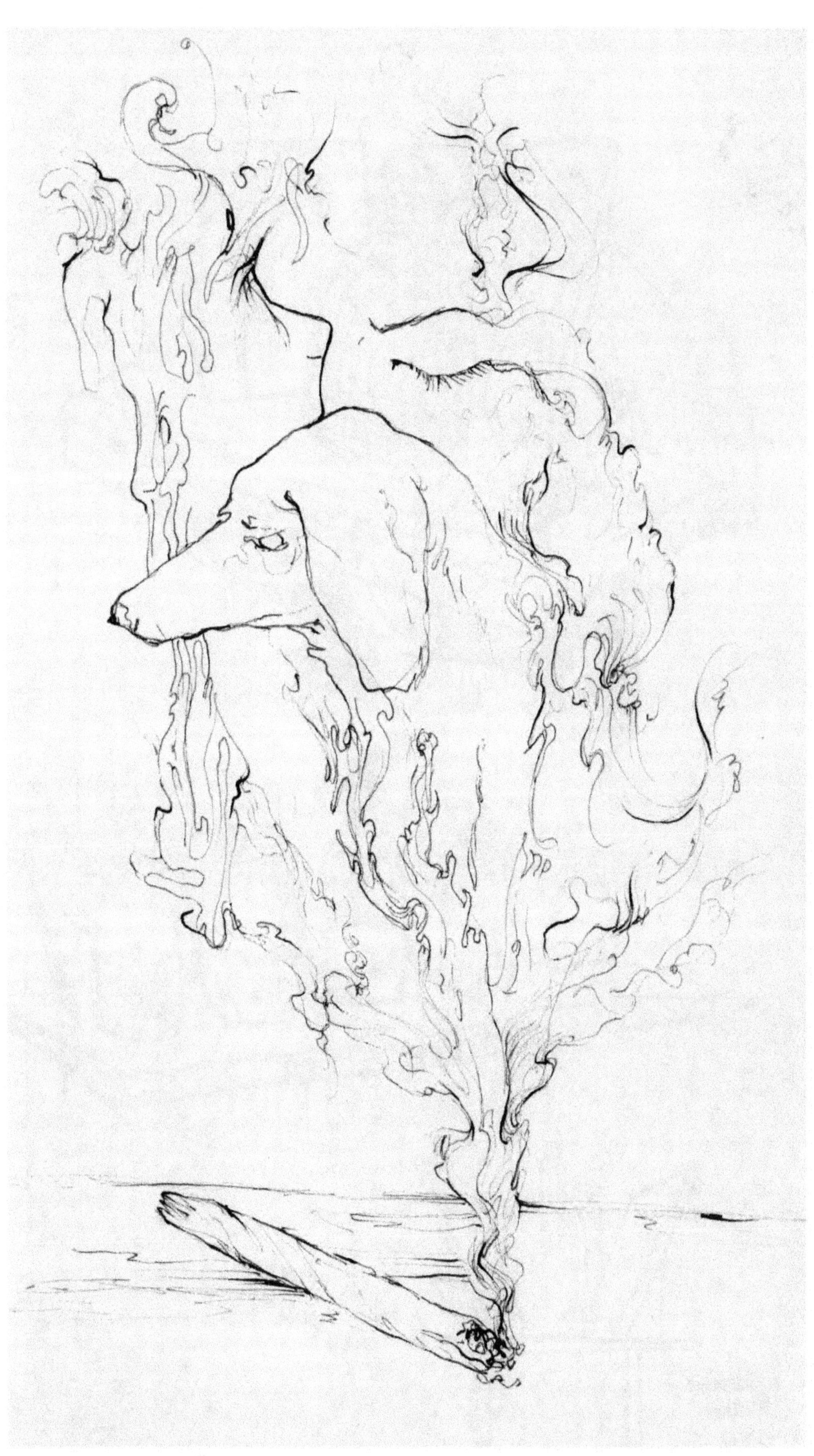

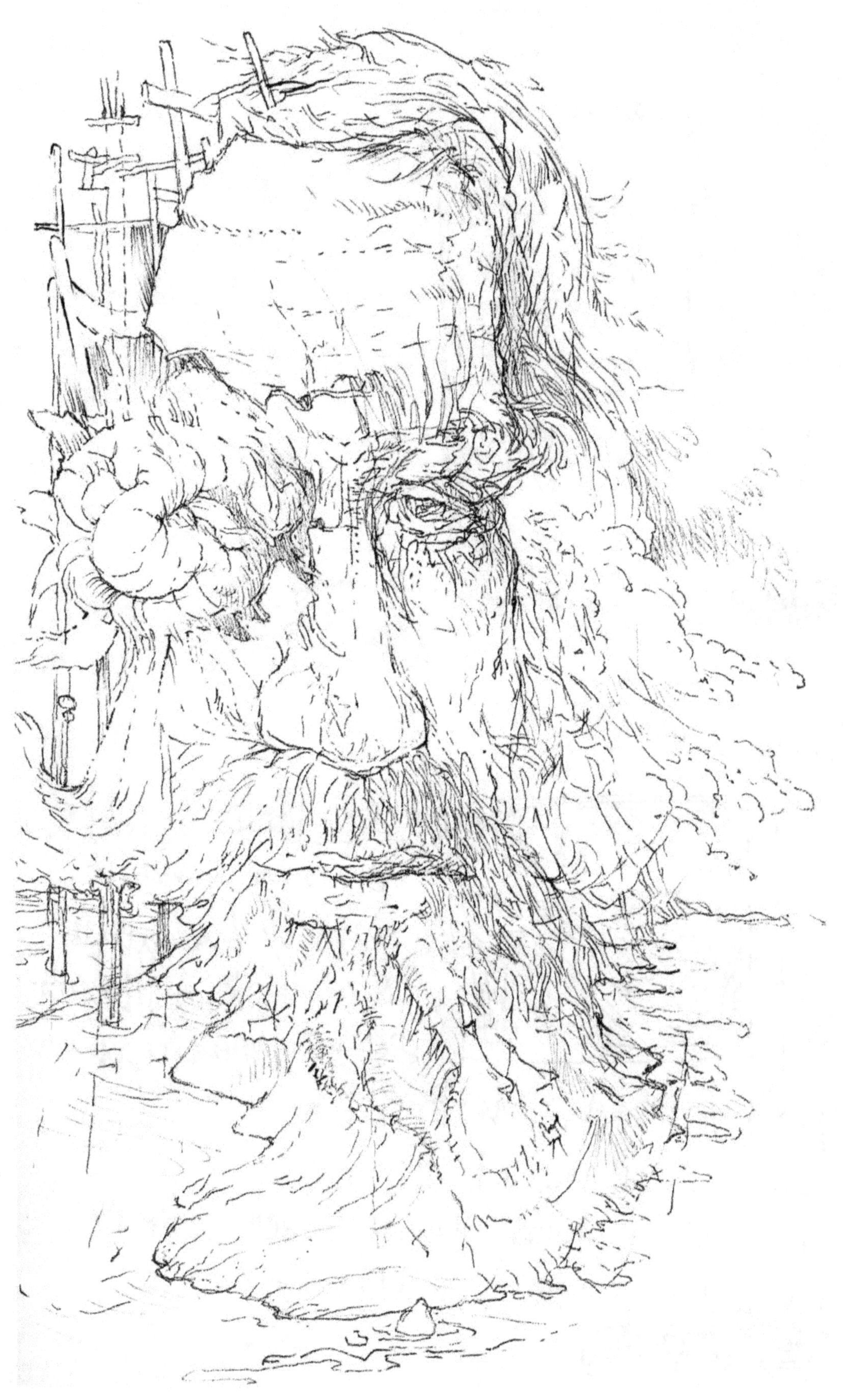

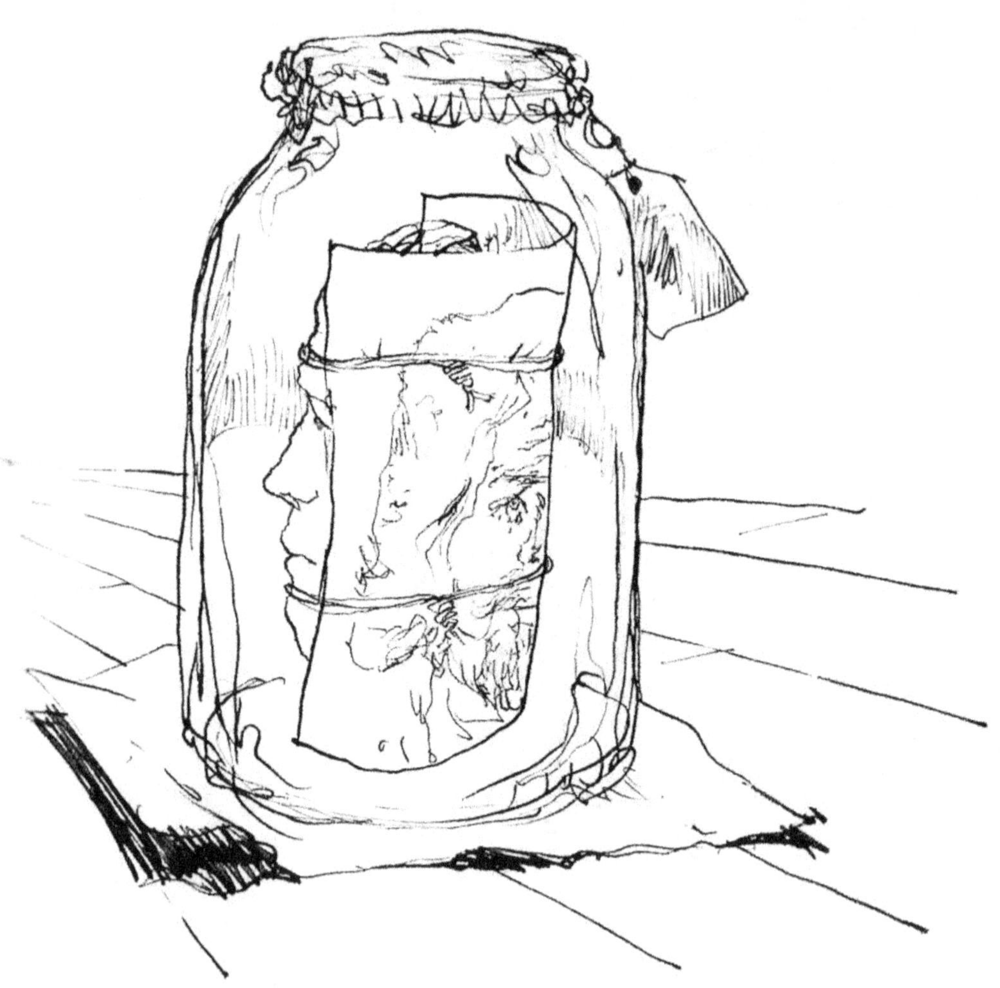

Vortex

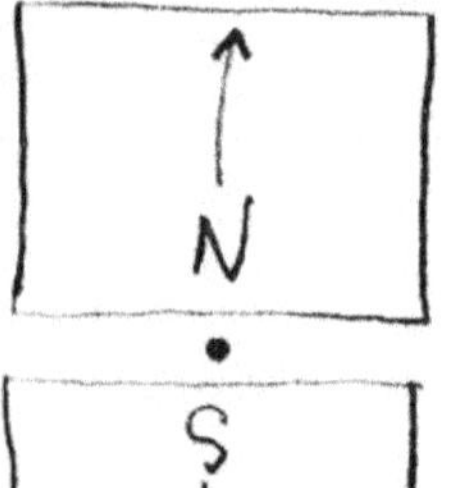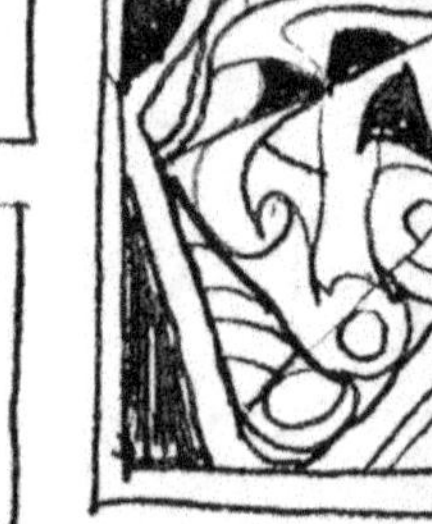

Are Vortex's real?
How come I never
heard of this except
as a trick or illusion
put in a mountain.

gravity — visual distortion.
vision is chemical-electric
sunspots causes event/electric scramble
the moon — tides, menstration

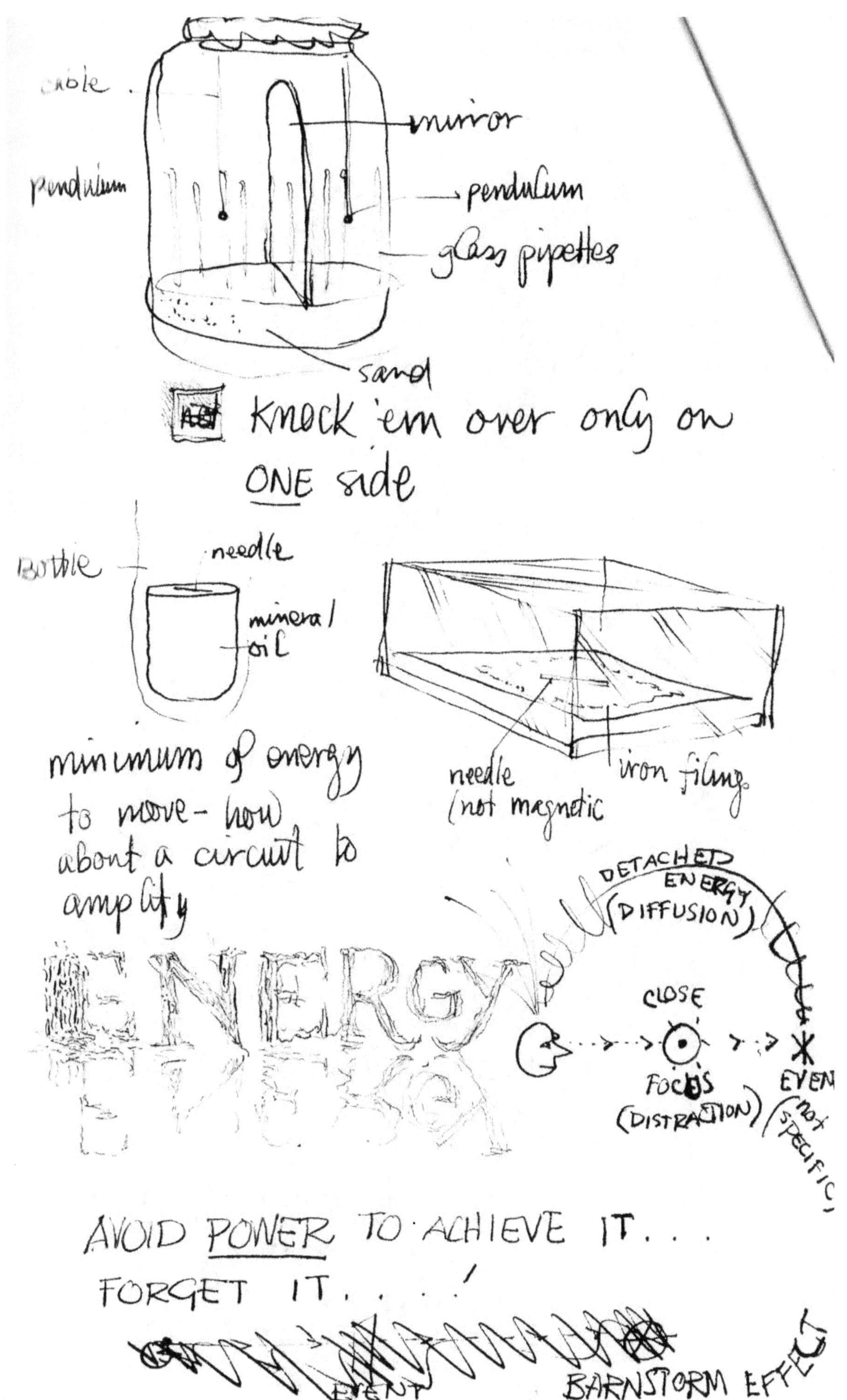

cable
pendulum
mirror
pendulum
glass pipettes
sand
Knock 'em over only on ONE side
Bottle
needle
mineral oil
needle (not magnetic
iron filing
minimum of energy to move - how about a circuit to amplify
ENERGY
DETACHED ENERGY (DIFFUSION)
CLOSE
FOCUS (DISTRACTION)
EVEN (not specific)
AVOID POWER TO ACHIEVE IT....
FORGET IT.....!
EVENT
BARNSTORM EFFECT

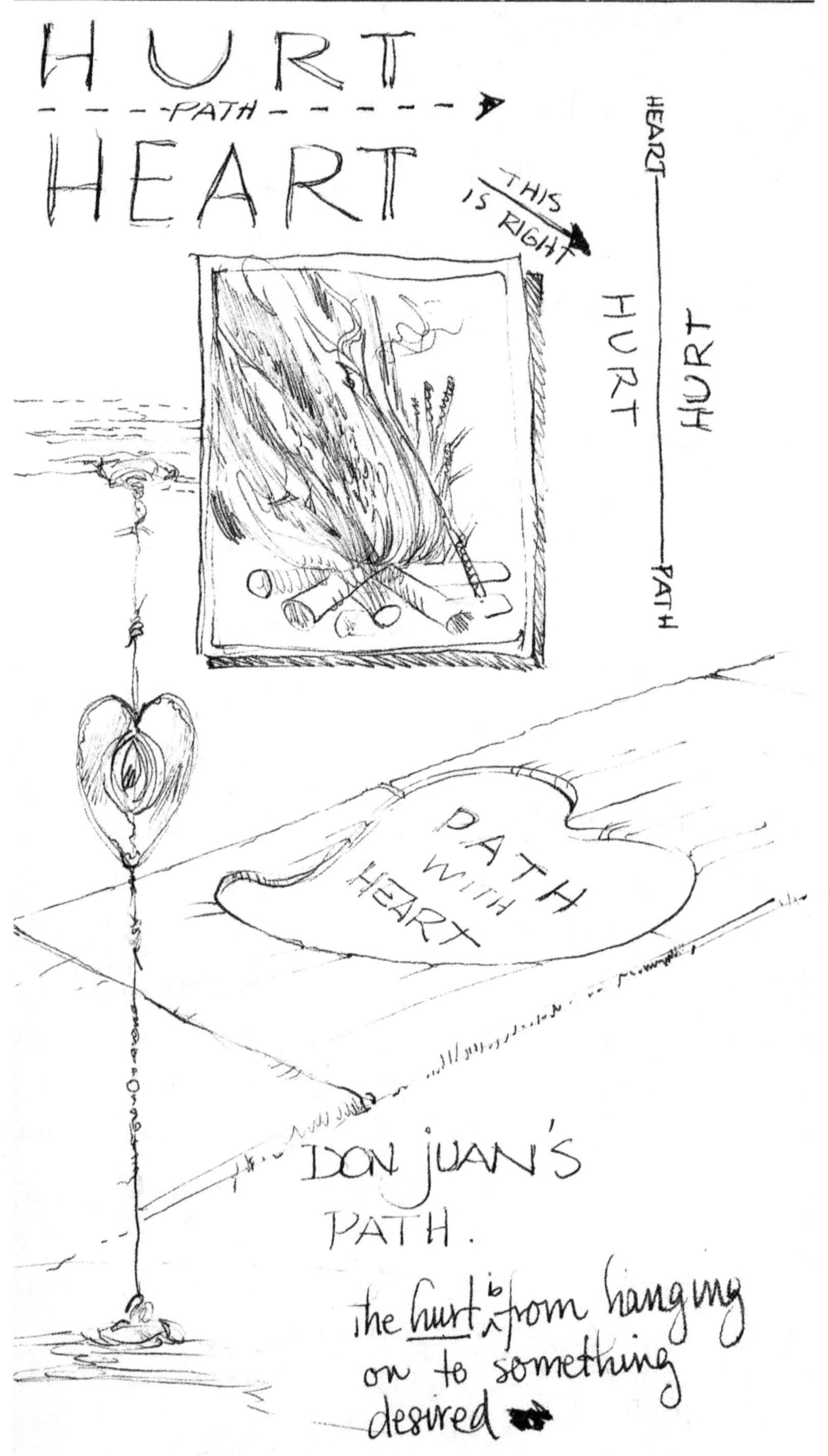

HURT
PATH
HEART
THIS IS RIGHT
HEART
HURT
HURT
PATH
PATH WITH HEART
DON JUAN'S PATH.
the hurt is from hanging on to something desired

As Looking at a page and not
seeing words — seeing shapes
lines & spaces. Keep staring
but don't "Look" — Find something.
else - but don't think - The Mind
You can do it easy in Japanese
unless you can read the calligraphy

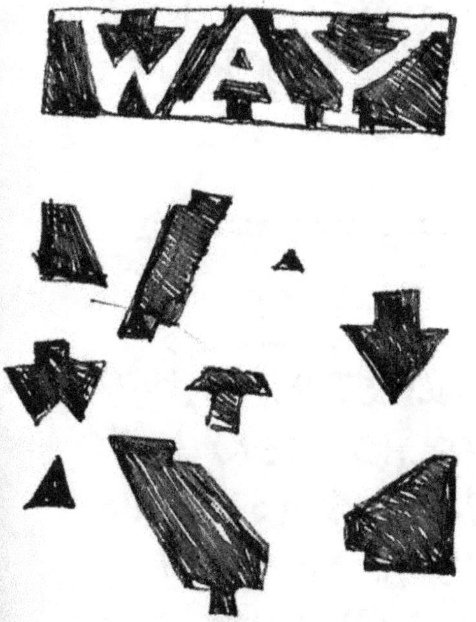

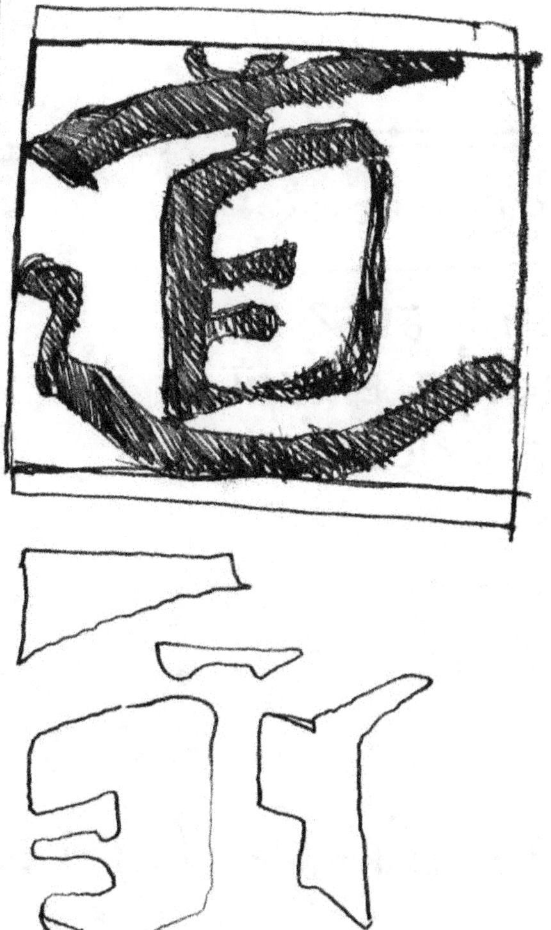

Parts of
the Way

Figure and ground shows the way...
Life - Book - same thing we focus on only
one thing - SEE the page and you also get the
information

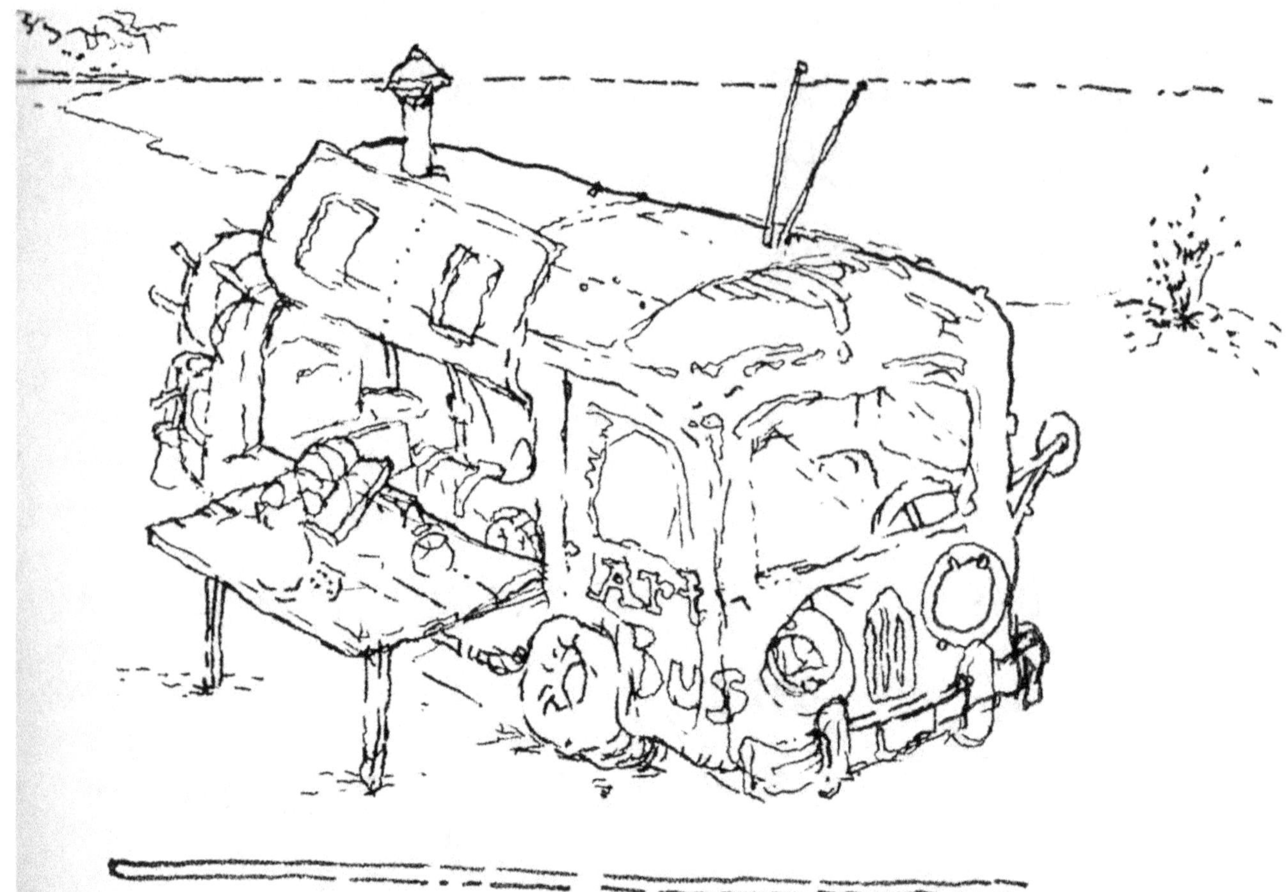

BUSINESS	ART
NOTHING EVER CHANGES EXCEPT THE PRICE	GALVESTON IS TO HOUSTON AS HOUSTON IS TO DALLAS AS DALLAS IS TO NEW YORK AS NEW YORK IS TO WORLD MARKET. NOTHING EVER CHANGES . . .

The changes that never change
are coming faster and faster!

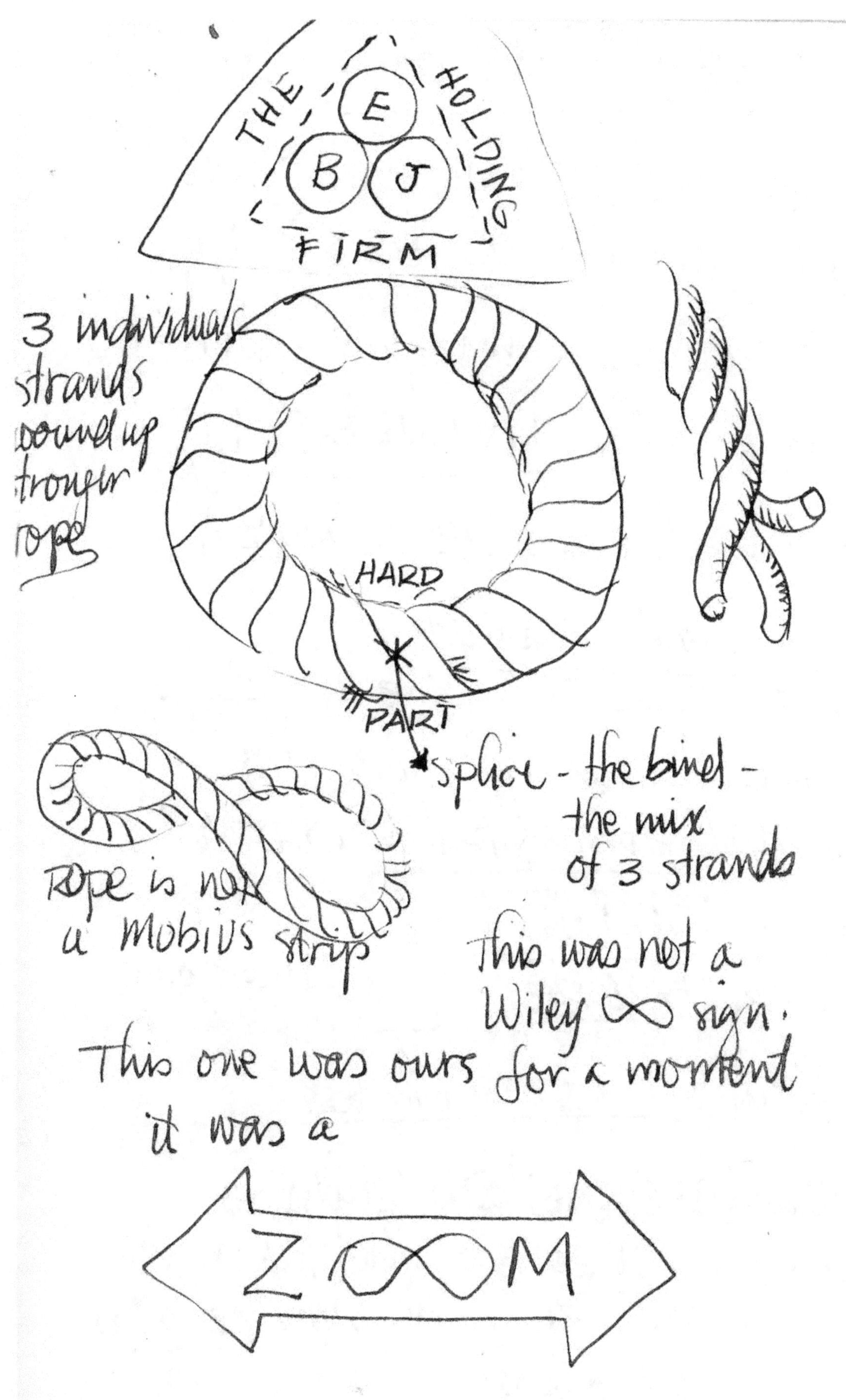

THE HOLDING FIRM
E
B J
3 individual strands wound up stronger rope
HARD PART
splice - the bind - the mix of 3 strands
rope is not a Mobius strip
this was not a Wiley ∞ sign.
This one was ours for a moment
it was a
ZOOM

<u>Failure is its own Reward!</u>

Do you ever imagine yourself
seen as a <u>SUCCESS</u>? ☐☐
                Y N

Do you ever imagine yourself
seen as a <u>FAILURE</u>? ☐☐
              Y N

Give best example (scenario)
of <u>each fantasy</u>.
A. ______________ B. ______________

Which do you do the
most <u>fantasizing</u> about?

  A. [SUCCESS] ____
  B. [FAILURE] ____   check one

Why? ___ 25 words or less. ___

~~Answer the question~~ Reply to
the statement at the Beginning.
      <u>FAILURE IS ITS OWN REWARD</u>
in a short essay.

           this completes the test

reverse until balanced
until both can REACH

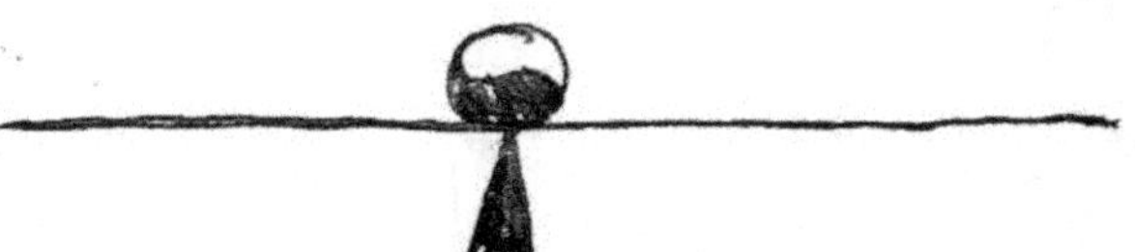

equilibrium - but precarious

The only game in town is see-saw*

*DON JUAN'S
. . . SEEING

HOW FAR DO YOU TRAVEL BEFORE
YOU CAN STOP
CENTERED

EXTREME

CAN YOU   KEEP YOUR

BALANCE

if not — where do you place yourself
on the see-saw of:

- MANIC - DEPRESSIVE - INTERIOR EXT &
- GOOD - ~~KINDS~~ EVIL - INT & EXT.
- ~~OPTIMISM - PESSIMISM - INT & EXT~~
- MALE - FEMALE (SUBJ.) INTER.
- MALE - FEMALE (RELATIONSHIP) EXT.

- other kinds of action

add weight as
you move
toward
CENTER

WHEN ONE DOWN
ON EITHER END
NO GAME

UNTIL ONE
MOVES IN OR OUT

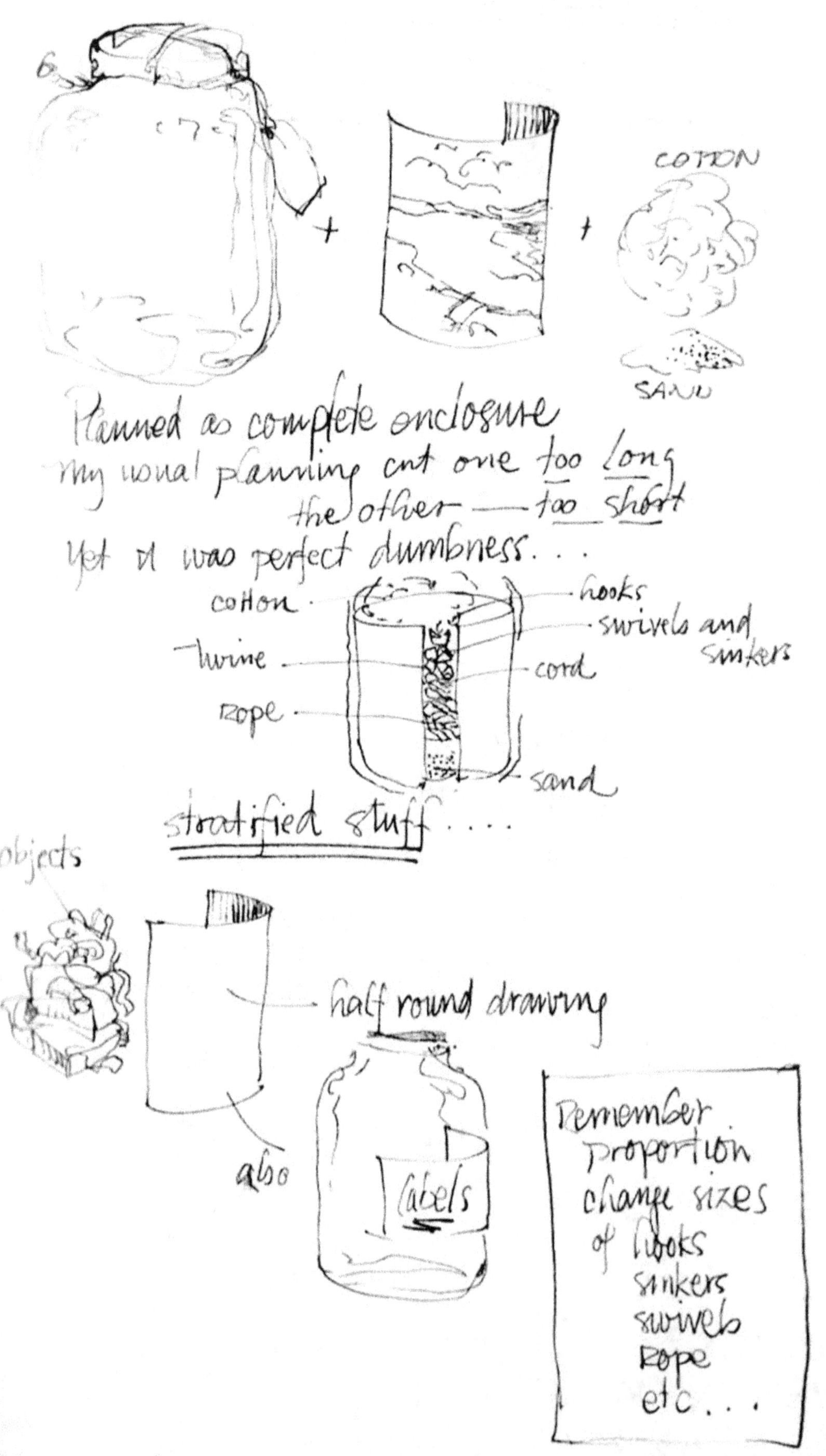

Planned as complete enclosure
my usual planning cut one too long
the other —— too short
Yet it was perfect dumbness. . .

stratified stuff . . . .

Since anything can turn into Phenomena how do you focus and not stop _seeing_. Find what phenomena cause the rising hackle and visceral knot and look again and again- start anywhere — with _intensity_!!

Once you can "flip the switch" then try it on _everything_ - find your way.

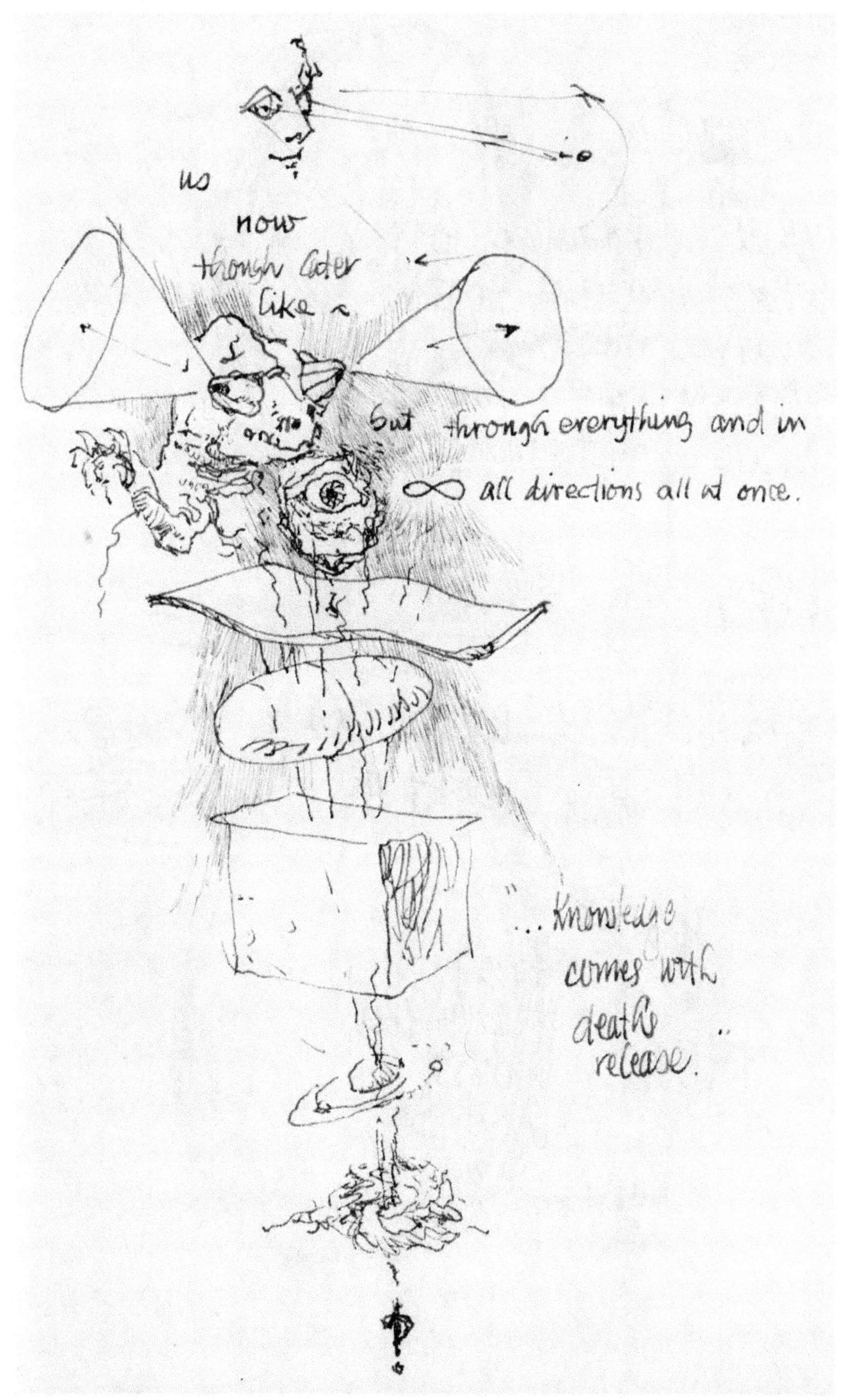
us
now
through later
like
but through everything and in
all directions all at once.
"...Knowledge
comes with
death
release."

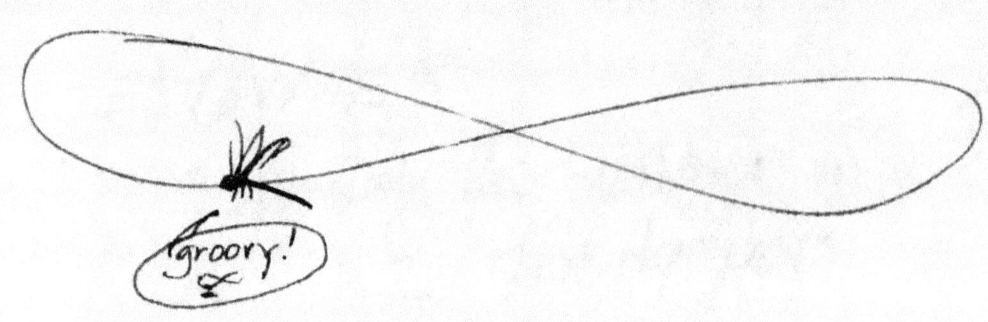

What's a meadow for . . . ?
whats a meta for . . . ?
whats a metaphor . . . ?
Whats a meta [more] [for] [us] ?
Whats a metamorphosis . . . ?

change the subject !

Okay, what do you want to
talk about ?

How about :
frogs
Butterflies
moths
locusts
cicadas
polyps

P

Walking in the jungle an
aborigine woman assaulted
mine and he struck her
on the head with his camera.
She stole his watch.

He has contracted ~~an~~ a
tropical infection

We shall hear more of this later —

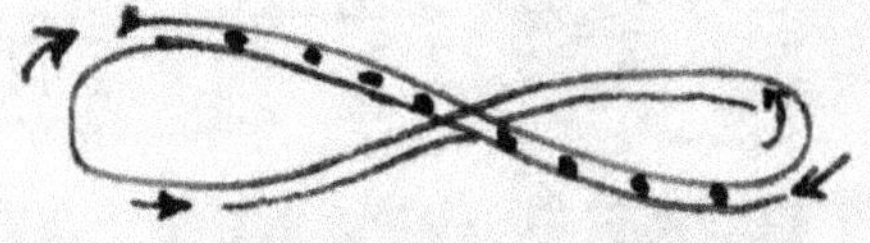

Four cups of coffee,
Then six cups of coffee;
a little later ⅓ of a PICKWICKBURGER,
and 3 cups of coffee and
finally in the afternoon break
Five cups of coffee...
                    a day in the
                    life of an artist

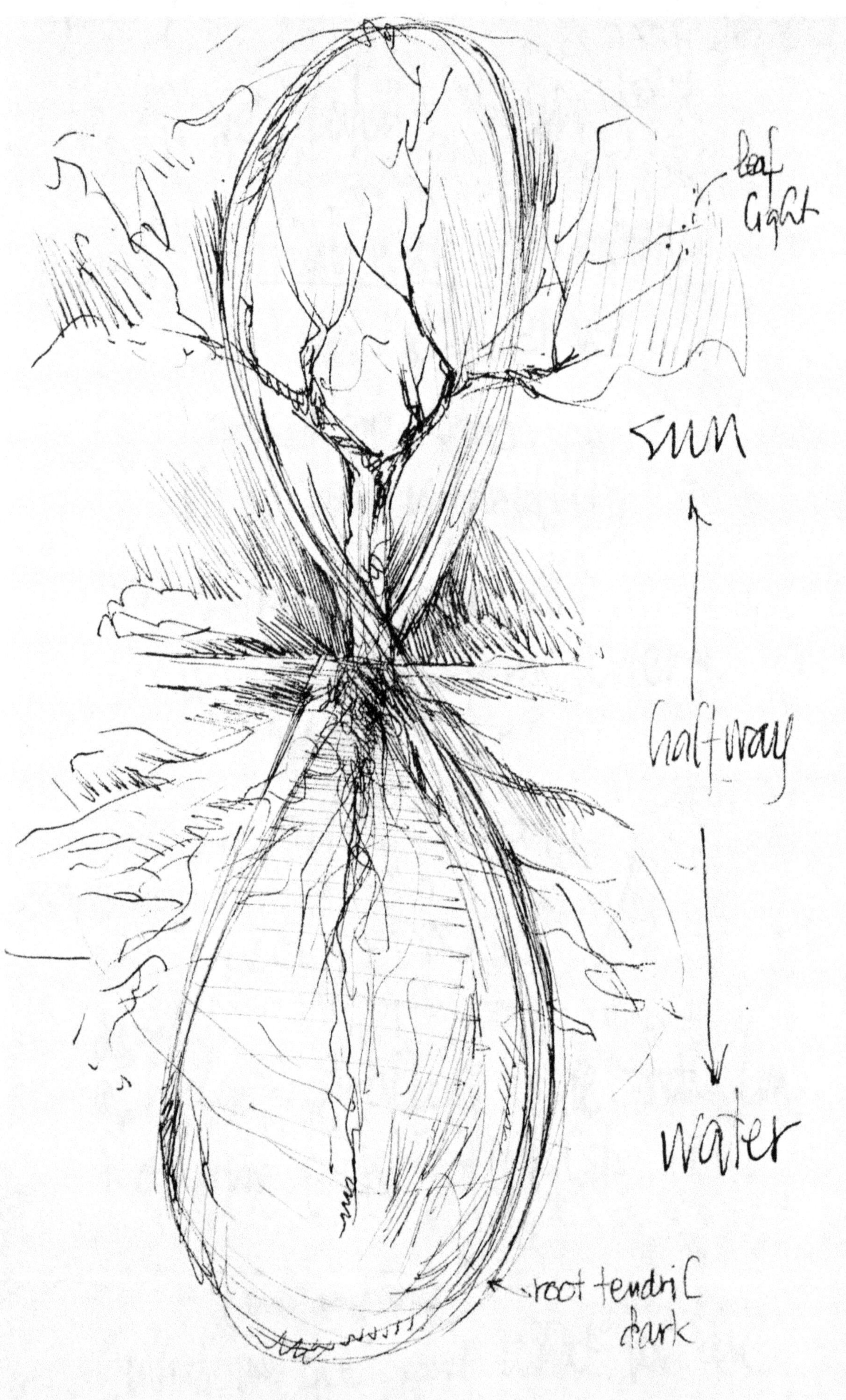

leaf
light
sun
halfway
water
root tendril
dark

a last thought
for 1973 —

we talked of
    changing the
        world,
he listened then
took 21¢ from
his coin purse to
pay for his coffee
and left . . .

1955   "Bob Camblin", Kansas City Art Institute, Kansas City, Missouri

1956   "Bob Camblin", Cottey College, Nevada, Missouri

"Bob Camblin - One-man Show of Paintings and Drawings", Kansas City, Missouri

1957   "Bob Camblin - Drawings and Paintings", Kansas City Art Institute, Kansas City, Missouri

"Fulbright Artists Exhibition", Schneider Gallery, Rome, Italy

"Exhibition of Self Portraits", Milan, Italy

"American Federation of Artists' International Traveling Show of Students' Work",

"62nd American Exhibition: Painting and Sculpture", Art Institute of Chicago, Chicago, Illinois

1958   "Collectors Market Exhibit", Nelson Gallery of Art, Kansas City, Kansas

"Childe Hassam Purchase Fund Show", American Academy of Arts and Letters, New York, N.Y.

"ART: USA 58", New York, New York

"Fulbright Painters", Institute for International Education, New York, N.Y., including

  Whitney Museum of American Art, New York City

  Akron Art Institute, Akron, Ohio

  Deleware Art Center, Wilmington, Delaware

  J.B. Speed Art Museum, Louisville, Kentucky

  Atlanta Public Library, Atlanta Georgia

  Rosicrucian Egyptian Oriental Museum, San Jose, California

  Colorado Springs Fine Arts Center, Colorado Springs, Colorado

  Santa Barbara Museum of Art, Santa Barbara, California

  University of Michigan, Ann Arbor, Michigan

  Lamont Art Gallery, Exeter, New Hampshire

  Mount Holyoke College, South Hadley, Massachusetts

  Brandeis University, Waltham, Massachusetts

  Oberlin College, Oberlin, Ohio

  Smithsonian Institution, Washington, D.C.

  University of Miami, Coral Gables, Florida

  George Thomas Hunter Gallery, Chattanooga, Tennessee

  George Peabody College, Nashville, Tennessee

  Springfield Art Museum, Springfield, Missouri

  Newcomb College, New Orleans, Louisiana

"Provincetown Art Festival", Provincetown, Massachusetts

"153rd Annual American Oil Painting and Sculpture", Detroit, Michigan

1959   "Five Artists", St. Armand's Gallery, Sarasota, Florida

"Two Fulbright Artists", Sarasota Art Association, Sarasota, Florida

1960   "Governor's All-Florida Show", John and Mable Ringling Museum of Art, Sarasota, Florida

"Bob Camblin", Museum of Art, Sarasota, Florida

"Bob Camblin", St. Armand's Gallery, Sarasota, Florida

"Bob Camblin", Southwestern College, Winfield, Kansas

"Bob Camblin", Kansas City Art Institute, Kansas City, Missouri

1961   "Bob Camblin", Oklahoma State University, Stillwater, Oklahoma

"Drawing Show", St. Armand's Gallery, Sarasota, Florida

1962   "Bob Camblin", University of Wisconsin, Madison, Wisconsin

1963   "Group Show", St. Armand's Gallery, Sarasota, Florida

1964   "Group Show", St. Armand's Gallery, Sarasota, Florida

1965   "Bob Camblin", University of Utah, Salt Lake City, Utah

"Bob Camblin", Windsor College, Windsor, Ontario, Canada

"Bob Camblin", Plumtree Gallery, Salt Lake City, Utah

1966   "Bob Camblin", Baker University, Baldwin City, Kansas

"Chrysalis Series", Plumtree Gallery, Salt Lake City, Utah

"Traveling Exhibition", Minnesota Museum of American Art, St. Paul, Minnesota,

1967   "Bob Camblin", Rice University, Allen Center, Houston, Texas

"Bob Camblin: Recent Drawings", Fred Jones Jr. Museum of Art, University of Oklahoma,
    Norman, Oklahoma, Feb. 4 - 28.

"Beaumont Annual", Beaumont, Texas

"Dickinson State College Exhibition", Dickinson, North Dakota
   Nelson Gallery of Art, Kansas City, Missouri
   Norfolk Museum of Art, Norfolk, Virginia

"Seventeenth Southwest Print & Drawing Exhibition", Dallas Museum of Art, Dallas, Texas

"Seventeenth Southwest Print & Drawing Exhibition", University of Wisconsin, Madison,
    Wisconsin

1968   "Bob Camblin", Rice University, Houston, Texas

"American Drawings 1968", Moore College of Art, Philadelphia, Pennsylvania

"Bob Camblin", Nelson Gallery of Art, Kansas City, Missouri

1969   "Bob Camblin", David Gallery, Houston, Texas

"Eighteenth Southwestern Print and Drawing Exhibition", Dallas Museum of Fine Arts, (toured
    10 museums and universities), Dallas, Texas

"Bob Camblin", University of Wisconsin, Madison, Wisconsin

1970   "Drawings in America", Museum of Fine Arts, Houston, Texas

"St. Paul Annual Drawing Show", Minnesota Museum of American Art, St. Paul, Minnesota

"The Highway Show", Rice University, Houston, Texas

"Drawings from Nine States: A Regional Exhibition", Museum of Fine Arts, Houston, Texas

"Bob Camblin", David Gallery, Houston, Texas

1971   "Project South/Southwest", Fort Worth Art Center, Fort Worth, Texas

"Tarrant County Annual", Fort Worth Art Center, Fort Worth, Texas

"Tattoo Show", B & E Productions, David Gallery, Houston, Texas

"Two-Man Exhibition", Cranfill Gallery, Dallas, Texas

"Drawings USA", Minnesota Museum of American Art, St. Paul, Minnesota

"Texas Sculpture and Painting Annual", Dallas Museum of Fine Arts, Dallas,Texas

"The Other Coast (10 Texas Artists)", California State Collage, Long Beach, California

1971 "3rd Biennial National Exhibition of Prints and Drawings", Dickinson State College, Dickinson, North Dakota

"Rice Art Faculty Exhibition, Sewall Art Gallery", Rice University, Houston, Texas

"Document Show", B & E Productions, David Gallery, Houston, Texas

"B & E Productions Show", St. Thomas Art Gallery, University of St. Thomas, Houston, Texas

1972 "Bob Camblin: Money is no object, Barter Show", David Gallery, Houston, Texas

"Faculty Exhibit", Rice University Gallery, Sewell Hall, Rice University

"Construction-Deconstruction Events 1 & 2", B & E Productions, Galveston, Texas, Flatonia, Texas

"Bob Camblin", Southern Illinois University Art Museum, Carbondale, Illinois

"The Former David Gallery Presents The Next to The Last Garage Sale", David Gallery, Houston, Texas

Main Street II, "Fort Worth, Dallas, Houston Invitational: 11 Artists", Houston's Chamber of Commerce's Cultural Affairs Committee, exhibitions at the Fort Worth Art Center, Fort Worth; The Contemporary Arts Museum, Houston; and The Dallas Museum of Fine Arts, Dallas, Texas

1973 "Faculty Exhibit", Rice University Gallery, Rice University, Houston, Texas

"Private Works: Works on Paper", Contemporary Arts Museum, Houston, Texas

"Extraordinary Realities", Whitney Museum of American Art, New York, New York (traveling exhibition)

"Hand Colored Prints", Brooke Alexander, Inc., New York, New York (traveling exhibition)

"Camping Show", St. Thomas Art Gallery, University of St. Thomas, Houston, Texas

"Joe Tate's Back Yard", St. Thomas Art Gallery, University of St. Thomas, Houston, Texas

"Contemporary Painting", Smither Gallery, Houston, Texas

"Houston Area Exhibition", The Sarah Campbell Blaffer Gallery, University of Houston, Texas

"Made in Houston", Louisiana Gallery, Houston, Texas

1974 "Drawings", Nancy Hoffman Gallery, New York City, New York

"Houston Artists", Cusack Gallery, Houston, Texas

1975 "Bob Camblin", Cusack Gallery, Houston, Texas

"Nineteenth National Print Exhibition", The Brooklyn Museum, New York, New York

"Holiday Show", Covo de longh Gallery, Houston, Texas

"Bob Camblin", Louisiana Gallery, Houston, Texas

"Objects from the Life of Bob Camblin", Union Art Gallery, Louisiana State University, Baton Rouge, Louisiana

"The Classic Revival", Illinois Bell Telephone, Chicago, Illinois; Traveled to Lakeview Center for the Arts, Peoria, Illinois; Quincy Art Canter, Quincy, Illinois; Illinois State Museum, Springfield, Illinois; Kirkland Gallery, Millikin University, Decatur, Illinois; Mitchell Museum, Mt. Vernon, Illinois; Ella Sharp Museum, Jackson, Michigan; University Gallery, University of Minnesota, Minneapolis, Minnesota

1976 "Bob Camblin: Watercolors and Prints", Baker University, Baldwin City, Kansas
"Bob Camblin", Covo de Iongh Gallery, Houston, Texas
"Bob Camblin", Louisiana State University, Baton Rouge, Louisiana
"Bob Camblin", Moody Gallery, Houston, Texas, November 12 - December 3
"Contemporary Images in Watercolor Exhibition", Akron Art Institute, Akron, Ohio & Indianapolis Institute of Art, Indianapolis, Indiana & The Memorial Art Gallery, University of Rochester, Rochester, New York
"Seven American Artists", Gulf Street, Kuwait City, Kuwait, November
"Houston Area Exhibition", Sarah Campbell Blaffer Gallery, University of Houston, Texas
"Made In Houston", Louisiana Gallery, Houston, Texas
"59 Works", The Collection of the Junior Service League of Longview, Longview, Texas
"Bob Camblin", Museum of Fine Arts, Houston, Texas
"Origin of the Birds", (with Bill Steffy), Covo de longh Gallery, Houston, Texas

1977 "N CompleatWorks: Bob Bilyeu Camblin in collaboration with the Anonymous Box Company", Moody Gallery, Houston, TX
"Little Egypt Enterprises: 13 Artists", Moody Gallery, Houston, Texas, June
"Joe Atteberry, Bob Camblin, and Bill Steffy", Moody Gallery, Houston, Texas,
"Moody Gallery Artists", Waco Art Center, Waco, Texas
"Houston Area Exhibition", Sarah Campbell Blaffer Gallery, University ofHouston, Houston, Texas

1978 "Bob Camblin", Projects Gallery, Art Museum of South Texas, Corpus Christi, Texas
"The Art of Texas", The Renaissance Society, University of Chicago, Chicago, Illinois
"Spirit of Texas", Kohler Arts Center, Sheboygan, Wisconsin
"Bob Camblin", Moody Gallery, Houston, Texas

1979 "Vanitas: Works of Bob Bilyeu Camblin and anonymous box co.", Moody Gallery, Houston, Texas
"Fire! An Exhibition of 100 Texas Artists", Contemporary Arts Museum, Houston, Texas
"Doors: Houston Artists", The Houston Festival, The Alley Theatre, Houston, Texas
"Five Artists From Texas", George Belcher Gallery, San Francisco, California
"Twenty-First Annual Invitational Operation Update, 1979", Longview Museum and Arts Center, Longview, Texas
"Works on Paper", Nave Museum, Victoria Regional Museum Association, Victoria, Texas

1980 "Contemporary Drawings and Watercolors", Memorial Art Gallery, University of Rochester, Rochester, New York
"David McManaway Works - Twenty Years", University Gallery, Meadows School of the Arts, Southern Methodist University, Dallas, Texas
"Inside Texas Borders", Corpus Christi State University, Corpus Christi, Texas
"Recent Works by Artists of the Southwest", Gensler and Associates/Architects, Houston, Texas
"Beehive Postcard Show", Salt Lake Art Center, Salt Lake City, Utah
"Bob Camblin", Moody Gallery, Houston, Texas

1981   "Collection '81, The Road Show", 2 Houston Center, Assistance League of Houston, Houston,
            Texas
        "The Image of the House in Contemporary Art", Lawndale Annex of the University of Houston,
            Texas
        "Little Egypt - Waterworkshop", Roberto Molina Gallery, Houston, Texas
        "Moody Gallery Exhibition", Linda Durham Gallery, Santa Fe, New Mexico
1982   "Art From Houston in Norway", Stavanger Kunstforening, Stavanger, Norway
1983   "Texas Images & Visions", Archer M. Huntington Gallery, University of Texas, Austin, Texas
1984   "Bob Camblin: A Houston Retrospective, 1968-1984", Midtown Art Center, Houston, Texas
        "1984 Show: An Exhibition of Contemporary Houston Art", 2 Houston Center,
            Houston Women's Caucus for Art, (listed in catalogue)
1985   "Fresh Paint: The Houston School", Museum of Fine Arts, Houston, Texas, Traveled to P.S. 1,
            Long Island City, New York, and the Oklahoma Art Center, Oklahoma City, Oklahoma
        "Self Images", Midtown Art Center, Houston, Texas
        "Propaganda, Too!", Midtown Art Center, Houston, Texas
        "Houston Drawing", Alfred C. Glassell, Jr. School of Art, Museum of Fine Arts, Houston, Texas
        "The New Nude", Midtown Arts Center, Houston, Texas
1986   "Texas Visions", Art League of Houston, Houston; Traveled to Museum of Western Art, Kerrville;
            Live Oak Art Club, Columbus; Abilene Fine Arts Center, Abilene; Lufkin Historical and
            Creative Art Center, Lufkin; Rockport Art Center, Rockport; McAllen International Museum,
            McAllen; Fort Bend County Museum, Richmond, Texas
        "Slides of the North Wall 1985-86", Anonymous Artists, Camblin's Studio, Houston, Texas,
            Funded by a grant from the Cultural Arts Council of Houston.
        "The Texas Landscape, 1900-1986", The Museum of Fine Arts, Houston, Texas
        "Collaborators: Artists Working Together In Houston 1969-1986", The Glassell School of Art,
            Houston, Texas
        "Bob Camblin", The Museum of Fine Arts, Houston, Texas, September 18 - October 19
1987   "Found", Diverse Works, Houston, Texas
        "Cinq X Cinq: Houston, Paris", Galerie Dario Boccara, Paris, France
1988   "Artists anonymous LAST DAZE silent auction", Studio exhibit at 1401 W.Gray, Houston, Texas
        "Handmade Paper", Little Egypt Enterprises, Houston, Texas
        "Robert Morris - Paintings/Bob Camblin - Paintings Drawings", Nave Museum, Victoria Regional
            Museum Association, Victoria, Texas, June
1989   "Bob Camblin", Rice University, Sewall Hall Gallery, Houston, Texas
        "Bob Camblin", Graham Gallery, Houston, Texas
        "Toy Show", Transco Gallery, Transco Energy Company, Houston, Texas, Nov.11 - Jan. 5
1990   "Printmaking in Texas: the 1980s", Modern Art Museum, Fort Worth, Texas
1991   "Texas Selections from the Menil Collection; A Tribute to the University of Texas Medical Branch
            Centennial Celebration", Galveston Art Center, Galveston, Texas
        "Bob Camblin", Graham Gallery, Houston, Texas

2003	"Collins House Exhibit of Baker University Collection", Baker University, Baldwin City, Kansas
2010	"Bob Camblin: Unframed Drawings and Paintings on Paper", Sarah Balinskas Fine Framing, Houston, Texas
2012	"Collection of Ursula Brinkerhoff", Canal Street Gallery, Houston, Texas
2014	"Flatbed Contemporary Print Fair", Flatbed Press, Austin, Texas
	"Art Bridge Party", Moody Gallery, Houston, Texas
2015	"Bob Camblin Paintings and Drawings", The Camblin Gallery
2016	"Bob Camblin: Hidden Realities", A 60-Year Retrospective, Running Man Press

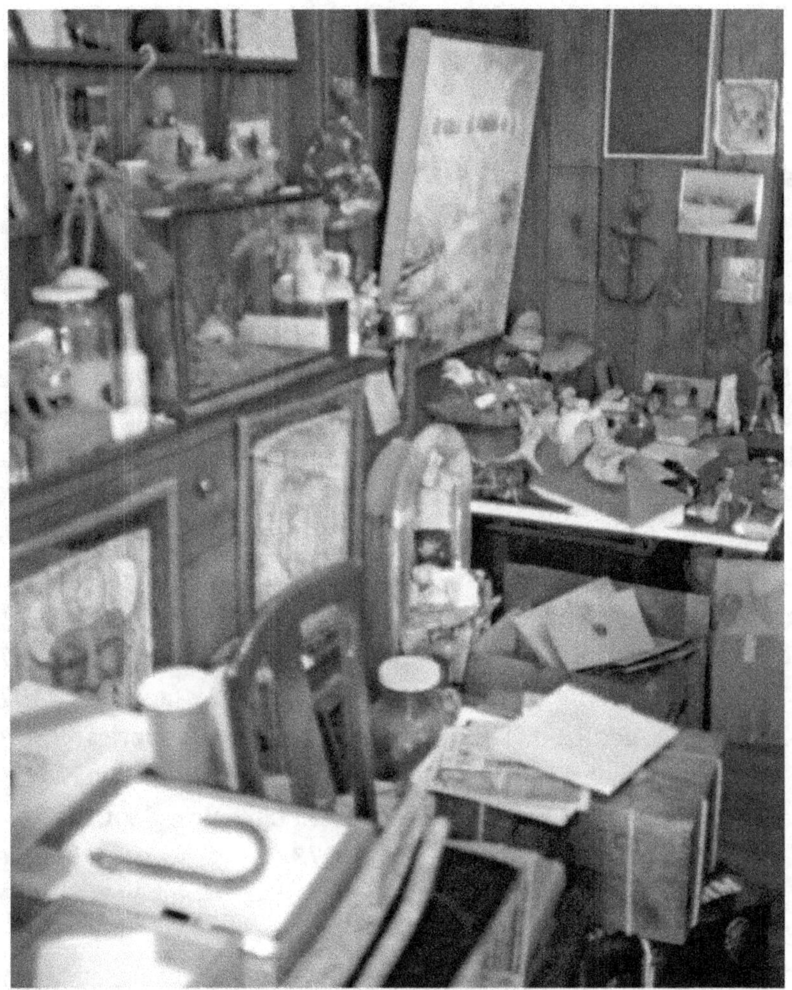

Bob Camblin's Houston studio, c. 1980s, with Atlas Powder dynamite crate

"62nd American Exhibition: Painting and Sculpture", Art Institute of Chicago,
Chicago, Illinois, 1957.

Time Magazine, "A Year Abroad", October 6,1958, p. 69.

Lewis, Jo Ann Sukel, "Fulbright Painters", Institute for International Education,
New York, N.Y., 1958.

"150 Objects Picked Here for Governor's Show", Sarasota Herald-Tribune, January 8,1960.

Solomon, Elke M., "American Drawings 1963-1973", Whitney Museum of American Art,
New York, N.Y., 1973.

Halliday, Bob, "U. Instructor to Exhibit New Work, Cites Artists Role to Effect Change",
The Salt Lake Tribune, November 20,1966, p. 18W.

"Metamorphosis", The Oklahoma Daily, University of Oklahoma, Norman, Oklahoma,
February 10,1967, p. 14.

"Eighteenth Southwestern Print and Drawing Exhibition", Dallas Museum of Fine Arts,
Dallas, Texas, Oct. 29,1969, press release.

Butterfield, Jan, "Dallas Galleries Feature Art of Talented Young Artists",
Fort Worth Star Telegram, November 12,1970, p. 6G.

"Drawings in America", Museum of Fine Arts, Houston, Texas, 1970

"The Highway Show", Rice Gallery, Rice University, Houston, Texas, 1970.

"Texas", Arts, Summer (Ete), 1971, pp. 49-50.

Holmes, Ann, "Where It's At [If You Can Find It]", The Art Gallery, May 20,1970, p. 37.

Freed, Eleanor, "Documenta", Houston Post, Art Section, Art Section, February 21,1971, p. 28.

Kutner, Janet, "Variety Exhibited by Camblin and David", Dallas Morning News, April 13,1971.

"The Other Coast (10 Texas Artists)", University of California, Long Beach, California, 1971.

Lunn, Judy, "Prowling Artists - Right in Your Backyard", Houston Post, July 21,1972, p. IB.

"The Last Garage Sale May Not Be", Houston Chronicle, Section 4, September 26.1972, p. 4.

Freed, Eleanor, "Texans, Titled and Subtitled", Houston Post, October 29,1972, p. IB.

"Oklahoma Acorns a Fair Trade", Houston Chronicle, Section 7, December 13,1972, p. 3.

Freed, Eleanor, "Montrose Bateau Lavoir", Houston Post "Spotlight", January 7,1973, p. 34.

Butler, Susan L., "So You Want To Be an Artist", Houston Chronicle, January 28,1973.

Doty, Robert, "EXTRAORDINARY REALITIES", Whitney Museum of American Art, 1973, p. 62.

Hopkins, Henry, "Contemporary Art in Texas: On the Road to Maturity", Art News, May 1973.

Butler, Susan L., Art Circles, "Private Works", The Houston Chronicle, Sept.1973.

Solomon, Elke M., "American Drawings: 1963-1973", 1973.

Ratcliff, Carter, "Hand Colored Prints", Brooke Alexander Gallery, New York, New Yor
November 1973. P. 9.

Hoffman, Nancy, "Drawings", Nancy Hoffman Gallery, New York, New York, May 1974.

Poster, Program Cover (front & last page) and Artist information for 'Der Rosenkavalier for the
Houston Grand Opera, January 1975, pp. front & back cover, 40 & 43.

Moser, Charlotte, "Master Printmaking in Houston", Houston Chronicle, May 31,1975.

Moser, Charlotte, "THE ART BOOM", Houston Chronicle, July 20,1975, p. 9.

Glauber, Robert H., "THE CLASSIC REVIVAL", Illinois Bell Telephone, Lobby Gallery,
Chicago, Illinois, (traveled to 8 museums and galleries), September 1975.

Dianne David interview by Louis J Marchiafava, Archive # OH036, The Houston Metropolitan
Research Center, Oral History Project Interviews, October 2,1975.

Fuller, Mary, "Marcel Duchamp Lives: One View of the Texas Art World", Currant,
October - November 1975, p. 18.

Butler, Susan L., "Art Circles", Houston Chronicle, Houston, Texas, January, 1976.

Moser, Charlotte, "Between Fantasy and Surrealism", Art News, April 1976, p. 66.

Moser, Charlotte, "Box is Both Form, Content of Developing Art", Houston Chronicle,
July 7,1976.

Smith, Roberta, "Twelve Days of Texas", Art In America, July/August 1976, p. 46.

"The Collection of the Junior Service League of Longview", The Collection,
Longview, Texas, Ca.1976, Pp. 32 & 36.

Crossley, Mimi, "Little Egypt rolls on", Houston Post, June 26,1977.

Crossley, Mimi, "Gallery Roundup - Bob Camblin: Paintings and Watercolors", Houston Post,
November 25,1977.

Moser, Charlotte, "Camblin's New Work Sparks Moody Show", Houston Chronicle,
August 19,1977.

"Camblin Paintings Merge Magic and Metaphysics", Houston Chronicle,
November 18,1977, p. 24.

Surls, James, "Fire! An Exhibition of 100 Texas Artists," Contemporary Arts Museum,
Houston, Texas, February 1979, p. 24.

Sween, Trudy, "Doors: Houston Artists," The Houston Festival, The Alley Theatre,
Houston, Texas, 1979, pp. 13-14.

"Doors Open Aesthetic Vistas at the Alley", Houston Chronicle. March 18,1979, p. 17.

Moser, Charlotte, "Art Celebrates Mexican 'Day of the Dead' Festival",
Houston Chronicle, April 7,1979, Sec. 3, p. 9.

Dunham, Judith, "Texas Overview", Artweek, April 21,1979, p. 4.

Olpin, Robert S., "Dictionary of Utah Art", Salt Lake Art Center. 1980, p. 30.

Smithsonian Institution, Archives of American Art, "440 Slides of Bob Camblin and his Work",
New York, New York, 1979.

Curtis, Sandra, "Texas Project", Archives of American Art Journal, Smithsonian Institution,
January 20,1980, p. 31.

"Recent Works by Artists of the Southwest", Gensler and Associates/Architects,
Houston, Texas, 1980.

Moser, Charlotte, "Playing Cowboys and Artists in Houston", Art News,
December 1980, pp. 124-128.

"1981 Houston Arts Calendar", Wordworks, Inc, Houston, Texas, 1981, pp. 7-8.

Johnson, Patricia, "The Image of the House Through Artists' Eyes", Houston Chronicle,
November 15, 1981, pp. 18-27; 47-49.

Freed, Eleanor, "Treasures of the Finding", Houston Arts Magazine,
    Society for the Performing Arts, September 1982, pp. 16-24.
Krantz, Les, "The Texas Art Review", 'Moody Gallery', Gulf Publishing in conjunction with
    The Krantz Company Publishers, Inc., Houston, Texas, 1982, p. 175.
Johnson, Patricia, "Print Show Lights Up Some of City's Masters in Field", Houston Chronicle,
    October 14,1982, p. 24.
Goetzmann/Reese,"Texas Images & Visions", Archer M. Huntington Gallery,
    University of Texas at Austin, Texas, 1983, pp 44 & 128.
Johnson, Patricia, "Camblin's Personal Artwork Explored", Houston Chronicle,
    March 23,1984. Sec. 5, p. 9.
Rose, Barbara & Kalil, Susie, "Fresh Paint: The Houston School", Museum of Fine Arts, Houston, Texas, 1984.
Larsen, Kay, "Art", New York Magazine, June 17,1985, p. 64.
"Texas Visions", Art League of Houston, Texas, 1985.
"Texas - A State of Mind", Archer M Huntington Art Gallery, University of Texas, Austin, Texas.
Landay, Janet, "Collaborators: Artists Working Together In Houston 1969 -1986",
    The Glassell School of Art, The Museum of Fine Arts, Houston, Texas, September, 1986, Introduction +
    Plates 3,4, 5.
"Glassell exhibit calls to mind 'the good old days' of art", The Houston Post,
    September 28, 1986, p.3F.
Kalil, Susie, "The Texas Landscape, 1900 - 1986", The Museum of Fine Arts,
    Houston, Texas, May 17 - September 7, 1986, pp. 47 & 91.
Carlozzi, Annette,"50 Texas Artists. A Critical Selection of Painters and Sculptors Working in
    Texas", Chronicle Books, San Francisco, California, 1986, pp. 28-29.
"Bob Camblin", Art, Seven One Three, Houston, Texas, 1988.
Falk, Peter H. [Editor], "Annual Exhibition Record of the Pennsylvania Academy of the Fine Arts, 1913-1968",
    Sound View Press, Madison, Connecticut, 1989.
Fisher, James L., "Forty Texas Printmakers", Modern Art Museum of Fort Worth, 1990,
    p. 6, 30, 31,105,106.
"1983-1993, DiverseWorks Artspace, The First Ten Years", "Found," Diverse Works,
    Houston, Texas, Exhibition: 1987, Published by DiverseWorks Artspace, Inc.,
    Houston, Texas, 1993.
Falk, Peter Hastings [Editor], "Annual Exhibition Record, 1914-1968",
    Pennsylvania Academy of the Fine Arts, 1999.
Dunbier, Lonnie Pierson [Editor], "The Artists' Bluebook", AskArt.com, 2005.
Stout, Richard, "Modernism in Houston Art: 1950-1970, Part 7", YouTube series done for
    Houston Modern Market Week Exhibition at the William Reaves Fine Art Gallery, Houston,
    Texas, April 28, 2012.
Glentzer, Molly, "Penny Cerling: A life of needles & pins", The Houston Chronicle, June 26, 2013.
Rice University, "Allen Center Open House, Nov. 1967", Rice History Corner from the Rice
    Archives [Sandy Havens' letter), June 24, 2013.

1928	Bob Bilyeu Camblin was born in the United States in Ponca City, Oklahoma
1946	Completes secondary education in Oklahoma
1948-49	Private First Class US Army
1950-51	A1C US Air Force
1951-54	Studies art at Kansas City Art Institute
1954-55	Master in Fine Art from Kansas City Art Institute
1956-57	Awarded a Fulbright Fellowship to study painting in Italy
1957-58	Cartographer for Trans World Airlines
1958-60	Art instructor at the John and Mable Ringling Museum of Art, Sarasota, Florida
1960-61	Art instructor at the University of Illinois, Urbana, Illinois
1961-65	Assistant Professor at the University of Detroit, Detroit, Michigan
1965-67	Assistant Professor at the University of Utah, Salt Lake City, Utah
1967-73	Assistant Professor at Rice University, Houston, Texas
1974	Professor at Rice University, Houston, Texas
1975-76	Visiting artist at Louisiana State University, Baton Rogue, Louisiana
1977	Instructor at University of Houston, Houston, Texas
2010	Died on December 4 in La Place, Louisiana

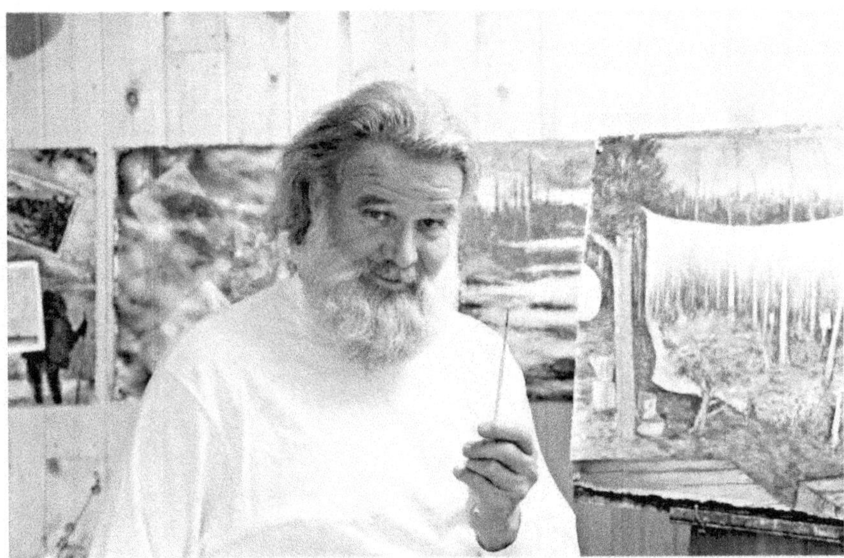

Image by Nancy Giordiano Echegoyen

www.ingramcontent.com/pod-product-compliance
Lightning Source LLC
Chambersburg PA
CBHW080255030726
47593CB00009B/2493